Why is 'Why' Unique?

Studies in
Generative Grammar

Editors
Norbert Corver
Harry van der Hulst

Founding editors
Jan Koster
Henk van Riemsdijk

Volume 142

Why is 'Why' Unique?

Its Syntactic and Semantic Properties

Edited by
Gabriela Soare

DE GRUYTER
MOUTON

ISBN 978-3-11-125870-6
e-ISBN (PDF) 978-3-11-067516-0
e-ISBN (EPUB) 978-3-11-067521-4
ISSN 0167-4331

Library of Congress Control Number: 2021938138

Bibliographic information published by the Deutsche Nationalbibliothek
The Deutsche Nationalbibliothek lists this publication in the Deutsche Nationalbibliografie;
detailed bibliographic data are available on the Internet at http://dnb.dnb.de.

© 2023 Walter de Gruyter GmbH, Berlin/Boston
This volume is text- and page-identical with the hardback published in 2021.
Typesetting: Integra Software Services Pvt. Ltd.
Printing and binding: CPI books GmbH, Leck

www.degruyter.com

Contents

Gabriela Soare
Introduction —— 1

Part 1: *Why* in a Gbe language

Leston Chandler Buell
Reason questions as a complementizer domain phenomenon: Evidence from Ewe —— 23

Part 2: Towards a cartography of high and low reason adverbials

Caterina Bonan and Ur Shlonsky
On 'why' in situ in Northern Italian dialects: Evidence from Trevisan —— 41

Aritz Irurtzun
***Why* questions break the residual V2 restriction (in Basque and beyond)** —— 63

Nicholas Catasso
Is German *warum* so special after all? —— 115

Norbert Corver
Why in Dutch? On *why*-stripping and high and low adverbials —— 151

Part 3: Wh-in-Situ languages: *Whys*, *hows*, and *whats*

Wei-Tien Dylan Tsai
On applicative *Why*-questions in Chinese —— 197

Lisa Lai-Shen Cheng
***What*-as-*Why* sentences in Cantonese** —— 219

Part 4: Some syntactic aspects of *how come*

Yoshio Endo
How come questions and diary English —— 249

Part 5: A special class of *why* rhetorical questions: Semantics and pragmatics

Lavi Wolf and Edit Doron
Why rhetorical questions? —— 273

Part 6: *Why* and the syntax-prosody interface

Giuliano Bocci, Silvio Cruschina and Luigi Rizzi
On some special properties of *why* in syntax and prosody —— 293

Index of subjects —— 317

Gabriela Soare
Introduction

1 *Why* – special syntactic and semantic properties

It has been known for about 30 years that the adjunct *why* differs from other wh-elements syntactically, semantically and pragmatically. Unlike other wh-elements, *why* can co-occur with focused elements and this imposes different conditions on what can count as a possible answer to a *why*-question (Bromberger 1992). Semantically speaking, *why*-questions trigger implicatures which are different from those of non-*why*-questions (Bromberger 1992). Syntactically, unlike other wh-phrases, *why* has been argued not to leave a trace or a copy within the IP (Rizzi 2001) and this has implications for its merge position. Several authors have argued that unlike other wh-elements, the adjunct *why* (and its equivalent in other languages) is externally-merged in the left periphery of the clause (Rizzi 1990, 2001, Hornstein 1995, Ko 2005, 2006, Stepanov and Tsai 2008, Thornton 2008, Endo 2015), or that it moves locally within the left periphery (Shlonsky and Soare 2011). The adjunct *why* is also different in that unlike other wh-phrases, it can occur in the surface pattern *why XP* and this XP can be of any phrasal category (De Villiers 1991, 1996). Another core property of *why* is that in some languages requiring subject inversion in *wh*-interrogatives (Italian, Romanian, Basque), *why* is exceptional in that it allows the non-inverted order *why*-subject-verb (Rizzi 2001). Actually different material, such as topics, foci and a subordinate clause can intervene between *why* and the subject in questions lacking inversion.

The syntactic behaviour of *why* has been studied in several languages, among which Romanian, a multiple wh-fronting language, in which wh-phrases are rigidly ordered (Rudin 1988, Alboiu 2002, Soare 2009, a.o.) Not only can *why* co-occur with other wh-elements, but it must also follow them. Mainly based on such ordering facts and on its interaction with negation, it has been claimed that 'why' in Romanian is externally-merged in a fairly low position inside the CP zone, labelled ReasonP (Shlonsky and Soare 2011), and moves locally to Rizzi's (2001) IntP in the absence of a wh-phrase. Similarly to movement languages, *why* in wh-in-situ languages (Korean, Japanese and Chinese) has been argued to be directly merged into SpecCP of the clause it modifies (Ko 2005). This also captures the peculiarity of *why* as opposed to other wh-phrases which are subject to other licensing mechanisms (for instance, Tsai's 1994 and Reinhart's 1998 Unselective Binding mechanism which is at stake for argumental wh-phrases as opposed to adjunct wh-phrases which are subject to covert LF-movement).

The peculiar properties of *why* extend to the PF interface as recent experimental research has shown that it exhibits special intonational contours. Preliminary experimental research has unveiled a prosodic asymmetry between *why* and other wh-phrases, which is attributed to the former's distinct syntactic derivation.

The adjunct *why* also shows interesting behaviour in point of acquisition. Child language often reveals linguistic distinctions that are opaque in the adult language but are transparent in other languages. Longitudinal diary studies have shown that in the grammars of some English-speaking children, *why*-questions are unlike those of other wh-questions in the sense that those children's *why*-questions consistently lack subject-auxiliary inversion (Labov and Labov 1978). In a longitudinal study of an English-speaking child, Thornton (2008) shows that the English child' grammar of *why*-questions resembles those of Italian: in matrix *why*-questions, a topic, a focused element or a subordinate clause can intervene between *why* and the subject. Conversely, in long-distance questions with tensed embedded clauses, the English child's grammar resembles the adult grammar in that lack of subject-auxiliary inversion is fairly consistent.

In a nutshell, the peculiarities of the adjunct *why* constitute in themselves a rich field of research that deserves further investigation. The papers that form this volume are thematically grouped into six sections. They provide a rich set of cross-linguistic data, illustrating further syntactic, semantic and prosodic aspects that set reason *why* apart from other wh-elements. Evidence comes from several language families, such as Gbe, Romance, Germanic, Chinese languages, Basque, and Semitic.

The chapters of this volume have emerged from preliminary research results that were presented at the workshop *Why is why unique? Its syntactic and semantic properties*, which the present author co-organised in 2017 in Zürich, part of the international conference *Societas Lingusitica Europaea* 50. The fruitful discussions of that workshop resulting in the present chapters are organised around six themes, each chapter being summarised in sections 6–11.

In sections 2–5 an overview of some of the main findings in the literature on *why* is provided.

2 *Why* and focus sensitivity

Ever since Bromberger (1992) it has been known that *why*-questions differ from non-*why*-questions with respect to the interaction with focused elements. This argument actually goes back to Dretske (1972). Consider the pairs in (1) and (2):

(1) a. Why did ADAM eat the apple?
    b. Why did Adam eat the APPLE?
    c. Why did Adam EAT the apple?
    d. Why did Adam eat the apple?

(2) a. When did ADAM eat the apple?
    b. When did Adam eat the APPLE?
    c. When did Adam EAT the apple?
    d. When did Adam eat the apple?

The contrast is two-fold. Firstly, focusing different constituents imposes different conditions on what counts as a possible answer in *why*-questions, but not in *when*-questions. While each of the questions in (1a-d) requires a different sort of answer, the questions in (2a-d) have the same answer and its truth or falsity does not depend on the focus value. This is shown by the contrast in (3) and (4).

(3) a. Because he (Adam) was the one that Eve worked on.
    b. Because it (the apple) was the only food around.
    c. Because he couldn't think of anything else to do with it.
    d. Because God intended that to happen.

(4) At 4 pm on August 15.

Secondly, *why*-questions and non-*why*-questions trigger different sorts of implicatures. For instance, as opposed to (1d) which is pronounced with normal intonation contour, (1a) in which *Adam* is stressed, implicates that someone else could have eaten the apple, but did not. In contrast, the stressed version of the *when*-question in (2a) necessarily implicates that someone else besides Adam has eaten the apple. (2a) can be uttered in a context in which several people ate the apple and the speaker is only interested in Adam. Bromberger's paradigm has been accounted by assuming that the focusing operator operates via existential closure and the binder for the existential closure is located in the left periphery. For the cases in (2), *when* is the scope of the focusing operators. For the cases in (1), the focusing operator is in the scope of *why*. In other words, the fact that *why* triggers different kind of implicatures in (1) as opposed to (2) is accounted for by the distinct ordering of quantifiers.

3 *Why* – its merge position

Rizzi (1990, 2001) provides a test in Italian similar to Bromberger's, which involves interaction of *perché* 'why' and contrastive focus. He notes that other wh-phrases cannot co-occur with focus (5). In contrast, *perché* can co-occur with a focused element and necessarily precedes it (6).

(5) *Che cosa A GIANNI   hanno   detto (non   a Piero)?
    What   TO GIANNI   have.3PL said   (not   to Piero)
    'What have they said to Gianni, (not to Piero)?'

(6) Perché QUESTO avremmo   dovuto dirgli, non qualcos'altro?
    Why   THIS   have.1PL should said   not something else
    'Why should we have told him this, not something else?'

The contrast shows that *perché* is first merged in the Spec of Int(errogative), while other wh-elements are moved from their first merge position to the Spec of Foc(us), lower than Int. According to this approach, *perché* does not bind any (syntactic) variable, since it is not associated with a trace or a copy.

More recently, essentially based on evidence from Romanian and from English infinitivals, Shlonsky and Soare (2011) have argued against the external merge of *why* in Spec IntP and in favour of a lower merge position, still inside the left periphery, Spec ReasonP. For many English speakers there is a stark contrast between (7a-f) and (7g) headed by *why*.

(7) I asked Bill   a. whether to serve spiced
                      aubergines for dinner.
                   b. who to serve.
                   c. what to serve the guests.
                   d. when to serve spiced aubergines.
                   e. how to serve spiced aubergines.
                   f. where to serve spiced aubergines.
                   g. ??why to serve spiced aubergines.
                      Shlonsky and Soare 2011 (4)

Assuming a truncation analysis in the sense of Rizzi (1993/4, Haegeman 2010, a.o.), the two authors argue that infinitival clauses are spliced at WhP below FocP. This is shown in (8).

(8) ~~ForceP > IntP > TopP > FocP~~ > WhP > FinP

Thus interrogative *why* cannot surface in the infinitival clause (7g) because it is specialized to interact with Int, not with Wh. Since IntP is part of the left periphery truncated in infinitivals, the ungrammaticality of (7g) results from the absence of an appropriate landing site for *why*. However, *why* can also be construed long-distance, that is, within the embedded infinitival clause (see also Cattell 1978, Ko 2005). Sentence (9) can be associated either with the reason of asking, or with the reason of resigning.

(9) Why did you ask her to resign?
    a. What is the reason x, such that for x, you asked her to resign? (short construal)
    b. What is the reason x, such that you asked her to resign for that particular reason x? (long construal)

The availability of (9b) indicates that *why* has an external merge position in the infinitival clause but it cannot remain there and moves to the finite matrix clause. This leads Shlonsky and Soare to propose Spec ReasonP as the external merge position of *why*, a position higher than negation. The derivation they propose for the long-distance construal reading in (9b) is provided in (10).

(10) ["CP"... [~~ForceP > IntP > TopP > FocP~~ > WhP > ... > ReasonP ...

Interrogative *why* cannot surface in the infinitival clause because it is specialized to interact with Int°, not Wh°. Since IntP is part of the truncated left periphery of the infinitival clause, the ungrammaticality of (7g) thus results from the absence of an appropriate landing site for *why* in the infinitival left periphery. Chapter 2 of this volume takes over the question of the merge position of the reason adjunct in a Gbe language, Ewe. The reason adjunct in Ewe is all the more interesting to investigate as it has a bipartite morphological make-up showing a sentence-final particle.

Cross-linguistically there are languages which distinguish between two lexical items expressing reason and the immediate question that arises is what is the merge position of such elements. Trevisan, a Venetan dialect spoken in the area of Venice, is a case in point as it has two distinct 'why' items: *parché* and *parcossa*. Caterina Bonan and Ur Shlonsky in Chapter 3 discuss the idea that a certain type of *why* may actually be merged sentence-internally. As will be discussed in Chapters 4 and 5, Basque and Dutch also exhibit distinct reason adverbials.

4 *How come* – its merge position

Rizzi's (1990, 2001) Spec IntP is not only the position hosting of a wh-phrase like *perché* 'why', but also the merge position of the Italian *come mai* 'how come'. However, Collins (1990) discusses the differences between *why* and *how come* and argues that *how come* is base-generated as the head of CP, while *why* is moved from inside IP. Shlonsky and Soare (2011) observe that *how come* is a phrase, not a head, and patterns with *why*, not with a head like *if* or *whether* in that it does not allow sluicing in sentences like the following.

(11) They thought John left early, but they didn't tell me a. why.
 b. how come.
 c. *whether/if.

Shlonsky and Soare (2011) adopt Rizzi's (2001) idea that Italian *come mai* is base-generated in Spec IntP in the CP system, and they also base-generate *how come* in Spec IntP.

(12) How come you said (that) John left?
 a. How come you said such-and-such a thing? (√short construal)
 b. How come John left? (*long construal)

Its base position then accounts for the availability of the short construal in (12a). Some other main differences between *why* and *how come* regard suject-auxiliary inversion, the licensing of the wh-in-situ and scope interactions with subject quantifiers. The first property is of special importance here. Subject-auxiliary inversion is obligatory in (root) *why*-questions and impossible with *how come*.

(13) a. Why did John resign?
 b. *Why John resigned?

(14) a. *How come did John resign?
 b. How come John resigned?

Collins attributes the ungrammaticality of (14a) to the impossibility of moving I° to C° as the latter is filled by *home come*. In Shlonsky and Soare's account, (English) subject-auxiliary inversion is triggered by interrogative operators that are linked to a syntactic variable. *How come* is not associated with a variable since it constitutes a trivial chain. It thus fails to trigger inversion. Endo's chapter contributes to the discussion of the English *how come* by putting forth and analysing one further special property, namely the possibility of subject drop attested in diary-style English (see, for instance, Haegeman 2013).

5 Wh-in-situ languages: *Whys, hows* and *whats*

There has been a growing body of literature on the merge posititon of reason *why* in wh-in-situ languages (Ko 2005, Tsai 2008, Stepanov and Tsai 2008, Tsai 2015, Endo 2015, 2020, a.o.). *Wh*-in-situ languages provide a window to peek through the surface distortion created by scrambling and *wh*-movement and are thus an opportunity to map out the origin of wh-adverbials more accurately. For instance, Tsai (2008) maps out the cartography of the structural placement of *how* and *why* in Mandarin Chinese and of their lexical counterparts, each one of them being associated with a distinct syntactic position (see also Huang 1982). Chinese, a 'hard-core' wh-in-situ language, distinguishes between two types of *why*-questions in (15)–(16).Consider the cases below containing a future modal. As shown in (15), *weishenme* 'why' can appear only before the modal.

(15) a. Akiu weishenme hui zou? (reason > modal)
       Akiu why   will leave
       'Why would Akiu leave?'
   b. *Akiu hui weishenme zou? (*modal > reason)
       Akiu will why   leave

(16) a. Akiu hui wei(-le) shenme cizhi? (modal > purpose)
       Akiu will for(-Prf) what   resign
       'For what purpose would Akiu resign?'
   b. ??Akiu wei(-le) shenme hui cizhi? (??purpose > modal)
       Akiu for(-Prf) what   will resign

By contrast, *wei(-le) shenme* 'for/because of what' has a strong tendency to stay in the scope of the future modal, and the result is a purpose question. Reason *weishenme* in (15) is a contraction of *wei shenme* 'for what' in Mandarin Chinese, and has evolved into a reason adverb. By contrast, *wei(-le) shenme* in (16) is a PP (i.e., with *wei* being a preposition) expressing a purpose question.

Mandarin Chinese (see also Cantonese, Chapter 8 in this volume) has alternative ways to ask reason/causal questions. It uses *zenme*, a simplex form of *how*, with two distinct interpretations.

(17) a. Akiu zenme qu Taipei?　　　　　　　　[irrealis: instrumental]
　　　　Akiu how　 go Taipei
　　　　'How will Akiu do to Taipei?'
　　b. Akiu zenme qu-le Taipei?　　　　　　　[realis/past: causal]
　　　　Akiu how　 go-Prf Taipei
　　　　'How come Akiu went to Taipei?'

Zenme has an instrumental reading with a bare tense clause, which is typically associated with irrealis mood (17a). By contrast, in (17b), it gets a causal reading in the presence of a perfective aspect marker, which has a strong tendency to be interpreted as past tense (cf. Tsai 1999). Furthermore, the contrast between (18a,b) shows that a modal can also separate instrumental *how* from causal *how*:

(18) a. Akiu keyi zenme(-yang) qu Taipei?　　　　[instrumental]
　　　　Akiu can　how(-manner)　go Taipei
　　　　'How can Akiu go to Taipei?'
　　b. Akiu zenme(*-yang) keyi qu Taipei?　　　　[causal/denial]
　　　　Akiu how(-manner)　can　go Taipei
　　　　'How come Akiu could go to Taipei?'
　　　　'Akiu can't/shouldn't go to Taipei.'

Premodal *zenme* in (18b) forms a causal question, while postmodal *zenme* forms an instrumental question in (18a) (there is also a morphological difference: postmodal *how* can alternate with a complex form *zenme-yang* 'how-manner', while premodal *how* cannot).

Thus, drawing on evidence from word order, the positioning with respect to lexical modals, scopal interaction, etc., Tsai (2008) cuts across sentential adverbs and vP-modifiers and puts forth a cartography of the *how-why* alternations. To be more precise, purpose *why* (16a) and instrumental *how* (17a)/(18a) appear in the vP periphery, wheres reason *why* (15a) and causal *how* (18b) are merged in the left periphery.

There are other wh-adjuncts asking for reason. A case in point is the wh-element *what*. This is a special type of *what* which is most appropriate in a context in which the speaker is emotionally affected (annoyance, surprise, etc). The syntax of *what* asking for reason has been studied by Ochi (2004) for languages like German, Hungarian and Serbo-Croatian, which all show overt wh-movement, and Japanese. This special reason *what* exhibits different properties in overt wh-movement languages and in-situ languages. Thus, as shown by Ochi (2004), in overt wh-movement languages, reason *what* patterns more with *how come* in that its interpretation is clause-bound. In the examples below in German, *warum* 'why', as opposed to the expletive *was* 'what', is a question about believing or about sleeping.

(19) a. Warum glaubst du, daß er so lange schläft?
    Why believe you that he so long sleeps
    'Why do you believe that he sleeps so long?' (ambiguous)
  b. Was glaubst du, daß er so lange schläft?
    What believe you that he so long sleeps
    'Why do you believe that he sleeps so long?' Ochi 2004, 36, (26)

In overt wh-movement languages, reason *what* cannot occur in multiple wh-questions and does not yield scope ambiguity either (Ochi 2004).

Conversely, in an in-situ language like Japanese, reason *what* patterns with *why*. *What* can be construed across a clause, can appear in multiple wh-questions, and yields scope ambiguity. In (20) below, *nani-o* 'what' having the meaning of *why* co-occurs with *dare-ga* 'who'.

(20) Dare-ga nani-o sawaideiru no?
    Who-Nom what-Acc clamouring Q
    'Who is clamoring why?' Ochi, 41, (39)

The question of why reason *what* shows the behaviour of *how come* in wh-fronting languages but patterns with *why* in a wh-in-situ language like Japanese deserves thorough investigation. Although such an investigation goes beyond the scope of this volume, a partial answer to explaining the asymmetry in the syntactic behaviour of reason *what*-questions is provided here through the lens of Mandarin and Cantonese.

In the sections below I will highlight the empirical and/or theoretical contributions of each chapter.

6 *Why* in a Gbe language

In Chapter 2, Leston Buell investigates *why*-questions in Ewe, a member of the Gbe subgroup of the Kwa language family. In Ewe the *why*-element is a bi-partite element consisting of the sentence initial *núkàtà* and the optional sentence-final *ɖó*.

(21) Núkàtà-(é) Kòfí lè hà dzí-ḿ (ɖô)?
    why-foc Kofi be.at singing sing-prog go.to
    'Why is Kofi singing?'

Analysing the interaction of this bi-partite form with negation and adopting an analysis of the latter as being high in the CP domain, with movement of the IP around it, the author suggests that *ɖó* heads Shlonsky and Soare's (2011) Reason head, while *núkàtà* originates in the specifier position. It then moves to Spec IntP. The author brings one further piece of evidence coming from VP nominalisation fronting to argue that *núkàtà* is merged in the complementizer domain. Furthermore, he shows that like the Italian *perché*, the Ewe *why* occupies a position higher than Focus and Topic, which sets it apart from other wh-elements in Ewe which cannot precede them.

To sum up, evidence from Ewe provides further support that reason questions are universally an exclusively complementizer domain phenomenon.

7 Towards a cartography of high and low reason adverbials

In Chapter 3 that deals with Trevisan, a Venetan dialect spoken in the area of Venice, Caterina Bonan and Ur Shlonsky investigate the syntactic properties of two truth-conditionally equivalents of *why*, *parché* and *parcossa*. On the basis of a close examination of the syntactic properties of the two wh-elements, they argue that only *parché* is externally-merged in the left periphery, whereas *parcossa* shows the properties of regular wh-words, i.e. it is sensitive to negation (22a) and cannot co-occur with a focus. Crucially, *parcossa* can also appear IP-internally, as in (23b). The authors discuss other syntactic properties distinguishing between the two items, such as the (im)possibility of co-occurrence with the complementizer *che* 'that' or the (im)possibility of triggering subject-clitic inversion.

(22) a. *Parcossa no si-tu vignuo?
       Why   Neg are-you come
       'Why didn't you come?'
    b. Parché no te si vignuo?

(23) a. Parcossa sì-tu ndàa al marcà?
       Why   are-you gone.F to the market
       'Why did you go to the market?'
    b. Sì-tu ndàa parcossa al marcà?

The distinct behaviour of the two reason *why*-elements leads to an analysis of *parcossa* as being merged IP-internally and optionally moving to the left periphery, presumably to Spec FocP.

The investigation of two distinct reason *why*-elements clearly indicates that Trevisan adds to the significant number of languages that support the characterisation that causal reason *why*-questions are universally an exclusively complementizer domain phenomenon, on the one hand, and that there is a low vP domain that hosts other reason adverbials, on the other.

As mentioned, this Northern Italian dialect is not the only language that exhibits two syntactically distinct reason *why*'s. Other languages studied in this volume are Basque and Dutch.

Aritz Irurtzun, in Chapter 4, discusses *why*-questions in Basque. Given that it is an SOV language, which also allows other word orders, it is in itself a good testing ground for the merge position of *why*. The author discussed the behaviour of regular wh-questions, which show the V2 phenomenon (see also Ortiz de Urbina 1989, 1999). As opposed to regular wh-questions, *why*-questions do not require the adjacency between the verb and wh-phrase and can also co-occur with Focus. As shown below, *zergatik* 'why' precedes Focus.

(24) a. Zergatik PEIOK eman die   albistea?
         Why   PEIO   eman AUX news
         'Why was PEIO who gave them the news?'
     b. *PEIOK zergatik eman die albistea?

Based on word order possibilities in matrix and embedded clauses as well as scope properties, the author argues that there are actually two types of *zergatik*: one that is merged in Spec ReasonP and then moves to Spec IntP and triggers residual V2, and another, that is merged in Spec IntP and does not require verb adjacency. In the author's analysis, the latter has the interpretation of *how come* rather than of *why*.

To summarise so far, whereas in Basque the same lexical element displays different syntactic distribution and is associated with two distinct interpretations, Trevisan, which encodes two distinct lexical entries, has one reason *why* that merges high in the left periphery, whereas the other patterns with other wh-elements. Let us consider other peculiar properties of *why*.

As mentioned in section 1, it has been argued by De Villiers (1991, 1996) that unlike other wh-phrases, *why* can occur in the surface pattern *why XP*. This is shown below:

(25) A: She will read this novel.   why + XP
     B: Why this novel?

(26) A: She will read this novel tomorrow.   *when + XP
     B: *When this magazine?

(27) A: She will read this novel in the park.   *how + XP
     B: *Where this magazine?

(28) A: She will read this novel pretty quickly.
     B: *How this magazine?

The two immediate questions that arise are: what underlies this asymmetry? What is the syntax of the pattern *why* + XP?

In Chapter 6, Norbert Corver considers these questions in Dutch and provides several arguments in favour of an analysis of the Dutch pattern *waarom XP*, known under the name of *Why*-Stripping, as a clausal structure where material has been sluiced, the only remaining element being the focalised constituent XP. More precisely, the reason adverb *waarum* 'why' moves from Spec ReasonP to Spec CP, which presumably corresponds to Rizzi's (2001) Spec IntP. The remnant XP undergoes movement to Spec FocusP. Crucially, in Corver's analysis, movement of *waarom* from Spec ReasonP does not yield a Relativised Minimality effect as ReasonP is located above FocusP. (29B) has the representation below.

(29) A: Zij   zal   Obama   interviewen.
        she   will   Obama   interview
        'She will interview Obama.'
     B: Waarom   OBAMA?
        Why   OBAMA
        'Why OBAMA?'

(30) [$_{CP}$ waarom$_j$ ... [$_{ReasonP}$ t$_j$ ...[$_{FocP}$ OBAMA$_i$ [$_{Foc'}$ Foc [$_{TP}$ ... t$_i$ ...]]]]]?

The reason wh-phrase *waarom* 'why' moves to Spec CP from a position higher than the focalised phrase *Obama* and thus no Relativised Minimality violation obtains.

As has been discussed for Trevisan and Basque, Corver's contribution shows that Dutch also has two distinct classes of reason adverbials. Thus, a distinction is made between (high) clausal reason adverbials and low reason adverbials. The latter are shown to be structurally low, being VP-modifiers. Crucially, movement of structurally low reason adverbials in such *Why*-Stripping contexts lead to an RM violation, i.e. movement of the low reason adverbial crosses the focalised XP element on its way to Spec CP. Interestingly, Corver extends the discussion of the distinction between high clause adverbials versus low VP-modifying adverbials to stripping patterns involving locational and temporal adverbials and shows that, given the appropriate context, they can also be clause adverbials.

Chapter 5 treats another OV language, German. Nicolas Catasso investigates the merge position of *warum* 'why'. Since modal particles are base-generated in the middle field of the clause in German (Cardinaletti 2011, Coniglio 2007, Coniglio et al. 2011), he discusses the interaction of *warum* and such modal particles. On the assumption that in Geman modal particles can surface in the left periphery on condition they are pied-piped by a *wh*-element, he provides an interesting set of data to show that *warum* 'why' actually originates in a position inside the middle field of the clause. On its way to the left periphery, it can optionally pied-pipe the modal particle. In (31), in Catasso's view, *warum* moves to the left periphery and pied-pipes the modal particle *denn*.

(31) a. Warum ist er denn weg?
 Why be-PRS.3SG he-NOM.SG denn away
 'Why has he left?'
 Warum denn$_i$ ist er t$_i$ weg?
 Why denn be-PRS.3SG he-NOM.SG away

If such an analysis is on the right track, it seems that German *warum* behaves like any other wh-element. If so, it would represent a counter-example to the generalisation that the reason *why*-element is externally merged in the left periphery of the clause.

Although such data are interesting, one question that arises is what drives the optionality of pied-piping. Furthermore, the examples provided contain particles which are merged high in the middle field of the clause, i.e. Mood or Mode particles.

8 The syntax of a special class of *what* based *why*-questions

Chapters 7 and 8 deal with a special class of *why*-elements in two in-situ languages, Cantonese and Mandarin. Drawing a comparison with other wh-in-situ languages, Wei-Tien Dylan Tsai's and Lisa-Lai Cheng's contributions to this volume analyse *what*-based *why*-questions Mandarin and Cantonese. What has got sparse attention in the literature is the postverbal *what*. Wei-Tien Dylan Tsai investigates a class of postverbal *what* questions that give rise to unexpected *why*-construals associated with a whining interpretation, as illustrated in (32) below.

(32) ni ku shenme?!
 you cry what
 'What the heck are you crying for?! (You shouldn't be crying.)'

In order to explain the postverbal position of these wh-expressions and their association with the peculiar pragmatics of whining as well as their negative deontic modal force, Tsai argues that these are applicative constructions in disguise (cf. Marantz 1984, 1993, McGinnis 2001, 2003, Harley 2002, Pylkkänen 2002, Tsai 2018, a.o.) More precisely, the object *shenme* in (32) is bound by a whining operator merged in the left periphery. Such special *what*-based questions involve an implicit light verb to which the main verb raises in overt syntax. This is shown below.

(33) a. ni   FOR   shenme   ku?!
         you   LV   what   cry
     b. ni   ku-FOR shenme   <ku>?!

In (33), the verb *ku* raises to the applicative head FOR. Tsai discusses experimental data to substantiate his claim (Yang and Tsai 2019). He thus shows that the verb carries the most prominent stress. The whining force of the wh-element involves stress shift from the object wh-element to the inner light verb, which is the locus of Focus. When the inner light verb is silent, it needs material to carry the prosodic weight and this triggers raising-to-FOR.

Tsai's analysis of Mandarin also accounts for the apparently ill-behaved *why*-questions in Vietnamese which are constructued on *how* and share the same whining force.

In Chapter 8 Lisa Cheng first discusses a special class of reason *why*-questions in Cantonese and Mandarin, those built on *what* and *how*. She then provides a thougough investigation of a special class of what looks like *why*-questions which are constructed with an initial *mat* 'what' element in Cantonese.

(34) a. lei^5 haam^3 mat^1 aa^3?
         you   cry   what   SFP?
     b. mat^1 lei^5 hai^2 dou^6 haam^3 ge^2?
         what/how you   PROG   cry   SFP
         'Why are you crying?'

Since Cantonese does not have wh-movement, the structure in (34b) is particularly interesting. Cheng discusses the morpho-syntactic and interpretative differences between sentence initial *mat*-questions and postverbal causal *mat*-questions and argues that *mat* in sentence initial questions is not derived by movement but is merged in the left periphery. Furthermore, sentence initial *mat*-questions are shown not to have the same denotation as *why*-questions. Given the similarities between *mat*-initial questions and exclamatives and in light of the special syntax of the *mat*-initial questions, the author concludes that this special class of questions are actually exclamatives which resemble German *was*-exclamatives in (35) and Dutch *wat/dat*-exclamatives in (36).

(35) Was (der) Otto seine Frau liebt!
 what the Otto his wife loves
 'How Otto loves his wife!'

(36) Wat springt zij ver!
 what jumps she far
 'Boy, she jumps high!'

Thus, *mat* in (34b) is not a typical *wh*-phrase, but rather a *wh*-exclamative of the Dutch/German type.

To summarise, in Mandarin, Cantonese and Taiwanese, the *what*-as-*why* questions (to take over Lisa Cheng's coinage) or the *how*-as-*why* questions which appear either postverbally or sentence-initially do not, after all, constitute exceptions to the cross-linguistic generalisation about the placement of *why*. Their contributions represent a significant step to sorting out the how of *what* and the what of *how*.

9 Some syntactic aspects of *how come*

Yoshio Endo, in Chapter 9, contributes to the discussion on *how come* in English sketched in section 4 by integrating another aspect, that of register. He discusses a novel phenomenon, namely the fact that *how come*-questions can exhibit subject drop in diary-style English, as exemplified below.

(37) How come <ec> can't use iPhone anymore?

As opposed to *how come*-questions, *why*-questions in diary English cannot appear with null subjects, as shown in (38).

(38) *Why can't <ec> use iPhone anymore?

He ties the subject-drop cases like (37) to the *that*-trace effects and the alleviating effect provided by intervening adverbial elements discussed by Rizzi and Shlonsky (2007) and Rizzi (2006, 2014) and exemplified below.

(39) This is the man who I think, next year, __ will sell the house.

Recall that in Rizzi's (2014) and Rizzi and Shlonsky's (2007) Fin-based approach, the nominal nature of Fin° merged above the subject position satisfies the criterial property of Subj(ect)° and as such the DP subject may skip Spec SubjP. Endo suggests an analysis in terms of recursion of Fin and proposes that *how come* directly licenses the lower Fin endowed with the [+N] feature. He further suggests that in diary style the null subject can only be licensed by the immediately adjacent Fin°[+N].

He then discusses the implications of his analysis to some special cases of *wanna* contraction.

(40) a. Who$_i$ do you want [t$_i$ to meet the president]?
     b. Who do you wanna meet the president?

As reported by the author, a minority of speakers accepts cases such as (40b). For these speakers the variable in (40a) does not the block the *wanna* contraction. The licensing of the subject position is accounted in terms of the same Fin-based approach that accounts for cases like (37) above.

10 The semantics and pragmatics of a special class of *why* rhetorical questions

Lavi Wolf and Edit Doron's contribution, Chapter 10, falls within the domain of semantics and pragmatics. It analyses the behaviour of *why* in rhetorical questions. An answer is provided here through the lens of a particular Hebrew construction that is dubbed Doubly-Marked Interrogatives (Khalaily and Doron 2016): a *why*-question embeds a regular *wh*-question, as in (41).

(41) lama   mi   ata
     why   who (are) you

This construction ostensibly asking for the identity of the addressee is conversationally used as a rejection act and may be uttered in a context in which the speaker uses an imperative, as in (42A).

(42) A: Clean the   room!
     B: lama   mi   ata
         why   who (are) you
         'Who are you (to tell me what to do)?'

Such special questions are attested in various dialects of Arabic and colloquial Modern Hebrew. The existence of such patterns is all the more interesting as Hebrew does not allow multiple questions. The authors show that doubly-marked interrogatives constitute a single intonational phrase and are marked by the falling intonation characteristic of rhetorical questions. Pragmatically, such questions serve to reject a previous speech act and imply that there is no justification in asking, for instance, the *who*-question and that there is only one alternative, which is shared both by the speaker and the addressee. The authors claim that the DMI is made up of an embedding metalinguistic question and an embedded rhetorical question and that the relationship between the two gives rise to a challenging rhetorical question effect which rejects a previously performed speech act.

11 *Why* and the syntax-prosody interface

The chapters dicussed thus far have dealt with the peculiarities of *why*-questions in terms of its syntax, semantics and pragmatics. One may also wonder how *why* behaves with respect to prosody. Is the prosody of *why* similar to that of other wh-elements? Does the merge position of *why* condition in any way its prosody?

In Chapter 11, Giuliano Bocci, Silvio Cruschina and Luigi Rizzi discuss the behaviour of *perché*-questions at the syntax-prosody interface in Italian. The authors discuss the results of an experimental study meant to test the focal nature of postverbal subjects in *perché*-questions (Bianchi, Bocci and Cruschina 2017). Thus, in neutral contexts, preverbal subjects are largely preferred (in 63% of the cases) and that is expected, whereas in contexts which are set to induce narrow focus on the subject, 66% of the paticipants prefer postverbal subjects. Bocci, Cruschina and Rizzi conduct a production experiment to compare the behavior of *perché* 'why' to that of other wh-phrases in direct questions. One of the main findings confirms the view that in non-*perché* questions the nuclear pitch accent is assigned to the lexical verb and never to the wh-element itself (Marotta 2001). The second major finding is that in direct *perché*-questions the main prominence falls on *why* and not the verb. The special behaviour of *perché*-questions is taken to be a consequence of their different syntactic derivation. In other wh-questions the assignment of the NPA to the lexical verb is a reflex of the successive cyclic movement of the bare wh-element, which tracks the intermediate positions. Since the syntactic derivation of *perché* is different, the asymmetry between *perché*-questions and other wh-questions is expected. *Perché* is thus the carrier of the focus-feature. The authors also consider some special cases of *why*-questions in Italian where main prominence is assigned to another constituent. This apparent exception to the pattern of the NPA in *why*-questions is explained by the fact that that particular element is the carrier of the focus featue. This is expected as *perché* and the fronted focus do not compete for the same position.

The chapter thus clearly shows that Italian *why*-questions behave differently from other wh-questions not only at the syntactic level, but also at the prosodic level.

Current work on *why* has both an empirical dimension – extending the investigation of its properties to other languages – and a conceptual or theoretical one. Four major aspects stand out, in particular, and are treated from different angles in the contributions to this volume:

1. Reason *why*-questions are universally an exclusively complementiser domain phenomenon and the questions that appear to run counter this generalisation are actually cases in which a truth-conditionally equivalent *why*-item is merged in the middle field of the clause and consequently show a whole array of distinct syntactic properties.
2. There is growing cross-linguistic evidence that there are high (i.e. clause-modifying) reason adverbials and low reason (i.e. VP-modifying) adverbials. What exactly is the hierarchy of such adverbials? What explains the particular order or hierarchy in which they appear? Can they co-occur in the same sentence?
3. What is the cartography of *what*-as-*why* questions (to use here Lisa Cheng's coinage) and *how*-as-*why* questions in wh-in-situ languages? Whereas some chapters in the present volume sketch out such an order, this domain of research clearly needs further exploring and extending to wh-movement languages.
4. How is *why* different prosodically from a typical interrogative question? How does syntax feed this peculiarity? Is the prosodic pattern of a *what*-as-*why* or of a *how*-as-*why* question any different from that of a typical interrogative question? If so, what explains this difference?

References

Alboiu, Gabriela. 2002. *The Features of Movement in Romanian*. University of Manitoba dissertation.

Bianchi, Valentina, Giuliano Bocci & Silvio Cruschina. 2018. The syntactic and prosodic effects of long-distance *wh*-movement in Italian. In Delia Bentley & Silvio Cruschina (eds.), *Non-Canonical Postverbal Subjects. Special Issue of Italian Journal of Linguistics* 30 (2). 59–78.

Bromberger, Sylvain. 1992. *On What We Know We Don't Know: Explanation, Theory, Linguistics and How Questions Shape Them*. Chicago: The University of Chicago Press.

Cardinaletti, Adriana. 2011. German and Italian modal particles and clause structure. *The Linguistic Review* 28. 493–531.

Cattell, Ray. 1978. The source of interrogative adverbs. *Language* 54. 61–77.

Collins, Chris. 1990. Why and how come. In Lisa Lai-Shen Cheng & Hamida Demirdache (eds.), *Papers on wh-movement*, 31–45. MIT Working Papers in Linguistics 13. Cambridge, MA: MIT, MIT Working Papers in Linguistics.

Coniglio, Marco. 2007. German Modal Particles in Root and Embedded Clauses. *University of Venice Working Papers in Linguistics* 17. 109–141.

Coniglio, Marco, Iulia Zegrean & Laura Brugè. 2011. Splitting up Force, evidence from discourse particles. 7–34. Università Ca' Foscari *University of Venice Working Papers in Linguistics*.

de Villiers, Jill. 1991. Wh-questions. In Thomas Maxfield and Bernadette Plunkett (eds.), *The Acquisition of wh*, 155–173. University of Massachusetts Occasional Papers in Linguistics 17. Amherst, MA: GLSA.

de Villiers, Jill. 1996. Defining the open and closed program for acquisition: The case of wh-questions. In Mabel Rice, (ed.), *Towards a genetics of language*. 145–184. Hillsdale, N.J.: Lawrence Erlbaum.

Dretske, Fred. 1972. Contrastive statements. *The Philosophical Review* 81. 411–437.

Endo, Yoshio. 2015. Two ReasonPs. In Ur Shlonsky (ed.), *Beyond functional sequence*, 220–231. New York: Oxford University Press.

Endo, Yoshio. 2020. Information structure, null Case particle and sentence final discourse particle. In Pierre-Yves Modicom & Olivier Duplatre (eds.), *Discourse particles and information structure*, 223–250. Amsterdam & Philadelphia: John Benjamins.

Haegeman, Liliane. 2010. The internal syntax of adverbial clauses. *Lingua* 120. 628–648.

Haegeman, Liliane. 2013. The Syntax of Registers: Diary Subject Omission and the Privilege of the Root. *Lingua* 130. 88–110.

Harley, Heidi. 2002. Possession and the double object construction. *Yearbook of Linguistic Variation* 2. 29–68.

Hornstein, Norbert. 1995. *Logical Form: From GB to Minimalism*. Oxford: Blackwell.

Huang, C.-T. James. 1982. *Logical relations in Chinese and the theory of grammar*. Cambridge MA: MIT dissertation.

Khalaily, Samir &Edith Doron. 2016. Colloquial Modern Hebrew Doubly-Marked Interrogatives and Contact with Arabic and Neo-Aramaic Dialects. In Edith Doron (ed.), *Language Contact and the Development of Modern Hebrew*. 112–127. Leiden: Brill.

Ko, Heejong. 2005. Syntax of *why*-in-situ: merge into [Spec, CP] in the overt syntax. *Natural Language & Linguistic Theory* 23(4). 867–916.

Ko, Heejeong. 2006. On the Structural Height of Reason Wh-Adverbials: acquisition and consequences. In Lisa-Lai Shen Cheng & Norbert Corver (eds.), *Wh-Movement Moving On*, 319–349. Cambridge, MA: MIT Press.

Labov, William, & Teresa Labov. 1978. Learning the syntax of questions. In Robin N. Campbell & Philip T. Smith (eds.), *Recent advances in the psychology of language. Vol. III*, 1–44. New York: Plenum Press.

Marotta, Giovanna. 2000. I toni accentuali nelle interrogative aperte (wh-) dell'italiano di Lucca. In Camilla Bettoni, Antonio Zampolli & Daniela Zorzi, (eds.), *Atti del II congresso di studi dell'Associazione Italiana di Linguistica Applicata*. 175–194. Perugia: Guerra Edizioni.

Marantz, Alec. 1984. *On the Nature of Grammatical Relations*. Cambridge, MA: MIT Press.

Marantz, Alec. 1993. Implications of asymmetries in double object constructions. In Sam Mchombo (ed.), *Theoretical aspects of Bantu grammar*, 113–150. Stanford: CSLI Publications.
McGinnis, Martha. 2001. Variation in the Phase Structure of Applicatives. *Linguistic Variation Yearbook* 1. 105–146.
McGinnis, Martha. 2003. Lethal Ambiguity. *Linguistic Inquiry* 35. 47–95.
Ochi, Masao. 2004. *How Come* and Other Adjunct *Wh*-phrases: A Cross-Linguistic Perspective. *Language and Linguistics* 5(1). 29–57.
Ortiz de Urbina, Jon. 1989. *Parameters in the Grammar of Basque: A GB approach to Basque Syntax*. Dordrecht: Foris.
Ortiz de Urbina, Jon. 1999. Focus in Basque. In G., Rebuschi & Laurice Tuller (eds.), *The Grammar of Focus*. 311–334. Amsterdam/Philadelphia: John Benjamins.
Pylkkänen, Lina. 2002. *Introducing Arguments*. Cambridge, MA: MIT dissertation.
Rizzi, Luigi. 1990. *Relativized Minimality*. Cambridge, MA: MIT Press.
Rizi, Luigi. 1993/1994. Some notes on linguistic theory and language development: The case of root infinitives. *Language Acquisition* 3. 371–393.
Rizzi, Luigi. 2001. On the position "Int (errogative)" in the left periphery of the clause. In Guglielmo Cinque & Georgi Salvi (eds.), *Current Studies in Italian Syntax. Essays offered to Lorenzo Renzi*, 287–296. Amsterdam: Elsevier North-Holland.
Rizzi, Luigi. 2006. On the Form of Chains: Criterial Positions and ECP Effects. In Lisa-Lai Shen Cheng & Norbert Corver (eds.), *Wh-movement: Moving on*, 97–134. Cambridge, MA: MIT Press.
Rizzi, Luigi. 2014. Some consequences of Criterial Freezing: Asymmetries, anti-adjacency and extraction from cleft sentences. In Peter Svenonius (ed.), *Functional Structure from Top to Toe – The Cartography of Syntactic Structures*. Vol. 9, 19–54. New York: Oxford University Press.
Rizzi, Luigi & Ur Shlonsky 2007. Strategies of subject extraction. In Hans-Martin Gärtner, Uli Sauerland, (eds.), *Interfaces + Recursion = Language? Chomsky's Minimalism and the View from Syntax-Semantics*, 115–60. Berlin: Mouton de Gruyter.
Rudin, Catherine. 1988. On multiple questions and multiple wh-fronting. *Natural Language and Linguistic Theory* 6. 455–501.
Shlonsky, Ur & Gabriela Soare. 2011. Where's 'Why'? *Linguistic Inquiry* 42(4). 651–669.
Soare, Gabriela. 2009. *The Syntax-Information Structure Interface: A view from Romanian*. Université de Genève dissertation.
Stepanov, Arthur & Wei-Tien D. Tsai. 2008. Cartography and licensing of wh-adjuncts: a cross-linguistic perspective. *Natural Language & Linguistic Theory* 26(3). 589–638.
Thornton Rosalind. 2008. Why continuity. *Natural Language & Linguistic Theory* 26(1). 107–146.
Tsai, Wei-Tien D. 2008. Left periphery and how-why alternations. *Journal of East Asian Linguistics* 17. 83–115.
Tsai, Wei-Tien D. 2015. A Tale of Two Peripheries: Evience from Chonese advrbials, light verbs, applicatives and object fronting. In Wei-Tien Dylan Tsai (ed.), *The Cartography of Chinese Syntax*, 1–32. New York: Oxford University Press.
Tsai, Wei-Tien D. 2018. High Applicatives are not High Enough: A Cartographic Solution. *Lingua Sinica* 4(1). 1–12.

Part 1: **_Why_ in a Gbe language**

Leston Chandler Buell
Reason questions as a complementizer domain phenomenon: Evidence from Ewe

1 Introduction

This paper[1] deals with reason questions (*why* questions) in Ewe, a member of the Gbe subgroup of the and spoken by more than 3,000,000 people, mainly in Ghana and Togo. An Ewe reason question, illustrated in (1), has a *why* component consisting of two non-adjacent elements: sentence-initial *núkàtà* and an optional sentence-final *ɖó*.

(1) *Núkàtà-(é) Kòfí lè hà dzí-ḿ (ɖô)?*
 why-FOC Kofi be.at singing sing-PROG go.to
 'Why is Kofi singing?'

Cross-linguistically, reason questions are particularly interesting because of certain syntactic and semantic properties that distinguish them from other question types. Some such differences in Italian led Rizzi (1999) to argue for two analytical points concerning the word *perché* 'why'. First, he argued that *perché* is first introduced in the complementizer domain rather than being moved there from a lower position. Second, he argued that *perché* occupies a position higher than other focused constituents.

This paper will show that Ewe *núkàtà . . . ɖó* also behaves differently from other *wh* phrases in the language. Furthermore, two of these unique characteristics will be argued to show that *núkàtà. . .ɖó*, just like Italian *perché*, is first merged in the left periphery and occupies a higher position than other focused constituents, and further that the bipartite nature of *núkàtà . . . ɖó* lends support to an independent ReasonP, lower in the complementizer domain than IntP (Shlonsky and Soare 2011).

---

[1] An earlier version of this paper appeared in M. Bowler, P. T. Duncan, T. Major, and H. Torrence (eds.) (2019), *Schuhschrift: Papers in Honor of Russell Schuh*, pp. 1–14, https://escholarship.org/uc/item/7c42d7th.
  The following abbreviations are used in the glosses: cj "conjoint", dj "disjoint", foc "focus", om "object marker", neg "negative", pl "plural", prog "progressive", prosp "prospective", pst "past", redup "reduplicant", rel "relative", sg "singular", sm "subject marker".

2 A morphological asymmetry

In this section, it will be shown that while the *ɖó* of the *núkàtà . . . ɖó* bipartite *why* component is homophonous with an element occurring in other types of adjuncts, it does not display the same morphological alternation, nor is it obligatory, unlike its non-reason counterpart. We begin with some basic facts about word order, questions, and adjuncts in the language.

Ewe is a language with SVOX word order, as illustrated by the simple sentence in (2). In *wh* questions, the questioned constituent obligatorily moves to a left-peripheral position and is often also followed by the focus marker *yé/-é*, as in (3). This focus marker is optional in most contexts, as in (4), a notable exception being any type of subject focus, in which case it is obligatory (Badan and Buell 2012), as in (5). Example (1) above further shows that *núkàtà*, like other *wh* phrases, can also be followed by the focus marker.

(2) Kòfí kpɔ́ Ámà lè àsìmè.
 Kofi see Ama be.at Market
 'Kofi saw Ama at the market.'

(3) Àmékà$_i$-é Kòfí gblɔ bé yè-kpɔ́ t$_i$ lè àsìmè?
 who-FOC Kofi say that LOG-see be.at market
 'Who$_i$ did Kofi say that he saw t$_i$ at the market?'

(4) Mángò-nyè-wó (yé) Kòfí ɖù.
 mango-1SG-PL FOC Kofi eat
 'Kofi ate MY MANGOES.'
 (Badan & Buell 2012)

(5) Àmékà *(yé) yì àfútà?
 who FOC go beach
 'Who went to the beach?'
 (Badan & Buell 2012)

Núkàtà 'why' is composed of three distinct morphemes. This composition and an illustration of its subparts are given in (6). Alongside *núkàtà . . . ɖó*, an alternative form *núkà ŋútí . . . ɖó* can also be used. Both of these forms end in a light postposition-like nominal element which can also be used as a body(part) noun: *tă* 'head' and *ŋútí* 'body'. No differences in interpretation or syntactic behavior were found between these two forms. All examples in this article use *núkàtà . . . ɖó*.

(6) nú-kà?   / nú-kà-tà?   / àvù kà?
    thing-which / thing-which-head / dog which
    'what? / why? / which dog?'

In other contexts, both as a content noun in the literal meaning of 'head' and in its use as a light nominal element, *tă* usually has a rising tone, rather than the low tone found in *núkàtà*, which shows that the word *núkàtà* has been lexicalized.

Ewe questions end with a low boundary tone, which is particularly salient when the final syllable is underlyingly high. In that case the final syllable surfaces as falling. The contrast is shown with the high-toned word *kpɔ́* 'see' in (7):

(7) a. *Kòfí ḍéká kò-é   wò-kpɔ́.*
       Kofi one   only-FOC   3SG-see
       'He only saw Kofi.'
    b. *Àmékà-é   wò-kpɔ̂?*
       who-FOC   3SG-see
       'Who did he see?'

It will be noted that the reason question in (1) ends in *ḍô*, with a falling tone, while in the expository text the form *ḍó*, with a high tone, has been used as the citation form. The final fall in the example questions is due to this final low boundary tone. In non-final positions *ḍó* is pronounced with a high tone rather than a falling one.

Many adjuncts in Ewe have the form V [DP (N)], in which the V is a light verb functioning like a preposition and the N is one of a handful of light nominal elements that behave roughly as postpositions. Some examples are given in (8).

(8) a. *Mè-kpɔ́ gà   hŏmè   áḍé [Lè   xɔ̀-á   mè.]*
       1SG-see money   amount some be.at room-the   inside
       'I found some money in the room.'
    b. *Àgbàlẽ̀ sìà   fò   nŭ [Tsó   àvù-wó   ŋú.]*
       Book   this hit   mouth go.from dog-PL   body
       'This book is about dogs.' (*fò nŭ* 'talk')
    c. *Mè-zɔ̀ [tó   tsì   ŋú.]*
       1SG-walk pass water body
       'I walked along the river.'

These adjuncts are relevant to the discussion because it will initially appear as if the sentence-final *ɖó* in a *núkàtà* question is identical to a light verb as used in other questions, while ultimately it will need to be considered a distinct lexical entry.

When the DP in such an adjunct phrase undergoes any type of A'-movement, the V is always stranded, while the light N is pied-piped (i.e., moved along with the noun), as shown in (9).[2]

(9) a. *wh* question
    [*Xɔ̀*   *kà*   *mè*]$_i$ *-é*   *nè-kpɔ́*   *gà*   *lá*   *lè t$_i$?*
    room   which   inside   -FOC   2SG-see   money   the   be.at
    'Which room did you find the money in?'
b. relative clause
    Ésìà   *nyé*   *tsì* [*sì*   *ŋú*]$_i$ *mè-zɔ̀*   *tó t$_i$*   *lá.*
    this   be   water   that   body   1SG-walk   pass   the
    'This is the river that I walked along.'

Ɖé is one of these preposition-like verbs,[3] and its use in adjuncts is illustrated in (10). Although *ɖé* typically designates movement ('onto', 'into', 'to', etc.), it is also used in many idiomatic contexts.

(10) a. *Dàdì-á*   *dzò*   *gé*   *ɖé*   *kplɔ̃-à*   *dzí.*   (movement)
       cat-the   jump   fall   go.to   table-the   top
       'The cat jumped onto the table.'
b. *Kòfí*   *kpé*   *ɖé*   *Ámà*   *ŋútí*   *ŋútɔ́.*   (idiomatic)
       Kofi   help   go.to   Ama   body   much
       'Kofi helped Ama a lot.'

Just as *ɖó* and *tà* are used to ask a reason question in *núkàtà . . . ɖó* questions, *ɖé* and *tǎ* can be used in statements to express a reason or goal, as in (11).

(11) *Mè-yì*   *Tógó*   *ɖé*   *tàkpékpé*   *áɖé*   *tǎ.*
     1SG-go   Togo   go.to   meeting   some   head
     'I went to Togo for a conference.'

---

[2] Ewe relative clauses often end in the article *lá*.
[3] *Ɖé* behaves like other preposition-like verbs except for the fact that it cannot be used as the main predicate, unlike the verbs *lè*, *tsó*, and *tó*, which appear in (6).

Now we come to the connection between ɖé and ɖó. When the complement of ɖé is extracted, as when it is questioned, ɖé normally takes the form ɖó, although four of my six informants also accept ɖé in this context:

(12) a. Kplɔ̃   kà   dzí-é   dàdì-á   dzò   gé   ɖô/%ɖê?
         table   which   top-FOC   cat-the   jump   fall   go.to
         'Which table did the cat jump onto?'
    b. Tàkpékpé   kà   Tă   nè-yì   Tógó   ɖô/%ɖê?
         meeting   which   head   2SG-go   Togo   go.to
         'What kind of conference did you go to Togo for?'

What distinguishes this ɖó (that from which a non-reason complement has been extracted) from the ɖó of núkàtà ... ɖó is that speakers who accept the form ɖé in the former context reject it in the latter context, as shown in (13).

(13) Núkàtà   xèvî-á   lè   dzò-dzò-ḿ   ɖô/*ɖê?
      why   bird-the   be.at   REDUP-fly-PROG   go.to
      'Why is the bird flying?'

The simplest analysis of distribution of ɖé and ɖó is one in which there are two separate lexical entries: one for the ɖé that for some speakers has the ɖé/ɖó alternation in extraction contexts and another without the alternation for any speakers.

The behavior of ɖé in extraction contexts has a parallel in the Dutch preposition *naar* 'to'. This preposition has two different (sets of) forms when its complement is extracted, depending whether it indicates a motion, as in (14), or something else, as in (15).

(14) a. De   bus   reed   naar   het   vliegveld.
         the   bus   rode   to   the   airport
         'The bus rode to the airport.'
    b. Waar   reed   de   bus   naartoe/heen/*naar?
         where   rode   the   bus   to
         'Where did the bus ride to?'

(15) a. Deze   zeep   ruikt   naar   lelietjes-van-dalen.
         this   soap   smells   to   lilies-of-the-valley
         'This soap smells like lily-of-the-valley.'
    b. Waar   ruikt   deze   zeep   naar/*naartoe/*heen?
         where   smell   this   soap   to
         'What does this soap smell like?'

In addition to the morphological asymmetry of reason and non-reason ɖé/ɖó, there is an additional asymmetry with respect to obligatoriness. Ðó is optional in reason questions, with no apparent consequence for interpretation:

(16) a. Kòfí lè mɔ́lì ɖù-ḿ.
kofi be.at rice eat-PROG
'Kofi is eating rice.'
b. Núkàtà-é Kòfí lè mɔ́lì ɖù-ḿ (ɖô)?
why- FOC Kofi be.at rice eat-PROG go.to
'Why is Kofi eating rice?'

The same is not the case for ɖé/ɖó in other types of questions. In (17), ɖó cannot be omitted, while in (18), it cannot be omitted in an out-of-the-blue context; the ɖó-less version requires some pragmatic context.

(17) a. Dàdì-á dzò gé ɖé kplɔ̃à dzí.
cat-the jump fall go.to table-the top
'The cat jumped onto the table.'
(Repeated from (10a).)
b. Kplɔ̃ kà dzí-é dàdì-á dzò gé *(ɖô)?
table which top-FOC cat-the jump fall go.to
'Which table did the cat jump onto?'

(18) a. Mèyì Tógó ɖé tàkpékpé áɖé tǎ.
1SG-go Togo go.to meeting some head
'I went to Togo for a conference.'
b. Tàkpékpé kà tǎ nèyì Tógó %(ɖô)?
meeting which head 2SG-go Togo go.to
'What kind of conference did you go to Togo for?'

In this section it was shown that the ɖó of reason questions is not an exponent of a morphological alternation like the ɖó of other adjuncts. In this way, reason adjuncts have been shown to differ in a certain way from other adjuncts. However, while this difference adds to the cross-linguistic evidence that reason questions are different from their non-reason counterparts, it says nothing about what position ɖó is merged in or occupies at the surface. We now turn to the first of these two questions.

3 Direct insertion of *núkàtà* in the left periphery

Evidence is accumulating that the merging of *why* directly in the complementizer domain is either universal or is at least a very strong cross-linguistic tendency. A particularly clear example of this evidence comes from Krachi, a Kwa language spoken in Ghana. As shown in (19), while other *wh* phrases can appear in a sentence-final position, 'why' must appear in sentence-initial position.

(19) a. Ɔʧɪw ɛ-mò bwatéo ɲfrɛ́/kɛmekɛê/nɛnɛ?
woman AGR-kill.PST chicken where/when/how
'Where/when/how did the woman slaughter the chicken?'
b. *Ɔʧɪw ɛ-mò bwatéo nání?
woman AGR-kill.PST chicken why
c. Nání jǐ ɔʧɪw ɛ-mò bwatéo?
why FOC woman AGR-kill.PST chicken
'Why (for what reason) did the woman slaughter the chicken?'
(Krachi; Kandybowicz and Torrence 2011)

However, at the same time, there clearly do exist types of *why* phrases that are introduced below the inflectional domain. An example of this is the clitic *i* 'what; why' in the Bantu language Sambaa.[4] As in other Bantu languages with a conjoint/disjoint alternation, the conjoint verb form in Sambaa can only appear when the element following it is inside the VP (Buell and Riedel 2008). Therefore, the clitic *i* in (20) is VP-internal.

(20) U-chi-ghul-iye-i?
2SG.SM-7OM-buy-PERF.CJ-why
'Why did you buy it?'
(Sambaa; Buell 2011: 813)

In such cases, it can usually be shown that the resulting question is essentially a purpose question rather than a reason question. While purpose questions can often be used as surrogates for reason questions, the two can be distinguished by the fact that purpose questions are generally incompatible with non-volitional predicates. Using that criterion, the examples in (21) show that Ewe *núkàtà* questions are genuine reason questions.

---

[4] While the clitic *i* is also used to mean 'what', it cannot have that interpretation in (20) because the direct object is encoded with the noun class 7 object marker *chi*.

(21) a. *Núkàtà wŏ-lè dɔ̀ lé-ḿ (ɖô)?*
　　　 why 3SG-be.at sickness suffer-PROG go.to
　　　 'Why is she sick?'
　　b. *Núkàtà gà àɖéké mé-lè é-sí (ɖó) ò?*
　　　 why money any NEG-be.at 3SG-hand go.to NEG
　　　 'Why doesn't she have any money?'

In the previous section, it was shown that the *núkàtà ... ɖó* word order closely resembles other cases in which a [DP+light N] constituent is extracted from the position which is complement to a light V. If 'why' were introduced in the same low position as other adjuncts, we would expect the *ɖó* of *núkàtà ... ɖó* to similarly be stranded in some low position below IP. Two types of evidence will now be presented to argue that, contrary to that expectation, *núkàtà ... ɖó* is first merged in the left periphery.

3.1 Negation

Buell (2011) connected Rizzi's (1999) idea that *why* first merges in the complementizer domain with negation, proposing that *why* cannot be merged under sentential negation. In English, the argument for this comes from the fact that *why* falls outside the scope of negation. One of these scopal effects is illustrated in (22), in which the sentence *But I have sung!* is felicitous as a response to a *why* question, but not to any other type of *wh* question.

(22) a. Why haven't you sung yet? But I have sung!
　　 b. What kinds of performances haven't you sung in yet? #But I have sung!
　　 c. Who haven't you sung for/with yet? #But I have sung!

The reason question in (22a) presupposes that no singing event took place. In contrast, the non-reason questions in (22b) and (22c) are incompatible with that same presupposition. Instead, they require a context in which there is a set of potential singing events, at least one of which went unrealized. This is explained if *why*, unlike the other *wh* phrases, leaves no copy or trace in a position under negation.[5]

---

[5] Shlonsky and Soare (2011) use the pair *Why/*How didn't Geraldine fix her bike?* to make the same claim in terms of Relativized Minimality. While *why* and *how* do not have the same status

At first glance, Ewe seems to constitute a clear counterexample to Buell's proposal, because for some speakers, *ɖó* can appear sandwiched between the two negative heads *mě* and *ò*, as in (23a), giving the impression that *ɖó* is lower than at least one of them.

(23) a. %*Núkàtà mě-gblɔ̃ ná Ámà bé Kòfí dzó ɖó ò?*
why 2SG:NEG-say to Ama that Kofi leave go.to NEG
'Why didn't you tell Ama that Kofi left?'
b. *Núkàtà mě-gblɔ̃ ná Ámà bé Kòfí dzó ò ɖô?*
why 2SG:NEG-say to Ama that Kofi leave NEG go.to

However, as (23b) shows, *ɖó* can also appear to the right of the second negative head, and that is the only word order accepted by all speakers. This fact leaves open the possibility sketched in Figure 1 that *ɖó* is not below either of the negative heads.

For independent reasons, Aboh (2004) has argued the very high position of the negative head *ò* in Figure 1 and the movement of IP around it.[6]

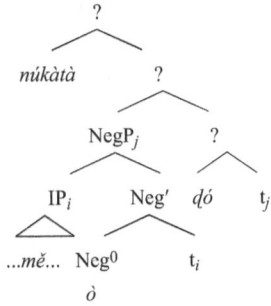

Figure 1: Structure with *ɖó* above both negative heads.

One argument that can be added for this high position is the fact that *ò* follows a complement clause when the matrix clause is negated, as in (24).

(24) *Nyè-mé-gblɔ̃ [CP bé Kòfí dzó] ò.*
1SG-NEG-speak that Kofi leave NEG
'I didn't say that Kofi left.'

---

in this pair, Buell (2011) shows that *how* actually can be used grammatically in such negative questions if a list of particular manners is context-salient. However, he also shows that the interpretation with respect to the scope of negation still differs between *why* and *how* in these cases.
6 See also Kandybowicz (2008) for a similar particle in Nupe.

This fact is easily explained if *ò* heads a projection somewhere above IP. The sentence-final position of *ò* in (24) is then explained by moving the entire matrix IP to the left of *ò*, without prior extraposition of the complement clause.

If the analysis in Figure 1 of sentence (23b) with *ò dó* is correct, then the problematic *dó ò* order in (23a) can be explained by assuming that a post-spell-out reordering has taken place that does not reflect the underlying syntactic hierarchy. This analysis is further supported by the fact that two of my six informants categorically reject the *dó ò* order. For those speakers, the only possible order is *ò dó*, which corresponds transparently to the syntactic structure in Figure 1.

The structure in Figure 1 is also compatible to Shlonsky and Soare's (2011) proposal, in which 'why' originates in a ReasonP in the complementizer region but can move to an IntP (the Interrogative Phrase first proposed by Rizzi 1999) even higher in the same region. Using data from Romanian, they argue for the following partial hierarchy of the complementizer domain.

(25)   . . . IntP > TopP > FocP > WhP > ReasonP . . .

Assuming the part of their analysis that places IntP above ReasonP and that allows 'why' to move from spec-ReasonP to spec-IntP, *dó* could head ReasonP while *núkàtà* originates in its specifier. The NegP in Figure 1 would then need to occupy a functional projection somewhere between IntP and ReasonP, and *núkàtà* would move from spec-ReasonP to spec-IntP. The resulting structure is depicted in Figure 2, which omits the silent Int⁰ and F⁰ heads.

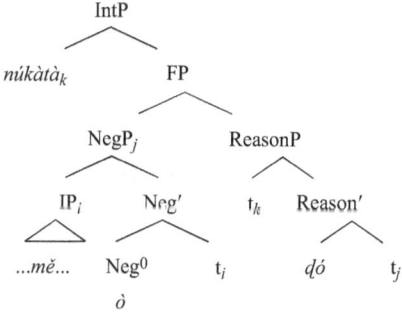

Figure 2: Structure with NegP in the specifier of a functional projection between IntP and ReasonP.

In addition to keeping 'why' entirely outside the c-command of both negation heads, this analysis, in which *dó* and *núkàtà* are first introduced as head and specifier of the same projection, nicely captures the fact that the two elements are related.

3.2 VP nominalization fronting

Although Ewe is an SVO language, in progressive and prospective aspect an inversion takes place in which the object comes to precede the verb, as in (26b). The verb is followed by a nominalizing particle (*ḿ* for progressive, *gé* for prospective) that indicates which of these two aspects is intended. The object, verb, and nominalizing particle form a constituent (Buell, 2012), which for convenience we can simply call a "(VP) nominalization." As illustrated in (27), this constituent can be preposed for focus, in an operation we can call "VP nominalization fronting."[7]

(26) a. S V O
    Ðèví lá ɖù àkɔ́ɖú.
    child the eat banana
    'The child ate a banana.' (default aspect)
  b. S Aux [O V Nom]
    Ðèví lá lè [àkɔ́ɖú ɖù-ḿ.]
    child the be.at banana eat-PROG
    'The child is eating a banana.' (progressive aspect)

(27) a. *Mè-lè [mɔ́lì ɖù gé.]*
    1SG-be.at rice eat PROSP
    'I'm going to eat rice.'
  b. *[Mɔ́lì ɖù gé] mè-lè.*
    rice eat PROSP 1SG-be.at
    'I'm going to EAT RICE.'

Instead of an object, this fronted constituent may contain a *wh* constituent (either an object or an adjunct), as in (28) and (29).[8] However, as shown in (30b), *núkàtà* 'why' is not compatible with VP nominalization fronting.

(28) [*Núkà ɖù-ḿ*] *nè-lè?*
    what eat-PROG 2SG-be.at
    'What are you eating?'

---

[7] VP nominalization fronting is a type of predicate focus. For a discussion of other types of predicate focus in Ewe, see Fiedler (2012), Badan and Buell (2012), and the references therein.
[8] Some speakers do not accept *áléké* 'how' in monoclausal examples of this construction. The full range of adjunct *wh* phrases in predicate focus is better shown in multiclausal questions, which are too complex to discuss here. See Buell (2012).

(29) [Áléké zɔ̀-ḿ   ] wŏ-lè?
       how   walk-PROG   3SG-be.at
   'How is he walking?'

(30) a. Núkàtà nè-lè   dzò-dzó-ḿ?
        why   2SG-be.at REDUP-leave-PROG
    'Why are you leaving?'
   b. *Núkàtà (dzò)-dzó-ḿ   nè-lè?
       why   REDUP-leave-PROG   2SG-be.at

Judgements on this point are so strong that when presented with them, speakers usually reject such questions after reading just the first two words, regardless of the length of the question. There is simply no way to complete a sentence starting with *núkàtà* followed by a verb stem and nominalizing particle.

The fact that a VP nominalization can contain clearly phrasal material, as in (31), in which the object is modified by a relative clause, shows that it is not formed by some extrasyntactic morphological process.

(31) Mè-lè   [[$_{DP}$ mɔ́lì sì Ámà ɖà lá] ɖù ḿ.]
     1SG-be.at   rice REL Ama cook the eat PROG
   'I'm eating the rice that Ama cooked.'

Aboh (2004, ch. 6) develops an analysis in which the nominalization is formed on the main line of projection. The nominalizing particle is merged somewhere below IP and above *v*P, and the verb stem and fronted element in the nominalization (i.e., the object or *wh* phrase) subsequently move above it.[9] Let us assume that analysis. If *núkàtà* is first introduced in the complementizer domain (somewhere above IP), then it is never in a position low enough to move to this sub-IP position above the nominalizing particle, as would be necessary to form part of the nominalization constituent. Merging *núkàtà* directly in the complementizer domain thus allows us to explain the distribution of VP nominalization fronting at no extra cost.

This gives us two arguments – negation and VP nominalization fronting – that Ewe *núkàtà ... ɖó*, just like Italian *perché* 'why', is first introduced in the complementizer domain. Now we turn briefly to the internal structure of that domain.

---

[9] Buell (2012) has argued that an alternative analysis requires an overly powerful Sidewards Movement mechanism.

4 Higher than focus

By showing that Italian *perché* 'why', unlike other *wh* phrases in the language, could be combined with fronted focused phrases and appear to their right, Rizzi (1999) showed that *perché* occupies a position higher than focused phrases in that language. Using the hierarchy in (25), these positions would correspond to spec-IntP and spec-FocP, respectively. The same results can be reproduced in Ewe, as shown in (32b), in which *núkàtà* is contrasted with *yèkáyì* 'when' in an embedded context, although the same pattern also holds in root questions and for other types of *wh* phrases. Of all types of *wh* phrases, only *núkàtà* can appear before a focused phrase.

(32) a. *Nyè-mé-nyá   núkàtà-(é)   Kòfí-é   wɔ   nú   sìà   ò.*
       1SG-NEG-know   why-FOC   Kofi-FOC make   thing   this   NEG
       'I don't know why KOFI did it.'
   b. **Nyè-mé-nyá   yèkáyì-(é)   Kòfí-é   dzó   ò.*
       1SG-NEG-know   when-FOC   Kofi-FOC leave   NEG
       intended: 'I don't know when KOFI did it.'

Thus, Ewe is similar to Italian not only in that 'why' is first merged in the complementizer domain, but also in that the position it occupies is higher than other focused elements.

Unlike other *wh* phrases, *núkàtà* can appear to the left of a topic, as shown in (33).

(33) a. *Núkàtà   Kòfí   yá   nè-fò   nũ   kplĩ́?*
       why   Kofi   TOP   2SG-hit   mouth   with:3SG
       'As for Kofi, why did you talk with him?'
   b. **Yèkáyì   Kòfí   yá   nè-fò   nũ   kplĩ́?*
       when   Kofi   TOP   2SG-hit   mouth   with:3SG
       intended: 'As for Kofi, when did you talk with him?'
   c. **Àfíkà   Kòfí   yá   nè-fò   nũ   kplĩ́?*
       when   Kofi   TOP   2SG-hit   mouth   with:3SG
       intended: 'As for Kofi, where did you talk with him?'

While perhaps surprising, such an ordering is predicted by the hierarchy in (25) to be possible.

5 Conclusion

In the previous sections three analytical points were addressed. First, it was shown that *núkàtà . . . ɖó* is morphologically different from other adjuncts involving extraction from *ɖé*. Second, using facts from negation and VP nominalization fronting, it was argued that *núkàtà* is first merged in the complementizer domain rather than being moved there from a low position such as from within the *v*P. Finally, it was shown that the same facts used by Rizzi in Italian to argue that 'why' occupied a higher position than focused phrases could be replicated in Ewe. Furthermore, both the bipartite nature of *núkàtà. . .ɖó* and the combined distribution of complementizer-domain elements were shown to lend support to Shonsky and Soare's (2011) proposed organization of the left periphery of the clause.

Ewe can thus be added to the growing number of languages that support the characterization that reason questions are universally an exclusively complementizer domain phenomenon.[10]

References

Aboh, Enoch Oladé. 2004. *The morphosyntax of complement–head sequences: Clause structure and word order patterns in Kwa*. Oxford: Oxford University Press.

Aboh, Enoch Oladé. 2007. Focused versus non-focused *wh*-phrases. In Katarina Hartmann, Enoch Oladé Aboh & Malte Zimmermann (eds.), *Focus strategies in African languages*, 297–298. Berlin: Mouton.

Badan, Linda & Leston Buell. 2012. Exploring expressions of focus in Ewe. *Nordic Journal of African Studies* 21(3). 141–163.

Buell, Leston. 2011. Zulu *ngani* "why": Postverbal and yet in CP. *Lingua* 121. 805–821.

Buell, Leston. 2012. A first look at Ewe VP fronting and derivation by phase. Available at <http://www.lingBuzz/001486>.

Buell, Leston & Kristina Riedel. 2008. The conjoint/disjoint alternation in Sambaa. TiN-Dag conference talk handout.

Collins, Chris. 1994. The factive construction in Kwa. *Travaux de recherche sur le créole haïtien* 23, 31–65. Université du Québec à Montréal.

Fiedler, Ines. 2012. Predicate-centered focus in Gbe. In Matthias Brenzinger and Anne-Maria Fehn (eds.), *Proceedings of the 6th World Conference on African Linguistics (WOCAL), Cologne, August 17–21, 2009*. 303–405. Köln: Rüdiger Köppe.

---

[10] I would like to thank my Ewe informants: Akuvi Adessou, Kokou Dzibril Amegan, Kate Dogbe, Jeannette Enaku, Nada Gbegble, and Elvis Yevudey. Thanks also go to Enoch Aboh, Ines Fiedler, Daan van Esch, and especially Jason Kandybowicz. This research was financed by Nederlandse Organisatie voor Wetenschappelijk Onderzoek (NWO) under project 360-70-300.

Kandybowicz, Jason. 2008. *The Grammar of Repetition: Nupe Grammar at the Syntax–Phonology Interface*. Amsterdam: John Benjamins.

Kandybowicz, Jason & Harold Torrence. 2011. Krachi *wh*-in-situ: A question of prosody. In Jaehoon Choi, E. Alan Hogue, Jeffrey Punske, Deniz Tat, Jessamyn Schertz & Alex Trueman (eds.), *Proceedings of the 29th West Coast Conference on Formal Linguistics*, 362–370. Somerville, MA: Cascadilla Proceedings Project.

Rizzi, Luigi. 1999. On the position of Int(errogative) in the left periphery of the clause. Unpublished manuscript. Università di Siena.

Shlonsky, Ur & Gabriela Soare. 2011. Where's 'why'? *Linguistic Inquiry* 42(4). 651–669.

Part 2: **Towards a cartography of high and low reason adverbials**

Caterina Bonan and Ur Shlonsky
On 'why' in situ in Northern Italian dialects: Evidence from Trevisan

1 Introduction

Trevisan is a Northeastern Italian dialect spoken in the Veneto region. In this paper, we concentrate on the variety of Trevisan described in detail in Bonan (2019), more precisely on the morphosyntax of two *why*-words: *parché* and *parcossa*.

We first present a brief overview of the main properties of the interrogative syntax of Trevisan. The language displays so-called 'optional wh-in situ' in genuine, answer-seeking questions: Regardless of whether wh-elements are lexically restricted, as in (1), or bare, as in (2), they are able to surface either fronted to the left periphery of the clause, or clause-internally:

(1) a. Che profesor ga-ea visto al marcà?
       What professor has=she seen at.the market
       'Which professor did she see at the market?'
    b. Ga-ea visto che profesor al marcà?
       Has=she seen what professor at.the market

(2) a. Chi ga-tu visto al marcà?
       Who have=you seen at.the market
       'Who did you see at the market?'
    b. Ga-tu visto chi al marcà?
       Have=you seen who at.the market

Not only can wh-elements surface clause-internally in matrix questions, such as those in (1) and (2), they are also licit 'in situ' in long construals. Observe the alternation in (3):

Acknowledgements: Research for this paper was funded by the Swiss National Science Fund (Grant #100012_156160 to Ur Shlonsky, (PI) and #P2GEP1_184384 to Caterina Bonan) which we gratefully acknowledge. A preliminary version of this paper was presented at the 50th meeting of the Societas Linguistica Europaea, Zürich, September 2017. We wish to thank the audience for their invaluable comments and suggestions, as well as our collaborators at the time, Giuliano Bocci and Lucas Tual. Thanks are also due to Gabriela Soare for her editorial suggestions and an anonymous reviewer for helpful comments.

https://doi.org/10.1515/9783110675160-003

(3) a. Chi   pensi-tu   chei   gabie   visto   al   marcà?
       Who   think=you that=they$_M$ have$_{SUBJ}$ seen   at.the   market
       'Who do you believe they met at the market?'
    b. Pensi-tu   chei   gabie   visto chi   al   marcà?
       Think=you that=they$_M$ have$_{SUBJ}$ seen who   at.the   market

Trevisan differs from the more widely known, closely-related variety of Bellunese known as Pagotto (Munaro 1995, Munaro et al. 2001, and related works), in which wh-in-situ is obligatory with bare wh-words, as shown in (4a-b), but disallowed with lexically-restricted ones, (4c,d).

(4) Pagotto (Munaro 1997)
    a.   Ha-tu   magnà   che?
           Have=you   eaten   what
           'What did you eat?'
    b. *   Che   ha-tu   magnà?
           What   have=you   eaten
    c.   Che   libro   ha-tu   ledest?
           What   book   have=you   read
           'Which book did you read?'
    d. *   Ha-tu   ledest   che   libro?
           Have=you   read   what   book

In its optionality and insensitivity to the lexical restrictedness of the the clause-internal wh-element, Trevisan resembles French. It differs from French however, and resembles Pagotto and many other North Italian dialects, in requiring subject-clitic inversion (SClI) in both ex-situ and in-situ wh-questions (Manzini & Savoia 2011, Bonan 2021, a.o.). In French, to recall, subject-clitic inversion is optional with wh-ex-situ and totally impossible with wh-in-situ. Compare Trevisan (5) and (6) and French (7).[1]

(5) a. Ga-tu   magnà   cuando?
       Have=you   eaten   when
       'When did you eat?'
    b. Cuando   ga-tu   magnà?
       When   have=you   eaten

---

[1] Like many Northern Italian dialects, Trevisan has two series of nominative clitics, one used in declaratives and one in interrogatives. Here, *te* is the declarative 2PS clitic, while *tu* is its interrogative counterpart. For further discussion, refer to Bonan (2019).

(6) a. * Te   gà   magnà   cuando?
         You=   have   eaten   when
         'When did you eat?'
    b. * Cuando te   gà   magnà?
         When   you=   have   eaten

(7) a. * As-tu   mangé   quand?   (French)
         Have=you   eaten   when
         'When did you eat?'
    b.   Tu   as   mangé   quand?
         You   have eaten   when
    c.   Quand as-tu   mangé?
         When   have=you   eaten
    d.   Quand tu   as   mangé?
         When   you   have eaten

The situation that we have just outlined is not completely reproduced in genuine wh-questions that contain a *why* word. This is expected under much recent work on the syntax of *why* (Rizzi 2001, Shlonsky & Soare 2011, Bocci et al. (this volume), a.o.)

In this paper, we first present novel data on the two *why*-words of Trevisan, *parché* and *parcossa*, and argue that one of the main peculiarities of the wh-interrogatives of this language is that while *parcossa* has the distribution of a regular wh-element (felicitous clause internally, requiring subject-clitic inversion, etc.), *parché* is distributionally a regular *why* word in the sense of Rizzi (2001) and resembles Italian *perché* and English *why* (§2). Then, in §3, we present and discuss data on intervention effects by negation and the co-occurrence of *why* words with contrastively focused constituents, all of which strongly suggest that *parché* is externally merged directly in the left periphery of the clause, while *parcossa* starts out TP-internally.

2 Trevisan *parché* vs *parcossa*: Data

The distribution of Trevisan *parcossa* parallels that of the wh-words in (2) and (3). This is unexpected if *why* words are indeed directly merged in the left periphery, ungrammatical in a clause-internal position and not obligatorily construed with subject-inversion in languages that otherwise require inversion in interrogatives (see Rizzi 2001 on Italian *perché*). These properties lead to a working hypothesis, which we will attempt to substantiate in the following sections: The differences between the two why-words of Trevisan are a consequence of their different external merge positions.

2.1 Distributional properties of *parché* and *parcossa*

Parcossa can appear either in-situ or in a clause-peripheral position. When *parcossa* is left-peripheral, it must either be combined with SCII or, for some but not all speakers, followed by the complementizer *che*. Observe the contrasts in (8):

(8) a.   Parcossa sì-tu ndàa al marcà?
         Parcossa are=you gone.$_F$ to.the market
         'Why did you go to the market?'
    b. * Parcossa te sì ndàa al marcà?
         Parcossa you= are gone.$_F$ to.the market
    c. % Parcossa che te sì ndàa al marcà?
         Parcossa that you= are gone.$_F$ to.the market

Parcossa is also perfectly fine clause-internally, as in (9):

(9) Sì-tu ndàa parcossa al marcà?
    Are=you gone.$_F$ parcossa to.the market
    'Why did you go to the market?'

Parcossa is obligatorily construed with a phonetically-realised *that* complementizer, *che*, in embedded questions, such as the one in (10). In this respect, *parcossa* behaves like all regular wh-words of Trevisan, as illustrated in the examples with *cuando*, 'when', in (11):

(10) Voria saver parcossa *(che) te sì ndàa al marcà
     Would$_{IPS}$ know parcossa that you= are gone.$_F$ to.the market
     'I'd like to know why you went to the market'

(11) a. Voria saver cuando *(che) te sì ndàa al marcà
        Would$_{IPS}$ know when that you= are gone.$_F$ to.the market
        'I'd like to know when you went to the market'
     b. Cuando *(che) te sì ndàa al marcà?
        When that you= are gone.$_F$ to.the market
        'When did you go to the market?'

The distribution and syntax of *parché* crucially differ from those of *parcossa*. First of all, *parché* is degraded clause-internally, with or without SCII.

(12) ?? Te   sì   ndàa   parché   al   marcà?
     You= are   gone.$_F$ parché   to.the market
     'Why did you go to the market?'

Secondly, it cannot be combined with subject-clitic inversion, as illustrated by the contrast in (13).

(13) a. * Parché   si-tu   ndàa   al   marcà?
           Parché   are=you gone.$_F$ to.the market
           'Why did you go to the market?'
     b.   Parché   te   sì   ndàa   al   marcà?
           Parché   you= are   gone.$_F$ to.the market

Thirdly, *parché* is incompatible with a following *che*, as illustrated in (14), in both direct and indirect questions:

(14) a. Voria   saver   parché (*che) te   sì   ndàa   al   marcà
         Would$_{1PS}$ know   parché that   you= are   gone$_F$ to.the market
         'I'd like to know why you went to the market'
     b. Parché (*che) te   sì   ndàa   al   marcà?
         Parché that   you= are   gone$_F$ to.the market
         'Why did you go to the market?'

Table 1 summarises the distributional properties of *parché* and *parcossa* discussed so far, compared to those of the regular wh-word *cuando*:

Table 1: Distribution of Trevisan wh-words.

	parché	*parcossa*	*cuando*
Ex situ + SCII	✗	✓	✓
Ex situ, NO SCII	✓	✗	✗
In situ + SCII	✗	✓	✓
In situ, NO SCII	✗	✗	✗
Compatibility with *that*-COMP	✗	✓	✓

In the next section, we briefly consider the different compatibilities of the *why* words of Trevisan with (lexical) subject-inversion.

2.2 Subject-inversion with *parché* and *parcossa*

What we have tried to show in §2.1 is that *parcossa* behaves like a regular wh-element, whereas *parché* does not. Another property shared by *parcossa* and other wh-elements is the impossibility for a lexical subject to appear to the immediate right of a fronted wh-element, as shown in (15).

(15) a. * Cuando to mama cant-ea?
     When your mother sings=she
     'When does your mother sing?'
   b.   Cuando cant-ea, to mama?
     When sings=she # your mother
     Literally: 'When does she sing, your mother?'
   c.   To mama, cuando cant-ea?
     Your mother # when sings=she
     'Your mother, when does she sing?'

Indeed, a fronted *parcossa* is incompatible with an immediately following lexical subject, as illustrated in (16a); the only available position for a lexical subject construed with a fronted *parcossa* is a dislocated one, as in examples (16b-c). Note that we make use of the symbol "#" to signal that the constituents that immediately precede and follow it constitute independent intonational phrases:

(16) a. * Parcossa to mama cant-ea?
     Parcossa your mother sings=she
     'Why is your mother singing?'
   b.   Parcossa cant-ea, to mama?
     Parcossa sings=she # your mother
     Literally: 'Why is she singing, your mother?'
   c.   To mama, parcossa cant-ea?
     Your mother # parcossa sings=she
     'Your mother, why is she singing?'

Differently from *parcossa*, *parché* is compatible both with a directly following lexical subject, as in (17a), as well as with a dislocated lexical subject, as in (17b-c):

(17) a. Parché to mama a canta?
Parché your mother she= sings
'Why is your mother singing?'
b. Parché a canta, to mama?
Parché she= sings # your mother
Literally: 'Why is she singing, your mother?'
c. To mama, parché a canta?
Your mother # parché she= sings
'Your mother, why is she singing?'

Optional subject-inversion characterizes *perché* in Italian (Rizzi 2001), as illustrated in (18). In contrast, all other wh-words in Italian, like *parcossa* or *cuando* in Trevisan, require subject-inversion, as in (19):

(18) a. Perché ha cantato Gianni?   (Standard Italian)
Perché has sung Gianni
'Why did Gianni sing?'
b. Perché Gianni ha cantato?
Perché Gianni has sung

(19) a. Quando ha cantato Gianni?   (Standard Italian)
When has sung Gianni
'When did Gianni sing?'
b. * Quando Gianni ha cantato?
When Gianni has sung

Given the distributional differences between *parché* and *parcossa* discussed so far, we now outline a theoretical analysis of the syntax of both *why* words of Trevisan.

3 *Parcossa* vs *parché*: Analysis

The data presented and discussed in §2 clearly suggest that the two *why* words of Trevisan, *parché* and *parcossa*, despite being truth-conditionally equivalent, are syntactically different. As previously mentioned, *why* has been argued to be cross-linguistically different from other wh-elements: Instead of being externally-merged within TP and then moved to the left periphery of the clause, *why* is either externally-merged directly in the specifier of the left-peripheral Int(errogative)P

(Rizzi 2001), or internally-merged there from a lower, left-peripheral projection (ReasonP in Shlonsky & Soare's 2011 terms, see also Chandler Buell (this volume)).

In section §3.1, we outline a brief summary of the existing literature on *parché* and *parcossa* in Venetan (see Bonan 2019 for a more detailed discussion), and then discuss the different compatibilities of *parché* and *parcossa* with *that* complementizers (§3.2). Afterwards, we test intervention effects on the two *why* words of Trevisan caused by negation in matrix and long-distance questions (§3.3), and in constructions with contrastively focused constituents (§3.4).

3.1 *Parché* and *parcossa* in the literature

The morphosyntax of *parché* and *parcossa* has received limited attention in the literature on Venetan dialects. Munaro (1997) states that in Pagotto, *parché* can only be licensed in a fronted position, as in (20a), whereas the sentential element *par far che* (literally, 'to do what') can only surface clause-internally, as in (20b):

(20) Pagotto (Munaro 1997)
    a. Parché   no   sje   vesti?
        Parché   NEG   are$_{2PP}$ come
        'Why didn't you come?'
    b. Sje-o   vesti   par   far   che?
        Are=you come to   do   What
        'Why did you come?'

Munaro (2005) notes that *parcossa*, which was available in Venetan in the past, has disappeared from Northern sub-varieties over the last century, but has been retained in Central Venetan. Munaro & Poletto (2004) show that *parché* is the only wh-element of Pagotto that can be directly followed by the sentential particle *po*, as in (21). This peculiar distibutional property of Pagotto *parché* suggests, on the one hand, that *parché* is a regular left-peripheral *wh*-element and, on the other hand, that *po* might be the phonetic realization of the head of Rizzi's (2001) IntP:

(21) Pagotto (adapted from Munaro 1997)
      Parché po eli   'ndadi via?
      Parché po have=they gone   away
      'Why did they go away?'

Only in Mendrisiotto, a Lombard dialect spoken in Southern Switzerland, has *parché* been attested clause-internally (Poletto & Pollock 2009), as illustrated in (22):

(22) Ta   vet   via   parché?
     You   go   away   why
     'Why are you going away?'
     Mendrisiotto (Poletto & Pollock 2009)

According to Poletto (1993), Padovano displays the same *parché-parcossa* alternation that we described for Trevisan in §2, with *parché* incompatible with (otherwise obligatory) subject-clitic inversion. The special properties of *parché*, namely, infelicity in clause-internal position, impossibility of co-occurrence with the complementizer *che*, etc., are due, in her view, to the fact that *parché* is a bi-partite wh-element composed of the preposition *par* ('for') and the complementizer *che* ('that') (or of the wh-phrase *par* and the the complementizer *che* in Poletto & Vannelli 1993). The bimorphemic nature of *parché* underlies Poletto & Pollock's (2004) and Benincà & Poletto's (2005) explanation of the impossibility of doubling *parché* in what they call 'wh-doubling constructions', i.e., wh-questions which, despite the presence of two wh-words (one fronted and one in situ), have the semantics of *single* wh-questions. Poletto and Vannelli's characterization of *parché* as bimorphemic cannot be straighforwardly transposed to Trevisan because *parché* and *parcossa* appear to be both multi-morphemic.

3.2 (In)compatibility with *that* complementizers

In this section, we account for the obligatory absence of *che* to the right of *parché*, its optional appearance with *parcossa* and support our claim that *parché* is externally merged in the Left Periphery while *parcossa* is externally merged inside TP.

Consider the following paradigms of data, illustrating the appearance of *che* in Trevisan *why* questions:

(23) a. % Parcossa   che   te   sì   ndàa   al   marcà?
             Parcossa   that   you=   are   gone$_F$ to.the   market
             'Why did you go to the market?'
     b.   Voria   saver parcossa *(che) te   sì   ndàa   al   marcà
             Would$_{1PS}$ know   parcossa that   you=   are   gone$_F$ to.the   market
             'I'd like to know why you went to the market'

(24) a. Parché (*che) te sì ndàa al marcà?
Parché that you= are gone_F to.the market
'Why did you go to the market?'
b. Voria saver parché (*che) te sì ndàa al marcà
Would_IPS know parché that you= are gone_F to.the market
'I'd like to know why you went to the market'

We assume that movement from TP to the Left Periphery transits through FinP (Cardinaletti 2010, Shlonsky (to appear)) and that *che* lexicalizes a Fin-head through the specifier of which a wh-expression has transited on it way to its final landing site in SpecFocusP or higher. Under these assumptions, the absence of *che* following *parché* (in 24) follows from the hypothesis that this expression is merged higher than FinP and therefore does not transit through it.

Consider now the fact that, when *parché* appears in the root, but is construed with an embedded clause, *che* is obligatory in the embedded clause. Contrast short and long construals of *parché* in a matrix clause in (25):

(25) a. * Parché che a te gà ciamà?
Parché that she= you has called
'Why did she call you?'
b. Parché dizi-tu *(che) a te gà ciamà?
Parché say=you that she= you has called
'Why do you think she called you?'

The *che* in (25b) is not Fin° but rather Force°, the regular declarative complementizer in Trevisan. However, if *parché* were bi-morphemic and composed of *par* and *che*, as in Poletto (1993) and related work, one would expect *che* to be absent in (25b), contrary to fact.

We conclude that *parché* is (synchronically) monomorphemic and attribute the fact that it cannot co-occur with *che* as Fin° because it does not move through its specifier but is externally merged in a higher position. In contrast, *parcossa* can be followed by *che*, as in (23). We argue that this *why* word originates inside TP and either remains in situ or moves to the left periphery. Therefore, its movement proceeds through SpecFinP, and Fin° can be lexicalized.

We further argue that *parcossa* is a PP, consisting of the preposition *par* and the wh-word *cossa*. Trevisan wh-PPs can either remain in a clause-internal position or move to the left periphery, trigerring either SCLI, as in (26), or lexicalization of Fin° by *che*, as in (27).

(26) a. Ga-tu   magnà   co   chi?
       Have=you   eaten   with   who
       'Who did you eat with?'
    b. Co   chi   ga-tu   magnà?
       With   who   have=you   eaten

(27) Co   chi   che   te   gà   magnà?
     With   who   that   you=   have   eaten

As pointed out to us by a reviewer, whom we wish to thank, that *parcossa* is a PP suggests a resemblance with Chinese 'when/where' which, contrary to 'why', are analysed by Huang (1982) as being arguments of a null P that heads an adjunct PP.

To conclude this section, we have argued that *parcossa* is merged in a clause-internal adverbial position (the specifier of a functional head, as per Cinque 1999) and either remains in-situ or undergoes overt movement to the left periphery of the clause, in which case it transits through SpecFinP and either triggers SClI or contributes to the lexicalization of Fin°. We address the issue of the final landing site of *parcossa* in the left periphery in §3.4. Trevisan *parché*, we argue, is like Italian *perché*, externally merged in SpecIntP.

3.3 Intervention effects

To further explore the syntactic behavior of the two *why* words in Trevisan and provide additional motivation for our hypothesis concerning the different first-merge sites of *parcossa* and *parché*, we now investigate whether intervention in Rizzi's (2001) terms is present in the following cases:
i. when the *why* appears in matrix (§3.3.1) and long-distance (§3.3.2) questions with a phonetically-realised negation;
ii. in the presence of a contrastively focused constituent (§3.4).

3.3.1 *Why* words in the presence of negation

Wh-movement (of adjuncts) is blocked when it crosses over c-commanding negation, viz. Ross's (1984) Inner Islands, construed as Relativized Minimality violations in Rizzi (1990):

Relativized Minimality (Rizzi 1997)
Given the sequence X...Z...Y, a local relation between X and Y is disrupted when Z structurally intervenes between X and Y. Intervention is defined hierarchically through c-command: Z structurally intervenes between X and Y when Z c-commands Y and Z does not c-command X.

X and Y cannot form a licit chain wh chain when Z is negation. However, if a wh-element is not moved over negation, but externally merged above it, so that the configuration is either X...Z or X...Y...Z, negation does not intervene and the wh-question that contains it is, *ceteris paribus*, expected be grammatical. In light of this, consider (28):

(28) a.   Parché   no   te   me   gà   ciamà?
          Parché   NEG   you=   me=   have   called
          'Why didn't you call me?'
    b. * Parcossa no   me   ga-tu   ciamà?
          Parcossa NEG   me=   have=you   called
    c. * Parcossa no   te   me   gà   ciamà?
          Parcossa NEG   you=   me=   have   called

There is no intervention effect in (28a). This is consistent with our claim that *parché* is merged directly in the left periphery, i.e., above negation. (28b-c) are ungrammatical because of movement of *parcossa* across negation, as diagrammed in (29):

(29) * Parcossa$_i$ no   me   ga-tu   ciamà ___$_i$?

       Parcossa NEG   me=   have=you   called

The absence of (otherwise obligatory) SCIl in (28a) should be construed in the following terms: SCLI is implemented by moving the inflected verb to Fin, and the negative head blocks such movement in Trevisan. The ungrammaticality of (28b-c) shows that negation blocks movement of *parcossa* independently of any effect it might have on SCLI: Once it is controlled for, as in (28a) and again in (30b), *parcossa* is compatible with negation.[2]

---

[2] Note that the grammaticality of SCLI in French (i) should be taken to mean that T incorporates Neg and the two move to Fin° as a single head:

(i)   Pourquoi   ne   m'as-tu   pas   téléphoné?
      Why   NEG   me=have=you   NEG   called
      'Why didn't you call me?'

(30) a. * Noo   ciami-tu parcossa?
       NEG=him= call=you   parcossa
       'Why don't you call him?'
    b.   No   teo   ciami parcossa?
         NEG you=him=   call   parcossa

Let us further test the analysis sketched in (29). (31) shows that *parcossa* can be interpreted as questioning either the matrix verb *dizi* ('say') (short construal), or the embedded verb *ciamà* ('call') (long construal). In contrast, *parché* can only be short-construed, as in (32):

(31) a. Short construal
       Parcossa$_i$ dizi-tu ___$_i$ [che a   te   gà ciamà] ?
       Parcossa   say=you   that she= you= has called
       'Why are you saying that she called you?'
       Answer: 'Because I think you should be aware of this'
    b. Long construal
       Parcossa$_i$ dizi-tu [che a   te   gà ciamà ___$_i$] ?
       Parcossa   say=you   that she= you= has called
       'Why do you think she called you?'
       Answer: 'Because she wanted to tell me about her promotion'

(32) a. Short construal
       Parché te   dizi [che a   te   gà ciamà]   ?
       Parché you= say   that she= you has called
       'Why are you saying that she called you?'
       Answer: 'Because I think you should be aware of this'
    b. Long construal (regular *parché*-syntax: no SCII)
       Parché$_i$ te   dizi [che ___$_i$ a   te   gà ciamà] ?
       Parché   you= say   that   she= you has called
       'Why do you think she called you?'
       Answer: 'Because she wanted to tell me about her promotion'

Long-construal of *parché* becomes possible when subject-clitic inversion takes place, as in the example in (33). Recall that SCII is obligatorily triggered by interrogative movement into the left periphery of the clause:

Trevisan negation does not permit this option so that T can only move *across* Neg, yielding a violation of Relativized Minimality.

(33) Long construal (obligatory SCII)
Parché$_i$ dizi-tu [che ___$_i$ a te gà ciamà] ?
↑___ SCII ___|
Parché say=you that she= you has called
'Why do you think she called you?'
Answer: 'Because she wanted to tell me about her promotion.'

In 3.3.2, we investigate the effects of negation on long-extraction of *parché* and *parcossa*.

3.3.2 Long-extraction of *why* words across negation

Given that *parcossa* is moved to the left periphery, while *parché* is merged there, we now expect the short construal of *parcossa* but not of *parché* to be sensitive to the presence of negation. This expectation is confirmed by the contrast in (34); indeed, negation only intervenes in constructions with a short-construed *parcossa*, as in (34a):

(34) Short construal (matrix negation)
    a. * Parcossa$_i$ no me ga-tu dito ___$_i$ che a te
         ←___x___|
        Parcossa NEG me have=you said that she= you
        gà ciamà?
        has called
        'Why didn't you tell me that she called you?'
        Answer: 'Because I know you're a jealous guy'
    b. Parché$_i$ no te me gà dito che a te gà ciamà?
        Parché NEG you me have said that she= you has called

We have shown that matrix negation only intervenes in the movement of *parcossa* across it, while *parché* is perfectly licit with matrix negation because it never crosses it. In (34b), *parcossa* in the matrix clause has moved over negation in the same clause, resulting in a violation of Relativized Minimality. We now predict that in the company of embedded negation, short construal of both *parcossa* and *parché* should be licit. This is confirmed by (35):

(35) Short construal (embedded negation)
   a. Parcossa$_i$ me ga-tu dito ___$_i$ che no a te
      Parcossa me have=you said   that NEG she= you
      gà ciamà?
      has called
      'Why did you tell me that she didn't call you?'
   b. Parché$_i$ te me gà dito che no a te gà ciamà?
      Parché you me have said that NEG she= you has called

In (35), *parcossa* and *parché* do not cross over embedded negation, and there is no violation of Relativized Minimality. Clearly, then, it is not the presence of negation *per se* in a clause that leads to the ungrammaticality of wh-movement, but only of negation in a position that structurally intervenes in the formation of the wh-chain.

We also expect differences between *parcossa* and *parché* to arise in case of long construals. With matrix negation, long-extraction of both *parché* and *parcossa* should give rise to a Relativized Minimality effect. This is confirmed by (36):

(36) Long construal (matrix negation)
   a. * Parcossa$_i$ no te dizi [che a me gà ciamà ___$_i$] ?
          ←——x——————————————————————⎦
      Parcossa NEG you= say that she= me has called
      'Why don't you say that she called me?'
   b. * Parché$_i$ no te dizi [che ___$_i$ a me gà ciamà] ?
          ←——x——————————⎦
      Parché NEG you= say that   she= me has called

The situation is expected to be different with long-construed *why*-words when negation is embedded. If *parcossa* is moved from a position below negation in the embedded clause, intervention is indeed predicted. If *parché* is moved to the matrix from a base position in the embedded left periphery, it should not be sensitive to negation in the embedded clause, since it would never cross it. These predictions are confirmed by the data in (37):

(37) Long construal (embedded negation)
    a. * Parcossa$_i$ dizi-tu [che no a me gà ciamà ___$_i$] ?

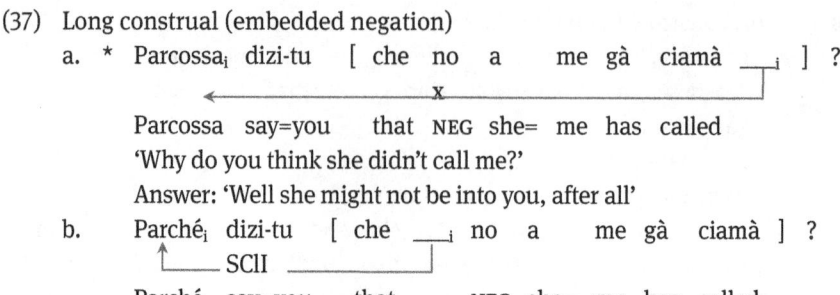

        Parcossa say=you   that NEG she= me has called
        'Why do you think she didn't call me?'
        Answer: 'Well she might not be into you, after all'
    b.   Parché$_i$ dizi-tu [che ___$_i$ no a me gà ciamà] ?
            SCII
        Parché say=you   that   NEG she= me has called

Note that long-extraction of *parché* obligatorily triggers SCII (in the matrix clause), as illustrated in (37b). Indeed, a long-extracted *parché* is not felicitous in the absence of subject-clitic inversion, as shown in (38):

(38) Long construal
    * Parché$_i$ te dizi che ___$_i$ no a me gà ciamà?
      Parché you= say that   NEG she= me has called
      'Why do you think she didn't call me?'
      Answer: 'Well she might not be into you, after all'

We therefore conclude that *parcossa* is externally merged below negation (and moved into the Left Periphery of the clause), whereas *parché* is always merged directly in the Left Periphery, presumably in SpecIntP. Therefore, negation only intervenes when something crosses over it, which happens systematically with *parcossa*, and with *parché* only when it undergoes movement from a subordinate left periphery to a matrix left periphery in long-construal questions.

3.4 (In)compatibility with focus

In this section, we discuss the incompatibility of contrastive focus with regular wh-elements (including *parcossa*) as contrasted with the compatibility of focus and *parché*. The data discussed provide supporting evidence to our claims concerning the different external-merge positions of *parché* and *parcossa*.

In Trevisan, as in many languages, matrix wh-questions and contrastive foci are incompatible. In (39), the wh-element is fronted, and the focus is clause-internal, while in (40), the focalized constituent is peripheral (presumably in SpecFocusP) and the *wh*-element is clause-internal (see below):³

(39) a. * Cuando ghe ga-tu dato I POMI (no i peri?)
        When DAT have=you given the apples NEG the pears
        Literally: 'When did you give THE APPLES to John, (not the pears)?'
   b. * Cuando ghe ga-tu dato A GIANNI (no a Toni)?
        When DAT have=you given to John NEG to Toni
        Literally: 'When did you give TO JOHN the apples (not to Toni)?'

(40) a. * I POMI ghe ga-tu dato quando a Gianni,
        The apples DAT have=you given when to John
        (no i peri?)
        NEG the pears
        Literally: 'THE APPLES you gave to John when (not the pears)?'
   b. * A GIANNI ghe ga-tu dato quando i pomi,
        To John DAT have=you given when the apples
        (no a Toni)?
        NEG to Toni
        Literally: 'TO JOHN you gave when the apples (not to Toni)?'

One way to exclude these sentences is to suppose that the focused constituent in (39) and the wh-element in situ in (40) need to move covertly to SpecFocus, in the Left Periphery of the clause, but since that position is filled, they are barred from doing so.⁴

Bonan (2021), however, argues that argumental foci and wh-elements move to a *v*P-peripheral SpecFoc position in Trevisan (see Belletti 2004, distinguished from the left-peripheral FocusP of Rizzi 1997). They are thus not literally in situ. Under this approach, the focused constituent in (39) does not move covertly and in fact, cannot move, as it is criterially frozen in the *v*P-peripheral focus position (Rizzi 2006 and subsequent work). However, the clause would then contain two foci: the wh-element in the left-peripheral SpecFocusP and the contrastively focused constituent in the *v*P-peripheral SpecFoc. The resultant sentence is ungrammatical, be it because the complement of the left-peripheral focus head, the presupposition, cannot itself contain a focus (Rizzi 1997) or because

---

3 In ditransitive constructions, the clitic *ghe* doubles the dative constituent, and is obligatory in the variety of Trevisan under investigation.
4 One must also assume that the Focus-head can only have a single specifier or landing site for movement.

of the non-satisfaction of question-answer congruence, as argued for in Bocci et al. (2020). In (40), the focused consitutent is in the left periphery and the wh-element is in situ. Here, the option of moving the wh-element to a clause-internal SpecFocP is presumably unavailable, because *cuando* is merged higher than *v*P. We suppose that it therefore undergoes covert movement but cannot access the left peripheral SpecFocusP, which is filled.

Observe now, that *parcossa* is also incompatible with foci.

(41) a. ?? Parcossa ghe ga-tu dato I POMI aa Maria?
Parcossa DAT have=you given the apples to.the Mary
Literally: 'Why did you give THE APPLES to Mary?'
b. ?? Parcossa ghe ga-tu dato AA MARIA i pomi?
Parcossa DAT have=you given to.the Mary the apples
Literally: 'Why did you give TO MARY the apples?'

(42) a. I POMI ghe ga-tu dato parcossa aa Maria?
The apples DAT have=you given parcossa to.the Mary
Literally: 'THE APPLES why did you give to Mary?'
b. * AA MARIA ghe ga-tu dato parcossa i pomi?
To.the Mary DAT have=you given parcossa the apples
Literally: 'TO MARY why did you give the apples?'

Clearly, what is relevant here is that *parcossa* moves to the left periphery either overtly, in (41) or covertly, in (42). It stands to reason that the landing site of *parcossa* is the left-peripheral SpecFocusP and not SpecIntP (as is presumably the case with long-extracted *perché* in Italian, cf. Rizzi 2001 and Shlonsky & Soare 2011). The pattern that we observe with *parcossa* is therefore the same as with *cuando* in (39) and (40) and the analytic options sketched out for these examples carry over to (41) and (42).

In contrast, the co-occurrence of a wh-element and a focus in the same clause is grammatical when the wh-element is *parché*, as illustrated in the sentences in (43):

(43) a. Parché te ghe gà dato i POMI aa Maria?
Parché you= DAT have given the apples to.the Mary
Literally: 'Why did you give THE APPLES to Mary?'
b. Parché te ghe gà dato aa MARIA i pomi?
Parché you= DAT have given to.the Mary the apples
Literally: 'Why did you give TO MARY the apples?'

Just like Italian *perché*, Trevisan *parché* is merged in SpecIntP, above FocusP. There is no reason to believe that a filled *v*P-peripheral FocP (under Bonan's 2021 analysis of (43)) should be any different from a filled left-peripheral FocusP. Both are indeed compatible with a why-word merged in SpecIntP.[5]

Before moving to the conclusions, it must be noted that 'reason why' has been argued to merge directly in the Left Periphery of the clause, while 'purpose why' is widely believed to be merged TP-internally, with its occurrences in the left periphery attributed to movement (Stepanov & Tsai 2008 and related works). It would therefore be legitimate to wonder whether *parcossa* is an instance of 'purpose why', as opposed to 'reason why' *parché*. However, this does not seem to be the case: both why-words can be used to ask purpose questions ('in order to P' as opposed to a 'because P'). In support of this claim, in (44) we provide un example of un unmistakably 'reason use' of *parcossa*:

(44) Butei   parcossa i   persegheri, de sta   stajon?
     Blossom=they parcossa the peach-trees   in this season
     'Why are the peach trees blossoming so early?'

4 Conclusions

Based on the intervention effects by negation in long-distance extraction and the co-occurrence restrictions on wh and focus, we conclude that, like its Italian counterpart *perché*, Trevisan *parché* is externally merged directly in the left periphery of the clause (IntP of Rizzi 2004, or ReasonP of Shlonsky & Soare 2011), while *parcossa* must start out TP-internally like all other regular wh-words. This analysis explains why *parcossa* triggers subject-clitic inversion, whereas *parché* does not; why *parcossa* can be licensed clause-internally, whereas *parché* cannot; and also why *parcossa* cannot be directly followed by a lexical subject, while *parché* can.

---

5 The reasons for which *why* is semantically compatible with focus remain to be determined, see Stepanov & Tsai (2008) and Bocci et al. (2020). Crucial here is Rizzi's idea that the external merge position for Italian *perché* and, arguably, for Trevisan *parché* is higher than any focus projection.

References

Belletti, Adriana. 2004. Aspects of the low IP area. In Luigi Rizzi (ed.) *The Structure of IP and CP. The Cartography of Syntactic Structures*. Oxford University Press.

Benincà, Paola & Cecilia Poletto. 2005. On some descriptive generalizations in Romance. In Guglielmo Cinque & Richard Kayne (eds.), *The Oxford Handbook of Comparative Grammar*, 221–258. Oxford University Press.

Bocci, Giuliano, Valentina Bianchi & Silvio Cruschina. 2020. Focus in wh-questions. *Natural Language & Linguistic Theory*. Springer. 1–51.

Bonan, Caterina. 2019. *On clause-internally moved wh-phrases. Wh-to-Foc, nominative clitics, and the theory of Northern Italian wh-in situ*. Université de Genève dissertation.

Bonan, Caterina. 2021 Romance Interrogative Syntax. Typological and formal dimensions of variation. Linguistik Aktuell / Linguistics Today 266. John Benjamins. doi:10.1075/la.266.

Cardinaletti, Anna. 2010. On a (wh-)moved topic in Italian, compared to Germanic. In Artemis Alexiadou, Jorge Hankamer, Thomas McFadden, Justin Nuger & Florian Schäfer (eds.), *Advances in Comparative German Syntax*. 3–40. Amsterdam: John Benjamins.

Cinque, Guglielmo. 1999. *Adverbs and Functional Heads: A Cross-Linguistic Perspective*. Oxford Studies in Comparative Syntax. Oxford: Oxford University Press.

Huang, James Cheng-The. 1982. *Logical Relations in Chinese and the Theory of Grammar*. MIT dissertatation.

Munaro, Nicola. 1995. On nominal wh-phrases in some North-Eastern Italian dialects. *Rivista di Grammatica Generativa* 20. 69–110.

Munaro, Nicola. 1997. Proprietà distribuzionali dei sintagmi interrogativi in alcuni dialetti veneti settentrionali. *Quaderni di lavoro ASIS* 1. 63–74.

Munaro, Nicola. 2005. Grammaticalization, reanalysis, and CP layering. In Montserrat Battlori, Maria-Lluïsa Hernanz, Carme Picallo & Francesc Roca (eds.), *Grammaticalization and Parametric Variation*. New York: Oxford University Press. 29–47.

Munaro, Nicola & Cecilia Poletto. 2004. On the diachronic origin of sentential particles in North-Eastern Italian dialects. *Nordic Journal of Linguistics* 28(2). 247–267.

Poletto, Cecilia. 1993. Subject Clitic-Verb Inversion in North Eastern Italian Dialects. *Working Papers in Linguistics* 3(1). 95–137.

Poletto, Cecilia & Jean-Yves Pollock. 2004. On wh-clitics and wh-doubling in French and some North Eastern Italian Dialects. *Probus* 16. 241–277.

Poletto, Cecilia & Jean-Yves Pollock. 2009. Another look at wh-questions in Romance: the case of Medrisiotto and its consequences for the analysis of French wh-in-situ and embedded interrogatives. In W. Leo Wentzel (ed.), *Romance Languages and Linguistic Theory 2006: Selected papers from 'Going Romance'*, 7–9 December 2006. Amsterdam: John Benjamins.

Poletto, Cecilia & Laura Vannelli.1993. Gli introduttori delle frasi interrogative nei dialetti italiani. In Emanuele Banfi, Giovanni Bonfadini, Patrizia Cordin & Maria Iliescu (eds.), *Atti del Convegno Italia Settentrionale: Crocevia di Idiomi Romanzi*. Max Niemeyer Verlag. 145–158.

Rizzi, Luigi. 1990. *Relativized Minimality*. Cambridge, MA: MIT Press.

Rizzi, Luigi. 1997. The Fine Structure of the Left Periphery. In Liliane Haegeman (ed.) *Elements of Grammar*. Kluwer International Handbooks of Linguistics. Springer. 281–337.

Rizzi, Luigi. 2001. On the position "int(errogative)" in the left periphery of the clause. In *Current studies in Italian syntax: Essays offered to Lorenzo Renzi*, ed. Guglielmo Cinque & Giampaolo Salvi, 267–296. Amsterdam: Elsevier.

Rizzi, Luigi. 2004. On the Cartography of Syntactic Structures. In Rizzi, Luigi (ed.), *The Structure of CP and IP. The Cartography of Syntactic Structures* II. Oxford Studies in Comparative Syntax. Oxford University Press. 223–251.

Rizzi, Luigi. 2017. Che and weak islands. *In Linguistic variation: structure and interpretation*. Maria Rita Manzini: Festschrift for her 60th birthday.

Rizzi, Luigi. 2006. On the form of chains: criterial positions and ECP effects. In Lisa Lai-Shen Cheng & Norbert Corver (eds.), *WH-movement: Moving on*. 97–134. Cambridge, MA: MIT Press.

Ross, Haj. 1984. Inner Islands. *Proceedings of the Tenth Annual Meeting of the Berkeley Linguistics Society*. 258–265.

Shlonsky, Ur & Gabriela Soare. 2011. Where's why? *Linguistic Inquiry* 42(4). 651–669.

Shlonsky, Ur. 2021. Cartography and selection in subjunctives and interrogatives. In Susan Si Fuzhen & Luigi Rizzi (eds.), *Current issues in syntactic cartography: A cross-linguistic perspective*, 15–25. Amsterdam: John Benjamins.

Stepanov, Arthur & Wei-Tien Dylan Tsai. 2008. Cartography and licensing of wh-adjuncts: A crosslinguistic perspective. *Natural Language and Linguistic Theory* 26. 589–628.

Aritz Irurtzun
Why questions break the residual V2 restriction (in Basque and beyond)

1 Introduction

Why questions –interrogative sentences that inquiry about reasons, causes, and purposes– are particular in many respects. In this paper I address the main properties of *why*-questions in Basque and contrast them with the patterns attested cross-linguistically. I show that there are two main construals (constructions with and without V2) and that they are accompanied by different semantic nuances. Adopting Shlonsky & Soare's (2011) richly articulated CP, I propose that in *why*-questions with V2, the interrogative phrase is first-merged in Spec-ReasonP and then moved successive cyclically, which is accompanied by movement of the verb (T-to-C movement), whereas in non-V2 constructions the interrogative phrase is externally merged in a very high position, where it is frozen, and takes scope over the whole clause.

The paper is organized as follows: Section 2 offers a brief introduction to the syntax of interrogatives (and foci) in Basque. Section 3 then addresses the particular behavior of *why*-questions in this language from a comparative perspective. In Section 4 I present my analysis of the different construals and finally Section 5 closes the chapter with the conclusions.

2 Standard question and focalization strategies

Basque is both an SOV and a 'discourse configurational' language, which means that even if the neutral word order is SOV, alternate word orders are also grammatical, but with a marked information structure. For instance, an informationally neutral statement would have the word order in (1), that is, SOV. An alternative word order such as the SVO of (2), even if grammatical, would be unacceptable as an informationally neutral sentence (this rather corresponds to a focalization over the subject (see below)):

Acknowledgements: Many thanks to M. Duguine, R. Etxepare, C. Mounole and an anonymous reviewer for their helpful comments. Many thanks also to G. Soare for her invitation. This research was funded by the following grants: ANR-18-FRAL-0006 UV2 (ANR-DFG), ANR-17-CE27-0011 BIM (ANR), and PGC2018-096870-B-I00 and FFI2017-87140-C4-1-P (MINECO).

https://doi.org/10.1515/9783110675160-004

(1) Jonek   ura   edan   du.
    Jon   water   drink   AUX
    'Jon drank water.'

(2) #Jonek   edan   du   ura.
    Jon   drink   AUX   water
    'Jon drank water.'

In a similar vein, subject *wh*-questions cannot maintain the neutral SOV word order (3) and necessarily display adjacency between the interrogative phrase and the verb (4). Otherwise it generates strong ungrammaticality (more so than in Spanish, *cf.* Dold (2018)):

(3) *Nork   ura   edan   du?
    who   water   drink   AUX
    'Who drank water?'

(4) Nork   edan   du   ura?
    who   drink   AUX   water
    'Who drank water?'

These patterns are generally analyzed as instances of *wh*-movement followed by the verb, which constitutes a 'residual V2'. 'Residual V2' is defined by Rizzi (1996, 64) as "such construction-specific manifestations of I-to-C movement in a language (like English and the modern Romance languages except Rætho-Romansch) which does not generalize the V2 order to main declarative clauses".

In Basque, this property generalizes to both embedded and matrix interrogative clauses, and just as in (4), in example (5) we observe a leftward position of the interrogative phrase followed by O-V inversion in the embedded clause, and S-V inversion in the matrix clause. Failing to display residual V2 in either embedded (6), matrix (7), or both clauses (8) produces ungrammaticality (see Irurtzun, 2016, for an overview of the syntax of interrogatives):

(5) Nork   esan   du   Jonek   [edan   duela   ura]?
    who   say   AUX   Jon   drink   AUX.C   water
    'Who did Jon say that drank water?'

(6) *Nork   esan   du   Jonek   [ura   edan   duela]?
    who   say   AUX   Jon   water   drink   AUX.C
    'Who did Jon say that drank water?'

(7) *Nork Jonek esan du [edan duela ura]?
    who Jon   say AUX drink AUX.C water
    'Who did Jon say that drank water?'

(8) *Nork Jonek esan du [ura edan duela]?
    who Jon   say AUX water drink AUX.C
    'Who did Jon say that drank water?'

Alternatively, the whole embedded clause can be fronted, but again this requires adjacency between the interrogative phrase and the verb in the embedded clause, as well as adjacency between the whole embedded clause and the matrix verb (9). This is known as a 'clausal pied-piping' construction (Ortiz de Urbina (1989), et seq.). Again, failing to render residual V2 in either embedded (10), matrix (11), or both clauses (12) generates ungrammaticality:

(9) [Nork edan duela ura]   esan du Jonek?
    who drink AUX.C water say AUX Jon
    'Who did Jon say that drank water?'

(10) *[Nork ura   edan duela] esan du Jonek?
     who   water drink AUX.C say AUX Jon
     'Who did Jon say that drank water?'

(11) *[Nork edan duela ura] Jonek esan du?
     who   drink AUX.C water Jon   say AUX
     'Who did Jon say that drank water?'

(12) *[Nork ura   edan duela] Jonek esan du?
     who   water drink AUX.C Jon   say AUX
     'Who did Jon say that drank water?'

Interestingly, focalization displays the very same pattern in Basque. As advanced above, focus on the subject necessarily affects the word order and instead of the neutral SOV, SVO is obtained, with residual V2 and adjacency between the focal phrase and the verb (cf. i.a. De Rijk (1978)):

(13) [Peiok]$_F$ edan du ura.
     Peio   drink AUX water
     '[Peiok]$_F$ drank Water.'

Such a pattern, again, generalizes to embedded clauses and the same restrictions that we saw for interrogatives hold (compare the focalization data in (14–17) with the question data in (5–8):

(14) [Peiok]_F esan du Jonek [edan duela ura].
     Peio   say AUX Jon   drink AUX.C water
     'Jon said that [Peiok]_F drank water.'

(15) *[Peiok]_F esan du Jonek [ura edan duela].
     Peio   say AUX Jon   water drink AUX.C
     'Jon said that [Peiok]_F drank water.'

(16) *[Peiok]_F Jonek esan du [edan duela ura].
     Peio   Jon   say AUX drink AUX.C water
     'Jon said that [Peiok]_F drank water.'

(17) *[Peiok]_F Jonek esan du [ura edan duela].
     Peio   Jon   say AUX water drink AUX.C
     'Jon said that [Peiok]_F drank water.'

The clausal pied-piping construction also exists for focalizations, with the same restrictions with respect to the necessity of residual V2 (compare (18–21) with (9–12)):

(18) *[[Peiok]_F edan duela ura] esan du Jonek.
     Peio   drink AUX.C water say AUX Jon
     'Jon said that [Peio]_F drank water.'

(19) *[[Peiok]_F ura edan duela] esan du Jonek.
     Peio   water drink AUX.C say AUX Jon
     'Jon said that [Peio]_F drank water.'

(20) *[[Peiok]_F edan duela ura] Jonek esan du.
     Peio   drink AUX.C water Jon say AUX
     'Jon said that [Peio]_F drank water.'

(21) *[[Peiok]_F ura edan duela] Jonek esan du.
     Peio   water drink AUX.C Jon say AUX
     'Jon said that [Peio]_F drank water.'

The standard analysis of *wh*-questions in Basque posits *wh*-movement to Spec-CP, which is then followed by T-to-C movement to check the Q-feature in a Spec-Head configuration –giving rise to the residual V2 configuration (see Ortiz de Urbina (1989) *et seq.*). Thus, sentence (22a) with a *wh*-question on the subject receives the analysis in (22b):

(22) a. Nork edan du ura?
 who drink AUX water
 'Who drank water?'

b.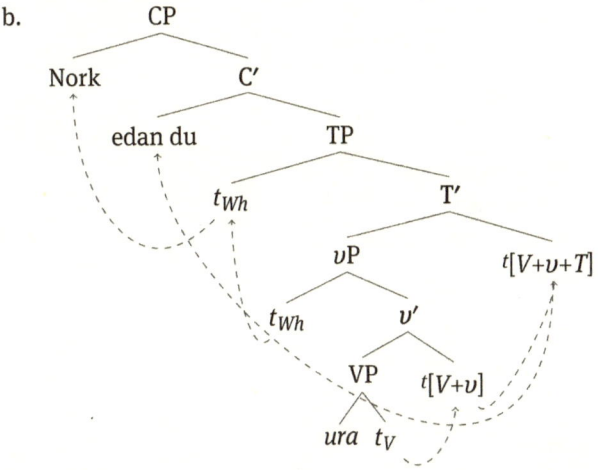

Likewise, an interrogative on the direct object as in (23a), showing V-S inversion would have the structure in (23b):

(23) a. Zer edan du Mirenek?
 what drink AUX Miren
 'What did Miren drink?'

b.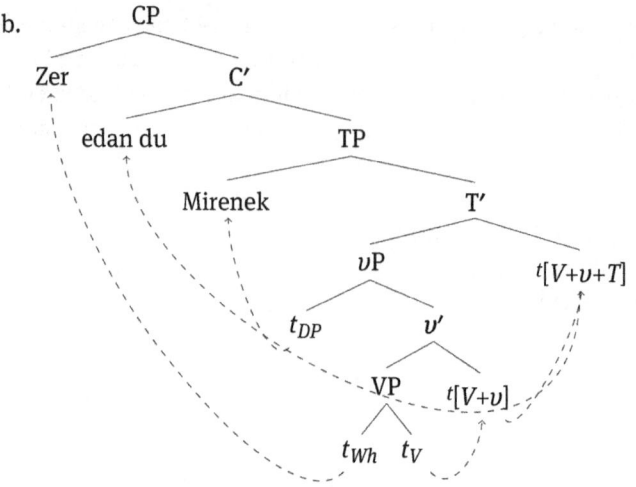

(24) a. [Mirenek]$_F$ edan du ura.
       Miren   drink AUX water
       '[Mirenek]$_F$ drank water.'

b.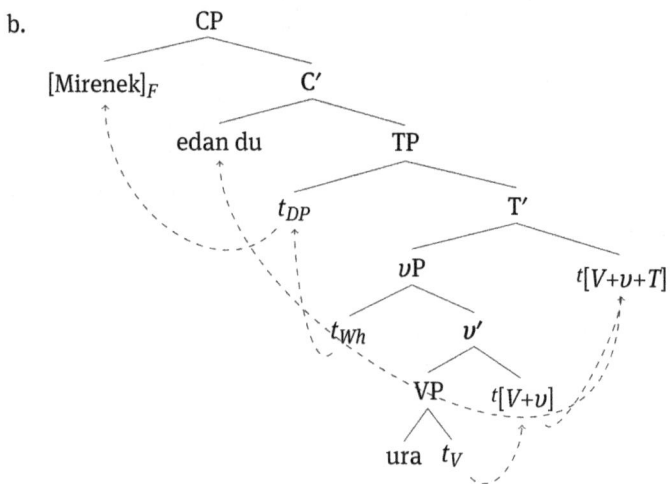

(25) a. [Ura]$_F$ edan du Mirenek.
       water drink AUX Miren
       'Miren drank [water]$_F$.'

b.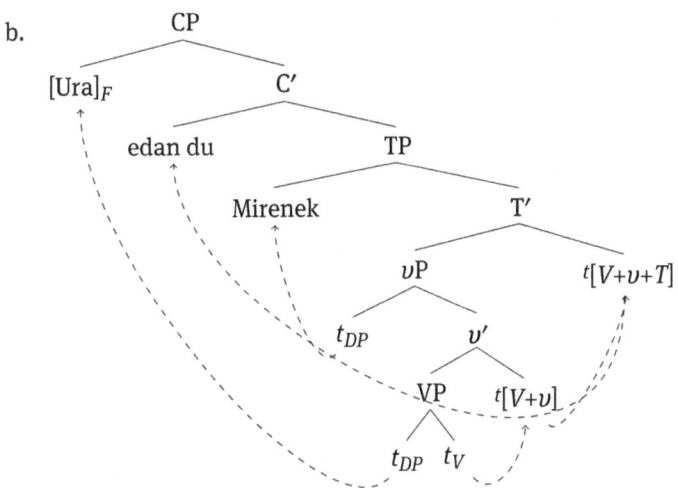

As I advanced, extraction out of embedded clauses takes place the same way successive cyclically, with the consequence that the residual V2 configuration is repeated in both clauses. Therefore, departing from the basic statement in (26), question (27a) on the subject of the embedded clause displays O-V inversion in the embedded clause as well as S-V inversion in the matrix clause, which derives from the structure depicted in (27b): the interrogative phrase undergoes movement to the specifier of the embedded CP first, followed by T-to-C movement of the embedded verb (which renders O-V inversion), and then it is extracted to the specifier of the matrix CP, which triggers again T-to-C movement of the matrix verb, resulting in S-V inversion:[1]

(26) Jonek [Peiok ura edan duela] esan du.
Jon Peio water drink AUX.C say AUX
'Jon said that Peio drank water.'

(27) a. Nork esan du Jonek edan duela ura?
who say AUX Jon drink AUX.C water
'Who did Jon say that drank water?'

---

[1] Again, the pattern for long-distance focalizations is the same. In the interest of space, I omit such examples and tree-structures.

b.

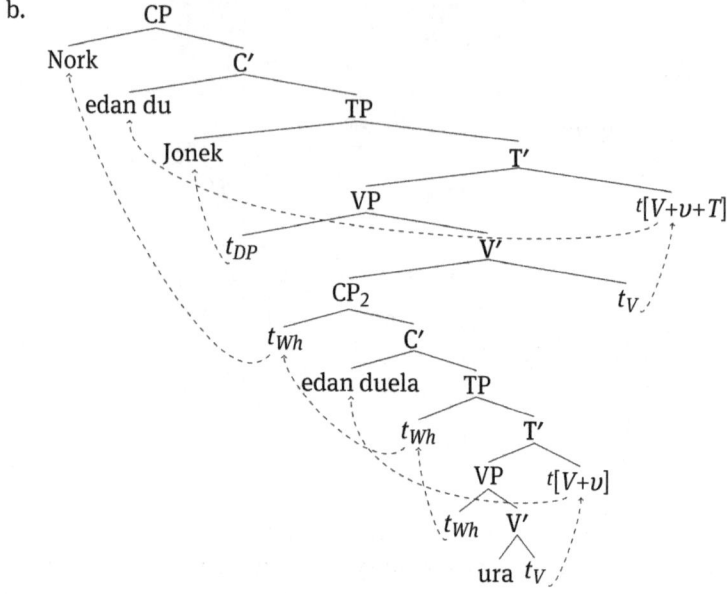

Finally, the first step of the pied-piping strategy that we saw in (9) –repeated here as (28)– is identical to that of the long-distance extraction: the *wh*-phrase is extracted to Spec-CP of the embedded clause, triggering movement of the verb (29a). However, the second step is different since then the whole embedded clause is extracted to the specifier of the matrix CP, which is followed by movement of the matrix verb to C (rendering the residual V2 effect), (29b):[2]

(28) [Nork edan duela ura] esan du Jonek?
 who drink AUX.C water say AUX Jon
 'Who did Jon say that drank water?'

---

[2] Here again I omit the examples and tree-structures for focalizations, as the displacements and syntactic configurations of each construal are identical for *wh*-constructions and focalizations.

(29) a.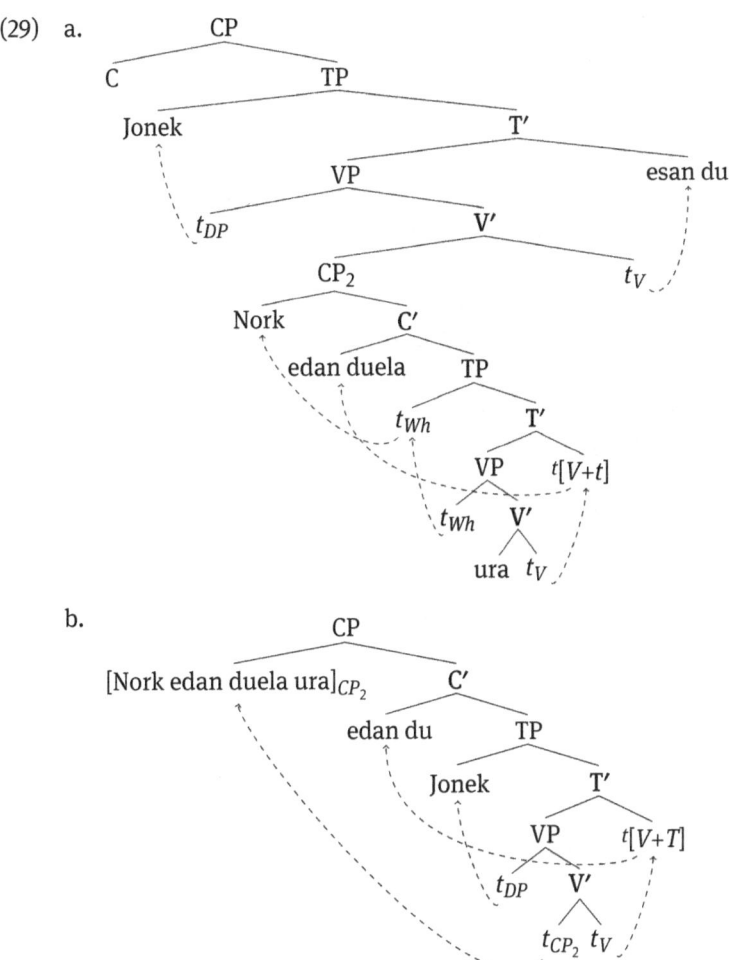

b.

Additional evidence in support of this analysis comes from the fact that extraction out of islands such as coordinate structures (30), adjuncts (31), left branches (32), and complex NPs (33) is fully deviant (again, the pattern is the same for both wh-constructions and focalizations):

(30) a. Jonek [salda eta legatza] nahi ditu.
Jon stock and hake want AUX
'Jon wants stock and hake.'
b. *Zer nahi ditu Jonek [salda eta t]?
what want AUX Jon stock and
Lit. 'What does Jon want stock and?'

c. Zer   nahi   ditu   Jonek   [*t* eta   legatza]?
   what   want   AUX   Jon   and   hake
   Lit. 'What does Jon want and hake?'

(31) a. Jon [abestia   entzun   duelako]   poztu   da.
        Jon   song.ART   hear   AUX.because   get.happy   AUX
        'Jon got happy because he heard the song.'
     b. *Zer   poztu   da   Jon   [*t* entzun   duelako]?
        what   get.happy   AUX   Jon   hear   AUX.because
        Lit. 'What did Jon got happy because he heard?'
     c. *[Abestia]$_F$ poztu   da   Jon   [*t* entzun   duelako].
        song.ART   get.happy   AUX   Jon   hear   AUX.because
        Lit. 'Jon got happy because he heard [the song]$_F$.'

(32) a. Mirenek   [Jonen   liburua]   irakurri   du.
        Miren   Jon.GEN   book   read   AUX
        'Miren read Jon's book.'
     b. *Noren   irakurri   du   Mirenek   [*t* liburua]?
        whose   read   AUX   Miren   book
        'Whose book did Miren read?'
     c. [Jonen]$_F$ irakurri   du   Mirenek   [*t* liburua].
        Jon.GEN   read   AUX   Miren   book
        'Miren read [Jon's]$_F$ son.'

(33) a. [Jonek   liburu   bat   idatzi   duelako   zurrumurrua]   entzun   duzu.
        Jon   book   one   write   AUX.C.P   rumour   hear   AUX
        'You heard the rumour that Jon wrote a book.'
     b. *Zer   entzun   duzu   [Jonek   *t* idatzi   duelako   zurrumurrua]?
        what   hear   AUX   Jon   write   AUX.C.P   rumour
        Lit. 'What did you hear the rumour that Jon wrote?'
     c. *[Liburu bat]$_F$ entzun   duzu   [Jonek   *t* idatzi   duelako   zurrumurrua].
        book   one   hear   AUX   Jon   write   AUX.C.P   rumour
        'You heard the rumour that Jon wrote [a book]$_F$.'

Summarizing, the main characteristics of *wh*-questions and focalizations are the following ones:
– Movement of the focus/*wh*-phrase to Spec-CP.
– T-to-C movement.
– Focus/*Wh*-movement is cyclic.
– The usual restrictions on extraction (islands) apply.

Now, since the syntax of foci and *wh*-questions is uniform, constructions combining a *wh*-question and a focalization are ungrammatical. This is illustrated by the ungrammaticality of both *Wh*»Foc (35) and Foc»*Wh* (36) with respect to the grammaticality of the simpler *wh*-question in (34):

(34) Nork edan du ura?
 who drink AUX water
 'Who drank water?'

(35) Nork [ura]$_F$ edan du?
 who water drink AUX
 'Who drank [water]$_F$?'

(36) [Ura]$_F$ nork edan du?
 water who drink AUX
 'Who drank [water]$_F$?'

From the Principles and Parameters model, such pattern has been analyzed as a clash deriving from two elements (the *wh*-phrase and the focal phrase) targeting the same position:

(37)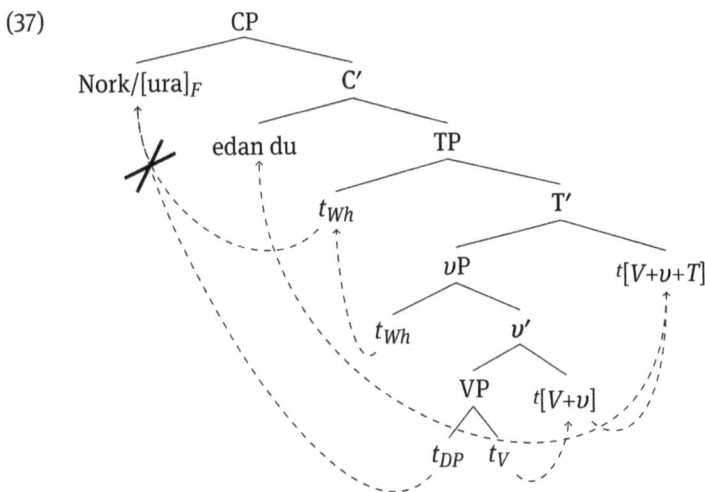

In the next section I will analyze the special behavior of Basque *why*-questions from a cross-linguistic perspective. I will argue that in many languages *why*-questions behave in particular ways with respect to other argument and adjunct questions and, furthermore, that often *why*-questions show a special syntax in patterned ways. In particular, I will show that when fronted they tend to not require the otherwise general adjacency to the verb (hence, no V2) and that they are compatible with foci. I will propose that such patterns derive from a very high merger of the causal interrogative.

3 Why

A longstanding observation is that not all *wh*-phrases necessarily require adjacency to the verb. In particular, researchers such as Mitxelena (1981); Uriagereka (1999) or Etxepare & Ortiz de Urbina (2003) observed that "the operator-verb adjacency is occasionally absent, especially with *zergatik* "why" and other causal *wh*-words" (Etxepare & Ortiz de Urbina, 2003, 465). For instance (38b) is (indeed) grammatical, alongside the general –residual V2– construction of (38a):

(38) a. Zergatik hil zuen zaldunak herensugea?
       why   kill AUX knight   dragon
       'Why did the knight kill the dragon?'
    b. Zergatik zaldunak herensugea hil zuen?
       why   knight   dragon   kill AUX
       'Why did the knight kill the dragon?'

That is, in contrast to (38a), in (38b) we do not observe O-V inversion, but contrary to what we saw in examples such as (3) and the following, the result is grammatical with a *why*-question.

There are some small dialectal differences with respect to the morphology of the interrogative element employed for *why*-questions: Southern dialects employ *zergatik* which is composed of the interrogative item *zer* 'what' + a motivative postposition, producing a *wh*-item with the value of 'why'. This element can be reinforced in some varieties with the addition of an inessive marker *-n*, producing *zergatikan* with no apparent change in meaning. In Northern dialects the interrogative item corresponding to *why* is composed of *zer* 'what' + the possessive *-ren* + the destinative postposition *-dako*: *ze(re)ndako* = 'why/for what purpose'.

In Northern dialects (which are the dialects that have *wh-in-situ* alongside *wh*-movement (*cf.* Duguine & Irurtzun, 2014)) lack of V2 in *why*-questions is more widely available than in Southern dialects. Thus, it is not uncommon to find in Northern Basque examples such as (39) or (40):³

(39) Zendako itxurari   ez darraiko bethi izana?
     why   appearance.DAT NEG follow always being
     'Why doesn't always come the being after the appearance?'

(40) Zendako nere   aintzinian jarri zira?
     why   me.POSS   front.INESS sit   AUX
     'Why did you sit down in front of me?'

3.1 The special behavior of why-questions

The particular behavior of *why*-questions is by no means an idiosyncratic property of Basque.⁴ For instance, a classical observation on the literature in French syntax is that French has both *wh in situ* and *wh*-movement questions and while all *wh*-phrases tend to behave similarly in both constructions, *pourquoi* 'why' escapes this general pattern (Kayne, 1972; de Cornulier, 1974; Kayne & Pollock, 1978; Rizzi, 1990; Hamann, 2000). To begin with, the basic word order in French being SVO, in the *wh in situ* strategy *wh*-phrases occupy the same position as the phrase they substitute. See for example the case of a direct object in (41):

(41) a. Tu veux [un vin].   [French]
        you want one wine
        'You want a wine.'
     b. Tu veux quoi?
        you want what
        'What do you want?'

The same happens with adjuncts such as *où* 'where':

(42) a. Tu vas [au   restaurant].   [French]
        you go   to.ART restaurant
        'You are going to the restaurant.'

---
3 Example (39) extracted from Jean Etxepare's *Buruxkak*; example (40) from a tweet by user @lamiscarreb.
4 See the contributions in this volume, Buell's and Bonan and Shlonsky's in particular.

b. Tu vas où?
   you go where
   'Where are you going?'

However, *pourquoi* cannot appear in the same position as its corresponding phrases (43b); it must obligatorily appear in the left periphery (43c):

(43) a. Tu verses de l'eau [parce que tu as soif] [French]
        you pour PART ART.water because you have thirst
        'You pour water because you are thirsty.'
     b. Tu verses de l'eau pourquoi?
        you pour PART ART.water why
        'Why do you pour water?'
     c. Pourquoi tu verses de l'eau?
        why you pour PART ART.water
        'Why do you pour water?'

In *wh*-movement questions the general SVO word order is altered with S-V inversion, ending up in a residual V2 configuration, both in argument (44a) and adjunct questions (44b–44c):

(44) a. Que fait Pierre?   [French]
        what does Pierre
        'What is Pierre doing?'
     b. Comment votera Pierre?
        how vote.FUT Pierre
        'How will Pierre vote?'
     c. Quand votera Pierre?
        when vote.FUT Pierre
        'When will Pierre vote?'

However, in questions with *pourquoi*, subject-verb inversion is deviant (45a), and a *pourquoi*-subject-verb order is grammatical (45b).[5]

---

[5] Speakers tend to prefer a variant of (45b) with a clitic attached to the verb (*Pourquoi Pierre votera-t-il?*) but since this is optional I kept the bare (45b) for a better comparison with (45a) and (46a).

(45) a. */?Pourquoi votera Pierre? [French]
       why   vote.FUT Pierre
       'Why will Pierre vote?'
   b. Pourquoi Pierre votera?
       why   Pierre vote.FUT
       'Why will Pierre vote?'

Last, note that this only affects *why*-question *pourquoi* since a question on a segmentally homophonous adjunct such as *pour quoi* 'for what' (seeking an answer such as 'For the abolition of the law') is ungrammatical if it does not involve subject-verb inversion (46a–46b):

(46) a. Pour quoi votera Pierre? [French]
       for what vote.FUT Pierre
       'What will Pierre vote for?'
   b. *Pour quoi Pierre votera?
       for what Pierre vote.FUT
       'What will Pierre vote for?'

The general pattern in Spanish *wh*-questions (an SVO language too) is that *wh*-questions involve *wh*-movement followed by movement of the verb (and hence, residual V2):

(47) a. Qué querían esos dos? [Spanish]
       what wanted those two
       'What did those two want?'
   b. *Qué esos dos querían?
       what those two wanted
       'What did those two want?'

But questions with *por qué* 'why' can optionally avoid the V2 pattern, and alongside the regular V2 patterns of (48a) and (49a), non-V2 constructions are also grammatical with *por qué* (48b), (49b) (Torrego, 1984; Uriagereka, 1988; Kaiser et al., 2019):[6]

---

[6] In Spanish orthography it is customary to write clause-initial inverted question marks. However, in order to avoid confusion with acceptability judgements, such question marks were omitted here.

(48) a. Por qué quiere Juan salir   antes que los demas? [Spanish]
       why   wants Juan go.out before than the rest
       'Why does John want to leave before the rest?'
    b. Por qué Juan quiere salir   antes que los demas?
       why   Juan wants go.out before than the rest
       'Why does John want to leave before the rest?'

(49) a. Por qué ha   dicho Pedro que Juan quiere a María? [Spanish]
       why   AUX say   Pedro that Juan loves   María
       'Why did Pedro say that Juan loves María?'
    b. Por qué Pedro ha   dicho que Juan quiere a María?
       why   Pedro AUX say   that Juan loves   María
       'Why did Pedro say that Juan loves María?'

Something similar happens in Italian. In general, *wh*-movement has to be accompanied by V2. Hence (50a) with no S-V inversion (no residual V2) is ungrammatical whereas (50b) with adjacency between the *wh*-phrase and the verb is perfectly grammatical:

(50) a. *Che cosa Maria ha   detto?   [Italian]
        what thing Maria AUX said
        'What did Maria say?'
    b. Che cosa ha   detto Maria?
       what thing AUX said Maria
       'What did Maria say?'

The same pattern is observed with adjunct *wh*-phrases such as *dove* 'where' (51a) and *come* 'how' (51b), which require a residual V2 construal. However, this is not the case with *perché* 'why', which appears in a clause initial position as in (51c), not triggering movement of the verb (Rizzi, 1996, 2001):

(51) a. Dove è   andato Gianni?   [Italian]
        where AUX went   Gianni
        'Where did Gianni go?'
    b. Come è   partito Gianni?
       how   AUX left   Gianni
       'How did Gianni leave?'
    c. Perché Gianni è   venuto?
       why   Gianni AUX came
       'Why did Gianni come?'

In New Testament Greek argument questions on direct objects *tí* require *wh*-movement and residual V2 (52a), but *why*-questions with *dià tí* do not, and are perfectly grammatical with a *Wh»Subj* word order (52b–52c) (Kirk, 2012).

(52) a. è: tí dó:sei ánt^hro:pos antállagma tê:s psukhê:s autoû? [NTG]
or what give man price the soul his
'Or what price will a man give for his soul?'
b. Dià tí toûto tò múron ouk epráthe:?
why this the ointment NEG sell
'Why was this ointment not sold?'
c. Dià tí hoi methe:taí sou parabaínousin tè:n parádosin tô:n presbutéro:n?
why the disciple your transgress the teaching the elder
'Why do your disciples transgress the teaching of the elderly?'

Likewise, in Romanian *wh*-phrases tend to require residual V2 construals, as shown with the pair in (53) (Shlonsky & Soare, 2011):

(53) a. Cui i-a cumpărat Ion un CD? [Romanian]
who.DAT him-has bought Ion a CD
'For whom did Ion buy a CD?'
b. *Cui Ion i-a cumpărat un CD?
who.DAT Ion him-has bought a CD
'For whom did Ion buy a CD?'

However, such a restriction does not hold for *de ce* 'why', which allows both V2 (54a) and non-V2 (54b) construals:

(54) a. De ce a cumpărat Ion un CD pentru el? [Romanian]
why has bought Ion a CD for him
Why did Ion buy him CD?
b. De ce Ion a cumpărat un CD pentru el?
why Ion has bought a CD for him
Why did Ion buy him a CD?

In Syrian Arabic the basic VSO word order is changed into Wh-V-S in wh-questions in general, as represented in (55), from Suleiman (2017):

(55) a. shw ḥaka basem? [Syrian Arabic]
    what said.3SG.M Basel
    'What did Bassel say?'
  b. *shw basem ḥaka?
    what Bassel said.3SG.M
    'What did Bassel say?'

However, the *Wh-V* adjacency becomes optional in questions with *lesh* 'why'. Compare the grammaticality of (56b) with the deviance of (55b):[7]

(56) a. lesh tdday?-et mary? [Syrian Arabic]
    why Upset-3SG.F Mary
    'Why did Mary get upset?'
  b. lesh mary tdday?-et?
    why Mary Upset-3SG.F
    'Why did Mary get upset?'

The pattern of Singapore English *wh*-questions is a bit different. In this language, *wh*-phrases show optional fronting and may be optionally accompanied by a question particle *ah* in either sentence-final or second position (Yeo, 2010):

(57) a. You buy what áh? [Singapore English]
    you buy what Q
    'What did you buy?'
  b. What you buy áh?
    what you buy Q
    'What did you buy?'
  c. What áh you buy?
    what Q you buy
    'What did you buy?'

But *why*-questions show the particularity that *why* has to be obligatorily in the clause-initial position, otherwise, the sentence is clearly deviant (58c):[8]

---

[7] Actually, the translation provided for V2 (56a) and non-V2 (56b) in Sulaiman (2017, 328) is 'What did upset Mary?' but from the discussion and the context it is clear that it is a *why*-question.
[8] *How* also behaves similarly in this language.

(58) a. Why John like Mary ah? [Singapore English]
        why John like Mary Q
        'Why does John like Mary?'
    b. Why ah John like Mary?
        why Q John like Mary
        'Why does John like Mary?'
    c. *John like Mary why ah?
        John like Mary why Q
        'Why does John like Mary?'

Similarly, in Persian in general, *wh*-phrases can remain in situ (59a), or move to the focus position (59b–59c) (Kahnemuyipour, 2001; Karimi, 2005):

(59) a. Kimea diruz   ketâb-ro be ki   dâd?   [Persian]
        Kimea yesterday book-râ to who gave
        'Who did Kimea give the book to yesterday?'
    b. Kimea be ki diruz   ketâb-ro dâd?
        Kimea to who yesterday book-râ gave
        'Who was it that Kimea gave the book to yesterday?'
    c. Be ki   Kimea diruz   ketâb-ro dâd?
        to who Kimea yesterday book-râ gave
        'Who was it that Kimea gave the book to yesterday?'

The only exception to this general pattern is *cherâ* 'why', which obligatorily surfaces in the left periphery (even in an echo-reading) (60b–60c):

(60) a. Ali bâ   Maryam ezdevâj kard chon   dust-esh dâsht. [Persian]
        Ali with Maryam marry   AUX because friend-her AUX
        'Ali married Maryam because he loved her.'
    b. *Ali bâ   Maryam ezdevâj kard cherâ?
        Ali with Maryam marry   AUX why
        'Why did Ali marry Maryam?'
    c. Ali cherâ bâ   Maryam ezdevâj kard?
        Ali why   with Maryam marry   AUX
        'Why did Ali marry Maryam?'

In Krachi *wh*-phrases can appear both in situ (61a) as well as in the left peripheric focus position (61b) (Kandybowicz & Torrence, 2012):

(61) a. ɔtʃíw   ɛ-mò   bwatéo   momo?   [Krachi]
       woman   AGR-kill.PST chicken which
       'Which chicken did the woman slaughter?'
   b. Bwatéo   momo   jí   ɔtʃíw   ɛ-mò?
      chicken which   FOC   woman   AGR-kill.PST
      'Which chicken did the woman slaughter?'

This is general across all wh-phrases (*nse* 'who', *ne* 'what', *n̦fr̂ɛ́* 'where', *kɛmekɛ́* 'when', *nɛnɛ* 'how'. . .), with the exception of *nání* 'why', which unlike the rest, cannot surface in the clause-internal position (62a) and has to be necessarily fronted (62b):

(62) a. ɔtʃíw   ɛ-mò   bwatéo   nání?   [Krachi]
       woman   AGR-kill.PST chicken why
       'Why did the woman slaughter the chicken?'
   b. Nání   jí   ɔtʃíw   ɛ-mò   bwatéo?
      why   FOC   woman   AGR-kill.PST chicken
      'Why did the woman slaughter the chicken?'

In Irish a different externalization pattern suggests a similar underlying structure: in this language, there are two different overt complementizers, *aN* –which is used when Spec-CP is occupied directly by external merge–, and *aL* –which is used when Spec-CP is filled *via* internal merge, *i.e.* movement (McCloskey, 2002, 2003). Thus, for instance, when the clause hosts A'-binding of a moved element, it is headed by *aL* (63a), but when it hosts A'-binding of a resumptive pronoun, it is headed by *aN* (63b):

(63) a. an   ghirseach   a   ghoid   na   síogaí   [Irish]
       the   girl   aL   stole   the   fairies
       'the girl that the fairies stole away.'
   b. an   ghirseach   a-r   ghoid   na   síogaí   í
      the   girl   aN-past stole   the   fairies her
      'the girl that the fairies stole away.'

Interestingly for our discussion, *why*-questions behave differently with respect to the other *wh*-questions. Whereas argument and adjunct *wh*-questions in general surface with the *aL* complementizer (64a), *why*-questions necessarily surface with *aN* (65):

(64) a. Cá   fhad   a   bhí   tú   ann?   [Irish]
       how   long   aL   be.past   you   there
       'How long were you there?'

b. *Cá fhad a raibh tú ann?
   how long *aN* be.past you there
   'How long were you there?'

(65) a. Cad chuige a ndeachaigh tú ann? [Irish]
     why   *aN* went   you there
     'Why did you go there?'
   b. *Cad chuige a chuaigh tú ann?
     why   *aL* went   you there
     'Why did you go there?'

This pattern extends beyond the simple 'why' *cad chuige* to more complex reason questions composed with *cén fáth* 'what reason':

(66) Cén fáth a-r dúirt tú sin? [Irish]
    what reason *aN*-[PAST] say you that
    'Why did you say that?'

(67) *Cén fáth a dúirt tú sin?
    what reason *aL* say you that
    'Why did you say that?'

In Sinhala (Kishimoto, 2018) a specificity of *wh*-adjuncts such as *æi* 'why' and *mokə də* 'why' is that they are not associated with a separable Q particle: *æi* must stand alone (68a), and the Q element *də* appearing in *mokə də* is fixed in a position next to the *wh*-word, and cannot be separated from it (contrary to what happens with other *wh*-elements). Thus the ungrammaticality of (68a) and (68b):[9]

(68) a. *Ranjit [Chitra æi də aawe kiyəla] dannəwa. [Sinhala]
       Ranjit Chitra why Q came.E that know.A
       'Ranjit knows why Chitra came.'
    b. *Ranjit [Chitra mokə aawa də] kiyəla] dannəwa.
       Ranjit *Chitra* why came.A Q that know.A
       'Ranjit knows why Chitra came.'

All in all, the broad picture that we obtain from this quick cross-linguistic comparison is that across languages of different families and types *why*-questions display dif-

---

9 Remarkably, these *wh*-adjuncts are restricted to have short-distance scope.

ferent patterns with respect to the rest of *wh*-questions. In particular, the *wh*-phrase corresponding to *why* tends to be in a higher position and (as a consequence) it tends not to require movement of the verb in the languages that generally have it (residual V2) and/or not to display the characteristic properties of *wh*-movement.[10,11]

3.2 An early acquired and early set pattern

The relative difference between *why*-questions and other *wh*-questions with respect to the requirement (or not) of residual V2 is an early acquired pattern. For instance, Barreña (1995) reports the following data on the acquisition of Basque:

(69) a. Hau nok ipini dau? (2;04;24)
 this who put AUX
 'Who put this?'
 b. Nok apurtu dau holakue? (2;04;24)
 who break AUX like.this
 'Who broke the one like this one?'
 c. Nun daoz nire egurrek? (2;06;05)
 where are my woods
 'Where are my woods?'

As can be seen, by the age of 2;04 subject questions (69a-69b) as well as locative adjunct questions (69c) trigger movement of the verb attracting it to be right-adjacent to the *wh*-phrase. This contrasts sharply with the patterns of *why*-questions, which even at much later ages do not necessarily show V2 effects:

(70) a. Zeatik honek jo ein bi dau trena? (2;08;13)
 why this hit do have AUX train
 'Why does this one have to hit the train?'

---

10 In Khmer too, "The behavior of *mec* "how, why" is comparable to that of the similarly homophonous words in Chinese (Li & Thompson, 1980, 523-4) and other languages. When the word means "how", it appears wherever manner adverbs are found, but when it means "why" it typically occurs clause initially (Haiman, 2011, 234). Likewise, with Dhao *ngaa tao* 'why', which "[u]nlike other interrogatives, *ngaa tao* never occurs in clause final position." (Balukh, 2020, 133).
11 See also the behavior of Zulu *ngani* 'why' which surfaces postverbally as other *wh*-phrases, but requires its preceding verb to be appear in disjoint or neutral form, whereas all other *wh*-phrases require a preceding verb in conjoint or neutral form. Buell (2011) builds on this evidence to propose that even if it surfaces postverbally, *ngani* is in the CP area (an Int° head). This contrasts with the rest of *wh*-phrases, which appear inside the VP.

b. Zegatik Arantzan zalduna bota dozu? (3;01;12)
why Arantza.Poss knight throw AUX
'Why did you throw Arantza's knight?'
c. Zegatik azeriek untxie jaten dabie? (3;09;11)
why foxes rabbit eat AUX
'Why do foxes eat rabbit?'

Similar differential patterns in acquisition have also been found in other languages such as English (Labov & Labov, 1978; Stromswold, 1990; Berk, 2003; Thornton, 2004, 2008; Conroy & Lidz, 2007), French (Hamann, 2000, 2006), or Korean (Ko, 2006) and Japanese (Ikeda et al., 2019) among others.

Besides, so far I have mentioned contemporary Basque data, but absence of V2 in *why*-questions is attested across all the history of Basque literature. In Ancient and (Post-)Classical Basque *wh*-movement was only optionally accompanied by V2 (Ortiz de Urbina, 1989; Aldai, 2011; Duguine & Irurtzun, 2014), but by far the *wh*-phrase that appears the less often left-adjacent to the verb (*i.e.* in a V2 construction) is *zergatik*.[12] Observe the examples below from 16th century Lazarraga (71a) and Leizarraga (71b); or the 17th century Axular (71c), Haranburu (71d), or Belapeyre (71e):

(71) a. Cegaiti lauoi bardin on erechi ez derausteçu euren
why four.DAT equally well consider NEG cause their
amoreetan?
loves.in
'Why didn't you make the four of them love each other?'
b. Cergatic haur hunela blasphemio erraiten ari da?
why this thus blasphemy saying PROG AUX
'Why is this one saying blasphemies like that?'
c. Cergatic bada gorputceco eritasunagatic eguiten duçuna
why then body.from sickness.for do aux.R.NEG
eztuçu arimacoagatic eguinen?
AUX soul.for do.FUT
'Why then won't you do for the sickness of the soul that that you do for the sickness of the body?'

---

12 For instance, studying a sample from the New Testament translations by Leizarraga (1571), Haraneder (c. 1740) and Etcheandy (1999) (the Gospels of Matthew and John), Aldai (2011) finds 14 examples of *wh*-V non-adjacency *vs.* 7 examples of adjacency with *zergatik*, but only 1 example of non-adjacency with *zer vs.* 15 examples of adjacency, or no examples of non-adjacency *vs.* 5 examples of adjacency with *non* 'where'.

d. Cergatic ni neror bakharric vtzten nauçu?
   why me me.contrast alone leave AUX
   'Me, why do you leave me alone?'
e. Cergatic egun oroz goiçan, egüerditau, eta arraxen
   why day all morning.at noon.at and afternoon.at
   hirourna cegnu khaldi emaiten dira eliçan?
   three.each sign hit give AUX church.at
   'Why are everyday in the morning by noon and in the afternoon three signs given at the church?'

3.3 Antisuperiority effects

A remarkable observation made in the literature on *why*-questions is that they may be subject to 'antisuperiority effects' in multiple *wh*-constructions. Such is, for instance, the case of Japanese (*cf. i.a.* Hornstein, 1995; Takita & Yang, 2014). In Japanese, as is well known, *wh*-phrases do not need to front and can remain in situ, which renders SOV word order (72a). However, Japanese has scrambling operations that can produce alternative word orders such as OSV, where the object is scrambled over the subject (72b). Both sentences are perfectly grammatical as there is no superiority effect:

(72) a. Dare-ga nani-o katta no?   [Japanese]
       who-NOM what-ACC bought Q
       'Who bought what?'
    b. Nani-o$_i$ dare-ga t_i katta no?
       what-ACC who-NOM bought Q
       'Who bought what?'

However, in multiple *wh*-constructions involving *naze* 'why' sentences such as (73a) –where *nani* 'what' precedes *naze* 'why'– are perfectly grammatical, but sentences such as (73b) –where *naze* precedes *nani*– are ungrammatical. Such a restriction is known as an 'antisuperiority effect':

(73) a. Taroo-ga nani-o naze katta no?   [Japanese]
       Taroo-NOM what-ACC why bought Q
       'What did Taroo buy why?'
    b. *Taroo-ga naze Nani-o katta no?
       Taroo-NOM why what-ACC bought Q
       'What did Taroo buy why?'

Korean displays a similar behavior: the word order *why»what* is ungrammatical (74a), whereas *what»why* is perfectly grammatical (74b) (Jeong, 2003):

(74) a. *Wae mwues-ul ne-nun sa-ess-ni? [Korean]
 why what-ACC you-TOP buy-PAST-Q
 'Why did you buy what?'
 b. Mwues-ul wae ne-nun sa-ess-ni?
 what-ACC why you-TOP buy-PAST-Q
 'Why did you buy what?'

Tibetan is also a language with scrambling operations whereby *wh*-phrases can surface in different positions. For instance, *garebyadnas* 'why' can either precede (75a) or follow (75b) the direct object:

(75) a. Bkrashis-lags-gi gyag garebyadnas gzigs-gnang-pa-red? [Tibetan]
 Tashi-HON-ERG yak why buy-HON-PAST-AGR
 'Why did Tashi buy a yak?'
 b. Bkrashis-lags-gi garebyadnas gyag gzigs-gnang-pa-red?
 Tashi-HON-ERG why yak buy-HON-PAST-AGR
 'Why did Tashi buy a yak?'

But if we substitute the direct object with interrogative *gagi* 'which/what', the antisuperiority effect arises and while the order *what»why* is grammatical (76a), the order *why»what* is not (76b) (Richards, 1997):

(76) a. Bkrashis-lags-gi gagi garebyadnas gzigs-gnang-pa-red? [Tibetan]
 Tashi-HON-ERG which why buy-HON-PAST-AGR
 'Why did Tashi buy what?'
 b. *Bkrashis-lags-gi garebyadnas gagi gzigs-gnang-pa-red?
 Tashi-HON-ERG why which buy-HON-PAST-AGR
 'Why did Tashi buy what?'

The same pattern can be found in Hungarian, where in multiple *wh*-questions *ki* 'who' must precede *miért* 'why' (Kiss, 2002):

(77) a. Ki miért hazudott? [Hungarian]
 who why lied
 'Who lied why?'

b. *Miért ki hazudott?
      why who lied
      'Who lied why?'

In Romanian too, *de ce* 'why' may co-occur with other *wh*-phrases in multiple *wh*-questions, but always following them, as shown in (78) and (79) (Shlonsky & Soare, 2011):

(78) a. Cine de ce a plecat? [Romanian]
        who why has left
        'Who left and why?'
     b. *De ce cine a plecat?
        why who has left
        'Who left and why?'

(79) a. Pe cine de ce ai întrebat despre accident? [Romanian]
        ACC who why have asked
        'Who did you ask about the accident and why?'
     b. *De ce pe cine ai întrebat despre accident?
        why ACC who have asked about accident
        'Who did you ask about the accident and why?'

In Basque, we find an analogous behavior: the word order in (80a), where *zer* 'what' precedes *zergatik* 'why' is grammatical, but the reverse word order, illustrated in (80b) is deviant:

(80) a. Zer erosi duzu zergatik?
        what buy AUX why
        'Why did you buy what?'
     b. ?Zergatik erosi duzu zer?
        why buy AUX what
        'Why did you buy what?'

Takita & Yang (2014) provide an analysis of Japanese antisuperiority facts that treat *naze* as a "defective" element and where the antisuperiority effect is an illicit case of feature valuation of C, which is induced by the defective feature specification of *naze*. Extending their analysis to the Basque data is a nontrivial task, since both languages differ in the interrogative strategy employed (*wh in situ* in Japanese; *wh*-movement in Basque) and in the availability of 'free' scrambling. I would like to conjecture that the deviance of constructions such as (80b) may be rather due to discursive reasons: first, note that they improve in embedded contexts. Thus, both (81a), with the order *what»why*, and (81b), with *why»what*, are perfectly grammatical:

(81) a. Esadazu [zer   erosi duzun zergatik].
         tell.me what buy   AUX.C why
         Lit. Tell me what you bought why.
     b. Esadazu [zergatik erosi duzun zer].
         tell.me why   buy   AUX.C what
         Lit. Tell me why you bought what.

But furthermore, multiple *wh*-constructions seem to be subject to the D-linking requirement of the leftmost *wh*-phrase (Bolinger, 1978), which is generally harder to satisfy for *why*-questions. In order to show the D-linking requirement of the leftmost *wh*-phrase, Bolinger (1978) provides the following paradigm:

(82) It's nice to have all those times scheduled but when are you doing what?
     (# . . .but what are you doing when?)

(83) It's nice to have all those activities ahead of you, but what are you doing when?
     (# . . .but when are you doing what?)

That is, when the set that the *wh*-phrase stands for is discursively given, it can be fronted to the leftmost position. Extending this analysis to the Basque data, we can observe that D-linking the *zergatik*-phrase ameliorates substantially the acceptability of *zergatik»zer* patterns (compare example (84) with (80b)):

(84) Gauza horiek guztiak erosteko arrazoi asko eman dituzu
     things those all   buy.for   reason many give AUX
     baina zergatik erosi duzu zer?
     but   why   buy   AUX what
     'You gave many reasons for buying all those things but why did you buy what?'

So, all in all, there may not be an absolute 'antisuperiority' restriction on multiple *wh*-constructions with *zergatik*, and the pattern observed in Basque and in other languages may be due to discursive factors.

3.4 Why+focus

We saw in Section 2 that in Basque *wh*-questions and focalizations are in general incompatible with each other. This is not a particularity of Basque, but one that has been observed language after language. In Italian, for instance, there is no possible combination of a focalization with a *wh*-question such as *a chi* 'to whom', and both *Wh»Foc* and *Foc»Wh* word orders are ungrammatical (Rizzi, 2001):

(85) a. *A chi [questo]$_F$ hanno detto? [Italian]
    to whom this AUX said
    'To whom did they say [this]$_F$?'
 b. *[Questo]$_F$ a chi hanno detto?
    this to whom AUX said
    'To whom did they say [this]$_F$?'

There is a caveat though, since *why*-questions tend to allow for focalizations, as Rizzi (2001) observes. However, in these combinations *perchè* 'why' must precede the focal phrase:

(86) a. Perchè [questo]$_F$ avremmo dovuto dirgli? [Italian]
    why this AUX should say.CL
    'Why should we have said [this]$_F$ to him?'
 b. *[Questo]$_F$ perchè avremmo dovuto dirgli?
    this why AUX should say.CL
    'Why should we have said [this]$_F$ to him?'

This is in line with what other researchers have observed in other languages. As Partee (1991, 171) puts it, "WHY-questions are focus-sensitive in a way that other WH-questions are not". But interestingly, language after language the same patterns of combination seem to emerge. In Romanian for instance, *wh*-questions in general cannot be combined with focalizations in any order (Shlonsky & Soare, 2011):

(87) a. *Cui [un CD]$_F$ i-ai cumpărat? [Romanian]
    who.DAT a CD him-AUX bought
    'To whom is it a CD that you bought?'
 b. *[Un CD]$_F$ cui i-ai cumpărat?
    A CD who.DAT him-AUX bought
    'To whom is it a CD that you bought?'

However, *de ce* 'why' can be combined with focalized constituents, but only with the *Why»Foc* order:

(88) a. De ce [un CD]_F ai cumpărat pentru el? [Romanian]
　　　 why　 a　 CD　 AUX bought　 for　　 him
　　　 'Why is it a CD that you bought for him?'
　　b. *[Un CD]_F de ce ai cumpărat pentru el?
　　　 　a　 CD　 why AUX bought　 for　　 him
　　　 'Why is it a CD that you bought for him?'

A similar pattern is also observed in Japanese. Endo (2015) provides the following paradigm combining a *wh*-question and a focalization with *dake* 'only':

(89) a. Nan-de [John-dake]_F naiteiru no? [Japanese]
　　　 why　　 John-only　　 crying　 Q
　　　 'Why is only John crying?'
　　b. ??[John-dake]_F nan-de naiteiru no?
　　　 　John-only　　 why　 crying　 Q
　　　 'Why is only John crying?'

As can be seen, the order *Why»Foc* is grammatical (89a), whereas the order *Foc»Why* is deviant (89b).[13]

A similar pattern can be observed in Hungarian, which is known for having a designated preverbal focus position, like in Basque (Kiss, 2002; Horvath, 2013). In this language, both *wh*-movement and focus movement are taken to target the same position (the immediately preverbal one) and hence, their combination produces ungrammaticality (in any of the logically possible orders):

(90) a. *[Pétert]_F kinek　 mutattad　 be? [Hungarian]
　　　 Péter.ACC who.DAT showed.2SG PRT
　　　 'To whom did you introduce [Peter]_F?'
　　　 *Kinek　 [Pétert]_F mutattad　 be?
　　　 who.DAT Péter.ACC showed.2SG PRT
　　　 'To whom did you introduce [Peter]_F?'

However, *wh*-questions with *miért* 'why' can be naturally combined with focalizations, provided they have the *Why»Foc* word order:

---

[13] See, however, Miyagawa (2017) for discussion on the strength of this evidence.

(91) a. Miért [Pétert]_F mutattad be Marinak? [Hungarian]
     why Péter.ACC showed.2SG PRT Mari.DAT
     'Why was it [Péter]_F that you introduced to Mari?'
  b. *[Pétert]_F miért mutattad be Marinak?
     Péter.ACC why showed.2SG PRT Mari.DAT
     'Why was it [Péter]_F that you introduced to Mari?'

Finally, the same pattern appears in New Testament Greek (Kirk, 2012): *why*-questions can be combined with focal elements such as *kaì humeîs* 'also/even you', but they always appear in the *Why»Foc* order:

(92) Dià tí kaì humeîs parabaínete tè:n entolè:n toû tʰeoû
     why also you transgress the commandment the God
     dià tè:n parádosin humô:n? [NTG]
     by the tradition your
     'Why do also you transgress the commandment of God by your tradition?'

And the pattern in Basque is exactly the same: the general impossibility of combining *wh*-questions and focalizations disappears with *zergatik*, and complex questions+focalizations can be formed. Such sentences share the same word order pattern that we saw for the other languages whereby the interrogative item has to precede the focus:

(93) a. Zergatik [Peiok]_F eman die albistea?
        why Peio give AUX news
        'Why was it Peio that gave them the news?'
  b. *[Peiok]_F zergatik eman die albistea?
     Peio why give AUX news
     'Why was it Peio that gave them the news?'

Furthermore, the V2 pattern may not be kept in such constructions and the verb may surface right-adjacent to the focal element (V3, as in (93a)). Nonetheless, placing the verb in the position after *zergatik*, that is, sandwiched between *zergatik* and the focus is also grammatical:

(94) Zergatik eman die [Peiok]_F albistea?
     why give AUX Peio news
     'Why was it Peio that gave them the news?'

As expected, leaving the verb in the sentence-final position is ungrammatical (as this would go against the general pattern of both *wh*-questions and focalizations):

(95) *Zergatik [Peiok]_F albistea eman die?
     why   Peio   news   give AUX
     'Why was it Peio that gave them the news?'

Last, note that *zergatik*-questions are also compatible with a particular type of focalization construal whereby instead of the sentence-initial position, the focus appears in the sentence-final position:[14]

(96) a. Zergatik esan die Peiok [egia]_F?
        why   tell AUX Peio   truth
        'Why did Peio tell them [the truth]_F ?'
     b. Zergatik esan die egia   [Peiok]_F?
        why   tell AUX truth Peio
        'Why did [Peio]_F tell them the truth?'

The fact that *why*-questions can be combined with focalizations makes them context and contrast-sensitive in a way that other *wh*-questions are not, as the philosophical literature has discussed (Partee, 1991; Bromberger, 1993; Cox, 2019). As a matter of fact, question (96a) can be naturally answered with an answer such as "because lying would be problematic", but not with an answer such as "because he was the only one around at the moment". On the contrary, (96b) clashes with an answer like "because lying would be problematic", but it is completely natural with an answer such as "because he was the only one around at the moment".

In conclusion, as in other languages, the syntax of *why*-questions in Basque seems to be characterized by a couple of particularities. It can behave like any other *wh*-question but (i) in some construals it does not generate the otherwise general residual V2, and (ii) it can be combined with focalizations (always with the *Why*»*Foc* word order). All this suggests that *zergatik* can be merged very high in the structure, so much so that the position of the verb may not be affected by it. This is what I will explore in the next sections proposing that there are two different construals: one where *why* is merged below the core complementizer area (in SpecReasonP) and then moved to IntP successive cyclically (generating

---

[14] These constructions tend to have a reinforced contrastive reading (see Ortiz de Urbina (2002) for discussion and a derivational proposal).

V2 effects), and another one where *why* is directly merged in SpecIntP, where it is frozen, and does not generate any V2 effects.

3.5 Long, short, and clausal construals

Regarding interpretation, the cross-linguistic literature on *why*-questions has uncovered that often *why*-questions can be ambiguous between the so-called short vs. long construals (cf. Cattell (1978); Ko (2005); Shlonsky & Soare (2011)). For example, question (97) could be interpreted in either of the two following ways:

(97) Why did you ask her to resign?
    1. What is the reason x such that for x, you asked her to resign?
       e.g. Because I didn't want to just tell her. (Short Construal)
    2. What is the reason x, such that you asked her to resign for that particular reason x?
       e.g. I asked her to resing because of her health, not because of her intelligence... (Long Construal).

The explicit syntax that Basque deploys in *wh*-questions helps disambiguating potential ambiguities with respect to short vs. long construals. In particular, the cyclicity of verbal movement and clausal pied-piping provides evidence of the extraction site of adjuncts which, in principle, can be extracted out of either the matrix or the embedded clauses. For instance, question (98) with *noiz* 'when' is eminently a question over the eventuality described in the matrix clause (*i.e. when→think*, not *when→finish*) since there is verbal movement in the matrix clause (signalled by S-V inversion) but not in the embedded clause (and hence no object-verb inversion):

(98) Noiz   pentsatzen du   Jonek [gerra bukatuko dela]?
when   think   AUX Jon   war   finish   AUX.C
'When is it that Jon thinks that the war will finish?'

Alternatively, in (99) the question is over the eventuality described in the embedded clause (*i.e. when→finish*), since there is verbal movement in both clauses, which signals that the extraction of *noiz* took place from the embedded clause:

(99) Noiz   pentsatzen du   Jonek [bukatuko dela   gerra]?
when   think   AUX Jon   finish   aux.c   war
'According to Jon, when will the war finish?'

Since clausal pied-piping is an alternative to long-distance extraction, it can only arise in questions on the embedded clause (*i.e. when→finish*), as shown in (100):

(100) [Noiz bukatuko dela gerra] pentsatzen du Jonek?
 when finish AUX.C war think AUX Jon
 'According to Jon, when will the war finish?'

The behavior of *zergatik* is the expected one given this syntax: the extraction site can be tracked down in the word order. Thus, the interpretation of (101a) is that of a short construal (*why→think*), in (101b) we have a long construal (*why→finish*) and in (101c) a long construal:[15]

(101) a. Zergatik pentsatzen du Jonek [gerra bukatuko dela]?
 why think AUX Jon war finish AUX.C
 'Why is it that Jon thinks that the war will finish?'
 b. Zergatik pentsatzen du Jonek [bukatuko dela gerra]?
 why think AUX Jon finish AUX.C war
 'Why is it that Jon thinks that the war will finish?'
 c. [Zergatik bukatuko dela gerra] pentsatzen du Jonek?
 why finish AUX.C war think AUX Jon
 'According to Jon, why will the war finish?'

(101a) shows S-V inversion in the matrix clause but no O-V inversion in the embedded clause, as a consequence, its reading is that of a question on the matrix clause (*why→think*). (101b) is an instance of long-distance extraction (with V2 in both clauses) and as a consequence its reading is that of a question on the embedded clause (*why→finish*). Last, the clausal pied-piping construction of (101c) is also a question on the embedded clause, hence its reading is *why→finish*.

Likewise, island structures provide good environments to assess the association between word order and interpretation. As we said in Section 2, *wh*-movement in Basque is impossible out of adjunct clauses. Thus, departing from the base in (102a), *wh*-extraction of the direct object such as in (102b) produces ungrammaticality:

---

15 Even if it is generally judged grammatical as such, example (101c) is more natural with *gerra* topicalized over *zergatik*.

(102) a. Jon [abestia entzun duelako] poztu da.
Jon song hear AUX.because get.happy AUX
'Jon got happy because he heard the song.'
b. *Zer poztu da Jon [t entzun duelako]?
what get.happy AUX Jon hear AUX.because
Lit. 'What did Jon got happy because he heard?'

Such behavior helps explaining the pattern in (103) below. Example (103a) with V-S inversion in the matrix clause and no inversion in the embedded clause is perfectly grammatical because *zergatik* can only be understood as coming from the matrix clause (hence its effect in the movement of the matrix verb, and its lack thereof in the embedded clause). Accordingly, its intended meaning questions why Jon got happy because he heard a song. Contrariwise, movement of the embedded verb over the direct object *abestia* in (103b) could only be due to a residual V2 of the movement of *zergatik* form the embedded clause to successive cyclically move to the specifier of the matrix clause (triggering again movement of the matrix verb). However, such an extraction out of an adjunct clause is illicit, hence the ungrammaticality of (103b):

(103) a. Zergatik poztu da Jon [pro abestia entzun duelako]?
why get.happy AUX Jon song hear AUX.because
'Why did Jon got happy because he heard the song?'
b. *Zergatik poztu da Jon [entzun duelako pro abestia]?
why get.happy AUX Jon hear AUX.because song
'Jon got happy because why did he hear the song?'

Now, regarding the ambiguity that we saw in (97) on the short *vs.* long construal, a Basque variant as in (104a) is also ambiguous between the short and long construal readings (even though the short construal reading is more prominent). This derives from the fact that having *zergatik* in clause-initial position, and then followed by the matrix and the embedded verbs can correspond to extraction from any of the clauses; both construals provide the same word order. However, a word order such as (104b) can only correspond to a long construal reading, which would be derived via the clausal pied-piping operation: first, movement of the *wh*-word to the specifier of the embedded CP, movement of the verb of the embedded clause to C (V2), and then movement of the whole embedded clause to the specifier of the matrix clause, which is again followed by movement of the matrix verb. It is the clausal pied-piping movement that produces the $[_{CP}$ *wh* V] V word order:

(104) a. Zergatik eskatu zenion uko   egiteko?
         why   ask   AUX   renunciation do
         'Why did you ask her/him to resign?'
      b. Zergatik uko   egiteko eskatu zenion?
         why   renunciation do   ask   AUX
         'Why did you ask her/him to resign?'

However, there is a third reading that questions such as (104b) can get: a 'clausal' reading. In the next sections I will argue that example (104b) can correspond to the clausal-pied piping construction (with its associated reading), but also to a construction where *zergatik* is directly first-merged in the left periphery, and there is no verbal movement whatsoever (thus, similar to the construction that we saw in (38b) and to the ones attested in other languages). In such cases, the interrogative element takes clausal scope and a reason interpretation similar to that of English *how come* or *why is it that*.

3.6 Clausal 'zergatik'

The clausal reading, as indicated by the name, does not inquire about the reasons of the VP/vP but about the whole TP. Hence it does not question on the motives of the subject/initiator. It rather questions why it is that the whole eventuality described by the sentence took place (thus, it is similar to the meaning of English *how come*).

Imagine the following scenario:

(105) *Context*: We leave Leire -an infant- with a caregiver for the morning. We know that she is very tired, since she spent a large part of last night awake and playing, but we need the caregiver to keep Leire from getting asleep, otherwise in the afternoon it will be difficult to get her to bed. When we come home at noon, we see that Leire is asleep.

In such a context, it would be pointless to ask a question like (106a), for we know the answer (she got asleep because she did not have enough sleep the night before and she was very sleepy). However, (106b) questions over the whole clause/ eventuality, and therefore it is coherent in this context as a recrimination of how come such an event took place, even if it was meant not to:

(106) a. #Zergatik lokartu da Leire?
   why get.asleep AUX Leire
   'Why did Leire get asleep?'
   [≈what were the reasons for her sleepiness?]
   b. Zergatik Leire lokartu da?
   why Leire get.asleep AUX
   'Why did Leire get asleep?'
   [how come she got asleep]

So in this pattern we would be in front of a very high *zergatik*, reminiscent of those that have been proposed for other languages.

Besides, regular *why*-questions tend to display ambiguity between a reason and a purpose reading (Stepanov & Tsai, 2008; Chapman & Kučerová, 2016). This is illustrated in example (107), from Chapman & Kučerová (2016):

(107) Why did she resign?
   a. ✓ *Purpose*: For what purpose did they resign? In order to earn more money next year.
   b. ✓ *Reason*: What was the reason for their resigning? Because they got a pay cut.

In Chapman & Kučerová's (2016) analysis, reason *why*-s are base-generated as TP adjuncts whereas purpose *why*-s are base-generated as adjuncts of CausP (a *v*P functional layer corresponding to agentive predicates having a volitional requirement).[16]

The same pattern arises in Basque with the V2 construal of *zergatik*:

(108) Zergatik utzi du lana?
   why leave AUX work
   'Why did they resign?'
   a. ✓ *Purpose*: For what purpose did they resign? In order to earn more money next year.
   b. ✓ *Reason*: What was the reason for their resigning? Because they got a pay cut.

---

16 This explains the fact that only agentive dynamic predicates allow for both readings; in particular neither passives, unaccusatives, nor locative existential predicates allow for purpose readings.

However, this ambiguity disappears with high *zergatik*, and the only available reading is the *how come* (reason) reading (≈ *Why is it that they resigned?*):

(109) Zergatik lana utzi du?
      why   work leave AUX
      'How come they resigned?'
   a. # *Purpose*: For what purpose did they resign? In order to earn more money next year.
   b. ✓ *Reason*: What was the reason for their resigning? Because they got a pay cut.

Very often, the clausal and the reason reading are hard to distinguish, as agents/initiators are which bring about the eventualities. However, we will see below that the clausal construction is particularly employed in conjectural or wondering situations such as rhetorical questions that wonder about the state of affairs and they often imply a counter-expectation (see Tsai (2008) for similar evidence).

Likewise, I mentioned in Section 3 that *zergatik* is composed of *zer* 'what' + "motivative" *-gatik*. Thus, a construction with *zergatik* can be ambiguous between being construed with the lexicalized *zergatik* 'why' or with the syntagmatic *zergatik* "what for". Below I provide some examples that show that regular constructions with V2 can display this ambiguity (the 'a' examples of (110a), (111a), and (112a)), thus they can be answered either with causes or with PP complements (as shown in their B and C answers). However, constructions with high *zergatik* (the 'b' examples of (110b), (111b), and (112b)) cannot; they only accept the causal reading, as shown in (110b-C), (111b-C), and (112b-C):[17,18]

(110) a. A. Zergatik   gaisotu da   Miren?
            why/what.for   get.sick aux Miren
            'Why did Miren get sick?' OR 'What did Miren get sick for?'
         B. Ez   babesteagatik.
            not protecting.for
            'Because she took no precautions.'

---

[17] Some of these examples are substandard and probably calques from Spanish.
[18] In Central Basque, ambiguous structures can be disambiguated by means of prosody: *zergátik* with the regular peninitial stress corresponds to the lexicalized "why", whereas *zérgatik* with initial stress on the syntagmatic "what for".

      C. Gaixotasun profesionalagatik.
         illness   profesional.for
         'Of an occupational disease.'
  b. A. Zergatik   Miren gaisotu da
       why/what.for Miren get.sick AUX
       'How come Miren got sick?'
     B. Ez babesteagatik.
       not protecting.for
       'Because she took no
       precautions.'
       C. #Gaixotasun profesionalagatik.
          illness   profesional.for
          'Of an occupational disease.'

(111) a. A. Zergatik   kondenatu dute Jon?
         why/what.for convict   aux Jon
        'Why did they convict Jon?' OR 'What did they convict Jon of?'
     B. Bere aurkako   frogak zituztelako.
       his   against.GEN proofs have.because
       'Because they had proofs against him.'
     C. Ogasun publikoaren aurkako   delituengatik.
       estate   public.GEN against.GEN crimes.for
       'Of crimes against public finances.'
  b. A. Zergatik   Jon kondenatu dute?
       why/what.for Jon convict   aux
      'How come they convicted Jon?'
     B. Bere aurkako   frogak zituztelako.
       his   against.GEN proofs have.because
       'Because they had proofs against him.'
     C. #Ogasun publikoaren aurkako   delituengatik.
       estate   public.GEN against.GEN crimes.for
       'Of crimes against public finances.'

(112) a. A. Zergatik   aldatu du   Peiok oparia?
        why/what.for change AUX Peio present.ART
       'Why did Peio change the present?' OR 'What did
       Peio change the present for?'
     B. Ez zitzaiolako   gustatzen.
       not AUX.because like
       'Because he didn't like it.'

  C. Beste batengatik.
    other one.for
    'For another one.'
 b. A. Zergatik Peiok oparia aldatu du?
    why   Peio   present   change   AUX
    'How come Peio changed the present?'
  B. Ez zitzaiolako gustatzen.
    not aux.because like
    'Because he didn't like it.'
  C. #Beste batengatik.
    other one.for
    'For another one.'

Further evidence in favor of the high merger of this *zergatik* is that the word order of an embedded clause cannot be affected by it. Thus, example (113a) is acceptable with initial *zergatik* followed by the rest of the elements of the clause in their base generated position, that is: S [S V]$_{CP}$ V. However, (113b) with S-V inversion in the embedded clause is not, since this inversion could only be triggered by a previous A'- movement to the specifier of the embedded CP. In (113b) it cannot be the case that *zergatik* originated in the embedded clause, for it would have triggered V2 in both the embedded and the matrix clauses. Thus the ungrammaticality of (113b). Alternatively, if *zergatik* was directly merged in the left periphery of the matrix clause we should not observe S-V inversion in the embedded clause (and hence, we would obtain (113a)):

(113) a. Zergatik Jonek [gerra bukatuko dela] pentsatzen du?
    why   Jon   war   finish   AUX.C   think   aux
    '{Why is it that/How come} Jon thinks that the war will finish?'
  b. *Zergatik Jonek [bukatuko dela gerra] pentsatzen du?
    why   Jon   finish   AUX.C   war   think   AUX
    '{Why is it that/How come} Jon thinks that the war will finish?'

However, the restriction on verb movement with 'high' *zergatik* is not an absolute one; it only holds if the movement can only be derivative of a purported movement of *zergatik* itself (as in the case of the embedded verb in (113b)), which clashes with the idea that *zergatik* was directly introduced in the left periphery. Verb movements are fine, provided that they piggy back on another displacement operation (say, a focalization), as in the case of (114a), where high *zergatik* is combbined with a focalization on the subject of the matrix clause (which in consequence shows O-V inversion). Again, (114b) is ungrammatical because besides the O-V inversion of the matrix clause, it also displays S-V inversion in the embedded clause. The former is due to the focalization of the subject (as in (114a)), but the latter could only be due to a *wh*-displacement in the embedded clause that generated the V2. The unavailability of such a movement suggests that in this construction *zergatik* is introduced directly high in the left periphery:

(114) a. ?Zergatik [Jonek]$_F$ pentsatzen du [gerra bukatuko dela]?
       why   Jon   think   AUX war   finish   AUX.C
       '{Why is it that/How come} Jon thinks that the war will finish?'
    b. *Zergatik [Jonek]$_F$ pentsatzen du [bukatuko dela   gerra]?
       why   Jon   think   AUX finish   AUX.C   war
       '{Why is it that/How come} Jon thinks that the war will finish?'

Besides focalized constituents, high *zergatik* can also be combined with topics and other intervening material which suggests its very high position in the clause. We already saw an example from Haranburu (17th c.) in (71d), repeated here as (115) where *zergatik* is followed by a reduplicated topical pronoun:

(115) Cergatic ni   neror   bakharric vtzten nauçu?
      why   me   me.contrast alone   leave AUX
      Lit. '{Why is it that/How come}, me, you leave me alone?'

But it can also be followed by series of adjuncts, as in example (71e), repeated here as (116) from Belapeyre (17th c.):

(116) Cergatic egun   oroz goiçan,   egüerditau, eta   arraxen
      why   day   all   morning.at   noon.at   and   afternoon.at
      hirourna   cegnu khaldi emaiten dira eliçan?
      three.each   sign   hit   give   AUX   church.at
      Lit. '{Why is it that/How come} everyday, in the morning, by noon, and in the afternoon three signs given at the church?'

Also by vocatives, as in example (117), from Uriarte (19th c.):

(117) Zergatik, Jauna, urrutira alde   egin dezu, desanparatu nazu
      why   Lord   far.to   side   do   AUX   abandon   aux
      denborarik   bearrenean,   naigabean?
      time.of   need.most.at   desperation.at
      'Why standest Thou afar off, o Lord? Why hidest Thou Thyself in times of trouble?'

In contemporary Basque high *zergatik* can even be associated with clauses with overt complementizers, as in the Basque variants of the reportative clauses analyzed by Etxepare (2010) for Spanish. Etxepare studies a set of constructions of Spanish which are characterized by having an overt initial complementizer *que*, which adds a reportative reading to the sentence. Thus, there is a difference between examples (118a) and (118b):

(118) a. Si   viene   mi   madre, el   tabaco es   tuyo.   [Spanish]
         if   comes   my   mother the   tobacco is   yours
         Lit. 'If my mother comes, the tobacco is yours.'
    b. Si   viene   mi   madre, que   el   tabaco es   tuyo.
         if   comes   my   mother C   the   tobacco is   yours
         Lit. 'If my mother comes, that the tobacco is yours.'

Etxepare (2010) imagines the following scenario: two teenagers (A and B) are secretly smoking in a room. Suddenly, fearing that his/her mother could show up and find out, A tells B (118a): *Si viene mi madre, el tabaco es tuyo*. By saying that, A asks B to act as if the tobacco was B's, if A's mother comes. However, by saying (118b), A asks B something more than just pretense: A asks B to *say* that the tobacco is B's. If B doesn't say so, B will not be complying with A's request.

Basque also has analogous constructions (119A), and high *zergatik* can appear with them (119B), as in the following scenario, where *nirea* 'mine' intervenes between *zergatik* and the verb:

(119) A. Nire   ama   etortzen ba-da, tabakoa zurea de-la.
         my   mother   come   if-BE   tobacco yours BE-C
         'If my mother comes, (say) that the tobacco is yours.'
    B. Zergatik nirea de-la?
         why   mine   BE-C
         '{Why is it that/How come} (I/we should say) that it is mine?'

By employing the complementizer *-la* (which surfaces attached to the verb) speaker A asks B to *say* that the tobacco is B's, but again by employing *-la* B complains asking why should she/he say that it is hers/his.

All this bears testimony to the fact that what I called *high zergatik* is very *high* in the clausal structure.

4 Analysis and discussion

Given that the wh-phrase corresponding to the meaning of *why* has such a particular behavior across languages, several authors have proposed that it is directly merged in a high position in the clause (see *i.a.* Hornstein, 1995; Rizzi, 2001; Ko, 2005). More recently, Shlonsky & Soare (2011) propose a richly articulated complementizer structure at the left periphery of the clause, arguing that English *why* (or Romanian *de ce*) is externally merged in Spec-ReasonP and then moved to Spec-IntP whereas *how come* is directly externally merged in Spec-IntP:

(120) IntP > TopP > FocP > WhP > ReasonP ...

Building on this richly articulated left periphery, I would like to propose that the differential patterns that we observed for Basque *zergatik* are due to the following two types of construals where *zergatik* participates:
1. *Zergatik* externally merged at Spec-ReasonP (above NegP); then moving to IntP successive cyclically followed by the verb and generating residual V2 effects. This gives rise to the canonical Short and Long construals.[19]
2. *Zergatik* directly merged at Int°, where it is frozen, takes clausal scope and as a consequence does not generate any verb movement (*i.e.*, high *zergatik*).

In this respect, high *zergatik* is a complementizer with the same syntax as English *how come*. There is no *wh*-movement and therefore no V2 effect in consequence (Collins, 1991).

It is also similar to Basque *nola* 'how', that beyond being a *wh*-adjunct in questions (121) can also serve as a complementizer in embedded clauses, not triggering movement of the verb. Thus, in (121a) we observe *nola*-verb adjacency and we have an embedded manner interpretation (hence the grammaticality of (121b) with *galdetu* 'ask' in the matrix clause, a question-embedding verb):

(121) a. Begira nola estali duen Jonek oparia.
          look   how wrap AUX.C Jon   present
          'Look how Jon wrapped the present.'
       b. Galdetu nola estali duen Jonek oparia.
          Ask   how wrap AUX.C Jon   present
          'Ask how Jon wrapped the present.'

---

19 I leave the question open as to whether in purpose-questions *zergatik* is introduced lower, as suggested by Chapman & Kučerová (2016).

In (122a) on the contrary we have complementizer *nola*; it implies a factive-like meaning and does not attract the verb. This complementizer cannot be combined with a question-embedding verb (122b):

(122) a. Begira nola Jonek oparia estali duen.
       look   how Jon present wrap AUX.C
       'Observe the fact that Jon wrapped the present.'
    b. *Galdetu nola Jonek oparia estali duen.
       Ask   how Jon present wrap AUX.C
       'Question the fact that Jon wrapped the present.'

Returning to *zergatik*, I mentioned already that high *zergatik* has an interpretation akin to that of English *how come* in that it generates speculative, wondering questions on how come the eventuality described by the clause happened. There is another interesting fact about *how come*: contrary to *why*, it always takes highest scope (*cf.* Collins (1991)). In (123a) the surface order *why*–∀ is ambiguous between the *Wh*»∀ and the ∀»*Wh* readings; however, (123b) with *how come* can only be interpreted with frozen scope *Wh*»∀:

(123) a. Why was every candidate elected?
       Wh»∀ / ∀»*Wh*
    b. How come every candidate was elected?
       Wh»∀ / *∀»*Wh*

If as I proposed high *zergatik* is externally merged in the same position as *how come*, the prediction would be that it should have a similar behavior with respect to scopal properties. Indeed, we observe the very same pattern: (124a) with V2 is ambiguous between the *Wh*»∀ and the ∀»*Wh* readings, but (124b) with high *zergatik* only has the *Wh*»∀ reading whereby *zergatik* takes highest scope:[20]

(124) a. Zergatik etorri dira ikasle   hauek guztiak?
       why   come   AUX   student these all
       'Why did all these students come?'
       [*Wh*»∀ / ∀»*Wh*]

---

[20] As a matter of fact, high *zergatik* can also be substituted by another *wh*-element with the same meaning that takes highest scope: *nolatan*.

b. Zergatik ikasle hauek guztiak etorri dira?
   why   student these all   come AUX
   '{Why is it that/How come} all these students came?'
   [Wh»∀ / *∀»Wh]

Likewise, English *how come* –as opposed to *why*– cannot appear in multiple *wh*-constructions, as represented in (125) (see Ochi (2004) for discussion). The same pattern is attested in Basque with high *zergatik*, which renders ungrammatical results when combined with another interrogative phrase. Compare the grammaticality of 'regular' *zergatik* with either multiple fronting in (126a) or with single fronting+*in situ wh* in (126b), with the ungrammaticality of high *zergatik* in (126c):[21]

(125) a. Why did John eat what?
      b. How come John ate what?

(126) a. ?Zergatik jan du   Jonek zer?
         why   eat AUX Jon   what
         'Why did Jon eat what?'
         '{Why is it that/How come} Jon ate what?'
      b. ??Zergatik zer jan du Jonek?
         why   what eat AUX Jon
         'Why did Jon eat what?'
      c. *Zergatik Jonek jan du zer?
         why   Jon   eat AUX what
         '{Why is it that/How come} Jon ate what?'

If high *zergatik* is a complementizer directly inserted in Int°, it follows that it is incompatible with any construction that targets that very same position.

Last, disjoint causal questions have a pair-list reading. Thus, question (127A) may ask about the reasons one may have for choosing either of the options, where (127B) could provide a coherent answer to it. (127A) can also be naturally answered with a single pair that focuses on the whole disjunct (127C):

---

21 As I explained in Section 3.3, 'antisuperiority-violating' constructions such as (126a) and (126b) are inherently degraded in matrix constructions.

(127) A. Zergatik hautatuko zenuke bata ala bestea?
    why   choose.FUT AUX   one.ART XOR other.ART
    'Why would you choose the one or the other?'
B. Bata   merkeagoa delako,   bestea   hobea delako.
    one.ART cheaper   BE.C.because other.ART better BE.C.because
    'The one because it is cheaper, the other one because it is better.'
C. Biak   ezin   ditudalako   erosi.
    two.ART impossible AUX.C.because buy
    'Because I can't buy both of them.'

Under the first reading, *zergatik* interacts with each of the disjuncts and generates a set of questions (a set of sets of propositions). Under the second reading, *zergatik* takes the whole clause as its sister and generates a single question.²²

As can be expected, the pair-list reading is unavailable with high *zergatik* (as represented in (128B)), the only available reading being the single-pair (128C):

(128) A. Zergatik bata   ala bestea   hautatuko zenuke?
    why   one.ART XOR other.ART choose.FUT AUX
    '{Why is it that/How come} you would choose the one or the other?'
B. #Bata   merkeagoa delako,   bestea   hobea delako.
    one.ART cheaper   BE.C.because other.ART better BE.C.because
    'The one because it is cheaper, the other one because it is better.'
C. Biak   ezin   ditudalako   erosi.
    two.ART impossible AUX.C.because buy
    'Because I can't buy both of them.'

The high merger of *zergatik* directly in Int⁰ makes it take scope over the whole clause as such. It is unsurprising then that high *zergatik* is particularly employed

---

22 This is similar to what happens in polarity questions with disjunction such as "Do you want tea or coffee?" which can be interpreted with a polar interpretation (one single question for which a possible answer could be "Yes."), or with an alternative interpretation (a pair/series of questions for which a possible answer could be "Tea.").

in rhetorical questions.²³ Below are some examples of rhetorical questions with high *zergatik*:²⁴

(129) a. Zergatik mundua hain gaizki banatua dago?
       why   world   so   badly share   AUX
       '{Why is it that/How come} the world is shared so badly?'

   b. Zergatik Jainkoak ez du bere izatearen froga edo
      why   God   NEG AUX its nature   proof or
      erantzunik ematen?
      response   give
      '{Why is it that/How come} God doesn't provide answers or proof of its nature?'

   c. Zeatikan beti   neska bat mutil baten   jarrera
      why   always girl one boy   one.POSS attitude
      matxistaz   kexatzen danen atea   bar da beste mutil
      macho.INSTR complain AUX.C get.out have AUX other boy
      bat esanez "not all man"?
      one saying "not all man"
      '{Why is it that/How come} whenever a girl complains about the macho attitude of a boy another boy comes saying "not all man [SIC]"?'

---

23 In this respect, it seems to be different from English *how come*: Fitzpatrick (2005) and Conroy (2006), when analyzing English *why* and *how come* mention examples such as (ia) and (ib), claiming that they show that *why*, as opposed to *how come* can be employed in forming rhetorical questions (for example, (ia) could be part of an exchange where someone asks, 'Did John leave?' and the response is 'No, why would John leave?', but (ib) cannot be used in such a case):

(i) a. Why would John leave?
(ii) b. *How come John would leave?

However note that these facts could be analyzed in a different manner: if *how come*, like Basque high *zergatik* is factive and takes the whole clause in its scope –hence asking about the whole eventuality– it could not perform a question (rhetorical or not) inquiring about John's motives for leaving. Whether *how come* cannot be really employed in rhetorical questions is a matter that deserves further investigation.

24 Example (129a) taken from a Fotolog entry, example (129b) from the Wikipedia webpage of Ingmar Bergman's film *Det sjunde inseglet*, example (129c) from a tweet by user @Iraultza8m (which employs the reinforced dialectal morphological variant *zeatikan* < *zergatik* + *-n* (inessive)), example (129d) from a tweet by user @EuskalHedabide and example (129e) from a tweet by user @beatxo.

d. Zendako herri batetan gure hizkuntza, bigarren hizkuntza da?
      why   town one.in   our language   second   language BE
      '{Why is it that/How come} our language is a second language in a town?'
   e. Zendako beti   eni   tokatzen zait aspiragailua pasatzea?
      why   always me.to touch   AUX hoover   pass.to
      '{Why is it that/How come} it is always my turn to do the hoovering?'

Rather than an innovation of recent years, such different behavior can be observed already in the Classical Basque literature.

5 Conclusions

Why-questions are special in many respects. As I showed, their syntactic pattern is particular in many languages, but their particularity seems to be homogeneous across them: they tend to surface at the left edge of the clause (outscoping topics, foci, etc.) and in languages generally requiring V2 this restriction disappears with *why*-questions. Also, they seem to be able to be first-merged in different positions in the clausal spine, and the very nature of infinite causal links makes it impossible to provide a fully exhaustive answer to a *why*-question. In consequence, any *why*-question can be answered with a series of propositions, each explaining further the information provided by the previous one: Q: *Why did John eat a sandwich?*, A: *Because he was hungry. And there was a sandwich in the plate. And there was no one around. And he knew that he was not going to have anything else until late. And...* This is particular of *why*-questions, as questions on arguments (*Who?*, *What?...*) or other adjuncts (*When?*, *Where?*) do not allow such infinity.[25]

The literature is converging on the idea that elements such as *why* can be first merged very high in the structure. Here I discussed evidence from Basque in support of this vision, providing evidence that we should distinguish different types of *why*-questions: (i) lower *why*-questions (for reasons and purposes) that show cyclicity effects and residual V2, and (ii) high *why*-questions where the interrogative element is a complementizer directly merged at Into and taking the whole clause as a complement. These are elements like English *how come* or Basque high *zergatik*, which are frozen and do not generate V2 effects.

---

[25] Maybe *how* also allows series of answers (even if they are more restricted than with *why*). This is another feature linking *why* and *how* together (cf. the discussion on Basque *nola(tan)* or English *how come* above.

References

Aldai, Gontzal. 2011. Wh-questions and SOV languages in Hawkins' (2004) theory: Evidence from Basque. *Linguistics* 49(5). 1079–1135. doi:10.1515/ling.2011.030.

Balukh, Jermy Imanuel. 2020. *A Grammar of Dhao: An Endangered Austronesian Language in Eastern Indonesia*. Amsterdam: LOT Dissertation Series.

Barreña, Andoni. 1995. *Gramatika jabekuntza-garapena eta haur euskaldunak*. Bilbao: University of the Basque Country UPV/EHU.

Berk, Stephanie. 2003. Why why is different. In Barbara Beachley, Amanda Brown & Frances Conlin (eds.), BUCLD 27: *Proceedings of the 27th annual Boston University Conference on Language Development*, 127–137. Sommerville: Cascadilla Press.

Bolinger, Dwight. 1978. Asking more than one thing at a time. In Henry Hiż (ed.), *Questions*, 107–150. Dordrecht: Springer. doi:10.1007/978-94-009-9509-3_4.

Bromberger, Sylvain. 1992. *On What We Know We Don't Know: Explanation, Theory, Linguistics and How Questions Shape Them*. Chicago: The University of Chicago Press.

Buell, Leston Chandler. 2011. Zulu ngani 'why': Postverbal and yet in CP. *Lingua* 121(5). 805–821. doi:10.1016/j.lingua.2010.11.004.

Cattell, Ray. 1978. On the source of interrogative adverbs. *Language* 54(1). 61–77.

Chapman, Cassandra & Ivona Kučerová. 2016. Two base-generated positions of why: Evidence from English. Paper presented at the DogDays syntax workshop, University of Toronto. Toronto, 18 August.

Collins, Chris. 1991. Why and How come. *MIT Working Papers in Linguistics* 15. 31–45.

Conroy, Anastasia. 2006. The semantics of how come: A look at how factivity does it all. In Nina Kazanina, Utako Minai, Philip J. Monahan & Heather Lee Taylor (eds.), *University of Maryland Working Papers in Linguistics* 14, 1–24. The University of Maryland Department of Linguistics.

Conroy, Anastasia & Jeffrey Lidz. 2007. Production/comprehension asymmetry in children's why questions. In Alyona Belikova, Luisa Meroni & Mari Umeda (eds.), *Proceedings of the 2nd Conference on Generative Approaches to Language Acquisition North America* (GALANA), 73–83. Sommerville: Cascadilla Proceedings Project.

Cox, Ryan. 2019. How why-interrogatives work. Synthèse doi:10.1007/s11229-019-02364-w.

de Cornulier, Benoît. 1974. "Pourquoi" et l'inversion du sujet non clitique. In Christian Rohrer, Nicolas Ruwet & Benoît de Cornulier (eds.), *Actes du Colloque Franco-Allemand de Grammaire Transformationnelle*. Vol. 1. *Études de syntaxe*, 139–163.Tübingen: Max Niemeyer.

Dold, Simon. 2018. *Basque-Spanish Language Contact: An Empirical Study on Word Order in Interrogatives*. Konstanz: Universität Konstanz dissertation.

Duguine, Maia & Aritz Irurtzun. 2014. From obligatory Wh-movement to optional Wh in situ in Labourdin Basque. *Language* 90.1. e1–e30. doi:10.1353/lan.2014.0006.

Endo, Yoshio. 2015. Two ReasonPs: What are*(n't) you coming to the United States for? In Ur Shlonsky (ed.), *Beyond Functional Sequence: The Cartography of Syntactic Structures*, Volume 10, 220–231. Oxford: Oxford University Press.

Etxepare, Ricardo. 2010. From hearsay evidentiality to samesaying relations. *Lingua* 120(3). 604–627. doi:10.1016/j.lingua.2008.07.009.

Etxepare, Ricardo & Jon Ortiz de Urbina. 2003. Focalization. In José Ignacio Hualde & Jon Ortiz de Urbina (eds.), *A Grammar of Basque*, 465–522. Berlin: Mouton de Gruyter.

Fitzpatrick, Justin. 2005. The Whys and How Comes of presupposition and NPI licensing in questions. In John Alderete, Chung hye Han & Alexei Kochetov (eds.), *Proceedings of the 24th West Coast Conference on Formal Linguistics*, 138–145. Sommervile, MA: Cascadilla Proceedings Project.

Haiman, John. 2011. *Cambodian khmer*. Amsterdam & Philadelphia: John Benjamins.

Hamann, Cornelia. 2000. The acquisition of constituent questions and the requirements of interpretation. In Marc-Ariel Friedemann & Luigi Rizzi (eds.), *The Acquisition of Syntax: Studies in Comparative Developmental Linguistics*, 170–235. London & New York: Routledge.

Hamann, Cornelia. 2006. Speculations about early syntax: the production of Wh-questions by normally developing French children and French children with SLI. *Catalan Journal of Linguistics* 5. 143–189.

Hornstein, Norbert. 1995. *Logical Form: From GB to Minimalism*. Oxford: Wiley-Blackwell.

Horvath, Julia. 2013. Focus, exhaustivity and the syntax of Wh-interrogatives: The case of Hungarian. In Johan Brandtler, Valéria Molnár & Christer Platzack (eds.), *Approaches to Hungarian: Volume 13: Papers from the 2011 Lund conference*, 97–132. Amsterdam & Philadelphia: John Benjamins.

Ikeda, Kanako, Tomohiro Fujii & Kyoko Yamakoshi. 2019. Why in the left periphery in Child Japanese: Evidence from children's word order. In Tatiana Bondarenko, Colin Davis, Justin Colley & Dmitry Privoznov (eds.), *Proceedings of the 14th Workshop on Altaic Formal Linguistics* (WAFL14), 91–102. Cambridge: MIT Working Papers in Linguistics #90.

Irurtzun, Aritz. 2016. Strategies for argument and adjunct focalization in Basque. In Beatriz Fernández & Jon Ortiz de Urbina (eds.), *Microparameters in the Grammar of Basque*, 243–263. Amsterdam and Philadelphia: John Benjamins.

Jeong, Youngmi. 2003. Deriving Anti-Superiority effects: Multiple wh-questions in Japanese and Korean. In Cedric Boeckx & Kleanthes K. Grohmann (eds.), *Multiple Wh-fronting*, 131–140. Amsterdam & Philadelphia: John Benjamins.

Kahnemuyipour, Arsalan. 2001. On wh-questions in Persian. *Canadian Journal of Linguistics/Revue canadienne de linguistique* 46(1–2). 41–61. doi:10.1017/S000841310001793X.

Kaiser, Georg A., Klaus von Heusinger & Svenja Schmid. 2019. Word order variation in Spanish and Italian interrogatives. The role of the subject in 'why'-interrogatives. In Natascha Pomino (ed.), *Proceedings of the IX Nereus International Workshop "Morphosyntactic and semantic aspects of the DP in Romance and beyond"*, 69–90. Konstanz: Universität Konstanz.

Kandybowicz, Jason & Harold Torrence. 2012. Krachi wh- in situ: a question of prosody. In Jaehoon Choi, E. Alan Hogue, Jeffrey Punske, Deniz Tat, Jessamyn Schertz & Alex Trueman (eds.), *Proceedings of the 29th West Coast Conference on Formal Linguistics*, 362–370. Somerville: Cascadilla.

Karimi, Simin. 2005. *A Minimalist Approach to Scrambling: Evidence from Persian*. Berlin: Mouton de Gruyter.

Kayne, Richard S. 1972. Subject Inversion in French Interrogatives. In Jean Casagrande & Bohdan Saciuk (eds.), *Generative Studies in Romance Languages*, 70–126. Rowley: Newbury House.

Kayne, Richard S. & Jean-Yves Pollock. 1978. Stylistic inversion, successive cyclicity, and Move NP in French. *Linguistic Inquiry* 9(4). 595–621.

Kirk, Allison. 2012. Word order variation in New Testament Greek wh-questions. In Ans M.C. van Kemenade & Nynke de Haa (eds.), *Historical Linguistics* 2009: *Selected papers from the 19th International Conference on Historical Linguistics, Nijmegen, 10-14 August 2009*, 293–314. Amsterdam & Philadelphia: John Benjamins.

Kishimoto, Hideki. 2018. Some asymmetries of long distance scope assignment in Sinhala. In Kunio Nishiyama, Hideki Kishimoto & Edith Aldridge (eds.), *Topics in Theoretical Asian Linguistics Studies in Honor of John B. Whitman*, 73–96. Amsterdam & Philadelphia: John Benjamins.

Kiss, Katalin É. 2002. *The Syntax of Hungarian*. Cambridge: Cambridge University Press.

Ko, Heejeong. 2005. Syntax of Why-in-situ: Merge into [SPEC, CP] in the overt syntax. *Natural Language & Linguistic Theory* 23(4). 867–916. doi:10.1007/s11049-004-5923-3.

Ko, Heejeong. 2006. On the structural height of reason wh-adverbials: Acquisition and consequences. In Lisa Lai-Shen Cheng & Norbert Corver (eds.), *WH-Movement: Moving on*, 319–350. Cambridge: MIT Press.

Labov, William & Teresa Labov. 1978. Learning the syntax of questions. In Recent advances in the psychology of language: Formal and experimental approaches, 1–44. New York & London: Plenum Press. doi:10.1007/978-1-4684-2532-1_1.

Li, Charles N. & Sandra A. Thompson. 1980. *Mandarin Chinese*. Berkeley: University of California Press.

McCloskey, James. 2002. Resumption, successive cyclicity, and the locality of operations. In Samuel David Epstein & T. Daniel Seely (eds.), *Derivation and Explanation in the Minimalist Program*, 184–226. Oxford: Blackwell.

McCloskey, James. 2003. Working on Irish. *GLOT International* 7(3). 63–72.

Mitxelena, Koldo. 1981. Galdegaia eta mintzagaia euskaraz. In *Euskal linguistika eta literatura: Bide berriak*, 57–81. Bilbao: Deustuko Unibertsitatea.

Miyagawa, Shigeru. 2017. *Agreement Beyond Phi*. Cambridge: MIT Press.

Ochi, Masao. 2004. How Come and other adjunct wh-phrases: A cross-linguistic perspective. *Language and Linguistics* 5. 29–57.

Ortiz de Urbina, Jon. 1989. *Some Parameters in the Grammar of Basque*. Dordrecht: Foris Publications.

Ortiz de Urbina, Jon. 2002. Focus of correction and remnant movement in Basque. In Joseba A. Lakarra & Xabier Artiagoitia (eds.), *Erramu boneta: A festschrift for Rudolph P.G. de Rijk*, 511–524. Bilbao: Euskaltzaindia.

Partee, Barbara. 1991. Topic, focus and quantification. In Steven K. Moore & Adam Zachary Wyner (eds.), *Proceedings of Semantics and Linguistic Theory* (SALT), 1, 159–188. Ithaca: Cornell University.

Richards, Norvin. 1997. *What Moves Where When in Which Language?* Cambridge: MIT dissertation.

de Rijk, Rudolph P. G. 1978. Topic fronting, focus pospositioning and the nature of the Verb Phrase in Basque. In Frank Jansen (ed.), *Studies on Fronting*, 81–112. Lisse: Peter de Ridder Press.

Rizzi, Luigi. 1990. *Relativized Minimality*. Cambridge: MIT Press.

Rizzi, Luigi. 1996. Residual verb second and the wh-criterion. In Adriana Belletti & Luigi Rizzi (eds.), *Parameters and Functional Heads: Essays in Comparative Syntax*, 63–90. Oxford: Oxford University Press.

Rizzi, Luigi. 2001. On the position "int(errogative)" in the left periphery of the clause. In Guglielmo Cinque & Giampaolo Salvi (eds.), *Current Studies in Italian Syntax: Essays Offered to Lorenzo Renzi*, 267–296. Amsterdam: Elsevier.

Shlonsky, Ur & Gabriela Soare. 2011. Where's 'why'? Linguistic Inquiry 42(4). 651–669.

Stepanov, Arthur & Wei-Tien Dylan Tsai. 2008. Cartography and licensing of wh- adjuncts: a cross-linguistic perspective. *Natural Language & Linguistic Theory* 26(3). 589–638. doi:10.1007/s11049-008-9047-z.

Stromswold, Karin J. 1990. *Learnability and the Acquisition of Auxiliaries*. Cambridge: MIT dissertation.

Sulaiman, Mais. 2017. Verb second not verb second in Syrian Arabic. In Laura R. Bailey & Michelle Sheehan (eds.), *Order and structure in syntax I: Word order and syntactic structure*, 325–331. Berlin: Language Science Press. doi:10.5281/zenodo.1117720.

Takita, Kensuke & Barry Chung-yu Yang. 2014. On multiple wh-questions with 'Why? in Japanese and Chinese. In Mamoru Saito (ed.), *Japanese Syntax in Comparative Perspective*, 206–227. Oxford: Oxford University Press.

Thornton, Rosalind. 2004. Why continuity. In Alejna Brugos, Linnea Micciulla & Christine E. Smith (eds.), *Proceedings of the 28th Boston University Conference on Language Development* (BUCLD 28), 620–632. Sommerville: Cascadilla Press.

Thornton, Rosalind. 2008. Why continuity. *Natural Language & Linguistic Theory* 26(1). 107–146. doi:10.1007/s11049-007-9031-z.

Torrego, Esther. 1984. On inversion in Spanish ans some of its effects. *Linguistic Inquiry* 15(1). 103–129.

Tsai, Wei-Tien Dylan. 2008. Left periphery and how-why alternations. *Journal of East Asian Linguistics* 17(2). 83–115. doi:10.1007/s10831-008-9021-0.

Uriagereka, Juan. 1988. Different strategies for eliminating barriers. In James Blevins & Juli Carter (eds.), *Proceedings of NELS* 18, 1987, 509–522. Amherst: GLSA.

Uriagereka, Juan. 1999. Minimal restrictions on Basque movements. *Natural Language & Linguistic Theory* 17. 403–444. doi:10.1023/A:1006146705483.

Yeo, Weichiang Norman. 2010. *Unifying Optional Wh-movement*. York: University of York dissertation.

Nicholas Catasso
Is German *warum* so special after all?

1 Introduction

Wh-extraction is a type of an A-bar dependency resulting from the application of language-specific rules for the formation of non-yes/no questions. For languages like English, in which run-of-the-mill *wh*-questions admit only one interrogative pronoun (*who*, *what*, etc.) or adverb (*when*, *how*, *where*, etc.) that surfaces to the left of the finite verb, it is generally assumed that the *wh*-element is first-merged in some VP position and raised into a dedicated CP specifier at PF in order to satisfy the relevant linearization constraints (1a). Assuming a Split CP in the spirit of Rizzi (1997), the surface position of the interrogative phrase may be taken to follow from movement to SpecFocP (1b):

(1) a. [$_{CP}$ *What* [$_{C°}$ *did* [$_{TP}$ *John* [$_{T°}$ ~~did~~] [$_{VP}$ *do* ~~what~~ *yesterday*]]]]?
    b. [$_{ForceP}$ [$_{TopP*}$ [$_{FocP}$ *What* [$_{Foc°}$ *did*] [$_{TopP*}$ [$_{FinP}$ [$_{TP}$ *John* [T° ~~did~~] *do* ~~what~~ *yesterday*?]]]]]

This, however, does not seem to be the case for all *wh*-interrogatives. Several authors have argued that differently from other *wh*-interrogatives, the adjunct causal *why* and its cross-linguistic counterparts are merged in a (Split) CP-internal position in a number of languages (cf. e.g. Hornstein 1995, Rizzi 2001, Ko 2005, Stepanov & Tsai 2008, Thornton 2008, Shlonsky & Soare 2011).

In his seminal paper, Rizzi (2001) assumes that *why* is externally merged in the specifier of the high left-peripheral functional projection, Int(errogative)P, as illustrated in (2):

Acknowledgements: Preliminary versions of this paper were presented at the 50th SLE meeting workshop 'Why Is 'Why' Unique? Its Syntactic and Semantic Properties' (Zurich, September 10th, 2017), at Cambridge Comparative Syntax 7 (Cambridge, May 11th, 2018), and at the Villa Vigoni workshop 'Dimensions of wh-words: A German-Italian question time' (Menaggio, May 7th, 2019). I would like to thank the audiences present on these occasions for most useful comments and questions on my presentations. I am especially indebted to Theresa Biberauer and Liliane Haegeman for discussing with me some important points concerning the data. For the judgments and thorough discussions on some of the Dutch examples, I am particularly grateful to Lena Karssenberg. I also thank an anonymous reviewer for his/her helpful comments on a previous version of this paper.

https://doi.org/10.1515/9783110675160-005

(2) ForceP > (TopP*) > **IntP** > (TopP*) > FocP > (TopP*) > FinP > (TP . . .)[1]

In short-distance construals, the interrogative adverb is linearized in the very position in which it is generated (3a). In the case of a long-construal structure, instead, *why* cannot be merged into the higher SpecIntP and behaves like any other *wh*-element, thereby moving to matrix-clause SpecFocP in the overt syntax (Rizzi 2001: 295). A sentence like (3a), which is ambiguous between these two readings, will therefore correspond to the syntactic derivation in (3b) if its semantic interpretation is 'Why did John utter those words?' (short construal) and to (3c) if the speaker is asking about the reason that John gave for Mary's leaving (long construal):

(3) a. *Why did John say Mary left?*
   b. [ForceP [TopP* [IntP *Why* [TopP* [FocP [TopP* [FinP *did* [TP *John* [T° *did*] *say* . . .]]]]]]]]?
   c. [ForceP [FocP *Why* [FinP [Fin° *did*] [TP *John* [VP [V° *say*] [CP [IntP *why* [FinP [TP [. . .]]]]]]]]]]?

Among the substantial evidence provided by Rizzi (2001) in favor of a higher position of the projection hosting *why*, the author notes that in languages like Italian, this *wh*-element is insensitive to the Wh-Criterion (Rizzi 1996), according to which:

(4) a. Each *wh*-operator must be in a Spec-Head relation with a +*wh* X°;
   b. Each +*wh* X° must be in a Spec-Head relation with a *wh*-operator.

While, indeed, the raising of non-causal interrogative phrases to Spec,FocP is associated with obligatory movement of the finite verb to Foc – which is witnessed by the fact that no other maximal or minimal projection may intervene between the *wh*-operator and the verb – (5a)-(5c), *perché* ('why') allows for arrangements like (5d), in which another constituent, here the subject, occurs in preverbal position to the right of the interrogative constituent:

(5) a. *Cosa*   (*Gianni)   ha   fatto   ([ok]*Gianni)*?
       what   Gianni   AUX.PRS.3SG   do-PTCP   Gianni
       'What did Gianni do?'

---

[1] This is a simplified representation of the Split CP which only includes the structure relevant to the present discussion. For a comprehensive treatment of the internal makeup of the left periphery (including the projections situated above ForceP), the interested reader is referred e.g. to Rizzi (2004, 2006, 2013), Benincà & Poletto (2004), Rizzi & Bocci (2017).

b. *Dove* (**Gianni*) *è* *andato* (ᵒᵏ*Gianni*)?
   where Gianni AUX.PRS.3SG go-PTCP Gianni
   'Where did Gianni go?'
c. *Come* (**Gianni*) *è* *partito* (ᵒᵏ*Gianni*)?
   how Gianni AUX.PRS.3SG leave-PTCP Gianni
   'How did Gianni leave?'
d. *Perché* (ᵒᵏ*Gianni*) *è* *partito* (ᵒᵏ*Gianni*)?
   why Gianni AUX.PRS.3SG leave-PTCP Gianni
   'Why did Gianni leave?'

Crucially, Rizzi (2001) shows that *perché* and focused phrases cannot occupy the same FP in Italian, since they may co-occur both in main and embedded clauses (6a)-(6b). This is not the case in sentences involving other types of *wh*-constituents:

(6) a. *Perché QUESTO vuoi dirgli (non qualcos'altro)?*
       why this want-PRS.2SG tell-INF-CL.DAT.3SG not something else
       'Why do you want to say this to him (and not something else)?'
   b. *Mi chiedo perché QUESTO vuoi*
       REFL.DAT.1SG ask-PRS.1SG why this want-PRS.2SG
       dirgli (non qualcos'altro).
       tell-INF-CL.DAT.3SG not something else
       'I wonder why you want to say this to him (and not something else).'

Shlonsky & Soare (2011) propose a slight revision of Rizzi's formalization, arguing that *why* is externally merged in the specifier of a dedicated low left-peripheral projection that they call 'ReasonP' and subsequently raised to Spec,IntP in short-distance construals (7a). As for long extraction of *why*, they contend that this interrogative is base-generated in the embedded Spec,ReasonP and moved to matrix Spec,WhP² via the highest specifier position in the subordinate structure (7b):

(7) a. [IntP *why* [TopP [FocP [WhP [ReasonP ~~*why*~~ [TP . . .]]]]]]   (short construal)
   b. [WhP *why* [FinP [TP [vP [CP ~~*why*~~ [ReasonP ~~*why*~~ [TP . . .]]]]]]]   (long construal)

---

2 Shlonsky & Soare (2011: 664) suggest, differently from Rizzi (1997, 2001) that *wh*-movement targets Spec,WhP and does not compete with focalized elements for the specifier position of FocP. This different configuration, however, is not relevant for the discussion at hand. For ease of exposition, in the next chapters of this paper I will label landing site of (non-causal) *wh*-interrogatives 'FocP'.

Advantages of this approach include the avoidance of any problems related to the formal status of IntP, which then preserves its obligatorily criterial nature, as well as the possibility to derive *why* clauses in multiple *wh*-languages such as Romanian, in which *why*, which systematically occurs as the lower of two clause-initial *wh*-XPs, can be assumed to remain in situ, cf. (8) (adapted from Shlonsky & Soare 2011: 658):

(8) a. *Pe   cine   de ce   ai   întrebat   despre   accident?*
         ACC   who   why   AUX.PRS.2SG ask-PTCP   about   accident
         'Who did you ask about the accident and why?'
   b. ... WhP$_{(i)}$ ... [$_{ReasonP}$ *de ce* [$_{TP}$ ... t$_{wh(i)}$ ...]]?

A further observation made by Shlonsky & Soare (2011: 656), whose relevance for the present discussion will become apparent in what follows, is that *why* does not seem to be sensitive to negation in the clause with which it is interpreted. Hence, the ungrammaticality of a sentence like (9b) (vs. (9a)) is to be understood as a Relativized Minimality violation induced by the intervention of negation (cf. Rizzi 1990):

(9) a. *Why didn't Geraldine fix her bike?*
   b. **How didn't Geraldine fix her bike?*

An immediate implication of this in cartographic terms is that ReasonP, whatever relative position it occupies in the clausal spine with respect to the other Split-CP projections and to the TP, must be positioned higher than NegP:

(10) a. *why*$_{(i)}$ ... t$_{why(i)}$ ... NegP
    b. **how*$_{(i)}$ ... NegP ... t$_{how(i)}$

In the next paragraphs, it will be argued on the basis of empirical data that languages like German behave differently concerning the Merge position of *why*, and that the facts discussed further, which possibly follow from more general syntactic principles, further strengthen the line of argumentation pursued in the recent cartographic literature on *why* in the other languages considered.

2 Why *why* is not as special in German

German is a single *wh*-movement V2-SOV language in which only one constituent can (and must) occupy the pre-verbal position both in declarative and non-yes/no questions. This means that in *wh*-questions, the interrogative pronoun/adverb is obligatorily raised to the relevant CP-specifier in which it appears in a Spec-Head configuration with the finite verb (11a) and that in embedded interrogatives, the *wh*-element surfaces in the CP, while the verb remains in situ (11b):[3]

(11) a. [_{FocP} *Was* [_{Foc°} *sagte* [_{TP} *Maria* [_{VP} *Maria was sagte*]]]]?
　　　　what　　　　say-PST.3SG　　Maria
　　　'What did Maria say?'
　　b. *Ich　　　frage　　　mich,*　　[_{FocP} *was* [_{TP} *Maria was sagte*]].
　　　　I-NOM.SG　ask-PRS.1SG　REFL.ACC.SG　　what　　Maria　　say-PST.3SG
　　　'I wonder what Mary said.'

The standard lexical item corresponding to *why* in German is *warum*. When we look at the distribution of this adverb in different syntactic contexts and compare it to that of the same element in other single-movement *wh*-ex-situ languages like Italian or English, we find at least two striking phenomena that apparently militate against the idea of a left-peripheral base-generation of *warum*. These two phenomena are illustrated in the next sections.

2.1 Modal-particle pied-piping

Modal particles are optional adverbial-like elements that appear most frequently in spoken interaction and perform the complex function of modifying the modality of the proposition in which they surface by encoding the speaker's intentions, beliefs or, more generally, disposition towards the information contained therein (cf., *inter alia*, Hentschel 1980, 1986, Thurmair 1989, 1991, Kwon 2005, Coniglio 2011, Abraham 2017a, 2017b, Müller 2018). These elements typically occur in languages with grammaticalized sentence brackets like German or Dutch, and are notoriously base-generated in the middle field, i.e. in the TP/VP area between the

---

3 All embedded clauses introduced by an overt (*wh-* or relative) pronoun/adverb or by a subordinating conjunction exhibit a verb-final word order in (Standard) German. By using the term 'in situ' when referring to the surface position of the verb in such configurations, I deliberately abstract away from an important – but controversial – issue. To be sure, if we proceed from the (non-Kaynian) postulate that the VP/TP in German is head-final, there are at least two possible ways to explain the verb-final arrangement of embedded clauses: (i) the bare verb raises from its Merge position in V° into the T° (in German, *to the right* of V°) to acquire the relevant inflectional features with which it is spelt out, or; (ii) the verb is genuinely in situ (in the sense that it surfaces in the very position in which it is merged) and receives its inflection through leftward affix hopping from T to V. This latter option corresponds, *mutatis mutandis*, to what is generally assumed for English (main and embedded) finite clauses, in which the verb remains in the VP, and the features in T percolate onto this projection.

lowest C-head and the VP (Coniglio 2007, 2011, Abraham 2010, Cardinaletti 2011). Indeed, modal particles (including e.g. *ja, doch, halt*, etc., all basically untraslatable into other languages) are generally placed in that area and may never autonomously surface in a left-peripheral position, irrespective of whether or not they are assumed to interact with the V2 arrangement of the clause. Cf. (12a)-(12c), in which the particle *ja* is inserted into a declarative V2 clause:

(12) a. Hans ist **ja** ein Netter.
Hans be-PRS.3SG ja a nice-one
b. *****Ja** ist Hans ein Netter.
ja be-PRS.3SG Hans a nice-one
c. *****Ja** Hans ist ein Netter.
ja Hans be-PRS.3SG a nice-one
(int.) 'Hans is a nice guy.'[4]

Such elements are at least in part clause-type specific. For instance, the particle *ja* illustrated above generally occurs in declarative clauses. Modal particles that often (but not exclusively) occur in *wh*-questions are *denn* and *nur*, which may modify the modality of a proposition individually (13a)-(13b) or in combination (13c). *Nur* expresses the speaker's consternation in (13a): (s)he asks about what the hearer has done to cause an infelicitous state of affairs that is at stake, and already imagines that it must be something appalling or embarrassing. In (13b), *denn* adds the implication that the speaker is curious about the content of the interlocutor's answer and/or that (s)he needs more information in order to be entirely satisfied with his/her knowledge of the facts. In (13c), these readings are simultaneously available: the speaker explicitly requires more information about something that the hearer must have done, and already has cues that the content of the answer will be sensational in a negative way. In (13), a rather neutral translation is given for all three examples:

(13) a. Was hast du **nur** getan?
what-ACC AUX-PRS.2SG you-NOM.SG nur do-PTCP
b. Was hast du **denn** getan?
what-ACC AUX-PRS.2SG you-NOM.SG denn do-PTCP

---

[4] In general, the semantic contribution of the particle *ja*, which is deliberately left untranslated in this example, can be of (at least) two types: it may stress an assertion made by the speaker (approximately corresponding to English *Hans is a really nice guy!*) or, alternatively, underline the presupposed status of the proposition, whose content is assumed by the speaker to be shared by the hearer (approximately corresponding to English *Well, as we both know, Hans is a nice guy*).

c. Was   hast   du   **denn nur** getan?
   what-ACC   AUX-PRS.2SG   you-NOM.SG   denn nur   do-PTCP
   'What have you done?'

The unmarked arrangement would have the particles surface in the middle field and the *wh*-interrogative obligatorily moved into the CP, as in (13c) above. However, as noted e.g. by Abraham (2010) and Bayer & Trotzke (2015), *wh*-pronouns like *was* ('what') in (13), but also interrogative adverbs such as *wie* ('how'), *wann* ('when'), *wo* ('where'), etc. can in principle also pied-pipe (multiple) modal particles to the left periphery. Bayer & Trotzke (2015: 27–28) associate the conjoint raising of *wh*-pronoun/adverb and modal particle(s) with the notion of 'emphasis for intensity': the speaker makes use of this construction in a *wh*-question as a syntactic strategy to amplify the meaning of the modal particle(s) as linked to the interrogativity of the clause in which it/they occur(s) and to give them special prominence. In (14a), both particles *denn* and *bloß* (the latter adding a rhetorical character to the question) are raised into the CP together with the interrogative element. In (14b), only *bloß* is pied-piped, while *denn* remains in situ. In (14c), the *wh*-pronoun moves into the left periphery, and the particles surface both in the middle field (sentences adapted from Bayer & Trotzke 2015: 23):

(14) a. [Wie **denn bloß**]$_i$ soll   ich   [t]$_i$ leben?
        how denn bloß   shall-PRS.1SG I-NOM.SG   live-INF
     b. [Wie **bloß**]$_i$ soll   ich   denn [t]$_i$ leben?
        how bloß   shall-PRS.1SG I-NOM.SG   denn   live-INF
     c. [Wie]$_i$ soll   ich   denn bloß [t]$_i$ leben?
        how   shall-PRS.1SG I-NOM.SG   denn bloß   live-INF
        'How am I supposed to live?'

As for the syntactic derivation of the configuration illustrated in (14a), in which both particles are pied-piped to the landing site of the interrogative, Bayer & Trotzke (2015) propose to treat them as instantiations of sideward movement. In a nutshell, a copy of the XP *wie bloß* is merged with the phrase *wie denn* to form a complex [*wie denn* [*wie bloß*]]. The lower copy of the interrogative element is deleted ([*wie denn* [~~wie~~ *bloß*]]), and the constituent resulting from this operation is raised into the left periphery. This derivation is summarized in (15) (simplified from Bayer & Trotzke 2015: 25 and not considering the movement of the finite verb). Structures of the type in (14b) may be taken to simply result from movement of one complex [*wie bloß*] into the CP, while in (14c), the *wh*-item does not pied-pipe any of the particles:

(15) [[wie denn bloß] [~~wie denn bloß~~] ich [~~wie bloß~~] leben soll]

Abstracting away from the technical details of this analysis, what is relevant here is that the left-peripheral positioning of modal particles only results from a pied-piping operation, i.e. they cannot autonomously leave the middle-field position in which they are base-generated. In what follows, I will thus not discuss the single steps of the syntactic derivation relative to each example, but rather assume that it is only in combination with a *wh*-item that modal-particle fronting is allowed in modern German.

In principle, this is also possible with *wh*-elements like *was* ('what'), *wann* ('when'), *wo* ('where') and *wer* ('who'), as long as the modal-particle combination is semantically licit and the relevant emphasis conditions apply.

2.1.1 Particle pied-piping in matrix questions with *warum*

Crucially, modal-particle pied-piping is licensed in very much the same way in *warum*-clauses, in which one (16) or more (17) modal particles first-merged below C° may move along with the interrogative to the left periphery or be left behind in the middle field:

(16) a. [*Warum* **denn**]$_i$ ist er [t]$_i$ weg?
 why denn be-PRS.3SG he-NOM.SG away
 b. [*Warum*]$_i$ ist er [t]$_i$ **denn** weg?
 why be-PRS.3SG he-NOM.SG denn away
 'Why has he left?'
 (a. from: F. Ani, *Süden und die Frau mit dem harten Kleid*, ch.12)

(17) a. [*Warum* **denn bloß**]$_i$ hat der Schöpfer[t]$_i$
 why denn bloß AUX.PRS.3SG the-NOM.SG Maker-NOM.SG
 Adam und Eva verboten, von dem einen
 Adam-DAT and Eve-DAT forbid-PTCP from the-DAT.SG one-DAT.SG
 Apfelbaum zu essen?
 apple-tree-DAT.SG to eat-INF
 b. [*Warum* **denn**]$_i$ hat der Schöpfer [t]$_i$ **bloß**
 why denn AUX.PRS.3SG the-NOM.SG Maker-NOM.SG bloß
 Adam und Eva verboten, von dem
 Adam-DAT and Eve-DAT forbid-PTCP from the-DAT.SG
 einen Apfelbaum zu essen?
 one-DAT.SG apple-tree-DAT.SG to eat-INF

c. [Warum]ᵢ hat der Schöpfer [t]ᵢ **denn bloß**
why AUX.PRS.3SG the-NOM.SG Maker-NOM.SG denn bloß
Adam und Eva verboten, von dem einen
Adam-DAT and Eve-DAT forbid-PTCP from the-DAT.SG one-DAT.SG
Apfelbaum zu essen?
apple-tree-DAT.SG to eat-INF
'Why did God prohibit Adam and Eve from eating of that one tree?'
(a. from: W. Nein, *Das Ja zum Leben und zum Menschen*, p. 31)

Given that in V2 languages like German the prefield, i.e. the CP-internal area to the left of the finite verb in matrix clauses, may only host one constituent and modal particles cannot surface in the left periphery if not pied-piped by a *wh*-interrogative, these data indicate that *warum* originates in the middle field and moves to the left periphery just as any other *wh*-element, optionally taking the particle(s) along.

2.1.2 Particle pied-piping in embedded questions with *warum*

Optional movement of one or more particles to the left periphery together with *warum* is also possible in embedded contexts:

(18) a. *Ich fragte ihn,* [warum **denn bloß**]ᵢ *wir*
I-NOM.SG ask-PST.1SG he-ACC.SG why denn bloß we-NOM.SG
uns „in unserer Jugend" [t]ᵢ *Nicht besser Verstanden*
REFL in our-DAT.SG youth-DAT.SG NEG better understand-PTCP
hätten.
AUX.PST.SBJ.1PL
'I asked him why we hadn't had a better relationship when we were young.'
(M. Pirol, *Nach oben offen. Reflexe*, p. 34)
b. *Wir haben höflich nachgefragt,* [warum]ᵢ *er*
we-NOM.SG AUX.PRS.2PL politely ask-PTCP why he-NOM.SG
denn bloß *so krumm am Instrument*
denn bloß so crooked at-the-DAT.SG instrument-DAT.SG
sitze.
sit-SUBJ.3SG
'We asked (him) politely why he was sitting so crooked at his instrument.'
(*Spiegel.de*, 2016)

Also note that differently from *wh*-extraction in languages like English, short-distance and long-distance construals in German are strongly asymmetric in a number of ways (cf., *inter alia*, Fanselow 1997, Salzmann 2005 and Grewendorf 2005). For the purposes of the present discussion, what is interesting to note is that most speakers of German only marginally accept long extraction of a *wh*-adverb in cases in which the embedded clause is introduced by an overt complementizer (19a).[5] In such cases, the *wh*-element is preferably extracted from its base-generation site and moved to the local CP specifier, in which it is bound to appear at PF. To guarantee the correct interrogative reading without violating the corresponding locality constraints, a syntactic placeholder (systematically lexicalized as *was*, lit. 'what', irrespective of the nature of the lower *wh*-interrogative) is inserted into the higher Spec,Foc (19b) (cf. e.g. McDaniel 1989, Brandt et al. 1992, d'Avis 2000, Lohnstein 2000: 166–167). What is generally acceptable, however, is a similar structure in which the extracted *wh*-adverb is raised to the CP-area of the matrix clause and the embedded clause is not introduced by a complementizer, but exhibits a linear V1 arrangement (19c) (cf. Reis 1995):

(19) a. ?(*)Wie   glaubst   du,   dass ich   das
            how   believe-PRS.2SG you-NOM.SG that I-NOM.SG this-ACC.SG
            tun   sollte?
            do-INF   shall-PST.SBJ.1SG
     b. Was   glaubst   du,   wie   ich   das
        was   believe-PRS.2SG you-NOM.SG how   I-NOM.SG this-ACC.SG
        tun   sollte?[6]
        do-INF   shall-PST.SBJ.1SG

---

[5] The factors determining the widespread dispreference for this construct are, to the best of my knowledge, still quite unclear. Some speakers regard this construction as fully grammatical at least in spoken German, others reject it even in colloquial registers. This difference does not seem to be uniquely related to regional variation, as generally assumed in the literature. Some of my (dialect-speaking) informants of Bavarian and Swabian German background do not accept long extraction of a *wh*-element when an overt complementizer introduces the embedded clause irrespective of register, and surprisingly enough, one of my informants from North Germany judges it as perfectly grammatical at least in spoken interaction.

[6] The construction illustrated in this example has been variously addressed in the literature (see references above). Most authors assume that *was* functions as a scope-operator-like element in this structure, which is generally argued to imply *partial movement*. The letter term is used to refer to 'incomplete' movement of the relevant *wh*-element, which is only raised to the embedded CP. The 'partial' interpretability of the interrogative clause resulting from the lower positioning

c. Wie   glaubst   du,   sollte   ich
    how   believe-PRS.2SG you-NOM.SG   shall-PST.SBJ.1SG I-NOM.SG
    das   tun?
    this-ACC.SG   do-INF
    'How do you think I should do this?' (long-distance construal)[7]

In the two contexts illustrated in (19b) (with *was* as a placeholder in the left periphery of the matrix CP) and (19c) (with long-distance extraction and V1 word order in the subordinate clause), modal-particle pied-piping and modal-particle 'stranding' (exemplified by the particle *denn* here) are possible with all *wh*-

---

of the *wh*-pronoun/adverb is resolved by generating a scope element in the form of *was* into the higher clause. For the time being, I do not have much more to say about the formal status of this element. However, it is to be noted that following the line of argumentation pursued in this paper, we may assume that this scopal operator is not merged directly into the higher Spec,CP, but in the middle field. In fact, this element allows both particle pied-piping and particle 'stranding', and there is no reason to think that in the clause in which it surfaces such particles may behave differently. In the following examples, this is shown for the extracted *wh*-adverb *wie* ('how') and the modal particle *wohl*, which may appear adjacent to scope-marking *was* (i) or below C (ii) in the matrix clause. However, this is possible with virtually all *wh*-interrogatives extracted from a subordinate clause, provided that the relevant conditions apply:

(i) Was   wohl   meinst   du,   wie   wir   in   der
     was   wohl   think-PRS.2SG you-NOM.SG   how   we-NOM.SG   in   the-DAT.SG
     klirrenden   Kälte   gelitten   hätten?
     biting-DAT.SG cold-DAT.SG   suffer-PTCP   AUX.PST.SBJ.1PL

(ii) Was   meinst   du   wohl, wie   wir   in   der
     what   think-PRS.2SG you-NOM.SG   wohl   how   we-NOM.SG   in   the-DAT.SG
     klirrenden   Kälte   gelitten   hätten?
     biting-DAT.SG cold-DAT.SG   suffer-PTCP   AUX.PST.SBJ.1PL
     'How much do you think we would have suffered in the biting cold?'
     (J. Saunders, *Patty Brian*, p. 101)

7 To be sure, it cannot be excluded that in this last example, *glaubst du* might be some sort of 'V1 parenthetical' and not an embedding matrix clause, in the spirit of Giorgi & Pianesi's (1997) treatment of some uses of Italian *credo* 'I believe' and as already mentioned by Freywald (2013: 324) for German. If that were the case, then this clause would correspond to a monoclausal matrix structure in which the *wh*-phrase has been moved to a local CP specifier and a parenthetical has been inserted between the interrogative phrase and the finite verb. For the sake of clarity, it is assumed here that the sentence in the (c)-example above is made up of a matrix and an embedded clause, from which the presence of the comma between the subject *du* and the finite verb of the subordinate predicate *sollte* follows.

elements (exemplified by *was* 'what' here (20a)-(20b)), including *warum* (21a)-(21b):

(20) a. Was   denkst   du,   [was]ᵢ   ich   [t]ᵢ
        was   believe-PRS.2SG   you-NOM.SG what-ACC   I-NOM.SG
        denn hier   mache?
        denn   here   do-PRS.1SG
        'What do you think I am doing here?'
        (K. Stickelbroeck, *Mieses Faul*, p. 41)
   b. [Was   **denn**]ᵢ glaubst   du,   soll
      what-ACC   denn   believe-PRS.2SG   you-NOM.SG   shall-PRS.1SG
      ich   [t]ᵢ tun?
      I-NOM.SG   do-INF
      'What do you think I should do?'
      (*Bote vom Untersee*, 1950)

(21) a. [Warum]ᵢ   denkst   du,   habe   ich   [t]ᵢ
        why   believe-PRS.2SG   you-NOM.SG AUX-PRS.1SG   I-NOM.SG
        denn   dieses   Thema   eröffnet?
        denn   this-ACC.SG topic-ACC.SG   open-PTCP
        'Why do you think I have opened this thread?'
        (*ameisenforum.de*, 2008)
   b. [Warum **denn**]ᵢ glaubst   du,   habe
      why   denn   believe-PRS.2SG   you-NOM.SG   AUX-PRS.1SG
      ich   dich   damals [t]ᵢ erkennen   und
      I-NOM.SG   you-ACC.SG back-then   recognize-INF   and
      verstehen   können?
      understand-INF   can-INF
      'Why do you think I could recognize and understand you back then?'
      (H. Hesse, *Der Steppenwolf*, p. 62)

In this section, it has been shown that both in main and embedded clauses, *warum* behaves just as any other *wh*-interrogative with respect to modal-particle pied-piping. This seems to indicate that *warum*, differently from English *why*, Italian *perché*, Romanian *de ce* etc. is not directly merged into a left-peripheral specifier, but rather originates in the middle field, from which it moves along together with the particle(s) to the CP area. In the next chapter, it will be demonstrated that particle pied-piping is not the only domain in which the behavior of *warum* suggests that the standard causal interrogative adverb in this language dramatically differs from most of its cross-linguistic counterparts.

2.2 'Split' aggressively non-D-linked *wh*-expressions

The term 'aggressively non-D-linked phrase' (Pesetsky 1987) refers to interrogative XPs consisting of a *wh*-constituent and a DP or PP intensifier of the *the hell*-type (*what the heck, when on earth*, etc.). In Modern German, virtually all *wh*-elements can optionally appear in 'split' aggressively non-D-linked configurations (Catasso 2019). This means that phrasal *wh*-intensifiers like *zur Hölle* ('the hell'), which modify an interrogative pronoun/adverb generating complex phrases of the type *was zur Hölle* ('what the hell') or *wo in aller Welt* ('where on earth'), may undergo movement together with the *wh*-element to the left periphery (22a)-(23a) or, in a slightly more marked construction, remain in the lower area as a litmus test of the trace of the interrogative in that position (22b)-(23b). With respect to non-causal interrogatives in general, indeed, there is no evidence whatsoever that should lead us to assume that these might be first-merged directly into Spec,CP:

(22) a. [*Was* **zur Hölle**]ᵢ *hat der da* [t]ᵢ *zu suchen?*
    what-ACC to-the-DAT.SG hell-DAT.SG have-PRS.3SG he-NOM.SG there to look-for-INF
    'He has no place here!' (= lit. 'What the hell does he have to look for here?')
    (*myofb.de*, 2015)
   b. [*Was*]ᵢ *hat der* [[t]ᵢ **zur Hölle**] *da gedacht?*
    what-ACC AUX-PRS.3SG he-NOM.SG to-the-DAT.SG hell-DAT.SG there think-PTCP
    'What the hell was he thinking?'
    (*gamestar.de*, 2019)

(23) a. [*Wo* **in aller Welt**]ᵢ *hast du das* [t]ᵢ *her?*
    where in all-DAT.SG world-DAT.SG have-PRS.2SG you-NOM.SG this-ACC.SG V.PRT
    'Where on earth do you have that from?'[8]
    (K. Rhodes, *Im Totengarten*, p. 91)

---

[8] In the original text: *Where on earth did you get it?*

b. [Wo]$_i$ hast   du   [[t]$_i$ **in aller   Welt**]$_i$
   where   have-PRS.2SG   you-NOM.SG   in   all-DAT.SG   world-DAT.SG
   das   schöne   Gedicht   her?
   the-ACC.SG   beautiful-ACC.SG   poem-ACC.SG   V.PRT
   'Where on earth do you have that beautiful poem from?'[9]
   (A.E. Brachvogel, Friedemann Bach, p. 67)

If we proceed from the assumption that the *wh*-element and the intensifier must be merged together – note that in languages like English or Italian, the interrogative pronoun/adverb and the *the-hell*-constituent are in fact inseparable (cf. section 3.1) –, the example above shows that, expectedly, the pronoun *was* / the adverb *wo* is base-generated in some middle-field position and moved to the CP. In the unmarked case, it is accompanied by the intensifier, as in (22a)-(23a), but may optionally be raised to the left periphery leaving this PP in situ (22b)-(23b). Other *wh*-intensifiers that may occur in such continuous or discontinuous constructions are *zum Teufel*, *zum Henker* ('the hell', lit. 'to the devil' and 'to the hangman', respectively), and *in Gottes Namen* ('on earth', lit. 'in God's name').

What is relevant for the present discussion is that *warum* behaves exactly like *was*, *wo* and the other *wh*-elements in this respect:

(24) a. [*Warum* **in aller   Welt**]$_i$ sollte   er
         why   in   all-DAT.SG   world-DAT.SG   shall-PST.SBJ.3SG   he-NOM.SG
         [t]$_i$ sowas   schreiben,   wenn   dort   nichts
                        something-like-that-ACC   write-INF   if   there   nothing-NOM
         war?
         be-PST.3SG
     b. [*Warum*]$_i$ sollte   er   [[t]$_i$ **in aller**
         why   shall-PST.SBJ.3SG   he-NOM.SG   in   all-DAT.SG
         Welt   sowas   schreiben,   wenn   dort
         world-DAT.SG   something-like-that-ACC   write-INF   if   there
         nichts   *war?*
         nothing-NOM   be-PST.3SG
         'Why should he write something like that if nothing happened there?'
         (b. from: *lovetalk.de*, 2010)

---

9 In the original text: *Where on earth did you get it?*

Crucially, this is also the case in embedded *warum*-clauses, where the *wh*-adverb undergoes movement to the CP together with the intensifier in the standard case, but may optionally leave it behind in the middle field:

(25) a. Ich   frage   mich,   [warum   zum   Teufel]$_i$
         I-NOM.SG   ask-PRS.1SG   REFL   why   to-the-DAT.SG   devil-DAT.SG
         ich   mich   [t]$_i$ nicht   in   dich   verlieben
         I-NOM.SG   REFL   NEG   in   you-ACC.SG   fall-in-love-INF
         kann.
         can-PRS.1SG
         'I wonder why the hell I can't fall in love with you.'
         (R. Pilcher *Wechselspiel der Liebe*, p. 51)
     b. Will   wissen,   [warum]$_i$ du   [[t]$_i$ zum
         want-PRS.1SG   know-INF   why   you-NOM.SG   to-the-DAT.SG
         Teufel]   nicht   an   deinem   Platz   bist.
         devil-DAT.SG   NEG   at   your-DAT.SG   place-DAT.SG   be-PRS.2SG
         'I want to know why the hell you're not in your place.'
         (V. McDermid, *Nacht unter Tag*, p. 23)

The facts discussed in this section strongly suggest that *warum*, differently from its cross-linguistic counterparts *perché*, *why*, *de ce*, etc., is not base-generated in the left periphery of the clause, but exhibits a syntactic behavior that is comparable to that of the other *wh*-elements. In what follows, it will be demonstrated on the one hand that the phenomena addressed above are not available in the languages considered so far in the literature on causal *wh*-adverbs (chapter 3.1), and on the other hand that German does not seem to represent the only 'exception' among Indo-European languages, since in another language displaying a syntactic makeup very similar to that of German, namely Dutch, the same structures illustrated in chapter 2 are fully productive (chapter 3.2).

3 Testing the differences: A cross-linguistic perspective

3.1 Romance and English

As observed in 1, it has been shown in the literature that in languages like Italian, English and Romanian, the standard interrogative corresponding to *why* is not moved to, but rather base-generated in a left-peripheral specifier. Considering the

German data discussed in the previous section, it is now worth asking whether discontinuous configurations are possible in English and Romance and what consequences this may have for the present discussion and for the comparative approach adopted here. If the split configurations illustrated above were grammatical in these languages, then another explanation should be sought for particle and aggressively-non-D-linked pied-piping in German, since Rizzi 2001 and Shlonsky & Soare 2011 clearly show that *why* cannot be first-merged in the TP/VP area in Romance and English. It they were not possible, then one might at least tentatively assume that German is, in fact, different from these languages with respect to the generation site of this element. For both English and Romance, only aggressively non-D-linked constituents can be tested, since modal particles are generally assumed not to be present in these languages, at least not as perfect syntactic equivalents of the German particles.[10] The following examples illustrate that in no case (i.e. neither with causal nor with non-causal interrogatives) can

---

[10] A number of works address some discourse particles/desemanticized adverbs of English and Romance, labeling these 'modal particles' on grounds that they may express (covert) modality at least in some contexts (although the categorization of a discourse adverb-like element as a modal particle may sometimes be controversial). Cf., among many others, Rozumko (2015) and Egerland & Jonas (2016) for English *surely/for sure* and *already*, respectively; Coniglio (2011), Cardinaletti (2011), Catasso (2017) for Italian *poi, mica, sì*, etc.; Coniglio & Zegrean (2012) for Romanian *oare, doar*, etc.; I am certainly sympathetic with this lexical choice, because (some of) the German and English/Romance particles partly overlap functionally; however, it must be taken into account that the English and Romance items have very little to do with the German modal particles *from a syntactic point of view*. For instance, they can (or must) often autonomously appear in the left periphery, like Romanian *oare* in (i), which is a CP-only item, Italian *mica* in (ii), which can surface in the TP or in the CP, or English *enough*, whose position is apparently limited to the area to the right of the finite verb in V:

(i) *Oare   unde   va   pleca   Ion   mâine?*
     oare   where   AUX.PRS.3SG   leave-INF Ion   tomorrow?
     'Where will Ion leave tomorrow?' (Coniglio & Zegrean 2012. 22)

(ii) *Non   ci   vengo   mica! / Mica   ci   vengo!*
     NEG   CL   come-PRS.1SG   mica   mica   CL   come-PRS.1SG
     'I am certainly not coming!' (adapted from Catasso 2017: 237)

(iii) *Just call him already!* (Egerland & Jonas 2016: 17)

This entails – among other things – that these items are not (necessarily) first-merged in the area below the finite verb and can therefore not be investigated to test the validity of the assumptions made in this paper. Most importantly, many of the English and Romance particles discussed in the literature so far do not seem to be at all involved in *wh*-raising operations.

the *wh*-pronoun/adverb and the aggressive modifier surface in a split constituent in Italian (26), English (27) and Romanian (28):

(26) a. *Cosa   diavolo   hai   fatto?*   /   *Perché   diavolo*
         what   devil   AUX.PRS.2SG   do-PTCP   why   devil
         l'hai   fatto?
         CL-AUX.PRS.2SG   do-PTCP
     b. *Cosa   hai   {*diavolo}   fatto?*   /   *Perché   l'hai*
         what   AUX.PRS.2SG   devil   do-PTCP   why   CL-AUX.PRS.2SG
         {*diavolo}   fatto   {*diavolo}?
         devil   do-PTCP   devil

(27) a. *What the hell did you do? / Why the hell did you do that?*
     b. *What did you {*the hell} do {*the hell} / Why did you {*the hell} do that {*the hell}?*

(28) a. *Ce   dracu'   ai   făcut?*   /   *De ce   dracu'   ai*
         what   devil   AUX.PRS.2SG   do-PTCP   why   devil   AUX.PRS.2SG
         făcut   asta?
         do-PTCP   this
     b. *Ce   ai   {*dracu'}   făcut   {*dracu'}?*   /   *De ce*
         what   AUX.PRS.2SG   devil   do-PTCP   devil   why
         ai   {*dracu'}   făcut   {*dracu'}   asta?
         AUX.PRS.2SG   devil   do-PTCP   devil   this
         'What the hell did you do? / Why the hell did you do that?

The syntactic derivation of such constructs, in which the *wh*-element obligatorily surfaces adjacent to the aggressive modifier, is controversial. If we adopt Poletto & Pollock (2009) analysis e.g. of French *diable*-phrases (e.g. in *Qu'est-ce que diable tu as fait?* 'What the hell did you do?') for cases like (26)-(28), we should assume that the interrogative is extracted from its base-generation site and cyclically moved into the head of a '*diable*P' in the 'outer' left periphery (i.e. above ForceP), whose head is lexicalized as the aggressive intensifier (cf. the (simplified) adaptation to Standard Italian in (29)). This approach is very attractive. Under the assumption that causal interrogatives such as *pourquoi* ('why'), as well as the other Romance and English *why*-items, are merged in Spec,IntP/Spec,ReasonP, however, the additional assumption should be made that the head of IntP/ReasonP can host a base-generated aggressive *wh*-element; or we should account for further movement of *why* from Spec,Int/Spec,ReasonP into the specifier of the projection headed by the aggressive intensifier. On the basis of independent evidence, Kellert (2015) proposes for French and Italian (but this approach can be extended, *mutatis mutandis*, to English and Romanian) that both the interrogative and the intensifier are base-generated in the lower clause domain, then copied into Spec,FocP, where only the aggressive modifier is interpreted at LF, and into a higher specifier, in which the whole complex phrase is phonologically spelt out (cf. the adaptation in (30)):

(29) [$_{diavoloP}$ [cosa]$_i$ [$_{diavolo°}$ *diavolo* [$_{ForceP}$ [t]$_i$ *hai fatto* [t]$_i$]]]?
(Poletto & Pollock 2009: 246)

(30) PF: [$_{XP}$ *cosa diavolo* $_{X°}$ [$_{FocP}$ cosa diavolo [$_{TP}$ hai fatto cosa diavolo]]]?
LF: [$_{XP}$ cosa diavolo $_{X°}$ [$_{FocP}$ cosa *diavolo* [$_{TP}$ *hai fatto* cosa diavolo]]]?
(Kellert 2015: 221)

I will leave the question open of whether the (grammatical) structures in (26)-(28) are to be accounted for by assuming a movement-based derivation (29) or a Distributed-Deletion approach à la Fanselow & Ćavar (2002), which motivates Kellert's analysis (30). What is crucial here is the fact that the *wh*-interrogative and the modifier cannot be spelt out in a split configuration in these languages.

3.2 Dutch

German does not seem to be an outstanding typological exception in allowing for discontinuous *wh*-constituents. In Dutch, both phenomena discussed in chapter 2 for German *warum* are possible and fully productive. Note that Dutch is – like German and unlike English and Romance – an asymmetric V2 language in which V-to-C movement occurs in matrix clauses (where the prefield is empty in yes/no questions and imperatives and admits only one XP in declarative and non-yes/no interrogative clauses), but not in embedded structures introduced by a subordinating conjunction or pronoun.

In the first place, the Dutch interrogative adverb *waarom* ('why'), just like any other *wh*-element, can appear in a split structure with a modal particle. Modal particles in Dutch basically exhibit the same structural features as their German counterparts, the most important of which is that they must be assumed to be generated in the middle field, since they exclusively appear in that area unless they are raised to the CP together with a *wh*-phrase. In (31), this is illustrated for the *wh*-adverb *hoe* ('how') and the modal particle *toch* (approximately 'yet', 'anyway', similar to German *doch*). In (31a), the whole complex formed by the interrogative and the particle is moved into the CP, while in (31b), *toch* remains in the lower area:

(31) a. [Hoe **toch**]ᵢ kan de Religie [t]ᵢ te
　　　 wie toch can-PRS.3SG the-NOM.SG religion-NOM.SG　　 to
　　　 pas komen...?
　　　 step come-INF
　　b. [Hoe]ᵢ kan de Religie [t]ᵢ **toch**
　　　 wie can-PRS.3SG the-NOM.SG religion-NOM.SG　　 toch
　　　 te pas komen...?
　　　 to step come-INF
　　　 'How can religion reveal to be useful...?'
　　　 (a. from: A. Bosboom-Toussaint, *De Vrouwen Van Het Leycestersche Tijdvak*, p. 130)

This is also the case in root *waarom*-clauses: the interrogative can pied-pipe the particle into the left periphery (32a) or be raised into its surface position leaving the particle in the middle field (32b). Unsurprisingly, the same linear optionality is observed in embedded clauses (33):

(32) a. [Waarom **toch**]ᵢ heeft ze Judith [t]ᵢ wel
　　　 why toch AUX.PRS.3SG she-NOM.SG Judith-ACC　　 PRT
　　　 laten vallen?
　　　 let-INF fall-INF
　　　 'Why did she let Judith fall?'
　　　 (J. Brands, *De vijfde regel*, p. 2)
　　b. [Waarom]ᵢ heeft ze [t]ᵢ **toch** geen
　　　 why AUX.PRS.3SG she-NOM.SG　　 toch no-ACC
　　　 Talen gestudeerd?
　　　 language-ACC.PL study-PTCP
　　　 'Why didn't she study languages?'
　　　 (I. Rock, *Je wordt wat je denkt*, p. 39)

(33) a. ... en vraagt [waarom **toch**]ᵢ al die bases
　　　 and ask-PRS.3SG why toch all that-NOM.PL base-NOM.PL
　　　 in Brabant liggen.
　　　 in Brabant lie-PRS.3PL
　　　 '...and asks why all those bases are in the Province of Brabant.'
　　　 (ronvanzeeland.nl, 2010)

b. *Mychels   vader   vraagt   [waarom]ᵢ ik   [t]ᵢ*
   Mychel-GEN father-NOM.SG ask-PRS.3SG why   I-NOM.SG
   toch *zo   onzeker   ben.*
   toch   so   insecure be-PRS.1SG
   'Mychels father aks why I am so insecure.'
   (S. Heitinga & Stasia Köhler, *De onvrije oefening*, p. 46)

Moreover, aggressively non-D-linked *wh*-phrases can be split in very much the same way as in the German examples in (22)-(24) above. This phenomenon is licensed with both causal (34) and non-causal (35) *wh*-interrogatives. In *waarom*-clauses (just as with the other interrogative pronouns and adverbs), the continuous and discontinuous construction are also licit in subordinate clauses (36). My informants tell me that the Dutch split configuration in which the aggressive intensifier remains in the middle field is even less marked than in German, and the grammaticality judgments are very neat. In the following examples, this is shown for the aggressive modifier *in vredesnaam* (lit. 'in peace's name'):

(34) a. *[Waarom **in vredesnaam**]ᵢ heb   je   [t]ᵢ dat*
        why   in peace-name   AUX.PRS.2SG you-NOM.SG   that-ACC
        gedaan?[11]
        do-PTCP
        'Why on earth did you do that?'
        (R. Dahl 2014, *De verhalenmachine*, p. 15)

   b. *Maar   Augustine, [waarom]ᵢ heb   je   [[t]ᵢ **in***
      but   Augustine   why   AUX.PRS.2SG you-NOM.SG   In
      vredesnaam] *dat   Kind   hier   gebracht?*[12]
      peace-name   the-ACC.SG   child-ACC.SG   here   bring-PTCP
      'Oh Augustine, why on earth have you brought the kid here?'
      (H. Beecher-Stowe, *De hut van oom Tom*, p. 19)

(35) a. *[Wat **in vredesnaam**]ᵢ   zou   het   nut*
        what in peace-name   AUX.PST.3SG the-NOM.SG   utility-NOM.SG
        [t]ᵢ zijn ..?
              be-INF
        'What on earth would the point be in . . .?'
        (*higherlevel.nl*, 2016)

---

[11] In the original text: *What on earth did you do that for?*
[12] In the original text: *Augustine, what in the world did you bring her here for?*

b. [Wat]ᵢ heb   je   [[t]ᵢ **in vredesnaam**] met
   what AUX.PRS.2SG you-NOM.SG   in peace-name   with
   hem   gedaan?[13]
   he-DAT.SG do-PTCP
   'What the hell did you do with him?'
   (J.D. Robb, *Vermoord in extase*, p. 18)

(36) ... en   je   vraagt   jezelf af   waarom
         and you-NOM.SG ask-PRS.2SG   REFL   V.PRT   why
   {*in vredesnaam*} je   das   {*in vredesnaam*} doet.[14]
   in peace-name   you-NOM.SG that-ACC in peace-name   do-PRS.2SG
   '...and you wonder why on earth you are doing that.'
   (sentence with lower *in vredesnaam* from: A. Carr, *Stoppen met roken*, p. 21)

Again, the Dutch construction seems to be on a par with the German one. These data suggest that in both languages, *warum/waarom* is not base-generated in a CP-specifier, but in the middle field (where it may be merged with a modal particle or an aggressive intensifier), and then moved into its PF-position, thereby optionally leaving the particle/modifier in the lower domain of the clause (for a different perspective, see Corver (this volume)). In this sense, the syntactic behavior of the causal interrogative adverb does not diverge from that of the other *wh*-elements. These differences with respect to English and Romance are quite intriguing. A possibility to investigate would be that the V2-SOV syntactic arrangement of German/Dutch may have implications for the base generation of *why*. To determine whether this is the case, however, this hypothesis needs to be substantiated by data from further languages of this type (e.g. Frisian). What is crucial here is that on the basis of the evidence presented in this section, German/Dutch on the one hand and English/Romance on the other hand behave differently as for the Merge position of *why*.

4 The Merge position of *warum*

At this point, the question arises as to how the differences illustrated in the previous chapters are to be motivated syntactically. Shlonsky & Soare (2011: 656), on the basis of data from Romance and English, correctly predict that the Merge position

---

[13] In the original text: *What the hell did you do with him?*
[14] In the original text: *...you wonder why on earth you are doing it.*

of *why* in languages like English, Italian and Romanian must be above negation in order not to induce a Relativized-Minimality violation due to the intervention of NegP (cf. section 1). The presence of this projection, indeed, triggers the ungrammaticality of examples like (9b) (**How didn't Geraldine fix her bike?* vs. **Why didn't Geraldine fix her bike?*). If one were to assume that German *warum* behaves like the other *wh*-interrogatives in terms of base-generation in the middle field and not in the CP, one would probably expect *at first glance* that a sentence like (9b) should be possible in German, since its *warum*-counterpart is perfectly grammatical (37a). This is, however, not the case: (37b) is as ungrammatical as in English:

(37) a. *Warum hat Geraldine ihr Fahrrad nicht*
 why AUX.PRS.3SG Geraldine-NOM her-ACC-SG bike-ACC.SG NEG
 repariert?
 repair-PTCP
 'Why didn't Geraldine repair her bike?'
 b. **Wie hat Geraldine ihr Fahrrad nicht*
 how AUX.PRS.3SG Geraldine-NOM her-ACC-SG bike-ACC.SG NEG
 repariert?
 repair-PTCP
 '*How didn't Geraldine repair her bike?'

This fact can be motivated straightforwardly. As can already be observed in (37), the position of negation (*nicht*) in present-day German is much lower than in Romance. The expression of sentential negation in German is in phase 4 of Jespersen's cycle, in which the language only exhibits a low-TP/VP particle that acted as a reinforcing item in older stages of the language first 'duplicating' and eventually replacing the original high negation *ne*. The same goes for Dutch, where the present-day low element is *niet* and the original high particle, which has disappeared, was *ni*. In Romance and English, on the other hand, NegP is arguably placed to the immediate left of the TP (for a thorough discussion of the position of NegP cf. at least Belletti 1990):

(38) a. CP > TP > NegP > VP ... (German/Dutch)
 b. CP > NegP > TP > VP (English/Romance)

Now, a closer look at the unmarked structural position of *warum* and *wie* in the German clause reveals that NegP must be lower than the former, but – crucially – higher than the latter. The middle-field site reserved for causal phrases in run-of-the-mill declarative readings precedes *nicht* (39a). If a causal constituent follows the negation, its interpretation can only be contrastive (39b). The syntactic arrangement in (39b) would imply that she *would* be coming, but not because of a cold (rather because of something else). The standard answer to a *why*-question, however, is of course of the type in (39a), in which the relevant constituent is an information, not a contrastive focus. As far as *wie* is concerned, the corresponding manner adverbial (assuming that a *wie*-clause asks for the manner in which an action has been performed)[15] is positioned below NegP in the unmarked case, which suggests that this must be its original position in the cartography of the clause (40). The (light) manner adverb *gut* ('well') could be substituted for a more explicit and heavy constituent like *auf diese Art und Weise* ('this way'), and the (un)grammaticality effect would not change. Exactly the same state of affairs is true of Dutch (41):

(39) a. ... dass   sie   wegen   einer   Erkältung   **nicht**
            that   she-NOM.SG because-of   a-GEN   cold-GEN.SG   NEG
        kommen   würde.
        come-INF AUX.PST.SBJ.3SG
        '...that she wouldn't come because of a cold.' (unmarked arrangement)
    b. ... dass   sie   **nicht**   wegen   einer   Erkältung
            that   she-NOM.SG   NEG   because-of   a-GEN   cold-GEN.SG
        kommen   würde.
        come-INF AUX.PST.SBJ.3SG
        '...that she would come not because of a cold (but rather...)'
        (marked arrangement)

---

15 Note that not always does one and the same interrogative adverb convey exactly the same semantic content. Indeed, in some contexts, German *wie* (and English *how*) are causal, not modal *wh*-elements that basically do the same job as *why* (or, in other words, they *mean* 'why', even though they express some kind of mirative causal interrogativity). Unsurprisingly, in such cases, negation can intervene between the preposed interrogative without this leading to ungrammaticality (cf. (i) for English and (ii) for German): considering the observations made above, it can be assumed that these items lexicalized as *wie* and *how* but used to ask for the reason – and not the manner – of a given state of affairs are base-generated in the same syntactic positions in which *warum* and *why*, respectively, originate, namely Spec,IntP/Spec,ReasonP in (i) and the canonical middle-field *warum*-position in (ii):

(i) *How didn't you see me? I'm literally twice your height.*

(ii) Wie   hast   du   denn   nicht   alles   gleich   entdeckt?
     how   AUX.PRS.2SG   you-NOM.SG   denn   NEG   all-ACC.SG   immediately   discover-PTCP
     'How (= why) didn't you spot everything at the beginning?'

This fact does nothing but confirm one the one hand Rizzi's (2001) and Shlonsky & Soare's (2011) idea that English *why* is base-generated in the CP (i.e. above NegP in the higher domain of the TP) and the idea defended here that German *warum*, although exhibiting the same syntactic behavior as the other *wh*-elements, is first-merged to the left of the projection lexicalizing negation.

(40) ... dass   er   das   {**nicht**} gut {***nicht**} gemacht
         that   he-NOM.SG   that-ACC.SG NEG   well   NEG   do-PTCP
    hat.
    AUX.PRS.3SG
    '...that he didn't do it well.'

(41) a. dat   ze   wegens   een verkoudheid **niet** zou
         that she-NOM.SG because-of   a   cold   NEG   AUX.PST.3SG
         komen.
         come-INF
         '...that she would not come because of a cold.'
     b. dat   hij   het   {**niet**} goed {***niet**} heeft
         that he-NOM.SG   it-ACC.SG   NEG   well   NEG   AUX.PRS.3SG
         gedaan.
         do-PTCP
         '...that he didn't do it well.'

It seems, thus, that the assumption that *warum/waarom* in German/Dutch and *why* in English and in other languages behave differently from a syntactic point of view is confirmed both empirically and on theoretical grounds. Note that the data in (39)-(41) also corroborate Soare & Shlonksy's (2011) general idea that negation, being realized as a particle-like element, may function as sort of a minimality blocker for movement of the *wh*-interrogative into the left peripheral specifier in which it is supposed to surface in the standard case.[16]

---

[16] An anonymous reviewer points out that even assuming a general analysis in which *warum* is base-generated in the middle field, the grammaticality of (37a) might be due to an additional option of merging *warum* in a higher position, thereby circumventing the restriction imposed by Relativized Minimality. Of course, this cannot be ruled out *a priori*. However, the relevant *warum*-data addressed in this paper (including (37a)) all include standard readings of this element and of the corresponding structures. If an additional higher base-generation site were to be assumed, one would expect that this should entail a different interpretation of *warum* or of the resulting sentence with *warum* in first position, which does not seem to be the case here. Therefore, I will leave this issue for future research.

5 What about *how come*? A case of micro-variation in German and Dutch

With these facts in mind, the question now comes up as to whether the near synonyms of *why* in languages like German and Dutch also behave differently from English and Romance. The *wh*-interrogative *how come*, which is used informally to ask what the reason for a given situation or state of affairs is, must be first merged in a left-peripheral position in English, since it does not trigger Subject-Auxiliary-Inversion (42a) or, in other words, it seems to introduce a clause whose computation is insensitive to the presence of this adverb. In some (spoken) varieties of English, it may function as a relative operator (cf. Radford 2018: 242) (42b). Rizzi (2001) establishes that Italian *come mai* ('how come') must also be first-merged in the left periphery, since it displays syntactic features that are very similar to those of *perché* (insensitivity to the Wh-criterion, co-occurrence with focused constituents, etc.) (43a). Conroy (2006: 11) also notes that in contexts like (43b), only the upper reading of *come mai* is possible, which implies that besides being *perché*-like, it cannot even be extracted from a lower clause and trigger a long-distance construal:

(42) a. *How come you call her that?*
 b. *And you wanna know the reason how come I fired you?*

(43) a. *Come mai Gianni è partito?*
 how come Gianni-NOM.SG AUX.PRS.3SG leave-PTCP
 'How come Gianni left?'
 b. *Come mai Gianni ha detto che si*
 how come Gianni-NOM.SG AUX.PRS.3SG say-PTCP that REFL
 è dimesso?
 AUX.PRS.3SG resign-PTCP
 'How come Gianni said that he resigned?'

The *how-come*-like element *wieso* (lit. 'how-so'), however, is arguably base-generated in some lower middle-field position in German. Indeed, it displays a similar distribution to *warum* e.g. with respect to optional modal-particle and *wh*-intensifier pied-piping, although speakers' judgments vary to a certain extent. The following examples illustrate that in *wieso*-clauses, a modal particle can move along with the interrogative adverb into the CP or optionally be left in situ both in root (44) and embedded (45) structures:

(44) a. [Wieso]ᵢ haben wir [[t]ᵢ **denn**] nicht getankt?
how-come AUX.PRS.1PL we-NOM.SG denn NEG fill-up-PTCP
'How come we haven't filled up?'
(W. Hofmann, *Abenteuermond*, p. 37)

b. [Wieso **denn**]ᵢ kommst gerade du [[t]ᵢ auf
how-come AUX.PRS.1PL come-PRS.2SG just you-NOM.SG to
diesen Gedanken?
this-ACC.SG thought-ACC.SG
'How come you of all people conceive this idea?'
(H. Böhlau, *Der gewürzige Hund*, ch. 2)

(45) a. Wir werden gefragt, [wieso]ᵢ wir [[t]ᵢ
we-NOM.PL AUX.PRS.1PL ask-PTCP how-come we-NOM.SG
denn] so viel Stress machen würden.
denn so much stress-ACC.SG make-INF AUX.PST.SBJ.1PL
'We are asked how come we get on their case so much.'
(*juleblogt.de*, 2014)

b. Ich habe den Gatten gerade
I-NOM.SG AUX.PRS.1SG the-ACC.SG husband-ACC.SG just
gefragt, [wieso **denn**]ᵢ alle Hosen [t]ᵢ
ask-PTCP how-come denn all-NOM.SG trousers-NOM.PL
weg sind.
away be-PRS.3PL
'I just asked my husband why all trousers have disappeared.'
(*sueddeutsche.de* forum, 2017)

The same goes for aggressive intensifiers like *zum Teufel*, which can appear in a continuous or in a split configuration both in matrix (46) and in subordinate (47) clauses with a preposed *wieso*. Note that *nochmal* ('again') in (46a) is part of the same phrase; it can appear in virtually any aggressively non-D-linked expression in German to further reinforce the expression of the speaker's consternation:

(46) a. Aber [wieso]ᵢ ist das [[t]ᵢ **zum**
but how-come be-PRS.3SG this-NOM.SG to-the-DAT.SG
Teufel nochmal] so wichtig?
devil-DAT.SG again so important
'But why the hell is this so important?'
(*brigitte.de*, 2007)

b. [*Wieso* **zum** **Teufel**]ᵢ *habt* *ihr* [t]ᵢ
how-come to-the-DAT.SG devil-DAT.SG AUX-PRS.2PL you-NOM.PL
überhaupt gewettet?
at-all bet-PTCP
'Why the hell did you bet in the first place?'
(J. Cotton, *Cotton reloaded*, p. 29)

(47) a. ... *stellt sich mir die Frage,*
pose-PRS.3SG REFL I-DAT.SG the-NOM.SG question-NOM.SG
[*wieso*]ᵢ *das* [[t]ᵢ **zum** **Teufel**] *nicht*
how-come this-NOM.SG to-the-DAT.SG devil-DAT.SG NEG
geändert wird.
change-PTCP AUX.PRS.3SG
'...the question arises to me why the hell this won't be changed.'
(*comunio.de*, 2011)

b. *Ich habe mich halt gefragt,*
I-NOM.SG AUX.PRS.1SG REFL PRT ask-PTCP how-come
[*wieso* **zum** **Teufel**]ᵢ *man* [t]ᵢ *immer so wenig*
to-the-DAT.SG devil-DAT.SG one-NOM.SG always so little
schläft.
sleep-PRS.3SG
'I was just wondering how come one always sleeps so little.'
(*muscle-corps.de*, 2008)

Interestingly enough, German and Dutch do not behave uniformly in relation to the syntax of this element. Most (Standard) Dutch speakers, indeed, share the judgment that such structures are very marginal, if not unavailable with Dutch *hoezo* (which is lexically identical to *wieso*; it means literally 'how-so'). Very similar or the same grammaticality judgments hold when:

(48) a. ?*Hoezo* *heb* *je* *in vredesnaam* *dat*
how-come AUX.PRS.2SG you-NOM.SG in peace-name the-ACC.SG
Kind hier gebracht?
child-ACC.SG here bring-PTCP
'Why on earth have you brought the kid here?'

b. ?*Hans   heeft   me   gevraagd   hoezo   ik
   Hans-NOM   AUX.PRS.3SG   I-ACC.SG   ask-PTCP   how-come   I-NOM.SG
   in vredesnaam   dat   kind   hier   heb
   in peace-name   the-ACC.SG   child-ACC.SG   here   AUX.PRS.1SG
   gebracht.
   bring-PTCP
   (int.:) 'Hans asked me why on earth I brought the kid here.'[17]

These data suggest at least two distinct consequences: (i) on the one hand, that Dutch *hoezo* is arguably base-generated in the left periphery, like English *how come*. Given that *waarom*, parallel to German *warum*, may pied-pipe modal par-

---

17 This argument of course presupposes that the corresponding intensifierless constructions are possible, which is confirmed not only by the presence of data like (i) in a number of different sources of (conceptually oral or written) Dutch, but also by my informants. As for (i), it can be assumed with certainty that *hoezo* is a raised *wh*-adverb asking for the reason why the situation described in the sentence has occurred, since it is the only possible interpretation here and this information is even made explicit in the pre-context and in the post-context:

(i) Er   rijzen   bij   mij   wat   vragen.   Ten eerste: hoezo
     EXPL   rise-PRS.3PL   at   me-OBL.SG   what   question-NOM.PL   firstly   how-come
     heeft   je   gitaar   weer   een   beurt   nodig?
     AUX.PRS.3SG   your-NOM.SG   guitar-NOM.SG   again   a-ACC.SG   turn-ACC.SG   necessary
     Ten tweede: wat   is   je   doel...?
     secondly   what   be-PRS.3SG   your-NOM.SG   aim-NOM.SG
     'I have some questions. First of all: how come your guitar needs to be fixed again? Secondly: what is your aim...?' (*gitaarnet.nl*, 2011)

Liliane Haegeman (p.c.) points out to me that there is variation among speakers with respect to the status (and use) of *hoezo*. Some speakers, indeed, can only use *hoezo* in isolation, where it may be followed by a standard V2 sentence that repeats something in the context, as in (ii) (example provided by Liliane Haegeman). Basically, these speakers: only have a colon-reading available for *hoezo*, in which what follows is not a sentence with a truth value, but rather a mere repetition of what another speaker said, and; do not accept a structure like (i) above as part of their grammar:

(ii) A: Ze   kunnen   mijn   reiskosten   niet   betalen.
        they-NOM.SG   can-PRS.3PL   my-ACC.PL   travel-expenses-ACC.PL   NEG   pay-INF
        'They cannot pay my travel expenses.'
     B: Hoezo?   (ze   kunnen   uw   reiskosten
         how-come   they-NOM.PL   can-PRS.3PL   your-ACC.PL   travel-expenses-ACC.PL
         niet   betalen?)
         NEG   pay-INF

This point is interesting and certainly deserves further investigation, which I am not able to undertake here. For the moment, I will limit myself to considering the *hoezo* available for speakers of Dutch who judge (i) as grammatical.

ticles and aggressive intensifiers into the left periphery, there does not seem to be any reasonable motivation for *hoezo* not to do so except for it being similar to English and Romance *why* in terms of base-generation position; (ii) on the other hand, that German *wieso*, although being etymologically related to *hoezo*, must be a more *warum*-like (i.e. a less mirative) type of interrogative in German than in the other West-Germanic languages.[18] In fact, German *wieso* (49a) (but, crucially, not its Dutch lexical counterpart (49b)) can function as a pseudo-relative pronoun in contexts of the *this-is-the-reason-why*-type:

(49) a. Das   ist   der   Grund,   ᴼᴷwarum/ᴼᴷwieso
       this-NOM.SG be-PRS.3SG the-NOM.SG reason-NOM.SG   why   how-come
       es   so   ist.
       it-NOM.SG so be-PRS.3SG
    b. Dat   is   de   reden   ᴼᴷwaarom/*hoezo
       this-NOM.SG be-PRS.3SG the-NOM.SG reason-NOM.SG   why   how-come
       het   zo   is.
       it-NOM.SG so be-PRS.3SG
       'This is the reason why it is so.'

Following Shlonsky & Soare (2011), then, English *why* is base-generated in Spec,ReasonP and moves to IntP in short-distance construals or to RelP when it functions as a pseudo-relative; *how come* is first merged in the same position and can only marginally (i.e. in some registers, and not for all speakers) move to RelP. The data discussed above show that German *warum* and *wieso* are raised

---

18 Also note that *wieso* and *warum* behave in the same way (i.e. on a par with the other *wh*-elements) in long-distance construals: a syntactic placeholder is preferably inserted into the higher Spec,CP (cf. the examples in (19)) and the causal interrogative is only raised to the local left periphery. Again, what is generally possible with *warum*, *wieso*, as well as with all the other *wh*-elements, is a construction in which the *wh*-adverb is cyclically moved into the Spec,CP of the matrix clause and the embedded clause exhibits a linear V1 arrangement:

(i) Was   glaubst   du,   warum/wieso   ich   das
     was   believe-PRS.2SG you-NOM.SG why/how-come   I-NOM.SG that-ACC.SG
     getan   habe?
     do-PTCP AUX-PRS.1SG

(ii) Warum/wieso   glaubst   du,   habe   ich   das
     why/how-come believe-PRS.2SG you-NOM.SG AUX-PRS.1SG I-NOM.SG that-ACC.SG
     getan?
     do-PTCP
     'Why do you think I did that?' (long construal)

to FocP, but may optionally move to RelP when they act as pseudo-relativizers. Dutch *waarom* behaves like German *warum/wieso*. *Hoezo*, instead, is arguably base-generated in the CP and does not move in any case:

(50)

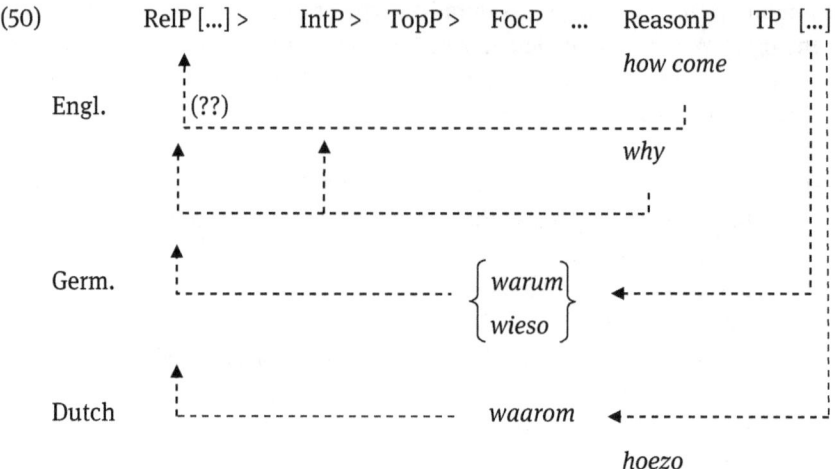

If this analysis is on the right track, the data presented in this paper unveil systemic differences on two levels. With respect to the syntax (and in particular to the base-generation site) of *why*, macro-typological contrasts have been discussed that are possibly interpretable as a correlate to more general grammatical principles. German and Dutch, two asymmetric-V2 languages, allow for continuous and split constituents with most *wh*-pronouns, including *warum/waarom*, whereas in other (non-V2) language systems like Italian, English and Romanian, this is not the case. This fact might call for a typological investigation implying a classification of languages based on the Merge site of causal interrogatives according to other basic grammatical rules. On a second (micro-variational) level, it has been shown that even closely related languages like German and Dutch can be assumed to behave differently in relation to the Merge position of another causal *wh*-adverb, namely *wieso/hoezo*. While *wieso* seems to be syntactically identical to *warum*, etymologically related *hoezo* appears to originate left-peripherally and be immovable.[19]

---

19 The question of whether Italian *come mai*, which is certainly first-merged CP-internally, allows for constructions of the type illustrated in (42b) for English is a controversial one. While most speakers of Standard Italian (including myself) judge sentences like (i) as completely ungrammatical, it must nevertheless be noted that this construction seems to be at least marginally possible in spoken colloquial Italian. Some of my informants tell me that it might be acceptable

6 Conclusions

In this paper, data from German are discussed that suggest that *warum* ('why') is not as special as some of its cross-linguistic counterparts (*why, perché, de ce*, etc.), but rather exhibits the same syntactic behavior as other interrogative *wh*-elements such as *was* ('what'), *wie* ('how') or *wann* ('when') as to its Merge position. For instance, this adverb can optionally pied-pipe modal particles and aggressive intensifiers to the left periphery. On the basis of the fact that modal particles are generally assumed to be base-generated in the middle field (and thus excluding rightward movement of these elements into the TP/VP area) and given the uniform behavior of *wh*-elements in German with respect to this rule, this is taken to be evidence for base-generation of *warum* in the middle field. At the same time, these data reinforce the assumptions made in the seminal studies by Rizzi (2001) and Shlonsky & Soare (2011) with respect to the syntax of *why* in other languages (cf. e.g. Shonsky & Soare's observations in support of the view that negation induces a Relativized Minimality violation, thereby preventing some *wh*-elements from being fronted in the overt syntax). Dutch *waarom* ('why') behaves in very much the same way as *warum*. In this sense, German and Dutch, two languages with an asymmetric-V2 grammar, represent an 'exception' to the generalizations made so far for other languages (which, in fact, have a non-V2 syntax).

A slightly different picture seems to hold for much less studied *how come*. Rizzi (2001) shows that this element originates in a left-peripheral position in English and Romance. In this paper, it is contended that German *wieso* ('how come') instead must be generated in some lower middle-field position, given that it has a distribution which is fairly identical to that of *warum* (e.g. with reference to particle and intensifier pied-piping). Despite the similarities observed for *warum* and *waarom*, in Standard Dutch these mechanisms are unavailable with *hoezo* ('how come'). Moreover, German *wieso* can function as a pseudo-relativizers, while Dutch *hoezo* (*contrary to waarom*) cannot. This demonstrates that *warum* and *waarom* are cross-linguistic realizations of one and the same element. On the

---

in unmonitored spontaneous Italian. As a matter of fact, it is occasionally found e.g. in online forums:

(i) *Molti   commenti   su   questo   blog   lasciano   intendere   il   motivo*
    many   comments   on   this   blog   let-PRS.3PL   understand-INF the   reason
    come mai   ci   ritroviamo   con   questa   classe   politica.
    how-come   REFL   end-up-PRS.1PL   with   this   class   political
    'Many comments on this blog let you understand why we have such a political establishment.'
    (*ilfattoquotidiano.it* forum, 2015)

other hand, *wieso* is a *warum*-like element, whereas *hoezo* behaves like Italian *come mai*.

The data presented here are intended to pave the way for further studies with broader typological scope that may reveal additional implications of general language(-family)-specific syntactic principles like asymmetric V2 for the grammar of *wh*-elements.

Sources

ameisenforum.de. 1 March 2008. Forum 'Eiweiß anbieten'. https://www.ameisenforum.de/post208085.html (accessed 22 September 2019).
Ani, Friedrich. 2002. *Süden und die Frau mit dem harten Kleid*. Knaur: Munich.
Beecher-Stowe, Harriet. 2011/1852. *De hut van oom Tom* (translation by Herman Smit). Houten: Van Goor.
Böhlau, Helene. 1916. *Der gewürzige Hund*. Berlin/Wien: Ullstein.
https://gutenberg.spiegel.de/buch/der-gewurzige-hund-7830/1 (accessed 1 October 2019).
Bosboom-Toussaint, Anna Louisa Geertruida. 1849/1850. *De Vrouwen van het Leycestersche Tijdvak*, vol 1.
http://cf.hum.uva.nl/dsp/ljc/bosboom/vrouleyc/vrouwl05.html (accessed 1 October 2019)
Bote vom Untersee. June 2nd, 1950. 'Aufruf zum Ja'. https://www.e-newspaperarchives.ch (accessed 25 September 2019)
Brachvogel, Albert Emil. 2012/1858. *Friedemann Bach*. Altenmünster: Jazzybee Verlag.
Brands, Jenne. 2009. *De vijfde regel*. Kampen: VLC.
brigitte.de. 3 January 2007. Forum 'Neu-Übende' http://bfriends.brigitte.de/foren/kinderwunsch-und-babyjahre/32872-neu-ubende- fruehjahr 2006-a-457.html (accessed 18 October 2019).
Carr, Allen. 2000. *Stoppen met roken* (translation by Eveline de Mooij). Amsterdam: Forum.
comunio.de. 11 October 2011. Forum 'So geht der Spaß an *comunio.de* definitive verloren'. https://classic.comunio.de/external/phpBB2/viewtopic.php?t=438625&postdays=0&postorder=asc&start=25&language=it_IT (accessed 26 October 2019).
Cotton, Jerry. 2017. *Cotton reloaded, vol 17*. Cologne: Bastei Lübbe.
Dahl, Roald. 1998/1953. *De verhalenmachine* (translation by Hans Edinga). Amsterdam: Meulenhoff. gamestar.de. 29 April 2005. Forum 'FIA Formel 1 – Saison 2019'. https://www.gamestar.de/xenforo/threads/fia-formel-1-saison-2019 (accessed 1 May 2019). gitaarnet.nl. 9 May 2011. Forum 'Stagg Les Paul 'pimpen'?' http://www.gitaarnet.nl/archive/index.php/t-145927.html (accessed 15 August 2019).
Heitinga, Simone & Köhler, Stasia. 2013. *De onvrije oefening. Ex top-turnsters over jarenlange fysieke en mentale intimidatie als trainingsmethode*. Breda: de Geus.
Hesse, Hermann. 2011/1927. *Der Steppenwolf*. Berlin: Suhrkamp Verlag.
higherlevel.nl. 11 March 2016. Forum 'Vennoot houdt zich niet aan opzegtermijn'. www.higherlevel.nl/forums/topic/52571 (accessed 15 August 2019).
Hofmann, Will. 2018. *Abenteuermond*. Berlin: Wiebers Verlag.

ifq.it (=ilfattoquotidiano.it). 17 January 2015. Forum 'Sicilia, il New York Times parla dei nostri vini, mica del petrolio'. https://www.ilfattoquotidiano.it/2015/01/17/sicilia-new-york-times-parla-dei-vini-mica-petrolio/1338567/ (accessed 19 October 2019).
juleblogt.de. 16 October 2014. Blog 'Er steht einfach nicht auf dich?'. https://blog.juleblogt.de/er-steht-einfach-nicht-auf-dich/ (accessed 1 November 2019).
lovetalk.de. 9 January 2010. Forum 'Probleme in der Beziehung'. http://www.lovetalk.de/probleme-in-der-beziehung/93257 (accessed 2 November 2019).
McDermid, Val. 2009. *Nacht unter Tag* (translation by Doris Styron) Knaur: Munich.
muscle-corps.de. 21 April 2008. Forum 'Schlafphasen nach Alkoholkonsum'. https://forummuscle-corps.de/threads/schlafphasen-nach-alkoholkonsum.2621/ (accessed 9 May 2019).
myofb.de. 10 October 2010. Blog 'Trailer zu *Hail Caesar* der Coen Brüder'. http://myofb.de/trailer-zu-hail-caesar-der-coen-brueder/ (accessed 11 May 2019).
Nein, Wolfgang. 2016. *Das Ja zum Leben und zum Menschen, Bd. 3: Predigten 2005–2006*. Nordstedt: BoD.
Pilcher, Rosamunde. 2014/1992. *Wechselspiel der Liebe* (translation by Dietlind Kaiser). Reinbek: Rowohlt.
Pirol, Moritz. 2011. *Nach oben offen. Reflexe*, Bd. 7. Hamburg: Orpheus und Söhne Verlag.
Robb, J. D. 1996. *Vermoord in extase* (translation by Textcase). Amsterdam: Boekerij.
Rock, Inge. 2013. *Je wordt wat je denkt*. Houten: Terra.
ronvanzeeland.nl. 10 July 2010. 'Vlieglawaai' (nl.). https://ronvanzeeland.nl/vlieglawaai-nl/ (accessed 15 November 2019).
Saunders, Jonathan. 2014. *Patty Brian*, vol. 1. Berlin: Novum.
Stickelbroeck, Klaus. 2011. *Mieses Faul*, 3rd ed. Hillesheim: KBV.
Rhodes, Kate. 2012. *Im Totengarten* (translation by Uta Hege). Berlin: Ullstein.
spiegel.de. 14 May 2016. Oh, Österreich! http://www.spiegel.de/politik/deutschland/news-des-tages-opel-oesterreich-pfizer-bedingungsloses-grundeinkommen-a-1092353.html (accessed 15 November 2019).sueddeutsche.de. 23 April 2017. Forum about the online article 'Habt Euch wieder lieb!'. https://www.sueddeutsche.de/medien/tatort-nachlese-habt-euch-wieder-lieb-1.3470470 (accessed 15 November 2019).

References

Abraham, Werner. 2010. Diskurspartikel zwischen Modalität, Modus und Fremdbewusstseinsabgleich (Theory of Mind). In Theo Harden & Elke Hentschel (eds.), In *40 Jahre Partikelforschung*, 33–77. Frankfurt: Peter Lang.
Abraham, Werner. 2017a. Modalpartikel und Mirativeffekte. In Werner Abraham, Yasuhiro Fujunawa, Elisabeth Leiss & Shin Tanaka (eds.), *Grammatische Funktionen aus Sicht der japanischen und deutschen Germanistik*, 75–108. Hamburg: Buske.
Abraham, Werner. 2017b. Modal particles and Verum focus. New corollaries. In Chiara Fedriani & Andrea Sansò (eds.), *Pragmatic markers, discourse markers and modal particles. What do we know and where do we go from here?*, 171–202. Amsterdam: John Benjamins.

Bayer, Josef & Trotzke, Andreas. 2015. The derivation and interpretation of left peripheral discourse particles. In Josef Bayer, Roland Hinterhölzl & Andreas Trotzke (eds.), *Discourse-oriented Syntax*, 13–40. Amsterdam & Philadelphia: John Benjamins.
Belletti, Adriana. 1990. *Generalized verb movement: Aspects of verb syntax*. Turin: Rosenberg & Sellier.
Benincà, Paola & Cecilia Poletto. 2004. Topic, Focus and V2. Defining the CP sublayers. In Luigi Rizzi (ed.), *The structure of CP and IP. The cartography of syntactic structures*, 52–76. Oxford: Oxford University Press.
Brandt, Margareta, Reis, Marga, Rosengren, Inger & Zimmermann, Ilse. 1992. Satztyp, Satzmodus und Illokution. In Inger Rosengren (ed.), *Satz und Illokution*, vol 1, 1–90. Tübingen: Niemeyer.
Cardinaletti, Anna. 2011. German and Italian modal particles and clause structure. *The Linguistic Review* 28. 493–531.
Catasso, Nicholas. 2017. *V2-Einbettung im Spannungsfeld von Hypotaxe und Parataxe*. Tübingen: Stauffenburg.
Catasso, Nicholas. 2019. On splittable aggressively non-D-linked expressions and their correlates in West Germanic. In Nina Topintzi, Nikolaos Lavidas & Maria Moumtzi (eds.), *Selected papers from the 23rd International Symposium on Theoretical and Applied Linguistics (ISTAL 23)*, 88–103. Thessaloniki: Aristotle University of Thessaloniki.
Coniglio, Marco. 2007. German modal particles in root and embedded clauses. *University of Venice Working Papers in Linguistics* 17. 109–141.
Coniglio, Marco. 2011. *Die Syntax der deutschen Modalpartikeln: Ihre Distribution und Lizensierung in Haupt- und Nebensätzen*. Berlin: Akademie Verlag.
Coniglio, Marco & Iulia Zegrean 2012. Splitting up Force: Evidence from discourse particles. *University of Venice Working Papers in Linguistics* 20. 7–34.
Conroy, Anastasia. 2006. The semantics of *how come*: A look at how factivity does it all. In Nina Kazanina, Utako Minai, Philip J. Monahan & Heather L. Taylor (eds.), *University of Maryland Working Papers in Linguistics* 14, 1–24. University of Maryland: Department of Linguistics.
Corver, Norbert. This volume. Why in Dutch? On why-Stripping and high and low adverbials. In Gabriela Soare (ed.), *Why is 'Why' Unique? Its Syntactic and Semantic Properties*, Berlin: De Gruyter Mouton.
d'Avis, Franz. 2000. On the *wh*-expletive *was* in German. In Uli Lutz, Gereon Müller & Arnim von Stechow (eds.), *Wh-Scope Marking*. Amsterdam: John Benjamins.
Fanselow, Gisbert. 1997. Minimal Link Effects in German. Ms., Universität Potsdam.
Fanselow, Gisbert & Damir Cavar. 2002. Distributed deletion. In Artemis Alexiadou (ed.), *Theoretical approaches to universals*, 65–107. Amsterdam: John Benjamins.
Freywald, Ulrike. 2013. Uneingeleiteter V1- und V2-Satz. In Jörg Meibauer, Markus Steinbach & Hans Altmann (eds.), *Satztypen des Deutschen*, 317–337. Berlin & New York: Mouton de Gruyter.
Giorgi, Alessandra & Pianesi, Fabio. 2004. Complementizer deletion in Italian. In Luigi Rizzi (ed.), *The structure of CP and IP. The cartography of syntactic structures*, vol. 2, 190–210. Oxford: Oxford University Press.
Grewendorf, Günther. 2005. The asymmetry of short and long *wh*-movement in German. In Hans-Georg Obenauer (ed.), *L'architecture propositionnelle: La syntaxe de la périphérie gauche*, 35–54. Saint Denis: Presses Universitaires de Vincennes.

Hentschel, Elke. 1980. Abtönungspartikeln als stilistische Merkmale des Alltagsgesprächs. In Wolfgang Kühlwein & Albert Rasch (eds.), *Sprache und Verstehen*, vol. 2, 142–145. Tübingen: Narr.

Hentschel, Elke. 1986. *Funktion und Geschichte deutscher Partikeln. Ja, doch, halt und eben*. Tübingen: Niemeyer.

Hornstein, Norbert. 1995. *Logical form*. Oxford: Blackwell.

Kellert, Olga. 2015. *Interrogative und Exklamative. Syntax und Semantik von multiplen wh-Elementen im Französischen und Italienischen*. Berlin & New York: Mouton de Gruyter.

Ko, Heejeong. 2005. Syntax of *why-in-situ*: Merge into [Spec, CP] in the overt syntax. *Natural Language and Linguistic Theory* 23. 867–916.

Kwon, Min-Jae. 2005. *Modalpartikeln und Satzmodus. Untersuchungen zur Syntax, Semantik und Pragmatik der deutschen Modalpartikeln*. Ludwig-Maximilians-Universität München dissertation.

Lohnstein, Horst. 2000. *Satzmodus-kompositionell. Zur Parametrisierung der Modusphrase im Deutschen*. Berlin: Akademie Verlag.

McDaniel, Dana. 1989. Partial and multiple *wh*-movement. *NLLT* 7. 565–604.

Müller, Sonja. 2018. *Distribution und Interpretation von Modalpartikel-Kombinationen*. Berlin: Language Science Press.

Pesetsky, David. 1987. Wh-in-situ: Movement and unselective binding. In Eric Reuland & Alice ter Meulen (eds.), *The representation of (in)definiteness*, 98–130. Cambridge, MA: MIT Press.

Poletto, Cecilia & Jean-Yves Pollock. 2009. Another look at *wh*-questions in Romance: the case of Medrisiotto and its consequences for the analysis of French *wh*-in-situ and embedded interrogatives. In Leo Wentzel (ed.), *Romance languages and linguistic theory 2006: Selected papers from Going Romance*, 199–258. Amsterdam: John Benjamins.

Radford, Andrew. 2018. *Colloquial English. Structure and variation*. Cambridge: Cambridge University Press.

Reis, Marga. 1995. Wer glaubst du hat recht? On so-called extractions from verb-second clauses and verb-first parenthetical constructions in German. *Sprache und Pragmatik* 36. 27–83.

Rizzi, Luigi. 1990. *Relativized Minimality*. Cambridge, MA: MIT Press.

Rizzi, Luigi. 1996. Residual Verb Second and the Wh-Criterion. In Adriana Belletti & Luigi Rizzi (eds.), *Parameters and Functional Heads*, 63–90. Oxford: Oxford University Press.

Rizzi, Luigi. 1997. The Fine Structure of the Left Periphery. In Liliane Haegemann (ed.), *Elements of Grammar*, 281–337. Dordrecht: Kluwer.

Rizzi, Luigi. 2001. On the position of Int(errogative) in the left periphery of the clause. In Guglielmo Cinque & Giampaolo Salvi (eds.), *Current studies in Italian syntax: Essays offered to Lorenzo Renzi*, 267–296. Amsterdam: Elsevier.

Rizzi Luigi. 2004. On the cartography of syntactic structures. In Luigi Rizzi (ed.), *The structure of CP and IP, The cartography of syntactic structures*, Vol. 2, 223–251. Oxford: Oxford University Press.

Rizzi Luigi. 2006. Selective Residual V-2 in Italian Interrogatives. In Patrick Brandt & Eric Fuß (eds.), *Form, structure and meaning: A Festschrift presented to Günther Grewendorf on occasion of his 60th birthday*. Berlin & New York: Mouton de Gruyter.

Rizzi Luigi. 2013. Notes on cartography and further explanation. *Probus* 25(1). 197–226.

Rizzi Luigi & Bocci, Giuliano. 2017. The left periphery of the clause – primarily illustrated for Italian. In Martin Everaert & Hans van Riemsdijk (eds.), *The Blackwell companion to syntax*, 2nd ed, 2171–2200. Hoboken: John Wiley and Sons.

Rozumko, Agata. 2015. The pragmatic functions of modal particles: a non-native speaker's perspective on dictionary definitions of *surely* and *for sure*. In Wojciech Malec & Marietta Rusinek (eds.), *Within language, beyond theories, vol. III: Discourse Analysis, Pragmatics and Corpus Studies*, 97–114. Newcastle Upon Tyne: Cambridge Scholars Publishing.

Salzmann, Martin. 2005. On an alternative to long A'-movement in German and Dutch. In Sylvia Blaho, Luis Vicente & Erik Schoorlemmer (eds.), *Proceedings of ConSOLE XIII*, 353–375. Leiden: Universiteit Leiden.

Shlonsky, Ur & Gabriela Soare. 2011. Where's 'Why'? *Linguistic Inquiry* 42(4). 651–669.

Stepanov, Arthur & Wei-Tien Dylan Tsai. 2008. Cartography and licensing of *wh*-adjuncts: A crosslinguistic perspective. *Natural Language and Linguistic Theory* 26. 589–638.

Thornton, Rosalind. 2008. Why continuity. *Natural Language and Linguistic Theory* 26. 107–146.

Thurmair, Maria. 1989. *Modalpartikeln und ihre Kombinationen*. Tübingen: Niemeyer.

Thurmair, Maria. 1991. Kombinieren Sie doch nur ruhig auch mal Modalpartikeln! Combinatorial regularities for modal particles and their use as an instrument of analysis. *Multilingua* 10(1/2). 19–42.

Norbert Corver
Why in Dutch? On *why*-stripping and high and low adverbials

1 Introduction

Just like English *why* (DeVilliers 1991, 1996), the Dutch question word *waarom* can occur in the surface pattern *Waarom XP?* ('why XP?'):

(1) A: *Zij   zal   Obama   interviewen.*
       she   will   Obama   interview
       'She will interview Obama.'
    B: *Waarom   Obama?*
       why   Obama
       'Why Obama?' ('Why will she interview Obama?')

Like English again (DeVilliers 1991, 1996), Dutch typically displays this pattern with the interrogative reason adverb *waarom*. It is less felicitous with other kinds of interrogative adverbs such as manner *hoe* 'how', temporal *wanneer* 'when', and locative *waar* 'where'.[1]

(2) A: *Zij   zal   Obama   vriendelijk   aankijken.*
       she   will   Obama   friendly   look.at
       'She will look at Obama in a friendly way.'
    B: **Hoe   Merkel?*
       how   Merkel
       'How will she look at Merkel?'

---

[1] For certain Dutch speakers, examples such as (2)–(4) get better when they are introduced by the coordinating conjunction *en* 'and'. We will briefly come back to this in Section 7.

Acknowledgments: Parts of this chapter were presented at the 2017 Workshop *Why is why unique? Its syntactic and semantic properties*, which was part of the conference Societas Linguistica Europaea, which took place in Zürich. I am grateful to the workshop participants for their comments and questions. I would also like to thank for constructive comments, an anonymous reviewer and the participants of my Comparative Syntax Class at the University of Connecticut during the Spring term of the academic year 2018–2019.

(3) A: *Zij zal morgen Obama interviewen.*
      she will tomorrow Obama interview
      'Tomorrow, she will interview Obama.'
   B: **Wanneer Merkel?*
      when   Merkel
      'When will she interview Merkel?'

(4) A: *Zij zal in Chicago Obama interviewen.*
      she will in Chicago Obama interview
      'She will interview Obama in Chicago.'
   B: **Waar Merkel?*
      where Merkel
      'Where will she interview Merkel?'

The question, obviously, arises as to what underlies the asymmetry between (1), on the one hand, and (2)–(4), on the other hand. Another question that should be raised concerns the structural representation of the Dutch sequence *Waarom XP?*. What does it look like? These and other questions will be addressed in the course of this chapter, which has the following organization. Section 2 addresses the question regarding the nature of the XP-part. It will be proposed that XP is a focalized constituent. In Section 3, it will be shown that the focalized XP ends up in the left periphery of the clause as a result of displacement. Section 4 provides an analysis of the contrast between (1) versus (2), that is, *Waarom XP?* versus **Hoe XP?*. In section 5, it will be shown that, besides the well-formed *Waarom XP?*-pattern, there are also $WH_{reason}+XP?$-patterns that are ill-formed. The question will be addressed as to what underlies this asymmetry. It will be argued that a crucial factor underlying this asymmetry is the structural prominence of the reason adverbial in the clause; that is, a distinction needs to be made between high (clausal) and low (VP) reason adverbials. It will be shown that the lower ones cannot be part of the $WH_{reason}+XP?$-template. Section 6 discusses some further properties of low and high reason adverbials. Section 7 presents an analysis of the spatio-temporal patterns *Wanneer XP?* (3) and *Waar XP?* (4). I will propose that also for these adverbials a distinction should be made between high (i.e. clausal) adverbials and low (i.e. VP-) adverbials. It will be shown that, in certain discourse contexts, patterns such as *Wanneer/Waar XP?* are actually possible. Section 8 provides a brief description of other surface manifestations of the *Waarom XP?*-pattern, both interrogative and non-interrogative ones. Section 9 concludes this chapter.

2 Some observations about the XP-part

This section examines the linguistic nature of the XP-component in the Dutch *Waarom XP?*-pattern. First of all, it should be noted that XP can be of any phrasal type:

(5) a. A: *Ik   heb   Jan   uitgenodigd.*
       I   have   Jan   invited
     B: *Waarom [_DP Jan]?*
        why   Jan
  b. A: *Jan   dook   naakt   het   zwembad   in.*
        Jan   dived   naked   the   swimming.pool into
     B: *Waarom [_AP naakt]?*
        why   naked
  c. A: *Je   moet   de   vis   langzaam   omdraaien.*
        you   must   the   fish   slowly   turn.around
     B: *Waarom [_AP langzaam]?*
        why   slowly
  d. A: *Jan   gaat   werken   in   Peoria.*
        Jan   goes   work   in   Peoria
     B: *Waarom [_PP in   Peoria]?*
        why   in   Peoria
  e. A: *Jan   deelde   mee   [_CP dat   hij   ging   verhuizen].*
        Jan   announced   PRT   that   he   would   move.house
     B: *Waarom (alleen) [_CP dat   hij   ging   verhuizen]?*
        why   (only)   that   he   would   move.house
  f. A: *Jan   heeft   zojuist   getennist.*
        Jan   has   just   played-tennis
     B: *Waarom [_VP getennist] (en   niet   gevoetbald)?*
        why   played-tennis (and   not   played-soccer)

XP has the following values in (5): DP (5a), AP (5b), adverbial AP (5c), PP (5d), CP (5e), and VP (5f).

Secondly, the element that follows *waarom* múst be a phrase; it cannot be a head (e.g. a finite verb).

(6) A: *Jan   kookt   morgen   de   vis   in   witte   wijn.*
       Jan   boils   tomorrow   the   fish   in   white   wine

B: *Waarom* [$_{AdvP}$ *morgen*] / [$_{DP}$ *de vis*] / [$_{PP}$ *in witte wijn*]?
why   tomorrow   /the fish   /in   white   wine
B:' **Waarom* [$_{Vfin}$ *kookt*] (*en niet bakt*)? *waarom + V$_{fin}$
why   boils   (and not bakes)

As (6) shows, phrasal constituents such as *morgen*, *de vis* and *in witte wijn* can occur after *waarom*. However, the finite verb *kookt*, which typically occurs in C° in Dutch main clauses —the so-called Verb Second phenomenon; see Koster (1975)— cannot.

Sometimes it appears as if a verbal head (V°) follows *waarom*, as in (7B), where the infinitival verb *koken* follows *waarom*:

(7) A: *Jan wil de vis morgen in witte wijn koken.*
       Jan wants the fish tomorrow in white wine cook
    B: *Waarom koken (en niet bakken)?*
       why   cook   (and not bake)

Upon closer inspection, however, *koken* constitutes a phrasal constituent, namely a VP consisting of a direct object trace and a verb. The trace results from scrambling of the direct object DP *de vis* to a position in the clausal middle field, as depicted in (8A). Under the assumption that XP in the *Waarom XP?*-pattern is a displaced constituent, *koken* in (7B) has undergone remnant-movement (Den Besten and Webelhuth 1987); that is, movement of a phrase that contains the trace of an extracted constituent (*in casu* the scrambled object DP *de vis*):

(8) A: *Jan wil* [$_{DP}$ *de vis*]$_i$ *morgen in witte wijn* [$_{VP}$ *t$_i$ koken*].
       Jan wants the fish   tomorrow in white wine   cook
    B: *Waarom* [$_{VP}$ *t$_i$ koken*] (*en niet bakken*)?
       why   cook   (and not bake)

A third property of the XP-component in the *Waarom XP*-pattern is the fact that XP bears phonological stress. Unstressed XPs, which have a D(iscourse)-linked interpretation, cannot follow *waarom*. This is exemplified in (9) and (10), where words written with small capitals carry phonological stress:

(9) A: *We hebben Jan uitgenodigd.*
       we have   Jan invited
    B: *Waarom JAN/DIE/HEM?*
       why   Jan/that.one/him

B': Waarom ?*[_DP de etter] / *'m_weak?
   why   the   jerk   /him

(10) A: Jan gaat werken in Peoria.
        Jan goes work   in Peoria
     B: Waarom [_PP in PEORIA] / [_PP DAAR_strong]?
        why   in Peoria   /   there
     B': *Waarom [_PP er_weak]?
         why   there

(9B) shows that phonologically strong (pro)nominal expressions can occur after *waarom*. As shown by (9B'), however, phonologically weak (pro)nominal expressions cannot occur in combination with *waarom*. In (10), we find the same contrast with locative expressions.

The contrast depicted in (9)-(10) suggests that the XP forms a focalized constituent. It is not unexpected then that XP can be accompanied by focus particles such as *alleen* 'only', *ook* 'also', and *zelfs* 'even'. This fourth characteristic of XP is illustrated in (11)-(12):

(11) A: Ze heeft Jan uitgenodigd.
        she has Jan invited
     B: Waarom [alleen JAN]?
        why   only   Jan

(12) A: Ze heeft Jan en Piet uitgenodigd.
        she has Jan and Piet invited
     B: JAN begrijp   ik, maar waarom [ook PIET]?
        Jan understand I   but why   also Piet
        'Jan I understand, but why also Piet?'

As an interim conclusion, it can be stated that the *Waarom XP?*-pattern can be represented as: *Waarom XP_focus?*. More precisely, the focalized XP represents contrastive focus: there is some kind of contrast between XP and an alternative piece of information. This alternative can be explicitly presented (13B) or presupposed (13B'):

(13) A: De commissie heeft Jan als voorzitter uitgekozen.
        the committee has   Jan as chairman   elected
     B: Waarom JAN, en niet PIET?
        why   Jan and not Piet

B:' Waarom JAN?
why Jan

A fifth property of the XP-component in the *Waarom XP*-pattern regards the number of focalized constituents that is permitted after *waarom*. In a discourse context in which the *Waarom XP?*-pattern is preceded by an all-focus sentence, the *Waarom XP?*-pattern typically contains a single instance of XP (14B). Thus, a pattern like *Waarom XP YP?* is excluded. This is shown in (14C-C"):

(14) A: Enkele Studenten lieten [_DP Jan] [_AdvP gisteren] [_AP naakt][_PP door een
some students let Jan yesterday naked through a
bos] fietsen.
forest cycle
'Yesterday, some students let John bike through a forest naked.'
B: Waarom [Jan] / [gisteren] / [naakt] / [door een bos]?
why Jan yesterday naked through a forest
C: *Waarom [Jan] [gisteren]?
why Jan yesterday
C': *Waarom [Jan] [naakt]?
C": *Waarom [Jan] [door een bos]?
C": *Waarom [gisteren] [naakt]?

In discourse contexts in which the preceding clause provides contrastive pairs, the *Waarom XP?*-pattern can contain two focalized phrases; that is: *Waarom XP YP?* This is exemplified in (15):

(15) A: Ze lieten [JAN] [door de STAD] fietsen en [PIET]
they let Jan through the city cycle and Piet
[door een BOS].
through a forest
'They let Jan bike through the city and Piet through a forest.'
B: Waarom [JAN] [door de STAD] en [PIET] [door
why Jan through the city and Piet through
een BOS]?
a forest
'Why did they let Jan bike through the city and Piet through the forest?'

In (15A), the pair {*Jan, door de stad*} is contrasted with {*Piet, door een bos*}. Each member of the contrastive pairs carries phonological stress.

In addition to having a contrastive meaning, the *Waarom XP?*-pattern also has a sense of surprise.² In (13B), for example, person B is surprised by the fact that the committee elected Jan and not Piet as chairman. Thus, *Jan* is unexpected information for person B. Given this surprise meaning component of XP, it is predicted that the expression *Waarom XP?* is infelicitous in discourse contexts in which XP is not unexpected. This is exemplified in (16):

(16) A: Van Gogh sneed zijn linker oor af.
         Van Gogh cut   his   left   ear off
     B: #Waarom Van Gogh?
         why   Van Gogh
     B': Waarom zijn linker oor (en   niet zijn rechter oor)?
         why   his   left   ear (and not   his   right   ear)

(16A) represents the well-known information that the painter Van Gogh cut off his ear. It belongs to the *common knowledge* of person A and person B. The fact that he cut off his left ear may be less well-known (more unexpected) and may trigger the question why he cut off his left ear and not his right ear.

3 Focus and displacement

Having discussed some basic properties of the *Waarom XP?*-pattern, I will now address the following question: What is the syntactic structure that corresponds to this string? Specifically, is *waarom XP?* a clausal structure —[$_{Clause}$ *waarom XP*]— or a non-clausal one —[$_{XP}$ *waarom XP*]? For example, does *Waarom Jan?* in (5a) have a structure like [$_{Clause}$ *waarom Jan β*], where β represents elided material, or a structure like [$_{DP}$ *waarom DP*], where *waarom* is an interrogative modifier directly attached (i.e., adjoined) to the focalized XP?

Under the clausal analysis, it is predicted that *waarom XP?* has the syntactic distribution of a clause; under the non-clausal (i.e., XP) analysis, *waarom XP?* should display the distributional behavior of XP. Now it turns out that the pattern has the distribution of a clause. A good diagnostic for clausal behavior is the possibility of occurring in postverbal position. In Dutch, noun phrases and adjective phrases cannot appear in postverbal position, clauses can.³ This contrast is

---
2 See Van Craenenbroeck (2010) for the observation that so-called SPD-patterns (Sluicing Plus Demonstrative) have a surprise reading.
3 In Dutch, PPs can also occur in post- and preverbal position (Koster 1974).

exemplified in (17), where the particle *af*, which is stranded as a result of Verb Second (i.e., movement of the finite verb to C°) in the main clause, marks the base position of the verb (Koster 1975).[4]

(17) a. *Ik vroeg me <*waarom Jan vertrokken was> **af**
         I   wondered REFL <why   Jan left   was> PRT
         <waarom Jan vertrokken was>.*
         <why   Jan left   was>
         'I wondered why Jan had left.'
     b. *Ik vroeg me dat <plotseling> **af** <*plotseling>.*
         I   wondered REFL that <suddenly> PRT <suddenly>
         'Suddenly, I asked myself that question.'

(17a) shows that the clause introduced by *waarom* must occur in postverbal position; that is, in a position following the particle *af*, which belongs to the displaced verb *vroeg*. (17b) shows that postverbal placement of the adverbial AP *plotseling* yields an ill-formed sentence.[5]

Consider now the mini-discourse in (18):

(18) A: *Jan is   vertrokken!*
        Jan has   left
     B: *Ik hoorde het. Ik vraag me **af** [waarom [$_{AP}$ zo PLOTSELING]]*
        I   heard it. I wonder REFL PRT why   so suddenly
        'I heard about it. But why so suddenly?'

Notice that the string *waarom zo plotseling* in speaker B's reply occurs in postverbal position. If the string were an AP, one would expect the sentence *Ik vraag me af waarom zo plotseling* to be ill-formed; compare (17b). But it is not. Its well-formedness suggests that the string *waarom zo plotseling* represents a full (interrogative) clause (CP). Notice, by the way, that this shows that the *waarom*

---

[4] '<α$_2$> ... <α$_1$>' designates that α occupies either syntactic position α$_1$ or syntactic position α$_2$.
[5] The *waarom* XP-pattern also occurs embedded within a noun phrase that is (semantically) headed by the noun *vraag* 'question':

(i) *[$_{DP}$ De vraag   [waarom Obama]] werd niet gesteld.*
         The question why   Obama   was not raised
    'The question why she will interview Obama was not raised.'

Since the noun *vraag* can combine with a CP but not with a bare (i.e., P-less) DP, an example like (i) provides further evidence in support of the clausal status of the string *waarom Obama*. In (i) the string constitutes an indirect question: *[$_{DP}$ De vraag [$_{CP}$ waarom Obama]]*.

XP-pattern does not only occur as a main clause, as for example in (5), but also as an embedded clause; see also example (i) of note 5.

A second reason for adopting a clausal analysis of *Waarom XP?* comes from the occurrence of sentence adverbs and discourse particles that typically occur in clausal contexts. As shown in (19), these elements can occur in a position in between *waarom* and the focalized XP (19B) or in a position following the focalized XP (19B'):

(19) A: Zij   zal   Obama   interviewen.
         she   will   Obama   interview
     B: Waarom   *{toch / nou / weer / trouwens / ...}*   OBAMA?
         why   {yet / PRT$_{int}$ / again / by.the.way / ...} Obama
     B:' Waarom   OBAMA   *{toch / nou / weer / trouwens / ...}*?

If *waarom XP?* is a clausal pattern, then part of the clause has been deleted, as in Sluicing (Merchant 2001) and fragment answers (Temmerman 2013):

(20) A: Zij   heeft   Jan   uitgenodigd.
         she   has   Jan   invited
         'She invited Jan.'
     B: [$_{CP}$ Waarom [$_{C'}$ C [$_{TP}$ zij Jan uitgenodigd heeft]]]?   (Sluicing)
         why   she Jan invited has
         'Why?' (that is, 'Why did she do that?')

(21) A: Wie   heeft   zij   uitgenodigd?
         who   has   she   invited
         'Who did she invite?'
     B: [$_{CP}$ JAN [$_{C'}$ C [$_{TP}$ zij t$_i$ uitgenodigd heeft]]].   (Fragment Answer)
         Jan
         'Jan.' (that is, 'She invited Jan.')

In the spirit of Sluicing/Fragment Answer analyses, and in line with Yoshida et al's (2015) and Weir's (2013) analyses of so-called *Why*-Stripping, I assume that the overt XP-remnant has been shifted to a high position in the clause before deletion of the lower clausal part takes place.[6] For example, the string *Waarom Jan?* in (5a), repeated here as (22), has the clausal representation in (23).

---

6 For the sake of discussion, I assume here that *waarom* 'why' is base-generated in [Spec,CP]. In Section 4, I will adopt Shlonsky and Soare's (2011) analysis according to which *why* undergoes

(22) A: *Zij heeft Jan uitgenodigd.*
      she has   Jan invited
   B: *Waarom JAN?*
      why   Jan

(23) [$_{CP}$ *Waarom* [$_{C'}$ C [$_{FocP}$ JAN$_i$ [$_{Foc'}$ Foc ~~[$_{TP}$ zij t$_i$ uitgenodigd heeft]~~]]]]?

As indicated in (23), I propose that the focalized DP *Jan* undergoes leftward movement to the specifier position of a Focus-projection (FocP). FocP is located below CP, which contains the interrogative reason adverbial *waarom*.[7]

I take the leftward Focus movement operation in (23) to be an A-bar movement operation. Evidence in support of (A-bar) movement comes from (i) island effects, (ii) reconstruction effects, and (iii) parasitic gap licensing. Let's first consider island effects. As shown in (24), extraction from a subject noun phrase is impossible in Dutch: the PP *over honden* cannot be moved out of the subject noun

---

movement from a clause-adverbial position (namely, the specifier position of ReasonP(hrase)) to the left periphery of the clause. For analyses that take *why* to be base-generated (that is, E(xternally)-Merged) in the left periphery of the clause, see among others Hornstein (1995), Ko (2005), Rizzi (1990, 2001), Stepanov and Tsai (2008), and Thornton (2008).

[7] The question could be raised as to whether the *Waarom XP?*-pattern is an underlying cleft construction. Under such an approach, *Waarom Jan?* in (22B) would be derived from a structure corresponding to *Waarom is het Jan die zij heeft uitgenodigd?* (Litt.: why is it Jan who she has invited); see (i) for a more specific structure which represents the stripping operation:

(i) [$_{CP}$ *Waarom* [$_{FocP}$ JAN$_i$ [$_{Foc'}$ Foc ~~het t$_i$ is [die zij t$_i$ heeft uitgenodigd]~~]]]

I will not adopt an underlying cleft analysis because the XP of the *Waarom XP?*-pattern can be a phrase that cannot occur as a focalized constituent in a cleft construction: specifically, an AP and a postpositional (directional) PP. Compare the clefts in (i) with the *Waarom XP?*-patterns in (ii).

(i) a. **Het is* [$_{AP}$ *LANGZAAM*] *dat Jan de vis omdraaide.*
       It is   slowly   that Jan the fish turned.around
   b. **Het was* [$_{PP}$ *DE BOOM in*] *dat Jan klom.*
       it was   the tree   into   that Jan climbed

(ii) a. A: *Je moet de vis* [$_{AP}$ *LANGZAAM*] *omdraaien.*
          you must the fish   slowly   turn.around
        B: *Waarom* [$_{AP}$ *LANGZAAM*]?
           why   slowly
     b. A: *Jan klom* [$_{PP}$ *DE BOOM in*].
           Jan climbed the tree   into
        B: *Waarom* [$_{PP}$ *DE BOOM in*]?
           why   the tree   into
           'Why into the tree?'

phrase. Notice now the ill-formedness of (25B), where *over honden* corresponds to a subpart of the subject noun phrase in (25A). If *over honden* is a displaced phrase, the ill-formedness of (25B) follows directly: the Subject island constraint is violated (Chomsky 1973, 1986). As shown by (25B'), the string *Waarom XP?* is fine when XP corresponds to the entire subject: *die over honden*.

(24) *[PP *Over HONDEN*]ᵢ heeft [DP die laatste documentaire tᵢ] me
      about dogs   has   that   last   documentary   me
      erg   *aangegrepen.*
      much   agitated
      'That documentary about dogs agitated me much.'

(25) A: [*Die documentaire over honden*] *heeft mij erg*
          that documentary about dogs   has   me   much
          aangegrepen.
          agitated
    B: **Waarom [over HONDEN]?*   (XP = part of subject)
        why   about dogs
    B': *Waarom [die over HONDEN]?*   (XP = subject)
        why   the.one about dogs

A second illustration of an island effect comes from left branch extraction. As shown in (26), the left branch (doubling) possessor *Marie* cannot be moved out of the direct object noun phrase. (26) violates Ross's (1967) Left Branch Condition (LBC; see also Corver 1990). Consider next the ill-formed pattern (27B), where the possessor *Marie* represents the XP in the *Waarom XP?*-pattern. Its ill-formedness is accounted for by an analysis which takes *Marie* to be a displaced constituent. Under such an analysis, (27B) is ruled out because of a violation of the LBC. As indicated by (27B'), it is possible to have the entire direct object noun phrase after *waarom*. In that case, the entire direct object is displaced and no island constraint is violated.

(26) *[MARIE]ᵢ heb ik [DP tᵢ [D' *d'r broer*]] *uitgenodigd.*   (LBC)
      Marie   have I   her brother invited
      'I invited Marie's brother.'

(27) A: *Ik heb [Marie d'r broer] uitgenodigd.*
          I have Marie her brother invited
          'I invited Marie's brother.'
    B: **Waarom MARIE?*   XP = left branch possessor
        why   Marie

B': *Waarom [DP die van MARIE]?*   XP = entire direct object
why   that of Marie
'Why Marie's (brother)?'

A final illustration of an island effect is given in (28), where it is shown that the adjectival modifier *hoe diep* can be extracted out of a complement-PP (28a) but not out of an adjunct-PP (28b). Thus, (28b) violates the Adjunct condition (Cattell 1976, Chomsky 1986, Corver 1990).

(28) a. [$_{DegP}$ *Hoe diep*]$_i$ *lag de schat* [$_{PP}$ t_i *onder de grond*]?
how deep lay the treasure under the ground
'How deep under the ground did the treasure lie?'
b. *[$_{DegP}$ *Hoe diep*]$_i$ *ontdekte hij de schat* [$_{PP}$ t_i *onder de grond*]?
how deep discovered he the treasure under the ground
'How deep under the ground did he discover the treasure?'

Notice now that we find exactly the same contrast in (29B) and (30B), where *zo diep* is interpreted, respectively, as a modifier of a complement-PP and a modifier of an adjunct-PP. The ungrammaticality of (30B) follows from an analysis that takes the adjectival modifier *zo diep* to be extracted from an adjunct-PP.

(29) A: *De schat lag* [$_{PP}$ *diep onder de grond*].
the treasure lay deep under the ground
B: *Waarom* [$_{DegP}$ *zo DIEP*]?
why so deep

(30) A: *Hij ontdekte de schat* [*diep onder de grond*].
he discovered the treasure deep under the ground
B: **Waarom* [$_{DegP}$ *zo DIEP*]?
why so deep

So far, it has been shown on the basis of island behavior that XP in *Waarom XP?* is a displaced constituent. The type of displacement can be characterized as A-bar movement. Evidence in support of this characterization comes from Reconstruction and parasitic gap licensing. Both phenomena have been argued to involve A-bar movement.

Let's first consider Reconstruction. As shown in (31), the reflexive pronoun *zichzelf* can instantiate XP in the *Waarom XP?*-pattern. The pronoun is interpreted as being coreferential with *Jan*. Thus, *waarom zichzelf* is interpreted as 'Why does Jan admire himself (and not somebody else)?'. In (32), *zijn linkerschoen* realizes XP. The possessive pronoun *zijn* receives a bound interpretation. That is, *waarom zijn linkerschoen* receives the interpretation 'Why is it the case that for every pupil x, x had to take off x's left shoe?'.

(31) A: *Jan$_i$ bewondert zichzelf$_i$*
 Jan admired himself
 B: *Waarom ZICHZELF?*
 why himself

(32) A: *[Iedere leerling]$_i$ moest zijn$_i$ linkerschoen uittrekken.*
 every pupil had.to his left.shoe take.off
 B: *Waarom ZIJN LINKERSCHOEN?*
 why his left.shoe

The interpretive dependency between (i) *Jan* and *zichzelf*, and (ii) *iedere leerling* and *zijn* follows immediately from an analysis in which XP is A-bar moved in narrow syntax and interpreted in its base position via Reconstruction. Under the copy theory of movement (Chomsky 1993; Corver and Nunes 2007), this reconstructed interpretation is made possible by the copy (in boldface) in the base position. Schematically, where strikethrough marks the unpronounced part of the clause:

(33) a. *[$_{CP}$ Waarom [$_{C'}$ C [$_{FocP}$ ZICHZELF [$_{Foc'}$ Foc [$_{TP}$ Jan$_i$ ZICHZELF bewondert]]]]?*
 b. *[$_{CP}$ Waarom [$_{C'}$ C [$_{FocP}$ ZIJN LINKERSCHOEN$_i$ [$_{Foc'}$ Foc [$_{TP}$ [iedere leerling] ZIJN LINKERSCHOEN uittrekken moest]]]]?*

Let's next consider parasitic gap licensing, which has been shown to exist in a language like Dutch (Bennis and Hoekstra 1984; Koster 1987). As shown in (34), the A-bar-moved noun phrase *de paprika's* is interpreted in the main clause in the position occupied by the wh-trace/copy (t_i), and in the embedded clause in the position occupied by *pg* (parasitic gap):

(34) *De paprika's$_i$ heeft Jan [na/zonder [PRO pg te hebben gewassen]]*
 the paprikas has Jan after/without to have washed
 in de pan t$_i$ gegooid.
 in the pan thrown
 'The paprikas Jan threw into the pan [after/without having washed them].'

Consider now the following example in which the *XP* element of the *Waarom XP?*-pattern consists of a coordinate structure, namely: *[[clause NP [adjunct clause ..pg..]] en [clause NP [adjunct clause ..pg..]]]*. As indicated, the prepositions introducing the adjunct clauses (*na, zonder*) are pronounced with contrastive accent, just like *de gele paprikas* and *de rode paprikas*.[8]

(35) A: Jan heeft de paprika's in de pan gegooid.
       Jan has   the paprikas in the pan thrown
       'Jan has just thrown the paprikas in the pan.'
   B: Ik weet het, maar waarom...
       I know it, but why
       DE GELE PAPRIKA'S [NA PRO **pg** te hebben gewassen]
       the yellow paprikas after   to have washed
       en DE RODE PAPRIKA'S [ZONDER PRO **pg** te hebben
       and the red paprikas without   to have
       gewassen]
       washed
       'I know, but why did he throw the yéllow parikas in the pan áfter having washed them, and why did he throw the réd ones in the pan withóut having washed them.'

Summarizing, I have shown in this section that the *Waarom XP?*-pattern involves A-bar movement of a focalized phrase (XP).

4 Towards an analysis of *Waarom XP?* versus **Hoe XP?*

Having shown that XP undergoes A-bar movement to [Spec,FocP], we can now address the question as to why the pattern *waarom XP?* is well-formed but the pattern *hoe/waar/ wanneer XP?* is not. In this section, I will first give an analysis of the contrast between the well-formed pattern *waarom XP?* (36) and the ill-formed pattern *hoe XP?* (37). This contrast will be related to the syntactic positions of the two types of adverbials in the hierarchical organization of the clause:

---

[8] Note that (35) instantiates the pattern *Waarom XP YP?*, with XP being the direct object noun phrase (*de gele paprika's, de rode paprika's*) and YP being the adjunct-PP (*na te hebben gewassen, zonder te hebben gewassen*).

hoe (manner, 'how') originates as a VP-adverbial and consequently occupies a relatively low position; *waarom* (reason, 'why'), on the contrary, originates as a clause-adverbial and consequently occupies a relatively high position in the clausal structure. Importantly, it will be shown in section 5 that certain reason adverbials start out as VP-adverbials. Importantly, those reason adverbials are nót permitted in the *Waarom XP?*-pattern. Section 7, finally, will examine the behavior of the temporal adverbial *wanneer* 'when' and the locational adverbial *waar* 'where'. Also with these adverbials, their status as VP-modifier or clausal modifier seems to matter for their occurrence in the *wanneer/waar XP?*-template.

Let's now start our discussion with the contrast between the well-formed pattern *waarom XP?* (36) and the ill-formed pattern *hoe XP?* (37):[9]

(36) A: *Zij zal Obama interviewen.*   (= (1))
       she will Obama interview
    B: *Waarom Obama?*
       why   Obama

(37) A: *Zij zal Obama vriendelijk aankijken.*   (= (2))
       she will Obama friendly   look.at
    B: **Hoe Merkel?*
       how Merkel
       'How will she look at Merkel?'

In the well-formed example (36), the reason adverbial *waarom* is followed by the focalized constituent *Obama*. In the ill-formed example (37), the manner adverbial *hoe* precedes the focalized constituent. The question obviously arises as to what causes this contrast in well-formedness.

In line with Shlonsky and Soare (2011), I assume that this contrast can be interpreted in terms of Rizzi's (1990) Relativized Minimality condition, which is stated in (38).

---

[9] A reviewer asks if the non-elliptical version of (36A) —that is, *Waarom zal zij Obama interviewen?*— is permitted as a reaction to (36B). The use of the non-elliptical sentence sounds a bit strange to my ear. I prefer the use of *zou* 'would' in this particular context: *Waarom zou zij Obama interviewen?* I presume this relates to pragmatic factors related to the modal interpretation of the verb *zullen* (see Broekhuis and Corver 2015:138–150). Notice, by the way, that both the elliptical pattern and the non-elliptical one are perfectly fine when we have *gaat* ('goes', with future interpretation 'will') instead of *zal*. Thus, both *Waarom Obama?* and *Waarom gaat zij Obama interviewen?* are acceptable reactions to person A's statement *Zij gaat Obama interviewen.*

(38) Relativized Minimality
In a configuration [...α...γ...β...], where α c-commands γ and γ c-commands β, γ blocks
a relationship between α and β iff γ is of the same type as α, where 'of the same type' is
understood as:
a. if α is a head, γ is a head;
b. if α is a phrase in an A-position, γ is a phrase in an A-position;
c. if α is a phrase in an A-bar-position, γ is a phrase in an A-bar-position.

Specifically, as will be shown in more detail below, (37B) violates Relativized Minimality because the manner wh-phrase *hoe* 'how' has been moved to an A-bar position (i.e., [Spec,CP]) across a displaced focalized constituent (*Merkel*) that also occupies an A-bar position. In other words, we have a configuration that corresponds to (38c); see (39b). In (36B), on the contrary, Relativized Minimality is not violated because the reason wh-phrase *waarom* 'why' moves to [Spec,CP] from a position higher than the focalized phrase *Obama*.[10] In other words, *waarom* does not move across an intervening phrase in an A-bar position; see (39a).

(39) a. $[_{CP}\ waarom_j \ldots\ [_{ReasP}\ t_j \ldots\ [_{FocP}\ OBAMA_{iq}\ [_{Foc'}\ Foc\ [\ldots t_i \ldots]]]]$ (36B)
 b. *$[_{CP}\ hoe_j \ldots [_{FocP}\ MERKEL_i\ [_{Foc'}\ Foc\ [\ldots t_j \ldots t_i \ldots]]]]$ (37B)

Let us look in slightly more detail at two important aspects of the analysis depicted in (39): first of all, the different syntactic placement of the reason adverbial and the manner adverbial, and, secondly, the location of the focalized constituent.

---

10 Potential evidence in support of displacement of *waarom* 'why' comes from patterns in which material (e.g., *in godsnaam*) that is associated with the wh-phrase is "stranded" (see Catasso (this volume)). Consider, for example, the sentences in (i):

(i) a. Waarom in godsnaam heb je toch Obama geïnterviewd?
 why in god's.name have you PRT Obama interviewed
 'Why on earth did you interview Obama?'
 b. Waarom$_i$ heb je [t$_i$ in godsnaam] toch Obama geïnterviewd?

Observe that the split and non-split pattern are also attested in the *Waarom XP?*-pattern:

(ii) A: Zij zal Obama interviewen.
 she will Obama interview
 B: Waarom in godsnaam toch OBAMA?
 why in god's.name PRT Obama
 B:' Waarom toch *in godsnaam* OBAMA?

In line with Cinque (1999, 2004), I assume that adverbials are base-generated in the specifier position of designated functional projections. Thus, a manner adverbial originates in the Spec-position of Man(ner)P(hrase), and a reason adverbial in the Spec-position of ReasonP(hrase); see Shlonsky and Soare (2011) for the latter proposal. Importantly, Dutch manner adverbials typically occupy a position low in the clausal structure whereas Dutch reason adverbials are located high in the clausal structure.[11] This difference in syntactic placement is reflected in their word order: reason adverbials typically precede manner adverbials, as in (40a). The order 'manner > reason' yields an ill-formed sentence, as shown in (40b).

(40) a. ...dat ze daarom$_{Reason}$ vriendelijk$_{Manner}$ Obama aankeek.
...that she for-that-reason friendly Obama at-looked
'...that, for that reason, she looked at Obama in a friendly way.'
b. *...dat ze vriendelijk$_{Manner}$ daarom$_{Reason}$ Obama aankeek.

The difference between *daarom* and *vriendelijk* as regards their syntactic placement and linearization corresponds to the distinction between clause adverbials and VP-adverbials (Jackendoff 1972). Manner adverbials such as *vriendelijk* 'friendly' are VP-adverbials; they restrict the denotation of the verbal predicate. Reason adverbials such as *daarom* 'for that reason' do not modify the eventuality expressed by the VP; they rather provide "additional" (*in casu*: reason/causal) information. Under the assumption that these adverbials occupy the specifier-position of designated functional projections, the structure assigned to (40a) corresponds to (41):[12]

(41) [$_{CP}$ dat [$_{FP}$ ze$_i$ [$_{F'}$ F [$_{ReasP}$ daarom [$_{R'}$ R^0 [$_{ManP}$ vriendelijk [$_{Man'}$ Man^0 [$_{VP}$ t$_i$ [$_{V'}$ Obama aankeek]]]]]]]]]

Dutch VP-adverbials can be distinguished from clause adverbials by means of a number of diagnostic tests. Firstly, a sentence containing a VP-adverbial can be paraphrased with a conjoined clause consisting of PRONOUN doet dat + ADVERB 'PRONOUN does that + ADVERB' (Van den Hoek 1972; Broekhuis and Corver 2016: 1123). This diagnostic test is exemplified in (42), where '→' represents "can be paraphrased as". The left conjunct in (42b) is a clause without the VP-adverbial.

---

[11] See Section 5, though, where it will be shown that there are also low reason adverbials.
[12] In (41), the subject pronoun *ze* 'she' occupies the specifier position of the phrasal projection 'F(unctional)P(hrase)'. I have left the exact (informational) nature of the layer FP implicit here. TopP (Rizzi 1997) or SubjP (Cardinaletti 2004) seem plausible candidates.

The right conjunct consists of the phrase *doet dat*, which substitutes for the VP in the left conjunct, and the VP-adverbial (*vriendelijk*).

(42) a. Ze   keek   Obama vriendelijk aan.   →   (42b)
         she   looked Obama friendly   PRT
         'She looked at Obama in a friendly way.'
   b. [Ze   keek   Obama an]   en   [ze   deed dat   vriendelijk].
         she   looked Obama PRT   and   she   did   that friendly

Notice now that the sentence adverbial *daarom* cannot be part of the right conjunct, that is: **ze deed dat daarom*:

(43) a. Ze   keek   Obama daarom   aan.   *→[13]   (43b)
         she   looked Obama for-that-reason   PRT
         'She looked at Obama for that reason.'
   b. [Ze   keek   Obama aan]   en   *[ze   deed   dat   daarom].
         she   looked Obama PRT   and   she   did   that   for.that.reason

A second diagnostic test yields a positive result for clause adverbials but a negative one for VP-adverbials (Broekhuis and Corver 2016: 1125). According to this test, a sentence with a clause adverbial can be paraphrased (→) as: "*Het is ADVERBIAL zo [$_{clause}$ dat . . . ..]*" (It is ADVERBIAL so [$_{clause}$ that . . ..]; 'it is ADVERBIAL the case that . . .').[14] In this paraphrase, the sentence adverbial has been placed external to the lexical domain of the clause and been made part of a copular clause. A sentence containing a VP-adverbial cannot be paraphrased this way. This contrast between clause adverbials and VP-adverbials is exemplified in (44). Sentence (43a), which features the clause adverbial *daarom*, can be paraphrased as (44a). On the contrary, sentence (42a), which features the VP-adverbial *vriendelijk*, cannot be paraphrased as (44b):[15]

---

13 *→ stands for "cannot be paraphrased as".
14 The *dat*-clause behaves like a sentential subject that is related to the subject pronoun *het* 'it' of the copular clause. The pronoun can also be replaced by the sentential subject, which yields the following variant of sentence (44a): *Dat ze Obama aankeek was daarom zo* (that she Obama looked.at was for.that.reason so, 'That she looked at Obama was the case for that reason.').
15 Importantly, the ill-formedness of (44b) is not related to the categorial status of the VP-adverbial. As shown in (i), a manner-adverbial PP is also excluded in the copular clause:

(i) a. Ze   keek   Obama [$_{PP}$ op vriendelijke wijze]   aan. (Compare (42a))
        she   looked Obama   at friendly   manner   PRT
   b. *Het   was   [$_{PP}$ op vriendelijke wijze] zo   dat   ze   Obama aankeek.
         it   was   at friendly   manner so   that she   Obama looked.at

(44) a. Het was daarom zo dat ze Obama aankeek.
    It was for.that.reason so that she Obama looked.at
    'For that reason, it was the case that she looked at Obama.'
  b. *Het was vriendelijk zo dat ze Obama aankeek.
    It was friendly so that she Obama looked.at

Notice at this point that *daarom* and *vriendelijk* can be separated from each other by propositional-modal adverbials such as *waarschijnlijk* 'probably', which are generally considered to be clear cases of clause-level modification.[16] The fact that *daarom* precedes the modal adverbial *waarschijnlijk* 'probably' confirms the idea that *daarom* in (40a) is a clause adverbial rather than a VP-adverbial.

(45) ...dat ze [ReasonP daarom [ModalP waarschijnlijk [ManP vriendelijk
    that she for.that.reason probably friendly
    [VP Obama aankeek]]]]
    Obama at.looked
    '..that, for that reason, she probably looked at Obama in a friendly way.'

The class of clause-adverbials includes also the following adverbials: Firstly, as exemplified in (46a), the polarity adverbials *niet* 'not' and *wel* (affirmation), and, secondly, the conjunctive adverbials *toch* 'nevertheless/yet', and *weer* 'again', which function as a sort of linkers indicating contingency relationships (e.g., contrast) between utterances in a discourse (Broekhuis and Corver 2016: 1155). These conjunctive adverbials typically follow the reason adverbial but precede the modal adverbial. Thus, we have the sequence 'reason > conjunctive > modal', as in (46b).[17]

---

16 Note that application of the two diagnostic tests directly shows that the modal adverbial *waarschjnlijk* 'probably' is a clause adverbial:
(i) a. Ze keek waarschijnlijk Obama aan.
    she looked.at probably Obama PRT
    'She probably looked at Obama.'
  b. [Ze keek Obama aan] en *[ze deed dat waarschijnlijk].
    She looked.at Obama PRT and she did that probably
  c. [Het was waarschijnlijk zo] dat ze Obama aankeek.
    It was probably so that she Obama looked.at
17 The sentences in (46) should be pronounced with phonological (sentence) stress on the direct object noun phrase *Obama*, which occupies the base position within VP.

(46) a. ..*dat ze* [$_{ModP}$ *waarschijnlijk* [$_{PolP}$ *niet/wel* [$_{ManP}$ *vriendelijk*
       that she   probably   not/AFFIRM   friendly
       [$_{VP}$ *Obama aankeek]]]*.
       Obama at.looked
       '..that she probably did not look at Obama in a friendly way.'
   b. ...*dat ze* [$_{ReasonP}$ *daarom* [$_{ConjunctiveP}$ *toch* [$_{ModalP}$ *waarschijnlijk*
       that she   for.that.reason   nevertheless   probably
       [Obama aankeek]]].
       Obama at.looked
       '..that she therefore nevertheless looked at Obama, probably.'

Having provided some insight into the hierarchical organization and (related) linearization of various Dutch adverbials, let us next consider the placement of the displaced focalized phrase in the middle field of the Dutch clause. With (46a,b) as base structures, the focalized phrase *Obama* (here abbreviated as O) displays the following distribution; '—' designates the base position of the direct object noun phrase *Obama*.

(47) ... *dat* <*O_4> *ze* <O_3> *waarschijnlijk* <O_2> *niet* <$^?$*O_1> *vriendelijk* -- *aankeek*.
         that   Obama she   probably   not   friendly   at-looked
    '..that she probably didn't look at Obama in a friendly way.'   (see (46a))

(48) *dat* <*O_4> *ze* <O_3> *daarom* <O_2> *toch* <O_1>   *waarschijnlijk*
     that   Obama she   for-that-reason   nevertheless   probably
     -- *aankeek*.
     at-looked
     '..that she probably didn't look at Obama in a friendly way.' (see (46b))

The following picture emerges from (47) and (48): the focalized phrase cannot occur in a position (O_4) preceding [Spec,FP], which is occupied by the weak pronoun *ze* (see (41)). In other words, the focalized constituent cannot occur in the leftmost position of the clausal middle field.[18] As shown by O_1 in (47), it is not possible to have the focalized phrase at the lower end of the middle field, that is, in between the polarity adverbial and the manner adverbial. Positions in which the focalized constituent can appear are those "in the middle of" the so-called middle field, such as O_2 and O_3 in (47), and O_1, O_2 and O_3 in (48).

---

18 In Broekhuis and Corver (2016: 1756) the middle field of the clause is defined as follows: "that part of the clause bounded to the right by the verbs in clause-final position (if present), and to the left by the complementizer in an embedded clause or the finite verb in second position of a main clause."

Starting from the assumption that focus movement targets the specifier position of a FocP (Rizzi 1997, Broekhuis and Corver 2016: 1639–45), I tentatively propose that placement of the FocP-layer is rather free with respect to adverbial layers in the middle field. An alternative way of looking at this free placement of the FocP, would be to say that there are two (or more) FocPs in the middle field: a relatively high one and a relatively low one (see Broekhuis and Corver 2016: 1640).[19, 20]

Potential support for the presence of two FocPs could come from patterns featuring two focalized phrases; see (15) and (35B). I leave an in-depth exploration of the various theoretical options for future research.

The possibility of placing the focalized phrase in a relatively high or relatively low position in the clausal middle field accounts for the facts in (19), repeated here as (49):[21]

(49) A: Zij   zal   Obama   interviewen.
         she   will   Obama   interview
     B: Waarom {toch / nou / weer / trouwens / ook alweer} OBAMA?
         why   {yet / PRT$_{int}$ / again / by.the.way / again} Obama
     B:' Waarom OBAMA {toch / nou / weer / trouwens / ook alweer}?

---

19 An alternative approach would be to say that there is just a single FocP but that the adverbs can be placed either above or below FocP depending on its scope relative to the contrastive focus. In Neeleman and Van der Koot (2008), yet another approach is taken. According to their analysis, focus movement can target *any* position from which the contrastively focused phrase may take scope over its background. This analysis has the obvious advantage that the rather free placement of the focalized phrase can be easily accounted for. A potential problem for this approach, however, is the fact that the contrastively focused phrase actually cannot target any position, as was shown in (47)-(48). Clearly, the debate on the landing site of focus movement is still ongoing. See Broekhuis and Corver (2016: 1639–1656) for further discussion.
20 See also Belletti (2004), Aboh (2007), and Zubizarreta (2010) for the idea that the clause contains a low and a high FocP.
21 These word order variants are also possible in embedded contexts:

(i) a. A: Ze   interviewde   gisteren   Obama.
           she   interviewed   yesterday   Obama
       B: Prima dat   ze   een   oud-president   interviewde.
           fine   that she a   former.president   interviewed
           'It's fine, of course, that she interviewed a former president.'
           Ik vraag   me   echter   wel   af   waarom   <Obama>
           I   wonder REFL however   AFF   PRT   why   Obama
           weer   <Obama>
           again
           'I do wonder, however, why it was again Obama whom she interviewed.'

In (49B), the focalized constituent occupies a low Focus position, whereas in (49B') it occupies a higher one. Importantly, under the assumpion that adverbs occupy a fixed position in the clausal structure (Cinque 1999), the word order variants in (49B,B') suggest that the deleted part of the clause can vary. In (49B), the deleted part corresponds to the complement of the Focus-head whose specifier position is occupied by *Obama*. In (49B'), on the contrary, the deleted part corresponds to the complement of the functional head whose specifier position is occupied by the adverbial element.[22]

5 Not all reason XPs are permitted in WH-XP: Low reason-adverbials

So far it has been shown that reason adverbial *waarom* 'why' can be part of the surface pattern *WH XP?*. In the spirit of Shlonsky and Soare (2011), I proposed that this pattern is well-formed because displacement of *waarom* to [Spec,CP] does not cross any intervening focalized phrase (i.e., XP). As a result of that, Relativized Minimality is not violated.

The aim of this section is to show that the statement that reason-XPs can always precede a focalized XP is too strong. There turn out to be reason-XPs that are excluded in the YP_{reason} XP_{focus}-pattern. It will be argued that these reason-XPs originate in a position low in the hierarchical organization of the clause, and, specificaly, lower than FocP. As a result of that, displacement of such reason-XPs across the (displaced) focalized constituent will yield a violation of the Relativized Minimality condition.

Let us now consider some of these low reason-XPs, which all have an adpositional shape (PP) and can be paraphrased by *vanwege* + DP, meaning 'because of *DP*'. The first example is given in (50), where the complement of *om* designates the object that is the reason of someone's emotional state expressed by the verb:

(50) A: *Ik   huil/lach   vaak   [$_{PP}$ om   dierenfilms].*
         I   cry/laugh   often   because.of   animal.movies
         'I often have a laugh/cry because of animal movies.'

---

[22] See also Weir (2014) for the claim the *Why*-Stripping can target different layers of the clausal structure.

B: *Waarom jij?
   why   you
   'Because of what do you often have a laugh/cry?'

The second example is given in (51), where the complement of *om* designates the reason of an act/action.

(51) A: Ik bewonder mijn dochter [PP om haar slimheid].
        I admire   my   daughter   for her smartness
        'I admire my daughter because of her smartness.'
     B: *En waarom   jouw zoon?
        and what.for your   son
        'And what do you admire your son for?'

Consider next (52), the third illustration, where the complement of *om* designates the person for whom one carries out a certain action. The person is the reason for one's action(s).

(52) A: Marie brak   [PP om de kinderen] haar danscarrière af.
        Marie broke   for the children   her dancing.career off
        'Marie broke off her dancing career because of the children.'
     B: *Om wie   haar zangcarrière?
        for whom   her singing.career
        'For/because of whom did she break off her singing career?'

The final example is given in (53), where the complement of *om* designates the source/reason of a certain state of affairs, especially a state of fame.[23]

(53) A: Nederland   is beroemd [PP om zijn tulpen].
        The.Netherlands is famous   for its tulips
        'The Netherlands is famous for/because of its tulips.'
     B: *Waarom Duitsland?
        what.for Germany
        'What is Germany famous for?'

---

23 Recall from example (16) that the *Waarom XP?*-pattern, besides expressing a contrastive meaning, also has a sense of surprise. A reviewer raises the question as to whether the sentences in (50B)-(53B) also convey a sense of surprise (even if they are ungrammatical). According to my intuitions, they do not.

Before giving an explanation of the ill-formedness of the B-examples in (50)-(53), I would like to point out that classifying these *om*-PPs as being adverbial is supported by their optionality: in (50A)-(53A), the *om*-phrase can easily be left out. Their status as VP-adverbials is supported by the two diagnostic tests that were introduced earlier. Firstly, the sentence containing the adverbial can be paraphrased with a conjoined PRONOUN *doet dat* + ADVERB (see (54a)).[24, 25] Secondly, the same sentence cannot be paraphrased with *Het is* ADVERBIAL *zo [$_{clause}$ dat ......]*. This is shown in (54b):

(54) a. Marie   brak   haar   danscarrière   af   en   ze   deed   dat
        Marie   broke   her   dancing.career   off   and   she   did   that
        om   de   kinderen.
        because.of   the   children
    b. *Het   was   om   de   kinderen   zo   dat   Marie   haar
        It   was   because.of   the   children   so   that   Marie her
        danscarrière   afbrak.
        dancing.career   broke.off

Their status as VP-adverbials is further corroborated by the fact that the *om*-phrase can occur in a position following the modal adverbial:

(55) Marie   brak   waarschijnlijk$_{Modal}$ daarom$_{Reason}$ haar   danscarrière   af.
      Marie   cut   probably   because.of.that   her   dancing.career   PRT

Having shown that Dutch has reason VP-adverbials besides reason clause-adverbials, we can now account for the ill-formedness of the *Waarom XP?*-pattern in (50B)-(53B). These examples are out for the same reason that *Hoe XP?* is out,

---

24 For semantic reasons —*doen dat* typically replaces a VP denoting an action— the first test cannot be applied to the copular construction in (53A).
25 The fact that the *om*-phrase can combine with the sequence PRONOUN *doet dat* shows that it is an adjunct-PP. Notice that a (non-reason) complement-PP, headed by *om* and selected by the verb, cannot occur in this template. Consider the following example, in which *denken om XP* (think about XP, 'to mind XP') represents the selectional relationship between the verb and the PP:

(i) De   operazanger   dronk   nooit   alcohol.   *Hij   dacht,   en   hij   deed
     the   opera-singer   drank   never   alcohol.   he   thought   and   he   did
     dat   om   zijn   stem
     that about   his   voice
     'The opera singer never drank any alcohol. He minded his voice.'.

namely: the interrogative VP-adverbial *waarom* moves across the focalized XP on its way to [Spec,CP]. This yields a configuration in which the displaced phrase occupying an A-bar position (namely, *waarom*) is separated from its trace by another displaced constituent in an A-bar position (namely, *XP*). Schematically, for sentence (51B), where small capitals indicate phonological stress:

(56)   *[$_{CP}$ Waarom$_j$ ...[$_{FocP}$ JOUW ZOON$_i$ [$_{Foc'}$ Foc [...t$_j$...t$_i$...]]]]   (51B)

In (56), the direct object noun phrase *jouw zoon* has undergone Focus movement to [Spec,FocP]. The reason VP-adverbial *waarom* is moved from a low adverbial position to [Spec,CP]. On its way to [Spec,CP], it crosses the displaced focalized phrase, which occupies an A-bar position. Consequently, the representation in (56) violates Relativized Minimality.

6 Clausal reason adverbials *versus* VP reason adverbials

From the discussion in section 5 we can draw the conclusion that besides high reason adverbials (section 4) there are also low reason adverbials. The former can be part of the *Waarom XP?*-pattern, the latter cannot. In this section, I will discuss some further properties of high and low reason adverbials that relate to this dichotomy.

A first property regards the formal appearances that these two types of adverbials can take. It turns out that the reason VP-adverbial permits a wider range of forms than does the reason clause-adverbial. Specifically, the VP-adverbial can take any R-pronominal form (57), the clause adverbial is restricted to *daarom* (58), and *waarom* 'why':

(57) a.   Ik   huil   vaak   [$_{PP}$ om   dierenfilms].
          I   cry   often   about   animal.movies
          'I often have cry about/because of animal movies.'
     b.   Ik   huil   vaak   [daar om]   [er   om]   [overal   om]
          I   cry   often   there about   there about   everything about
          [ergens   om].
          something   about
          'I often cry about/because of that/it/everything/something.'

(58) a. Ik ben erg emotioneel. Ik huil [daarom] zo vaak.
         I am very emotional. I cry for-that-reason so often.
         'I am very emotional. I therefore often cry.'
     b. *Ik huil [er om]/[overal om]/[ergens om] zo vaak.
         I cry it for everything for something for so often

The fact that the reason clause-adverbial *daarom* (and also *waarom*) canot be substituted for by any other R-pronominal form might be interpreted as evidence for their grammaticalized form. That is, they constitute unanalyzable, non-decomposable units. This is also corroborated by the fact that structurally low reason R-pronominal adverbials can be paraphrased by P + emphatic *wat(te)/dat(te)* in echo-sentences whereas structurally high reason adverbials cannot:

(59) a. Jij huilt vaak [WAAR om] / [om WAT(TE)]?
         you cry often what for for what
     b. Moet jij vaak [DAAR om] / [om DAT(TE)] huilen?
         must you often that for for that cry

(60) a. Oh, moet jij [DAAROm]/*[om DAT(TE)] zo vaak huilen?
         oh must you because.of.that so often cry
         'Oh, THEREfore you have to cry so often!'
     b. WAARom/*[om WAT(TE)] is het toch zo dat jij zo vaak moet huilen?
         why is it yet so that you so often must cry
         'WHY is it that you have to cry so often?!'

A second property regards the (im)possibility of extracting material out of the *om*-phrase, yielding a preposition stranding pattern. The VP-adverbial *om*-phrase permits subextraction (61), the clause-adverbial *om*-phrase does not (62):

(61) a. Daar$_i$ heb ik vaak [$_{PP}$ t$_i$ om] gehuild.
         (e.g., *daar* = animal movies)
         there have I often because.of cried
         'I often cried because of that.'
     b. Waar$_i$ heb jij vaak [$_{PP}$ t$_i$ om] gehuild?
         where have you often because.of cried
         'Because of what did you often cry?'

(62) a. Ik   ben   erg   emotioneel. *Daar$_i$ huil ik [$_{PP}$ t$_i$ om] zo vaak.
          I   am   very emotional   there   cry   I   because.of   so often
          'I am very emotional. That's why I cry so often.'
      b. *Waar$_i$ huil jij [t$_i$ om] zo vaak?
          where   cry   you because.of so often
          'Why is it that you cry so often?'

It should be noted that pied piping of the prepositional element *om* yields a well-formed pattern for the clausal adverb in (62): *Daarom huil ik zo vaak* (Compare (62a)); *Waarom huil jij zo vaak?* (Compare (62b)). In short, pied piping is obligatory. Notice further that pied piping is an option for the VP-adverbial *om*-phrase in (61): *Daar om heb ik vaak gehuild* (Compare (61a)); *Waar om heb jij vaak gehuild?* (Compare (61b)).

A third property that distinguishes VP reason adverbials from clause reason adverbials concerns the possibility of being part of a topicalized VP (Den Besten and Webelhuth 1987). As shown in (63B), the adverbial PP *om de kinderen* can be part of a displaced verbal projection. Notice also that the high (i.e., sentence) adverb *daarom*, which precedes the negative adverb *nooit* 'never', is not part of the fronted verbal projection. As a matter of fact, the sentence-level reason adverbial *daarom* cannot be part of a fronted verbal projection, as is shown by the ill-formedness of (64B). It must remain in clause-internal position, as exemplified in (64B').

(63) A: Marie houdt erg   van   haar   huidige baan.
          Marie loves a.lot of   her   current job
          'Marie really loves her present job.'
      B: [$_{VP}$ **Om** **de** **kinderen** haar baan opgeven]$_i$ zal   zij
          for   the   children   her   job   quit   will she
          daarom   vermoedelijk nooit t$_i$!
          therefore   presumably   never
          'She will therefore presumably never quit her job because of the children.'

(64) A: Marie   voert   haar taken uitstekend   uit.
          Marie   carries her   tasks excellently out
          'Marie carries out her tasks in an excellent way.'
      B: ***Daarom   ontslagen worden** zal   zij   nooit!
          therefore   fired   be   will she   never
          'Therefore, she will never be fired!'
      B:' [$_{VP}$ **Ontslagen worden**]$_i$ zal zij **daarom** nooit t$_i$!

Also at the interpretative level, there is a distinction between VP reason adverbials and clause reason adverbials. The former designate a more or less objective reason; there is a referent — an individual, as in (52A), or an object, as in (50a), (51A), (53A) — which represents the reason of the eventuality expressed by the clause. For example, in (50A), animal movies are the reason for my crying, and in (52A), children can be a reason for giving up a job. The clausal reason adverbial *daarom* in (58a), on the other hand, has a more conjunctive role in the sense that it links the utterance of which it is a part, to a preceding utterance. For example, in (58a), the eventuality of my crying is linked to my being emotional, which is expressed in the preceding utterance. Another characteristic of the clause-adverbial *daarom* is its more subjective meaning; that is, there is a greater involvement of a person (the speaker or someone else), who is responsible for constructing the causal relation. For example, in (58a), the speaker (*ik*, 'I') establishes a relationship between his regular crying and his emotional state of mind.[26]

Having shown that there is a strong empirical basis for distinguishing reason VP-adverbials from reason clause-adverbials, I would like to point out that this leads to the expectation that these two types of reason adverbials can co-occur in a single sentence. As shown in (65)-(66), this is indeed the case.

(65) *Marie houdt erg van haar huidige baan.*
Marie loves much of her current job
'Marie loves her current job a lot.'

*Zij zal **daarom** [$_{NegP}$ nooit [$_{VP}$ **om de kinderen** haar baan opgeven]].*
she will therefore never for the children her job quit
'For that reason she will never quit her job because of the kids.'

(66) *Marie hecht niet aan geld en status.*
Marie cares not about money and status
'Marie does not care about money or status.'

*Zij zal **daarom** [$_{NegP}$ nooit [$_{VP}$ **[daar om]** haar huidige baan opzeggen]].*
she will therefore never for.that her current job quit
'Therefore she will never quit her job for that reason.'

---

26 See Geerts *et al* (1984: 1163), Pander Maat and Sanders (2001), Stukker (2005) for different types of reason/causality marking in Dutch.

Notice that, if there are two types of reason adverbials —namely, a structurally high one and a structurally low one— the existence of the following *Waarom XP?*-pattern is entirely expected.

(67) A: Marie   bewondert Obama   [om   zijn   welsprekendheid].
         Marie   admires   Obama   for   his   eloquence
     B: *Waarom*_{clause-adverbial} (toch) [DAAR om]_{VP-adverbial}?
         why   yet   for.that
         'Why for (= because of) that (and not for something else)?'

Waarom is a reason clause-adverbial that has a base position higher than FocP, *daarom* is a reason VP-adverbial that has been moved to [Spec,FocP]. This is depicted in (68):

(68) [_{CP} *Waarom*_j ... [_{ReasP}   t_j ... [_{FocP} [_{PP} DAAR om]_i [_{Foc'} Foc [... t_i ...]]]]

So far I have shown that there are reasons for making a distinction between high reason adverbials and low reason adverbials. Furthermore, it was shown that, given these two classes of reason adverbials, it is not unexpected that we find the pattern *Waarom* DAAROM? (why because.of.that, 'Why for that reason?'), where the VP-adverbial *daarom* is a phrase that has undergone Focus-movement to [Spec,FocP]. Recall from section 4 that the placement of the focalized phrase is quite versatile; the focalized phrase displays a certain freedom of placement with respect to adverbials in the higher middle field of the Dutch clause (see, for example, (47)-(48)). We find the same freedom of placement with a reason VP-adverbial that has undergone Focus movement to [Spec,FocP]. This versatility is exemplified in (69); the use of small capitals indicates phonological stress.[27]

(69) Marie   houdt   erg   van   haar   huidige   baan.
     Marie   loves   much   of   her   current   job
     'Marie loves her current job a lot.'

---

[27] In line with the Freezing Constraint (Wexler and Culicover 1980, Corver 2006), extraction from the displaced focalized phrase is impossible. Extraction is possibly only from the lowest (i.e., base) position.

(i) DAAR_i   zal   zij <*t_i om> daarom   <*t_i om>   waarschijnlijk   <*t_i om>   nooit
    there   will   she   for for.that.reason   probably   never
    haar   baan   <t_i om> opgeven.
    her   job   give.up
    'She will therefore never give up her job for/because of that.'

a. *Zij   zal   daarom   waarschijnlijk   [om   de*
   she   will   therefore   probably   because.of   the
   ***KINDEREN]**ᵢ   nooit   [vp tᵢ   haar   baan   opgeven].*
   children   never   her   job   quit
   'For that reason she will never quit her job because of the kids.'
b. *Zij zal daarom [**om   de KINDEREN]**ᵢ waarschijnlijk nooit [vp tᵢ haar baan opgeven].*
c. *Zij zal [**om   de KINDEREN]**ᵢ daarom waarschijnlijk nooit [vp tᵢ haar baan opgeven].*

In line with what was stated in section 4, I tentatively propose that the Focus phrase to whose Spec-position the focalized constituent is moved, has a rather free placement in the clausal middle field. In (69a), it occupies a position in between the modal adverbial *waarschijnlijk* 'probably' and the negative temporal adverbial *nooit* 'never'. In (69b), it occurs in between the clause reason adverbial *daarom* 'therefore' and the modal adverbial *waarschijnlijk* 'probably'. In (69c), finally, it is located in a high position preceding the clause reason adverbial *daarom*.

For the sake of illustration, I have added a few more examples of sentences in which the reason VP-adverbial shows up in a high (displaced) position. These sentences have been drawn from the internet by means of a Google-search. All examples involve patterns in which the displaced low reason adverbial precedes the clause-level reason adverbial; compare (69c).[28]

---

[28] It is tempting to analyze the sequences *daarom daarom* (70a), *hierom daarom* (70b), and *om die reden daarom* (70c) as instantiations of a Spec-head configuration in which the first reason adverbial (i.e. the displaced VP-adverbial: *daarom, hierom, om die reden*) occupies the specifier position of a Reason-head, which is lexicalized by the second reason-adverbial *daarom*. Such an approach would be in line with Rizzi's (2006) idea of *criterial heads*. A criterial head is a head endowed with a specific feature (e.g., Q, Foc, Top, Neg) that attracts a phrase bearing that feature, thereby designating a position dedicated to the relevant type of interpretation. Under such an approach, a sequence like *daarom daarom* in (70a) would be assigned the representation: *[ReasonP daarom [Reason' daarom [....]]]*. In view of the examples in (69), where the reason VP-adverbial occupies a position lower than the reason clause-adverbial *daarom* (see (69a,b)), it is not entirely clear that a criterial approach is the right one for these "double reason-adverbial" patterns. I will leave a more in-depth investigation of these patterns for future research.

(70) a. *De eerste vulkaan ligt meer op de route en zal*
the first vulcano lies more on the route and will
daarom daarom sneller bezocht worden.
that-for therefore faster visited be
'The first vulcano is more along the same route and, because of that, chances are bigger that people will go there.'

b. *Ik weet dat ik een prima presentatie kan neerzetten*
I know that I an excellent presentation can give
en zal hierom daarom in de herkansing dit ook
and will this-for therefore in the second-chance this also
laten zien.
let show
'I know I can give an excellent presentation and, for that reason, I will therefore show this when I get a second chance.'

c. *Wanneer u als ondernemer een druk bedrijf runt, dan moeten*
when you as entrepreneur a busy company runs then should
de randzaken niet te veel aanwezig zijn. Overweeg om
the side-issues not too much present be consider for
die reden daarom een gietvloer.
that reason therefore a cast-floor
'When you are running a business as an entrepeneur, you should not be bothered by unimportant issues. For that reason you should therefore consider a cast floor.'

Summarizing, I have shown that reason VP-adverbials display different behavior from reason clause-adverbials. It was further observed that the two types of reason adverbials can co-occur in one and the same clause. In line with this, it was shown that the pattern *Waarom daarom?* ('Why for that reason?') is a well-formed linguistic expression in Dutch. Finally, it was observed that the reason VP-adverbial can be displaced to a position in the clausal middle field.

7 *Wanneer XP?* and *Waar XP?*

In section 4, I have given an account of the well-formedness of the pattern *Waarom$_{reason}$ XP?* (36), and the ill-formedness of the pattern *Hoe$_{manner}$ XP?* (37). The ill-formedness of the patterns *Waar ('where') XP?* (2) and *Wanneer ('when') XP?* (3) can be accounted for along the same lines as the ill-formedness of *Hoe$_{manner}$ XP?* Specifically, the locative adverbial *waar* 'where' and the temporal adverbial *wanneer* 'when' function as VP-adverbials in (2) and (3): they restrict the denotation of the predicate by anchoring the eventuality at a certain location or time. Their low placement in the hierarchical organization of adverbials is suggested by the fact that temporal and locative adverbials occur in a position following the modal adverbial:[29]

(71) a. ...*dat ze waarschijnlijk in Chicago/daar Obama zal interviewen.*
           that she probably in Chicago/there Obama will interview
      '...that she will probably interview Obama in Chicago/there.'
   b. ...*dat ze waarschijnlijk morgen/dan Obama zal interviewen.*
           that she probably tomorrow/then Obama will interview
      '...that she will probably interview Obama tomorrow/then.'

Focus movement of *Obama* yields a word order pattern in which *Obama* either immediately follows *waarschijnlijk* or immediately precedes it:

(72) ...*dat <*O_3> ze <O_2> waarschijnlijk <O_1> morgen/in Chicago -- zal ontmoeten.*

Since the displaced phrase *Obama* ends up in a position (namely [Spec,FocP]) that is structurally higher than is the temporal/locative adverbial (*morgen/in Chicago*), displacement of an interrogative temporal (*wanneer*) or locational (*waar*) adverbial to [Spec,CP] will yield a violation of the Relativized Minimality condition: the derived structure is a configuration in which a phrase in an A-bar position (*in casu* the wh-phrase in [Spec,CP]) is separated from its trace position by an intervening phrase in an A-bar position. To make things more concrete, consider again the examples in (2) and (3), which are repeated here as (73) and (74), respectively. I have added the modal adverbial *waarschijnlijk* in order to make clear that the spatio-temporal adverbial originates as a VP-adverbial.

---

29 In sentences containing both a temporal VP-adverbial and a locational VP-adverbial, the former typically precedes the latter, as shown in (i). The two VP-adverbials are most comfortable in a position preceding the manner adverbial (Broekhuis and Corver 2016: 1191):

(i) a. *Zij zal [waarschijnlijk] [om twee uur] [in het park] [luid]*
       she will probably at two o'clock in the park loudly
    gaan roepen.
    go shout
    'She will probably start shouting loudly in the park at two o'clock.'
  b. modal > temporal > locational > manner

(73) A: *Zij   zal   waarschijnlijk   morgen   Obama   interviewen.*
       she   will   probably   tomorrow   Obama   interview
   B: **Wanneer   Merkel?*
       when   Merkel
       'When will she interview Merkel?'

(74) A: *Zij   zal   waarschijnlijk   in   Chicago   Obama   interviewen.*
       she   will   probably   in   Chicago   Obama   interview
   B: **Waar   Merkel?*
       where   Merkel
       'Where will she interview Merkel?'

The derived structure of the B-examples is schematically represented in (75):

(75) **[$_{CP}$ wanneer$_j$/waar$_j$ .... [$_{FocP}$ MERKEL$_i$ [$_{Foc'}$ Foc [....t$_j$....t$_i$.....]]]*

This configuration clearly violates Rizzi's (1990) Relativized Minimality principle: the wh-phrase (*wanneer*/waar) in [Spec,CP] is separated from its trace by the intervening focalized phrase in [Spec,FocP], which is an A-bar position.

At this point, the following question arises: Do locational and temporal adverbials occur only as VP-adverbials or can they also occur as clause-adverbials, just like reason adverbials? The answer to this question is: "No, they do not only occur as VP-adverbials, and, yes, they can occur as clause-adverbials." As noted in Broekhuis and Corver (2016: 1150–1154), spatio-temporal adverbials are not only used as VP adverbials but also as clause adverbials. Examples (76a, b) which feature two temporal adverbials or two locational adverbials, separated by an intervening modal adverbial, suggest that the high (clause-modification) versus low (VP-modification) dichotomy is also found with spatio-temporal adverbials.[30]

---

[30] As noted in Broekhuis and Corver (2016: 1151), the two spatio-temporal adverbials in (76) obey certain ordering restrictions: the spatial domain or time interval referred to by the clause adverbial (*in New York, op Kerstavond*) must include the location or time referred to by the VP adverbial (*in het Ritz-hotel, om 10 uur*). The reverse ordering is infelicitous, as shown in (i). This ordering constraint does not seem to be due to syntactic factors. Rather, some semantic constraint seems to play a role here. A reason for thinking this is the fact that (i) becomes fully acceptable when the second (i.e., VP-adverbial modifer) is absent. This is exemplified in (ii).

(i) a. #*Ze zal in het Ritzhotel waarschijnlijk in New York een persconferentie geven.*
    b. #*Ze zal om 10 uur waarschijnlijk op Kerstavond een persconferentie geven.*

(ii) a. *Ze zal in het Ritzhotel waarschijnlijk een persconferentie geven.*
     b. *Ze zal om 10 uur waarschijnlijk een persconferentie geven.*

I have added example (76c) to show the parallel with sentences containing two different types of reason-adverbials.

(76) a. Ze   zal   in   New   York   waarschijnlijk   in   het   Ritz-hotel
         she   will   in   New   York   probably   in   the   Ritz-hotel
         een   persconferentie   geven.
         a   press.conference   give

  b. Ze   zal   op   Kerstavond   waarschijnlijk   om
     she   will   on   Christmas.Eve   probably   at
     10   uur   een   persconferentie   geven.
     10   o'clock a   press.conference   give

  c. Ze   zal   daarom   waarschijnlijk   om   de   kinderen
     she   will   therefore   probably   because.of   the   children
     haar baan   opzeggen.
     her   job   quit

Besides the evidence in (76) for the existence of high and low spatio-temporal adverbials, their existence is also supported by the two diagnostic tests that were introduced earlier. Specifically, under the VP-adverbial use of the spatio-temporal adverbial, the clause containing it can be paraphrased with a conjoined PRONOUN *doet dat* + ADVERB 'PRONOUN does that + ADVERB' clause; see (77). And under the clause-adverbial use, the sentence with the clause adverbial can be paraphrased as: '*Het is* ADVERBIAL *zo [$_{clause}$ dat .....]*' (It is ADVERBIAL so [$_{clause}$ that ....]); see (78).

(77) a. [Ze   zal   in   New   York   waarschijnlijk   een   persconferentie
        she   will   in   New   York   probably   a   press.conference
        geven]   en   [ze   zal   dat   doen   in   het   Ritz-hotel].
        give   and   she   will   that   do   in   the   Ritz-hotel

  b. [Ze   zal   op   Kerstavond   waarschijnlijk   een   persconferentie
     she   will   on   Christmas.Eve   probably   a   press.conference
     geven]   en   [ze   zal   dat   doen   om   10   uur].
     give   and   she   will   that   do   at   10   o'clock

(78) a. Het   zal   in   New   York   waarschijnlijk   zo   zijn   dat   ze
        it   will   in   New   York   probably   so   be   that   she
        in   het   Ritz-hotel   een   persconferentie   geeft.
        in   the   Ritz-hotel   a   press.conference   gives

b. Het zal op   Kerstavond   waarschijnlijk zo zijn dat
   it   will on   Christmas.Eve   probably   so be   that
   ze   om   10   uur   een   persconferentie geeft.
   she at   10   o'clock a   press.conference gives

Recall from section 6 that the existence of the pattern *Waarom* DAAROM? (see (67)), with *waarom* being a clause-adverbial and *daarom* being a VP-adverbial, is entirely expected. The question now arises as to whether we find the same type of pattern with spatio-temporal adverbials; that is: *Wanneer XP$_{temporal}$?* and *Waar XP$_{locational}$?*, where the wh-phrase is a sentence-adverbial and the focalized XP a VP-adverbial. The examples in (79)-(80) suggest that these patterns are possible in Dutch; small capitals indicate phonological stress:[31]

(79) A: Merkel   zal   in   twee   Amerikaanse   steden   een   persconferentie
        Merkel   will in   two   American   cities   a   press.conference
        geven.   Eén   in   het   Ritz-hotel,   de   ander in   het   Carlton.
        give   one   in   the   Ritz-hotel   the   other in   the   Carlton
     B: [Waar]   [in   het RITZ-HOTEL],   en   [waar]   [in   het
        where   in   the Ritz-hotel   and where   in   the
        CARLTON]?
        Carlton
        'Where (= in which city) in the Ritz hotel, and where (= in which city) in the Carlton hotel?'

(80) A: Merkel zal   in   twee   verschillende   maanden   een persconferentie
        Merkel will in   two   different   months   a press.conference
        Eén   op   een   woensdag   en   één   op   een   zaterdag.   geven.
        one   on   a   Wednesday   and   one   on   a   Saturday   give

---

31 Importantly, the locational wh-phrase *waar* and the PP that follows it, do not form a complex adpositional phrase in which *waar* acts as a (spatial) modifier of the PP. In other words, the strings *waar in het Ritz-hotel* and *waar in het Carlton* do not have the following structure: [$_{PP}$ waar [$_{P'}$ in het Ritz-hotel/Carlton]], where *waar* asks for a space (e.g., a room) located within the Ritz-hotel/Carlton. Notice that, under this structure and reading, *waar* typically carries emphatic stress.

B: [*Wanneer*] [*op een* WOENSDAG], *en* [*wanneer*] [*op een*
when on a Wednesday and when on a
ZATERDAG]?
Saturday
'When (= in which month) on Wednesday, and when (= in which month) on Saturday?'

In (79B), we have the pattern *Waar XP$_{locational}$?* Importantly, the explicit contrastive set-up (i.e. 'Where PP$_{Loc}$? and where PP$_{Loc}$?') makes the *Waar XP$_{locational}$?* more acceptable. The same holds for the *Wanneer XP$_{temporal}$?*-pattern. The derived structure of the two patterns can be schematically represented as follows (Compare (68)):

(81) a. [$_{CP}$ *Waar$_j$* ... *t$_j$* ... [$_{FocP}$ [$_{PP}$ *in het* RITZ-HOTEL]$_i$ [$_{Foc'}$ *Foc* [...*t$_i$*...]]]]   (79B)
b. [$_{CP}$*Wanneer$_j$*... *t$_j$* ... [$_{FocP}$ [$_{PP}$ *op een* WOENSDAG]$_i$ [$_{Foc'}$ *Foc* [...*t$_i$*...]]]]   (80B)

Now, if the patterns in (79B) and (80B) are possible, one would expect patterns featuring a focalized argument (e.g., a direct object noun phrase) to be possible as well. In other words, patterns such as (73B) and (74B) might not be so bad after all. What is important is that the contrastive context is sufficiently clear. For certain speakers (including myself), (73B) and (74B) already get better when they are introduced by the coordinating cojunction *en* 'and', as in *En wanneer Merkel?* (and when Merkel, 'And when will she interview Merkel?') and *En waar Merkel?* (and where Merkel, 'And where will she interview Merkel?').[32] I take *en* 'and' to be a regular coordinating conjunction by assuming that the silent left conjunct represents the alternative provided by the common ground. Thus, the expression *En wanneer/waar Merkel?* has the structure in (82):

(82) [$_{ConjP}$ $\emptyset_{common\,ground}$ [$_{Conj'}$ *en* [$_{CP}$ *wanneer/waar$_j$*
... *t$_j$* ... [$_{FocP}$[$_{DP}$ MERKEL]$_i$ [$_{Foc'}$*Foc* [... *t$_i$* ...]]]]]]

$\emptyset$ represents the silent left conjunct, the meaning of which is provided by the common ground 'She will interview Obama tomorrow/in Chicago'. The meaning of the common ground stands in opposition to the meaning of the right conjunct.[33]

---

32 Recall footnote 1.
33 See Broekhuis and Corver (2017) for discussion of another Dutch construction in which, at the surface, the coordinating conjunction *en* 'and' introduces the sentence. They call this construction the 'expressive *en maar* (and but) construction'. An example is given in (ia). They claim that the left conjunct of this coordinate structure is silent ($\emptyset$), and that this silent conjunct desig-

Another discourse context in which the use of the pattern *Wanneer Merkel?* considerably improves, is given in (83):

(83) A: *Zij zal   enkele wereldleiders interviewen.*
       she will some   world.leaders   interview
       Maandag OBAMA, Dinsdag MACRON, Woensdag   POETIN.
       monday   Obama   Tuesday Macron   Wednesday Poetin
   B: *Wanneer MERKEL?*
      when   Merkel
      'When will she interview Merkel?'

In (83A), a list of (contrastive) pairs is given, where the pairs consist of the one who is interviewed and the date at which the interview will take place. After speaker A has given a list of pairs, it is quite natural for person B to ask: *Wanneer Merkel?* Also in this example, adding *en* 'and' (*En wanneer Merkel?*) turns the utterance in a completely natural one.

Summarizing, I tried to show in this section that the patterns *Waar ('where') XP?* and *Wanneer ('when') XP?*, which are traditionally considered to be impossible, are in fact possible if the right discourse context, namely one in which a contrastive relationship holds, is sufficiently clear. It was further shown that both locational and temporal adverbials, just like reason adverbials, can be of two types: VP-adverbial and clause-adverbial. It is the latter type that can occur in the *Wanneer/Waar XP?*-pattern.

8 Variations on a theme

In section 4, I showed that the wh-phrase *waarom* can occur in combination with a focalized phrasal constituent, yielding the surface pattern *waarom XP?* Interest-

---

nates the common ground (*in casu* the alternative 'x listens') which is contrasted with the information provided by the right conjunct ('x does not listen'); see (ib).

(i) a. *En   maar niet luisteren!*
       and   PRT   not   listen
       'You keep on refusing to listen!'
    b. [ConjP ∅common ground [Conj' en [PRO maar niet luisteren]]]   (PRO = the addressee)

ingly, this surface pattern is found also with several other reason adverbials, both interrogative (84) and non-interrogative ones (85).[34]

(84) Dentist: *Poetst u elke dag uw tanden?*
brush you every day your teeth
Patient: **Vanwaar** [DIE VRAAG]?
from.where that question
'Why are you asking?'

(85) a. *Uw gebit is belangrijk.*
your teeth is important.
Vandaar[35]/**Daarom**/**Derhalve** DIT ADVIES: *Poets uw tanden!*
therefore this advice: brush your teeth
'Your teeth are important, whence this advice: Brush your teeth!'
b. *Jan heeft te fanatiek getraind.* **Zodoende** *die blessure.*
Jan has too fanatically trained so-doing/thus this injury
'Jan trained too fanatically. That's why he has that injury now.'

Also for these examples it can be shown that they have a clausal basis. As shown in (86), for example, particles/adverbs that typically occur in clausal environments can appear in between the left-peripheral reason-adverbial and the focalized XP:

(86) a. *Vanwaar {toch / nou / weer / dan}* [DIE KRITIEK]?
whence {yet / PRT$_{int}$ / again / then} that criticism
'Why are you criticizing me?'
b. *Vandaar {dus / vermoedelijk}* [DIE KRITIEK]: ...
therefore thus/presumably that criticism
'That explains that criticism.'

I assume that, just like *waarom*, the reason adverbials in (84)-(85) find their origin in the specifier position of the functional projection ReasP, which is located above

---

34 See English *whence*, *hence*, and *thence*. An example of a *whence XP*-pattern is given in (i):

(i) *This work is slow and dangerous, whence the high costs.*

35 Finite clauses (CP) are quite common after *vandaar*, as in (i):

(i) *Ik had die nacht slecht geslapen. Vandaar* [$_{CP}$ *dat ik zo moe was*].
I had that night badly slept whence that I so tired was
'I slept badly that night. That's why I was so tired.'

FocP. In other words, these reason adverbials start out as clausal modifiers. From there, the reason adverbial moves to the specifier position of CP. Schematically:

(87) a. $[_{CP}$ vanwaar$_j$ [... toch ...$[_{ReasP}$ t_j ... $[_{FocP}$ DIE KRITIEK$_i$ $[_{Foc'}$ Foc [... t_i...]]]]]
 b. $[_{CP}$ vandaar$_j$[... dus ... $[_{ReasP}$ t_j ... $[_{FocP}$ DIE KRITIEK$_i$ $[_{Foc'}$ Foc [...t_i ...]]]]]

The clause-adverbial status of the reason-adverbial elements in (84)-(85) is confirmed by the two by now familiar diagnostic tests (here illustrated by means of *vandaar*): Firstly, *vandaar* cannot occur as a modifier of *doet dat* 'does that', which suggests that it is not a VP-modifier but a clausal modifier (88b). Secondly, the sentence containing *vandaar* can be paraphrased as '*Het is* ADVERBIAL *zo* $[_{clause}$ *dat* ...]' (It is ADVERBIAL so $[_{clause}$ that ...]); see (88c). Example (88a) shows the sentence on which the variants (88b) and (88c) are based.

(88) De coach vond Messi niet goed spelen ...
 the coach considered Messi not well play
 'The coach thought Messi did not play well ...
 a. en heeft hem vandaar gewisseld.
 and has him thence replaced
 and replaced him for that reason.'
 b. *en heeft hem gewisseld, en hij deed dat vandaar.
 and has him replaced and he did that thence
 c. en het is vandaar zo dat hij hem gewisseld heeft.
 and it is thence so that he him replaced has
 and it is for that reason that he replaced him.'

The reason adverbials *vanwaar* and *vandaar* have a meaning relationship with the spatial expressions *van waar* 'from where' and *van daar* 'from there', which occur in sentences such as (89a) and (89b), respectively:

(89) a. Van waar heb je een mooi uitzicht op de krater?
 from where have you a nice view of the crater
 'From where do you have a nice view of the crater?'
 b. Van daar heb je een mooi uitzicht op de krater.
 from there have you a nice view of the crater
 'From over there you have a nice view of the crater.'

The combination of locative *waar/daar* 'where/there' and directional *van* 'from' yields a source interpretation 'from which/that place'. Under the reason-adverbial interpretation (see (85a), (88a)), the source is identified as the reason or cause of something. Although the spatial expressions *van waar* and *van daar* have the same phonological stress pattern as the reason adverbials *vanwaar* and *vandaar*, namely stress on *daar/waar*, there are reasons for assigning them different structural representations.[36] Specifically, the reason adverbials constitute (complex) words, whereas the spatial expressions are phrases. Evidence in support of this contrast comes from (i) the (im)possibility of having material that intervenes between *van* and *waar/daar*, and (ii) the (im)possibility of replacing *waar/daar* by a complex noun phrase (e.g., *die plek* 'that place'). As shown in (90), these manipulations are possible with the spatial expression *van daar* (here exemplified with *daar*):

(90) a. Van af daar *heb je een* mooi uitzicht op de krater.
from PRT there have you a nice view of the crater
'From there you have a nice view of the crater.'
b. Van die plek *heb je een* mooi uitzicht op de krater.
from that place have you a nice view of the crater
'From that place you have a nice view of the crater.'

The reason adverbial *vandaar* does not permit separation of *van* and *daar* (**vanafdaar*), nor does it allow replacement by a complex noun phrase: **van die reden* (of that reason; intended meaning: 'therefore/thence').

Having shown that the reason adverbials *vanwaar/vandaar* and the locative expressions *van waar/van daar* have different structural representations, I would like to draw your attention to another asymmetry: reason adverbials can be followed by a focalized XP, as was already shown in (84)-(85), the spatial expressions *van waar/van daar* cannot. This contrast is illustrated in (91):

(91) Context: Sue shows Bill pictures of her visit to Paris and says the following:
We stonden op de Eiffel toren.
we stood on the Eiffel tower
a. *Vandaar$_{Reason}$* [DIT UITZICHT]
from.there (= 'whence') this view
'Whence this view.' (as presented on the picture)
b. **Van daar$_{Spatial}$* [DIT UITZICHT].
from there this view
'From there we had this view.'

---

36 This is also visible orthographically. In spatial expressions, *van* and *waar/daar* are written as two separate elements. In reason-adverbial expressions, on the other hand, they are written as a single unit: *vanwaar/vandaar*.

The contrast between (91a) and (91b) can again be accounted for along the lines sketched in (92):

(92) a. $[_{CP}$ Vandaar$_j$...$[_{ReasP}$ t_j...$[_{FocP}$ DIT UITZICHT$_i$ $[_{Foc'}$ Foc[... t_i...]]]]$ (= (91a))
 b. *$[_{CP}$ Van daar$_j$... $[_{FocP}$ DIT UITZICHT$_i$ $[_{Foc'}$ Foc [... t_j... t_i...]]]]$ (= (91b))

Displacement of the (clausal) reason adverbial *vandaar* in (92a) does not yield a violation of the Relativized Minimality condition: *vandaar* does not cross the intervening focalized constituent *dit uitzicht*. In (92b), however, the locative expression *van daar* originates in a position hierarchically lower than FocP. As a result of that, movement of *van daar* to the left periphery of the clause crosses the intervening focalized phrase *dit uitzicht*. Consequently, Relativized Minimality is violated.

9 Conclusion

In this chapter, the Dutch pattern *Waarom XP?*, known under the name of *Why*-Stripping, was studied. It was proposed that the reason adverbial *waarom* moves from a clause-adverbial position (the specifier of ReasonP) to [Spec,CP]. The remnant XP that follows *waarom*, is a focalized constituent that undergoes movement to [Spec,FocP]. Importantly, on its way to [Spec,CP], the wh-phrase *waarom* does not cross the displaced focalized constituent, for the simple reason that the clause-adverbial position in which *waarom* originates, is located higher than [Spec,FocP]. Consequently, displacement of *waarom* does not yield a violation of the Relativized Minimality constraint. It was further shown that displacement of structurally low reason-adverbials (i.e. VP-modifiers) in *Why*-Stripping environments causes a violation of the Relativized Minimality constraint. Finally, I tried to show that the distinction between high (i.e., clause-modifying) versus low (i.e., VP-modifying) adverbials also matters for stripping patterns involving spatio-temporal adverbials. Manner-adverbials, being canonical VP-modifiers, typically do not occur in stripping environments. Finally, it was shown that the pattern 'Reason adverbial + XP' has different manifestations in Dutch, and also occurs with non-interrogative reason-adverbials.

References

Aboh, Enoch Oladé. 2007. Leftward focus versus rightward focus: the Kwa-Bantu conspiracy. *SOAS Working Papers in Linguistics* 15. 81–104.

Belletti, Adriana. 2004. Aspects of the low IP area. In L. Rizzi (ed.), *The structure of CP and IP. The cartography of syntactic structures, volume 2*. 16–51. Oxford/New York: Oxford University Press.

Bennis, Hans & Teun Hoekstra. 1984. Gaps and parasitic gaps. *Linguistic Review* 4. 29–87.

Besten, Hans & Gert Webelhuth. 1987. Remnant topicalization and VP structure in the Germanic OV languages. *GLOW Newsletter* 18. 15–16.

Broekhuis, Hans & Norbert Corver. 2015. *Syntax of Dutch. Verbs and verb phrases, Volume 1*. Amsterdam: Amsterdam University Press.

Broekhuis, Hans, and Norbert Corver. 2016. *Syntax of Dutch. Verbs and verb phrases, Volume 3*. Amsterdam: Amsterdam University Press.

Broekhuis, Hans, and Norbert Corver. 2017. The expressive *en maar*-construction. In Hilke Reckman, Lisa Lai-Shen Cheng, Maarten Hijzelendoorn & Rint Sybesma (eds.), *Crossroads semantics: computation, experiment and grammar*, 305–325. Amsterdam/Philadelphia: John Benjamins.

Cardinaletti, Anna. 2004. Towards a cartography of subject positions. In L. Rizzi (ed.), *The cartography of syntactic structures.* Vol 2., *The structure of CP and IP*, 115–165. New York/ Oxford: Oxford University Press.

Catasso, Nicolas. This volume. Is German *warum* so special after all? In Gabriela Soare (ed.), *Why is 'Why' Unique? Its Syntactic and Semantic Properties*, Berlin: De Gruyter Mouton.

Cattell, Ray. 1976. Constraints on movement rules. *Language* 52. 18–50.

Chomsky, Noam. 1973. Conditions on transformations. In Steven Anderson & Paul Kiparsky (eds.), *A festschrift for Morris Halle*. 232–286. New York: Holt, Rinehart and Winston.

Chomsky, Noam. 1986. *Barriers*. Cambridge, MA: MIT Press.

Chomsky, Noam. 1993. A Minimalist program for linguistic theory. In K. Hale and S. J. Keyser (eds.), *The view from building 20: Essays in honor of Sylvain Bromberger*, 1–52. Cambridge, MA: MIT Press.

Cinque, Guglielmo. 1999. *Adverbs and functional heads. A cross-linguistic perspective*. Oxford: Oxford University Press.

Cinque, Guglielmo. 2004. Issues in adverbial syntax. *Lingua* 114. 683–710.

Corver, Norbert. 1990. The syntax of left branch extractions. Tilburg University dissertation.

Corver, Norbert. 2006. Freezing effects. In: Everaert, Martin and Henk van Riemsdijk (eds.), *The Blackwell Companion to Syntax*, 2, 383–406. Malden, MA & Oxford: Blackwell.

Corver, Norbert & Jairo Nunes. (2007). *The copy theory of movement*. Amsterdam/Philadelphia: John Benjamins.

Craenenbroeck, Jeroen van. 2010. *The syntax of ellipsis. Evidence from Dutch dialects*. Oxford: Oxford University Press.

DeVilliers, Jill. 1991. Why questions? In Thomas L. Maxfield and Bernadette Plunkett (eds.), *University of Massachusetts Occasional Papers in Linguistics 17, special edition: The acquisition of* wh, 155–175. Amherst, MA: GLSA.

DeVilliers, Jill. 1996. Defining the open and closed program for acquisition: The case of wh-questions. In Mabel L. Rice, (ed.), *Towards a genetics of language*. 145–184. Hillsdale, N.J.: Lawrence Erlbaum.

Geerts, Guido, Walter Haesereyn, Joop de Rooij & Marten van den Toorn (eds.). 1994. *Algemene Nederlandse Spraakkunst*. Groningen/Leuven: Wolters.
Hornstein, Norbert. 1995. *Logical Form: From GB to Minimalism*. Cambridge, MA/Oxford: Blackwell.
Jackendoff, Ray. 1972. *Semantic interpretation in generative grammar*. Cambridge, MA: MIT Press.
Ko, Heejeong. 2005. Syntax of *why*-in-situ: Merge into [Spec,CP] in the overt syntax. *Natural Language and Linguistic Theory* 23. 867–916.
Koster, Jan. 1974. Het werkwoord als spiegelcentrum. *Spektator* 3. 601–618.
Koster, Jan. 1975. Dutch as an SOV language. *Linguistic Analysis* 1. 111–136.
Koster, Jan. 1987. *Domains and dynasties: The radical autonomy of syntax*. Dordrecht: Foris.
Merchant, Jason. 2001. *The syntax of silence. Sluicing, islands and the theory of ellipsis*. Oxford: Oxford University Press.
Neeleman, Ad & Hans van der Koot. 2008. Dutch scrambling and the nature of discourse templates. *The Journal of Comparative Germanic Linguistics* 11. 137–189.
Pander Maat, Henk & Ted Sanders. 2001. Subjectivity in causal connectives: An empirical study of language in use. *Cognitive Linguistics* 12. 247–273.
Rizzi, Luigi. 1990. *Relativized Minimality*. Cambridge, MA: MIT Press.
Rizzi, Luigi. 1997. The fine structure of the left periphery. In Liliane Haegeman (ed.), *Elements of grammar: Handbook in generative syntax*. Dordrecht: Kluwer.
Rizzi, Luigi. 2001. On the position of Int(errogative) in the left periphery of the clause. In Guglielmo Cinque & Giampaolo Salvi (eds.), *Current studies in Italian syntax: Essays offered to Lorenzo Renzi*, 267–296. Amsterdam: Elsevier.
Rizzi, Luigi. 2006. On the form of chains: Criterial positions and ECP effects. In Lisa Lai-Shen Cheng & Noerbert Corver (eds.), *WH-movement: Moving on*. 97–133. Cambridge, MA: MIT Press.
Ross, John Robert. 1967. Constraints on variables in syntax. PhD thesis, MIT [Published as *Infinite syntax!* 1986. Norwood, NJ: Ablex.]
Shlonsky, Ur & Gabriela Soare. 2011. Where's 'Why'?. *Linguistic inquiry* 42. 651–669.
Stepanov, Arthur & Wei-Tien Dylan Tsai. 2008. Cartography and licensing of *wh*-adjuncts: A cross-linguistic perspective. *Natural Language and Linguistic Theory* 26. 589–638.
Stukker, Ninke. 2005. Causality marking across levels of language structure. A cognitive semantic analysis of causal verbs and casual connectives in Dutch. PhD dissertation. Utrecht: LOT Publications.
Temmerman, Tanja. 2013. The syntax of Dutch embedded fragment answers. *Natural Language and Linguistic Theory* 31: 235–285.
Thornton, Rosalind. 2008. Wh continuity. *Natural Language and Linguistic Theory* 26. 107–146.
Weir, Andrew. 2013. *Why-stripping* targets voice phrase. In Hsin-Lun Huang, Amanda Rysling, & Ethan Poole (eds.), *Proceedings of NELS 43*, 235–248. Amherst, Mass.: GLSA.
Wexler, Ken & Peter Culicover. 1980. *Formal principles of language acquisition*. Cambridge, MA: MIT Press.
Yoshida, Masaya, Chizuru Nakao & Ivan Ortega-Santos. 2015. The syntax of *why*-stripping. *Natural Language and Linguistic Theory* 33. 323–370.
Zubizarreta, María Luisa. 2010. The syntax and prosody of focus: The Bantu-Italian connection. *Iberia: An International Journal of Theoretical Linguistics* 2. 131–168.

Part 3: **Wh-in-Situ languages: *Whys, hows,* and *whats***

Wei-Tien Dylan Tsai
On applicative *Why*-questions in Chinese

1 Introduction

It is generally observed across languages that *why*-questions are formed by merging the relevant *wh*-expression high up in the left periphery (cf. Rizzi 1990, 2001, Starke 2001, Ko 2005, 2006, Stepanov & Tsai 2008, Tsai 2008, Shlonsky & Soare 2011, Jedrzejowski 2014, Endo 2015, Miyagawa 2017, among others). This paper investigates a class of postverbal *wh*'s in Chinese which give unexpected *why*-construals with a touch of "whining" force (also cf. Tsai 2011; Pan 2014; Yang 2015, among others), as shown by the Mandarin example (1a):

(1) a. ni ku shenme   [Mandarin whining *what*]
       you cry what
       你 哭 什麼!
       'What the heck are you crying for?! (You shouldn't be crying.)'
    b. lí sī teh khàu ántsuánn!   [TSM whining *how*]
       you be Prg cry   how
       汝 是 咧   哭   按怎?!
       'How the heck are you crying?! (You shouldn't be crying.)'
    c. ni zenme zai ku?!   [Mandarin *how come*]
       you how   Prg cry
       你 怎麼   在   哭?!
       'How come you are crying?!'
    d. lí ántsuánn teh khàu?!   [TSM *how come*]
       you how   Prg cry
       汝 按怎   咧   哭?!
       'How come you are crying?!'

Acknowledgments: An early version of this paper was presented in the International Conference on the Grammatical Representation of Tense and Speech Acts (Hanoi, January 2020) and the 19th Seoul International Conference on Generative Grammar (Seoul, August 2017). I am grateful to the audience there for sharing their insights and criticisms. Also special thanks to Gabi Soare for her help and suggestions. The research leading to this article is funded by the Ministry of Science and Technology of Taiwan (MOST 109-2410-H-007-065-MY2 and NSC 101-2410-H-007-055-MY2).

https://doi.org/10.1515/9783110675160-007

Interestingly enough, instead of a *what*, Taiwan Southern Min (TSM, a Chinese dialect spoken in Taiwan, often called Taiwanese), elects to employ a *how* in a similar construal, as illustrated by the example (1b) taken from Lau & Tsai (to appear). It is also worthwhile to note that they are not *how come*-questions, where Mandarin *zenme* 'how' and Taiwanese *ántsuánn* 'how' both appear in a preverbal position, as shown in (1c) and (1d) respectively.¹

Furthermore, Cheng (this volume) presents an interesting comparison between *mat¹* 'what' and *dim²* 'how' in Cantonese with their Mandarin counterparts in both postverbal and sentence-initial positions. In particular, while both postverbal *mat¹* and sentence-initial *mat¹* share the "whining" construal, the latter is shown to have an additional "unexpectedness" reading. This is very similar to the mirative usage of sentence-initial *zenme* 'how' in Mandarin (cf. Tsai & Yang 2019). Cheng also notes that postverbal *mat¹* expresses dissatisfaction of some sort. It is therefore very much in line with Mandarin whining *what* mentioned above.

Our task is thus to explain the unusual syntactic position of these *wh*-expressions, as well as their association with the peculiar pragmatics and negative deontic modal force (in addition to the usual *why*-semantics). I would like to propose that (1a) and (1b) are actually applicative constructions in disguise (cf. Marantz 1984, 1993; McGinnis 2001, 2003; Harley 2002; Pylkkänen 2002; Tsai 2018; among others), where the whining *wh*'s in question are introduced by a silent applicative head (or an inner light verb to the same effect, cf. Tsai 2015a).

---

1 As a matter of fact, (1a) and (1b) are not *the hell*-question, either. This is because they are not aggressively D-linked (cf. Pesetsky 1987), and cannot be answered (i.e., completely lacking the option of exerting interrogative force). A genuine *the hell* question would be like (i), which can be answered if the addressee chooses to do so (cf. Huang & Ochi 2004).

(i) ni   daodi   weishenme   zai   ku?!
    you   on.earth   why   Prg   cry
    'Why the hell are you crying?!'

Moreover, when we add *daodi* 'on earth' to (1), the whining force actually dissipates, and the question can be answered again, as illustrated below. Special thanks to Michal Starke for raising the issue.

(ii) ni   daodi   ku   shenme?!
     you   on.earth   cry   what
     'What the hell are you crying for?!'

2 The syntax of silent applicatives

The gist of our analysis is that (1a) actually involves an implicit light verb FOR (or a silent applicative head to the same effect), to which the main verb *ku* 'cry' raises in overt syntax, as shown in the following derivation (LV: light verb):[2]

(2) a. ni   FOR   shenme   ku?!
         you   LV   what   cry
⇒ b. ni   ku-FOR   shenme   <ku>?!
         you   cry-LV   shenme   cry

Given that *weishenme*, a typical Mandarin *why*, actually evolves from a PP *wei (-le) shenme* 'for what' (similar to the relation between *pourquoi* and *pour quoi* in French). It is therefore not unreasonable to treat (1a) on a par with inner light verb construals as discussed in Lin (2001), Feng (2005) and Tsai (2015a, 2017), which typically involve either instrumental, locative, or benefactive arguments.[3] Take the instrumental usage such as (3a) for example: it can be paraphrased as a sentence with a lexical light verb *yong* 'use', as in (3b):

(3) a. ni   qie na-ba   dao,   wo   qie zhe-ba   dao.
         you   cut that-Cl knife   I   cut this-Cl   knife
         你切那把刀，我切這把刀。
         'You (will) cut with that knife, and I (will) cut with this knife.'
    b. ni   **yong**   na-ba   dao   wo   qie,   **yong**   zhe-ba   dao   qie.
         you   use   that-Cl knife cut, I   use   this-Cl   knife cut
         你用那把刀切，我用這把刀切。
         'You (will) cut with that knife, and I (will) cut with this knife.'
                                                                              [lexical light verb]

More specifically, we assume that there is a silent inner light verb USE in (3a), which corresponds to its lexical counterpart *yong* 'use' in (3b), and that the apparent direct

---
[2] Here we may consider the English expression *cry wolf* when interpreted as 'crying about wolves' or 'crying because of wolves'. See Tsai (2011) and Yang (2015) for a raising-to-FOR analysis in the same spirit.
[3] By contrast, *weishenme* 'why', a contracted form of *wei(-le) shenme* 'for what', functions as an adverbial, and is merged high in the left periphery, presumably to the Spec position of ReasonP along the lines of Shlonsky & Soare (2011). Given the strong uniformity in the sense of Chomsky (2001) and Miyagawa (2010), this may well result from placing focus in C according to the parameter setting of Chinese, i.e., Cδ-Tφ in Miyagawa's (2017) terms.

object *zheba dao* 'this knife' is actually an instrumental argument in disguise. The surface word order of (3a) can be derived by raising the main verb *qie* 'cut' to USE, as sketched in the following derivation:

(4) a. ni **USE** Na-ba dao qie, wo **USE** zhe-ba dao qie.
    you   that-Cl knife cut I   this-Cl knife cut.
                                                    [inner light verb]

⇒ b. ni qie_j+**USE** na-ba dao t_j, wo qie_k+**USE** zhe-ba dao t_k.
     you cut   that-Cl knife   I   cut   this-Cl knife
                                                    [raising-to-inner *v*]

It is also worthwhile to note that this insight is in line with Endo's (2015) observation that reason WHAT across languages are essentially *what...for*-questions (see also Ochi 2004), as exemplified below:

(5) Kimi-wa nani-o   sonnani naiteiru no   [Japanese whining *what*]
    You-top what-Acc so-much crying   Q
    'Why are you crying so much?'

This account can be further contrasted with Huang's (1994, 1997) raising-to-CAUSE analysis of (6a). First note that (6a) can be paraphrased as (6b) with a lexical outer light verb *rang*:

(6) a. na-dun fan   **chi-de** Akiu huomaosanzhang.
       that-Cl meal eat-Res   Akiu furious
       那頓飯吃得阿Q火冒三丈。
       'That meal made Akiu eat such that he became furious.'
    b. na-dun fan   **rang** Akiu **chi-de** huomaosanzhang.
       that-Cl meal cause   Akiu eat-Res   furious
       那頓飯讓阿Q吃得火冒三丈。
       'That meal made Akiu eat such that he became furious.'

In light of the light verb syntax presented above, we may well put forward the claim that there is an implicit eventuality predicate CAUSE in (6a), which corresponds to its lexical counterpart *rang* 'cause' in (6b). The silent outer light verb in turn attracts the main verb, resulting in the word order change, as illustrated in the following derivation:

(7) a. na-dun fan   CAUSE   Akiu chi-de   huomaosanzhang. [outer light verb]
       that-Cl meal Cause   Akiu eat-Res   furious
⇒ b. na-dun fan   **[chi-de]**$_k$**+CAUSE** Akiu t$_k$ huomaosanzhang.
       that-Cl knife eat-Res   Akiu   furious

[raising-to-outer *v*]

3 Evidence from PF operations

There are two pieces of evidence for our line of thinking: Our first argument has to do with the fact that the whining *wh*-construal in question allow the lower copy of the raised verb either to delete, as in (8a) or to remain in PF, as in (8b). Interestingly enough, a "split" deletion such as (8c) is also allowed (cf. Tsai 2011):

(8) a. ni   mai-yuan   shenme <mai-yuan>?!   [copy deleted]
       you   hold-grudge   what   hold-grudge
       你埋怨什麼?!
       'What are you holding grudge about?'
   b. ni   mai-yuan   shenme <**mai-yuan**>?!   [copy pronounced]
       you   hold-grudge   what   hold-grudge
       你埋怨什麼埋怨?!
   c. ni   **mai-**yuan   shenme <mai-**yuan**>?!   [split deletion]
       you   hold-grudge   what   hold-grudge
       你埋什麼怨?!

The pronunciation of the lower copy in (8b) is reminiscent of the following Chinese verb-copying constructions:

(9) wo   kan   dianshi   <**kan**-de>   huomaosanzhang.
     I   watch   TV   watch-Res   furious
     我看電視看得火冒三丈。
     'I have watched TV till I became furious.'

By contrast, the same verb copying mechanism is not available for typical preverbal *how come*-questions in Mandarin, as evidenced by the following example:

(10) *ni   ku   zenme   ku   le?!
      you cry   how   cry   Inc
      *你哭怎麼哭了?
      'What the heck are you crying for?!'

According to Cheng (2007), verb copying applies at failure to reduce a verb chain, as its lower copy has been fused with an aspect marker. In our case, raising to FOR is more in line with the raising to Foc along the line of Hornstein & Nunes (2002) and Nunes (2004): That is, it triggers a morphological fusion between the main verb and the light verb, even if the latter category is silent in Chinese (also cf. Tsai 2014).

Another revealing fact is that verb-copying is only available for inner light verb construals, as shown by contrast between (11a) and (11b). This indicates that the PF operation in (9) is confined to the vP phase, hence a result of cyclic spell-out:

(11) a. wo **qie**$_k$+**USE** na-bo dao **qie**$_k$-de huomaosanzhang.
       I cut that-Cl knife cut-Res furious
       我切那把刀切得火冒三丈。
       'I used that knife to cut till I became furious.' [inner v ⇒ verb copying]
   b. * na-dun fan **chi**$_k$+**CAUSE** wo **chi**$_k$-de huomaosanzhang.
       that-Cl meal eat I eat-res furious
       * 那頓飯吃我吃得火冒三丈
       'That meal made me furious while eating.' [outer v ⇒ *verb copying]

Our second argument is built on the distinct prosodic pattern of the whining construal. As reported by the recent experimental study of Yang & Tsai (2019), the verb in (12) carries the most prominent stress, as illustrated by Figure 1:

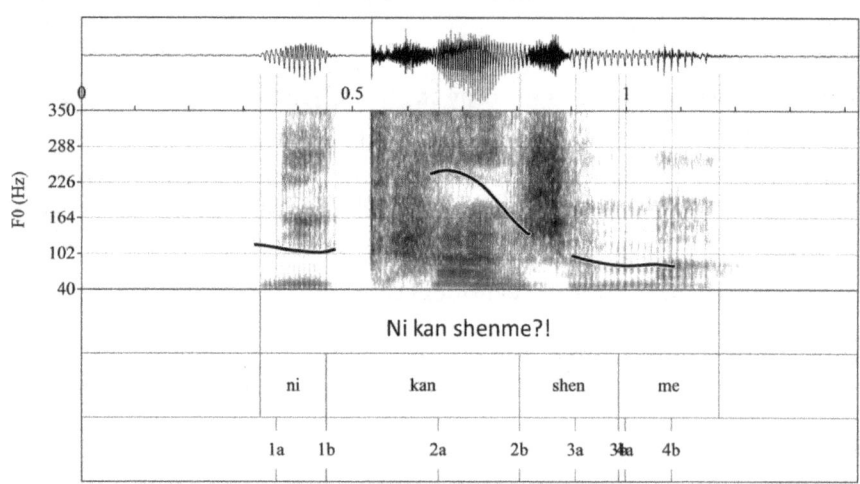

Figure 1: Waveform and sonogram of Mandarin whining *what*.

(12) ni   kan   shenme?!   [whining *what*]
     you   look.at what
     你   看   什麼
     'What are you looking at?!'

The intonation in question contrasts sharply with that of a typical interrogative question such as (13), which differs significantly from (12) with respect to pitch, duration and intensity, as shown by Figures 2–4 respectively:

(13) ni   kan   shenme?!   [interrogative *what*]
     you   look.at what
     你   看   什麼
     'What are you looking at?'

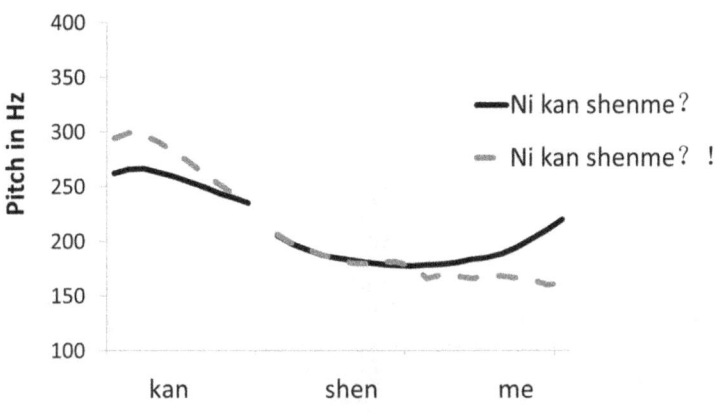

Figure 2: Mean F0 curves of *kan shenme* in (12) and (13).

The experimental study shows that the "force shift" from interrogative to whining has a lot to do with the change of the overall prosodic pattern (i.e., the distinctive intonation associated with clause-typing), as well as the stress shift from the object *wh* (i.e., the locus of nuclear stress) to the inner light verb (i.e., the locus of focus). Most importantly, when the inner light verb is silent, it needs something to carry the prosodic weight assigned to it. This in turn triggers raising-to-FOR as seen in (2b). Verb doubling associated with similar focus effects are also observed in Gungbe (Aboh 2004) and the Kwa languages (Landau 2007).[4]

---

[4] Special thanks to Alain Rouveret for pointing out to me the relevant discussions in the literature.

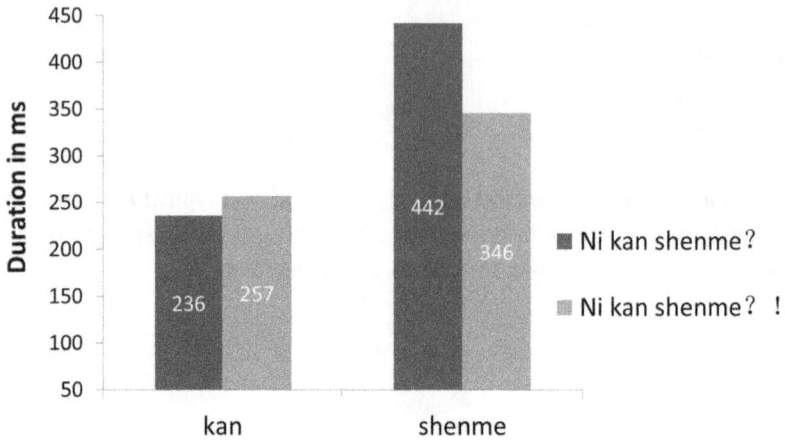

Figure 3: Mean duration of *kan shenme* in (12) and (13).

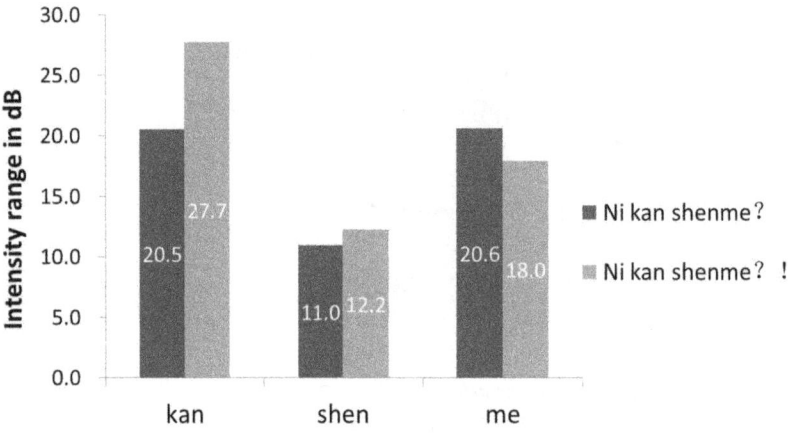

Figure 4: Mean intensity range of *kan shenme* in (13a-b).

Yang & Tsai (2019) further points out that the same observation applies to those cases where the lower verb copy is actually pronounced at PF, as in (14):

(14) ni [$_v$ kan] shenme [$_V$ kan]?! [verb copying of whining *what*]
     you look.at what look.at
     'What are you looking at?!'

Figure 5 shows that the pitch of the higher verb copy (*kan*$_v$) is consistently higher than that of the lower one (*kan*$_V$). Figure 6, on the other hand, shows that the

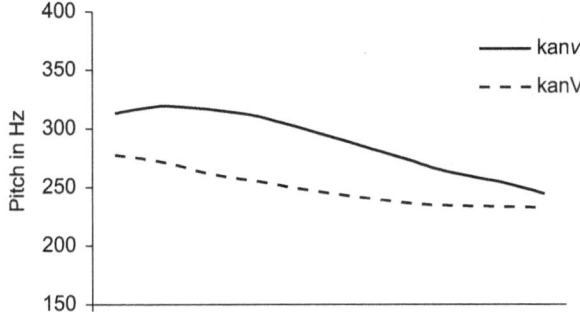

Figure 5: Mean F0 curves of the two verb copies in (14).

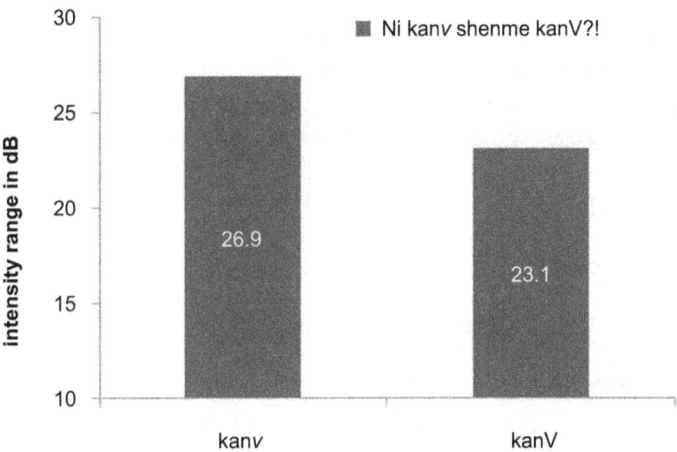

Figure 6: Mean intensity range of the two verb copies in (14).

intensity range of *kan$_v$* is also stronger than that of *kan$_V$*. This prosodic evidence substantiates our claim above that the verb copying of (14) is made possible by the focus property associated with the light verb FOR (hence the first verb copy on the surface, cf. Hornstein & Nunes (2002) and Nunes (2004)).

4 Robust analyticity and the typology of applicatives

On the typological front, it is worthwhile to note that Cheng & Sybesma (2015) offer an applicative analysis of subject-experiencer psych-predicates such as *danxin* 'worry' in (15a): They argue that the apparent transitive usage of *danxin* actually derives from a silent version of *dui* in (15b), a *de facto* applicative construction in Mandarin:

(15) a. Akiu   hen   danxin   Xiaodi.
         Akiu   Very   Worry   Xiaodi
         阿Q   很   擔心   小D
         'Akiu worries about Xiaodi.'
     b. Akiu   dui   Xiaodi   hen   danxin.
         Akiu   to   Xiaodi   very   worry
         阿Q   對   小D   很   擔心
         'Akiu worries about Xiaodi.'

As illustrated in (16a), when the applicative head is spelled out as *dui*, no verb movement is triggered in PF. Instead, *dui* raises over the applicative argument *Xiaodi* to the head of PredP. If the applicative head is not realized phonetically, as represented by TO, then the main verb *danxin* pick it up and raises all the way to Pred, as shown in (16b):

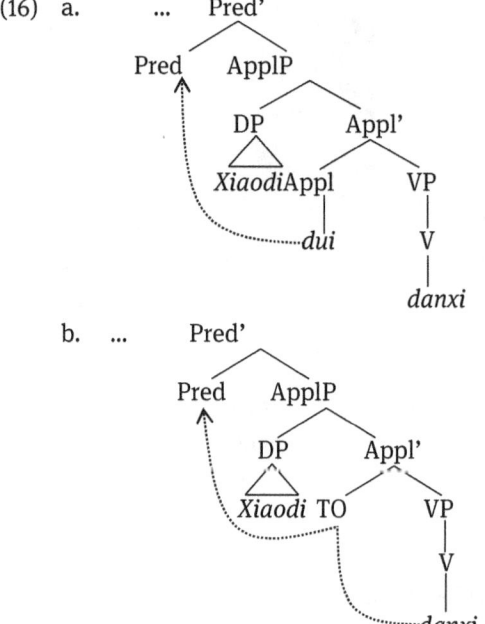

Interestingly enough, there is a strong conceptual connection between their proposal and the inner-outer dichotomy of light verbs advocated here: We entertain the idea that Chinese applicative expressions have a more pronounced topography along functional projections due to its robust analyticity (cf. Huang 2015; Tsai 2015a, 2018). Namely, while typical applicative morphemes are bound to the verb root in Bantu languages, as exemplified by the Kinyarwanda example (17) (cf. McGinnet 2001, 2003), their Mandarin counterparts are free, and have a much wider distribution accompanied by their respective applicative arguments, as shown in (18):

(17) úmwáalímu y-a-andik-iish-ijé-ho   ikíbáho   imibáre   íngwa.
     teacher   he-Pst-write-Inst-Asp-Loc   blackboard   math   chalk
     'The teacher wrote math on the blackboard with chalk.'

(18) laoshi   yong   fenbi   zai   heiban-shang   xie   shuxue.
     teacher use   chalk   at   blackboard-up   write   mathematics
     'The teacher wrote math on the blackboard with chalk.'

Along this line, we may well put forth the claim that Chinese inner light verbs are "analytic" versions of Bantu applicatives (see also Tsai 2017). As illustrated below, *dui* and TO are taken to be inner light verbs, achieving very much the same result as Cheng & Sybesma's treatment:

(19)   a.

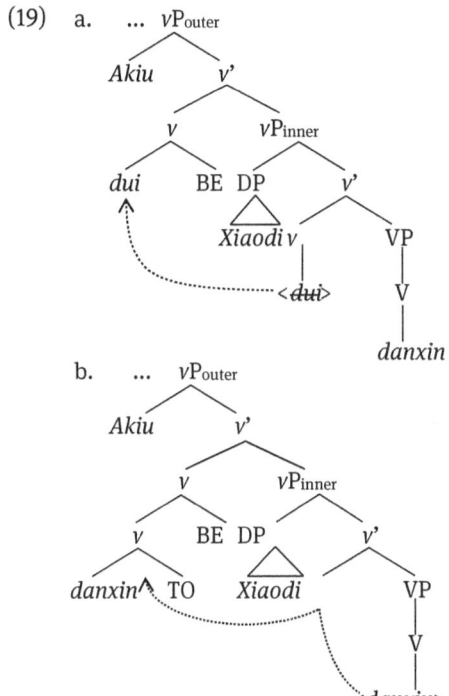

As a result, we are able to explain away the peculiar distribution of whining *what* in (1) by treating it as an "extra" argument in applicative-theoretic terms: That is, it is left in the apparent direct object position after the main verb *ku* 'cry' raises all the way to a silent outer light verb DO (or a voice head to the same effect) through the head position of a silent inner light verb FOR, as sketched in the following diagram:

(20)
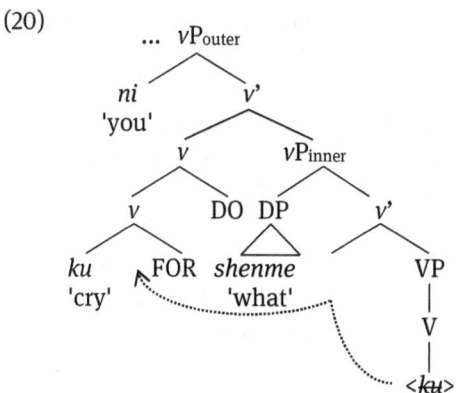

One of the advantages of this proposal is that, if the lower copy remains (or partially deleted) at PF, then the verb copying effects of (9) and (14) will be derived without further stipulations. Interestingly enough, similar verb copying phenomena is also attested in Vietnamese whining *what*, as illustrated by the following pair of examples (Tran Phan p.c.):

(21) a. Em **khóc** (cái) gì?!
     you cry Cl what
     'What the hell are you crying for?!'
  b. Em **khóc** (cái) gì mà **khóc**?!
     you cry Cl what MA cry
     'What the hell are you crying for?!'

This construal presents a sharp contrast with the typical causal *how*-question below, where *sao* 'how' occupies the sentence-initial position, and the whining force is distinctively absent:

(22) Sao mà em không đi?
     how.come MA you NEG go
     'How come you didn't go?'

5 Encoding force in syntactic terms

One of the main goals of the cartographic approach is to build an explicit clausal spine for pragmatic construals such as illocutionary forces, subjectivity, evidentiality, topicalization, focalization, etc. Along this line, we would like to suggest that the whining force in question is contributed by the force head in the left periphery (also cf. Pan 2014), which triggers a distinct intonation pattern very different from interrogative and indefinite *wh*-construals. As Yang (2015) have demonstrated quite convincingly, this kind of "force-shift" applies mostly in the root context, as evidenced by the absence of a whining construal for the indirect question below:

(23) wo xiangzhidao [ni ku shenme].
 I wonder you cry what
 我想知道你哭什麼。
 a. I wonder what you are crying for. [interrogative]
 b. #I wonder what the heck you are crying for. [#whining]

Here the interpretation is purely interrogative, which lends further support to our claim that the whining construal is built upon a *for what* question, where *shenme* 'what' is actually an applicative argument.

As noted by Krifka (2014), illocutionary acts can sometimes be embedded as arguments of force operators, e.g., verbs of saying or speech act adverbials. It is quite clear here that the interrogative construal in (23a) can be embedded as the complement of the matrix verb *xiangzhidao* 'wonder', whereas its wining counterpart in (23b) cannot. It is therefore no wonder people sometimes just give an answer to the embedded applicative *why*-question in (23) directly.

Curiously enough, it seems possible to embed the whining question under exclamative predicates such as *jingya* 'surprised' (cf. Abels 2007; Badan & Cheng 2015). As illustrated below, here the situation is somewhat reversed: the interrogative reading is blocked, while the whining construal survives.

(24) wo hen jingya [ni ku shenme].
 I very surprised you cry what
 a. #I am surprised what you are crying for. [#interrogative]
 b. I am surpsied what the heck you are crying for. [whining]

This shows that the force operator involved (call it a whining operator) does share some characteristics with the classic exclamative operator in expressing surprise/unexpectedness (cf. Zanuttini & Portner 2000, 2003).

Furthermore, the whining construal is also subject to a variety of locality effects, as evidenced by the negative island effect of (25):

(25) *ni bu   ku   shenme?!   [*whining *what* under negation]
     you not cry what
     *你不哭什麼?!
     'What the heck are you not crying for?!'

One way to think of the locality effect is to analyze whining *what* (L-WHAT in Yang's term) as an adverb subject to covert movement at LF. The other alternative is to suggest that the applicative *shenme* in question is bound by the whining operator (W-Op), which is merged directly to the Spec position of ForceP, as sketched in (26a):

(26) a. [ForceP W-Op$_x$ ... [TP *ni*   [$_{vP}$ *ku*-FOR   *shenme*(x)   <*ku*>]]]?!
                                  you   cry-LV   what   cry
     b. [ForceP W-Op$_x$ ... [TP *ni*   [NegP *bu* [$_{vP}$ *ku*-FOR *shenme*(x)   <*ku*>]]]]?!
                                  you   NEG   cry-LV what   cry

Since the resulting dependency is non-referential due to the applicative nature of whining *wh*, the deviance of (25) may be attributed either to inner island violation (cf. Rizzi 1990), or to negative operator intervention in the sense of Beck (1996, 2006) and Beck & Kim (1997), as illustrated in (26b). Under this treatment, W-Op can be conceived as a force operator taking the whining speech act as its argument along the line of Krifka (2014).

Along this line, we adopt a feature-based version of Relativized Minimality, as formulated by Rizzi (2004). It distinguishes the following four types of dependencies, and factors them in with regard to locality effects:

(27) a. Argumental: person, number, gender, case
     b. Quantificational: Wh, Neg, measure, focus...
     c. Modifier: evaluative, epistemic, Neg, frequentative, measure, manner, ...
     d. Topic

As a result, (25) can be ruled out straightforwardly by proposing that the quantificational dependency established by the operator binding has crossed over another quantifier, namely, the negation *bu* 'not', as illustrated below:

(28) a. [+Quan] ... [+Quan] ... [+Quan]

On the other hand, the negative deontic modal force can be treated as an implicature triggered by the whining operator, which is reminiscent of the negative modal force displayed by the following non-canonical usage of *shenme* 'what' and *nali* 'where' (also cf. Cheung 2009, among others):

(29) **shenme** Akiu qu-le xiancheng!
WHAT Akiu Go-Prf downtown
什麼阿Q 去了縣城！
'No way Akiu went downtown!'

As observed in Tsai (2011), the difference lies in the sentential scope taken by non-canonical *shenme* and *nali*. This height of interpretation triggers negation over epistemic modality, as indicated by the impossibility readings of (29). By contrast, the verbal scope of applicative *shenme* in (1a) only allows negation over deontic modality, which goes hand-in-hand with the whining force.[5]

From a comparative perspective, our position is further strengthened by similar construals attested in Taiwan Southern Min (henceforth TSM): The copula *sī* normally associated with reason *how* in (30a) must also appear to license the postverbal whining *ántsuánn* 'how' in (28b), where the presence of the assertive auxiliary *sī* is obligatory:

(30) a. Tsuísūn **sī-ántsuánn** teh khàu? [TSM reason *how*]
Tsuisun be-now Prg cry
水順是按怎咧哭？
'Why is Tsuisun crying?'
b. Tsuísūn *(**sī**) teh khàu **ántsuánn**?! [TSM whining *how*]
Tsuisun be Prt cry how
水順是咧哭按怎?!
'Why the hell is Tsuisun crying?!'

---

5 See Tsai (2015b) for evidence for placing Chinese epistemic modals in the complementizer layer (i.e., the left periphery, hence taking an IP scope), and their deontic counterparts in the inflectional layer (hence taking a VP scope).

Here *sī* serves as a scope marker for postverbal *ántsuánn* 'how' with the now familiar force shift from interrogative to whining. The following derivation of (30b) is adapted from Lau & Tsai (2020) in the spirit of our applicative analysis (W-Op: whining operator):

(31)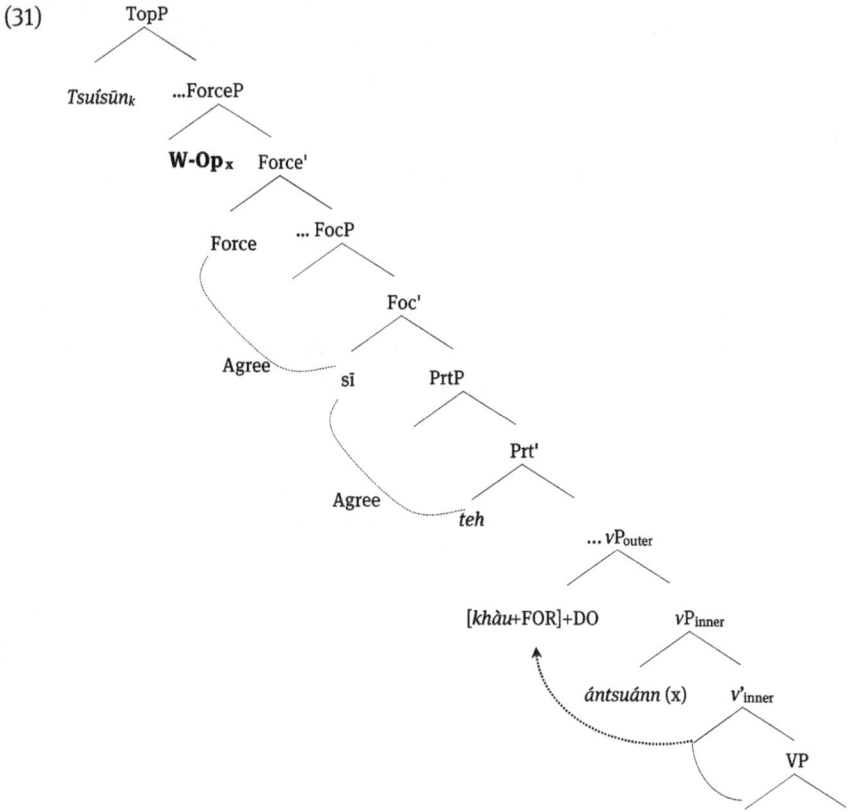

6 The hows of *what* and the whats of *how*

The question remains as to how to capture the similarity between whining *what* in Mandarin and whining *how* in TSM. Here we draw inspiration from a fine-grained study of Japanese *wh*-adverbials reveals that *nande* can be interpreted as either instrumental or reason, as in (32a,b):

(32) Mari-wa nande kaetta-no?
　　　Mari-Top nande left-Q
　　a. 　　'How did Mari leave?'
　　b. 　　'Why did Mari leave?'

Furthermore, the above construals can be disambiguated through morphosyntactic means (cf. Fujii et al. 2014): In (33a), when employing the non-contracted PP form *nani-de* 'what-with', only the instrumental reading is available (i.e., a *how*-question). By contrast, when accompanied by *mata* 'on.earth', as in (33b), the contracted adverbial form *nande* triggers the reason interpretation (i.e., a *why*-question):

(33) a. Mari-wa nani-de kaetta-no?
　　　　 Mari-Top what-with left-Q
　　　　 'With what (means) did Mari leave?' 　　　　[PP: instrumental]
　　 b. Mari-wa nande mata kaetta-no?
　　　　 Mari-Top NANDE on.earth left-Q
　　　　 'Why on earth did Mari leave?' 　　　　[Adv: reason]

Interestingly enough, only instrumental *nande* (call it *nande^I*) and its PP counterpart can appear below certain sentential adverbials such as *tokidoki* 'sometimes', as evidenced by the contrast between (34a,b):

(34) Hiroshi-wa **tokidoki** nande^I/nani-de okayu-o taberu-no?
　　　Hiroshi-Top sometimes how/what-with rice.congee-Acc eat-Q
　　a. 'How does Hiroshi sometimes eat rice congee?' 　　[instrumental]
　　b. #'Why does Hiroshi sometimes eat rice congee?' 　　[#reason]

Reason *nande* (call it *nande^R*), on the other hand, typically appears in conjunction with *mata* 'on earth' above *tokidoki*:

(35) Hiroshi-wa nande^R mata **tokidoki** okayu-o taberu-no?
　　　Hiroshi-Top why on.earth sometimes rice.congee-Acc eat-Q
　　a. #'How on earth does Hiroshi sometimes eat rice congee?' [#instrumental]
　　b. 'Why on earth does Hiroshi sometimes eat rice congee?' 　　[reason]

As mentioned above, Chinese *why* has its root in the applicative construal of its PP cognate, which pattern is observed cross-linguistically, as illustrated below:

(36) Chinese weishenme   vs. wei(-le)shenme
     French   pourquoi   vs. pour quoi
     Japanese nande   vs. nani-de
     English why   vs. for what

Interestingly enough, *why* also derives from the Old English *hwi*, an instrumental case form of *hwæt* 'what'. It can be interpreted either as 'for what purpose' (as in Mandarin) or 'by what means' (as in Japanese). Along this line, it is quite plausible to decompose TSM *how* further into a prepositional part *án* and a nominal part *tsuánn*. In certain constructions, it can even alternate with *siánn*, the real TSM *what* (cf. Lau & Tsai, to appear), as exemplified below:

(37) Tsuísūn sī teh khàu **siánn**?!   [TSM whining *what*]
     Tsuisun be Prg cry   WHAT
     'What the hell is Tsuisun crying for?! (He shouldn't be crying.)'

This *what-how* alternation in TSM is again attested in Vietnamese: Recall that we found a whining *what* in Vietnamese with the whining construals of (21a,b). As noted by Tran Phan (p.c.), it turns out that the same verb copying pattern also shows up with *sao* 'how' in a postverbal position, where the presence of a modal *được* 'can' appears to be obligatory, as evidenced by (38a,b):

(38) a. Em **khóc** sao được?!
        you cry   how can
        'How can you cry?!'
     b. Em **khóc** sao được mà **khóc**?!
        you cry   how can   MA cry
        'How can you cry?!'

Our account thus not only explains away the exceptions to the cross-linguistic generalization about the placement of *why*, but also reconstruct the correct cartography of those "ill-behaved" *why*-questions in both Mandarin and TSM. Hopefully this study will represent the first step to figure out the how of *what* and the what of *how*.

7 Concluding remarks

To sum up, we have presented evidence showing Mandarin postverbal *why*-question is actually an applicative construction in disguise, where the apparent object *shenme* 'what' is bound by a whining operator merged to the left periphery, resulting in the "force-shifting" construal in question. Our argument is based on the verb copying effects of the whining *wh*-construal of (39a): When the main verb *ku* 'cry' raises to the applicative head FOR, the lower copy left by the V-to-*v* movement can be either pronounced, as in (39b), or deleted at PF, as in (39c):

(39) a. ni   ku-FOR   shenme   <ku>?!
         you   cry-LV   what   cry
     b. ni   **ku**   shenme   **ku**?!   [the lower copy pronounce.d]
         you   cry   what   cry
     c. ni   ku   shenme?!   [the lower copy deleted]
         you   cry   what

Furthermore, the experimental study of Yang & Tsai (2019) shows a prosodic pattern clearly distinct from a typical interrogative question, where the focus has shifted from the usual nuclear stress position to the applicative head FOR. This not only suggests that the postverbal *why*-question involves *v*P-internal syntax, but also supports our claim that the whining force is associated with the overall rearrangement of the stress/intonation pattern. Cross-linguistic evidence is also drawn from a very similar construction in Vietnamese (cf. (21a,b)), where the sentence-final placement of *gì* 'what' also triggers the whining force, as well as the signature verb copying mechanism.

Finally, a morpho-syntactic study of *how* and *why* across languages reveals that the similarity shared by the whining construals of Mandarin *shenme* 'what' and TSM *ántsuánn* 'how' is not an accident, but has its root in the development of *how*- and *why*-questions through applicative usages akin to *with/by/for what* in English.

References

Abels, Klaus. 2010. Factivity in Exclamatives is a Presupposition. *Studia Linguistica* 64(1). 141–157.

Aboh, Enoch Oladé. 2004. *The Morphosyntax of Complement-Head Sequences*. New York: Oxford University Press.

Badan, Linda, and Lisa Lai-Shen Cheng. 2015. Exclamatives in Mandarin Chinese. *Journal of East Asian Linguistics* 24. 383–413.

Beck, Sigrid. 1996. Quantified structures as barriers for LF movement. *Natural Language Semantics* 4. 1–56.

Beck, Sigrid. 2006. Intervention effects follow from focus interpretations. *Natural Language Semantics*, 14. 1–56.

Beck, Sigrid & Shin-Sook Kim. 1997. On Wh- and operator-scope in Korean. *Journal of East Asian Linguistics* 6. 339–384.

Belletti, Adriana. 2004. Aspects of the low IP area. In Luigi Rizzi (ed.), *The Structure of CP and IP*, 16–51. Oxford: Oxford University Press.

Belletti, Adriana, 2005. Extended doubling and the VP periphery. *Probus* 17(1). 1–35.

Cheng, Lisa L-S. 2007. Verb copying in Mandarin Chinese. In Norbert Corver & Jairo Nunes (eds.), *The Copy Theory of Movement on the PF Side*, 151–174. Amsterdam: John Benjamins.

Cheng, Lisa L-S. This volume. *What*-as-*Why* Sentences in Cantonese. In Gabriela Soare (ed.), *Why is Why Unique? Its Syntactic and Semantic Properties*, Berlin: De Gruyter Mouton.

Cheung, Y. L. Lawrence. 2009. The Negative *Wh*-construction and Its Semantic Properties. *Journal of East Asian Linguistics* 18.4: 297–321.

Endo, Yoshio. 2015. Two ReasonPs: What are*(n't) you coming to the US for? In *Beyond Functional Sequence*, ed. Ur Shlonsky, 220–231. New York: Oxford University Press.

Eun, Dabin. 2017. *How-Why* Alternations in Chinese, Japanese and Korean. Ms., National Tsing Hua University.

Feng, Shengli. 2005. *Studies on Chinese Prosodic Grammar*. Peking University Press.

Feng, Shengli & Jing Su. 2016. Shanggu Hanyu Zhong De "Wei" Yu Qingdongci Jufa Zhong De Chouxiang Qingdongci [WEI and the syntax of abstract light verbs in Archaic Chinese]. Paper presented in Roundtable on Current Issues in Light Verb Syntax in Chinese.

Fujii, Tomohiro, Kensuke Takita, Barry Chung-Yu Yang & Wei-Tien Dylan Tsai. 2014. Comparative Remarks on *Wh*-adverbials in Situ in Japanese and Chinese. In Mamoru Saito (ed.), *Japanese Syntax in Comparative Perspective*, 181–205. New York: Oxford University Press.

Harley, Heidi. 2002. Possession and the double object construction. *Yearbook of Linguistic Variation* 2. 29–68.

Hornstein, Norbert & Jairo Nunes. 2002. On Asymmetries between Parasitic Gap and Across-the-board Constructions. *Syntax* 5. 26–54.

Huang, C.-T. James. 2015. On Syntactic Analyticity and Parametric Theory. In Li, Y.-H. Audrey, Andrew Simpson & Wei-Tien Dylan Tsai (eds.), *Chinese Syntax in a Cross-linguistic Perspective*, 1–48. New York: Oxford University Press.

Huang, C.-T. James & Masao Ochi. 2004. In *Proceedings of the 34th Conference of the North Eastern Linguistic Society*, 279–294. Amherst, MA: GLSA Publications, University of Massachusetts.

Jedrzejowski, Lukasz. 2014. Again on *why*. But why? Paper presented in FASL 22.

Ko, Heejeong. 2005. Syntax of *why*-in-situ: Merge into [Spec, CP] in the overt syntax. *Natural Language and Linguistic Theory* 23(4). 867–916.

Ko, Heejeong. 2006. On the Structural Height of Reason *Wh*-adverbials: Acquisition and consequences. In Lisa Lai-Shen Cheng & Norbert Corver (eds.), *Wh-movement moving on*, 319–349. Cambridge MA: MIT Press.

Krifka, Manred. 2014. Embedding Illocutionary Acts. In Tom Roeper & Margaret Speas (eds.), *Complexity in Cognition, Studies in Theoretical Pscholinguistics*, vol. 43: 59–87. Berlin: Springer.

Landau, Idan. 2007. EPP Extensions. *Linguistic Inquiry* 38(3). 485–523.
Lau, Seng-hian & Wei-Tien Dylan Tsai. 2020. On *How* and *Why* in Taiwan Southern Min. *Language and Linguistics* 21.2: 254–284.
Lin, T.-H. Jonah. 2001. *Light Verb Syntax and the Theory of Phrase Structure*. PhD Dissertation, University of California, Irvine.
Lu, Qinning. 2008. Hanyu Yiwen Daici Feiyiwen Yongfa De Lishi Kaocha [A historical study of the non-interrogative construals of Chinese *wh*-pronouns]. PhD Dissertation, Nankai University.
Marantz, Alec. 1984. *On the Nature of Grammatical Relations*. Cambridge, MA: MIT Press.
Marantz, Alec. 1993. Implications of asymmetries in double object constructions. In *Theoretical aspects of Bantu grammar*, ed. Sam Mchombo, 113–150. Stanford: CSLI Publications.
McGinnis, Martha. 2001. Variation in the Phase Structure of Applicatives. *Linguistic Variation Yearbook* 1. 105–146.
McGinnis, Martha. 2003. Lethal Ambiguity. *Linguistic Inquiry* 35. 47–95.
Miyagawa, Shigeru. 2010. Why agree? Why move? Unifying Agreement-based and Discourse-configurational Languages. Cambridge, MA: MiT Press.
Miyagawa. 2017. *Agreement Beyond Phi*. Cambridge, MA: MIT Press.
Nunes, Jairo. 2004. *Linearization of Chains and Sideward Movement*. Cambridge, MA: MIT Press.
Ochi, Masao. 2004. *How come* and other adjunct *wh*-phrases: A cross-linguistic perspective. *Language and Linguistics* 5. 29–57.
Pan, Victor Junnan. 2015. Mandarin peripheral construals at the syntax-discourse interface. *The Linguistic Review* 32(4). 819–868.
Paul, Waltraud. 2014. Why particles are not particular: sentence-final particles in Chinese as heads of a split CP. *Studia Linguistica* 68(1). 77–115.
Pesetsky, David. 1987. Wh-*in-Situ*: Movement and Unselective Binding. In Eric Reuland and Alice ter Meulen (eds.), *The Representation of (In)definiteness*, 98–129. Cambridge, MA: MIT Press.
Pylkkänen, Liina 2002. *Introducing Arguments*. PhD Dissertation, Cambridge, MA: MIT.
Rizzi, Luigi. 1990. *Relativized Minimality*. Cambridge, MA: MIT Press.
Rizzi, Luigi. 1997. The Fine Structure of the Left Periphery. In Liliane Haegeman, *Elements of Grammar*, 281–338. Dordrecht: Kluwer.
Rizzi, Luigi. 2001. On the Position "Int(errogative)" in the Left Periphery of the Clause. In Guglielmo Cinque and Giampaolo Salvi (eds.), *Current studies in Italian syntax: Essays offered to Lorenzo Renzi*, 267–296. Amsterdam: Elsevier.
Rizzi, Luigi. 2004. Locality and the Left Periphery. In *Structures and beyond: The cartography of syntactic structures*, vol. 3, ed. Adriana Belletti, 223–251. New York: Oxford University Press.
Roberts, Ian. 1985. Agreement Parameters and the Development of English Modal Auxiliaries. *Natural Language and Linguistic Theory* 3. 21–58.
Roberts, Ian. 1993. *Verbs and Diachronic Syntax*, Dordrecht: Kluwer.
Roberts, Ian & Anna Roussou. 1999. A Formal Approach to Grammaticalization. *Linguistics (Special Issue on Grammaticalization)* 37. 1011–1041.
Shlonsky, Ur & Gabriela Soare. 2011. Where's Why? *Linguistic Inquiry* 42(4). 651–669.
Starke, Michal. 2001. *Move dissolves into merge: A theory of locality*. PhD dissertation, Université de Genève.

Stepanov, Arthur & Wei-Tien Dylan Tsai. 2008. Cartography and Licensing of WH-Adjuncts: A Cross-linguistic Perspective. *Natural Language & Linguistic Theory* 26. 589–638.
Tsai, Wei-Tien Dylan. 2008. Left Periphery and *How-Why* Alternations. *Journal of East Asian Linguistics* 17. 83–115.
Tsai, W.-T. Dylan. 2011. Cong 'Zhe Hua Cong He Shuo Qi' Shuo Qi [Speaking from 'where does this come from?']. *Yuyanxue Luncong* 43. 194–208.
Tsai, Wei-Tien Dylan. 2014. Syntax-semantics Mismatches, Focus Movement and Light Verb Syntax. In Huang, James C.-T. and Feng-hsi Liu (eds.), *Peaches and Plums* (Language and Linguistics Monograph Series), 203–226. Taipei: Academia Sinica.
Tsai, Wei-Tien Dylan. 2015a. A Tale of Two Peripheries: Evidence from Chinese adverbials, light verbs, applicatives and object fronting. In Wei-Tien Dylan Tsai (ed.), *The Cartography of Chinese Syntax*, 1–32. New York: Oxford University Press.
Tsai, Wei-Tien Dylan. 2015b. On the Topography of Chinese Modals. In Ur Shlonsky (ed.), Beyond Functional Sequence, 275–294. New York: Oxford University Press.
Tsai, Wei-Tien Dylan. 2017. Jiwuhua, Shiyong Jiego, Yu Qingdongci Fenxi [Transitivization, Applicative Construction and Light Verb Analysis]. *Contemporary Research in Modern Chinese* 19. 1–13.
Tsai, Wei-Tien Dylan. 2018. High Applicatives are not High Enough: A Cartographic Solution. *Lingua Sinica* 4(1). 1–12.
Tsai, Wei-Tien Dylan & Ching-Yu Helen Yang (2019) "On the Syntax of Mirativity: Evidence from Mandarin Chinese," paper presented in the 3rd International Workshop on Syntactic Cartography, Beijing Language and Culture University, Beijing, October 2019.
Yang, Barry C.-Y. 2015. *What for* and adjunct *what*. Paper presented at the 10th International Workshop on Theoretical East Asian Linguistics (TEAL-10). Tokyo University of Foreign Studies, Tokyo, June 2015.
Yang, Yang & Wei-Tien Dylan Tsai. 2019. Nianli Yizhuan de Yunluyufa ji Shiyanyanjiu [An Experimental Study on the Prosodic Syntax of Force Shift]. *Chinese Teaching in the World*: 33(1). 36–46.
Zanuttini, Raffaella & Paul Portner. 2000. The Characterization of Exclamative Clauses in Paduan. *Language* 76(1). 123–132.
Zanuttini, Raffaella & Paul Portner. 2003. Exclamatives Clauses: At the syntax–semantics interface. *Language* 79(1). 39–81.

Lisa Lai-Shen Cheng
What-as-*Why* sentences in Cantonese

1 Introduction

Cantonese, like Mandarin, is a *wh*-in-situ language. Furthermore, it also has both preverbal *why* and sentence-initial *why* questions as shown in (1) and (2).[1,2]

(1) a. keoi⁵ dim²gaai² mou⁵   lei⁴?   (Cantonese)
       3SG   why   not.have come
    b. dim²gaai² keoi⁵ mou⁵   lei⁴?
       Why   3SG   not.have come
       'Why didn't s/he come?'

(2) a. tā   wèishénme méiyǒu   lái?   (Mandarin)
       3SG   why   not.have come
    b. wèishénme tā   méiyǒu   lái?
       why   3SG   not.have come
       'Why didn't s/he come?'

In both languages, there are alternative ways to ask causal/reason questions. First, both Cantonese and Mandarin can use their counterparts of *what* and *how* in expressing causal/reason questions (see (3a,b) and (4a,b)). It should be noted that the counterparts of *what* appear postverbally while the counterparts of *how* appear preceding a modal (see Tsai (2008), and Cheng (2019)).[3,4]

---

[1] See Ko (2005) for an analysis of the merge position of *why* questions in Mandarin.
[2] The following abbreviations are used in the glosses: CL = classifier, DE=de, DET =determiner, EXP = experiential, INF = infinitive, M = masculine, NEG = negative, PFV = perfective, PROG = progressive, PRT = particle, PTCP =participle, SFP =sentence final particle, SG = singular. The tones are marked by numbers in Cantonese and by diacritics in Mandarin.
[3] Note that the interpretation of these sentences is not exactly the same as the English translation. We'll discuss this further in section 3.
[4] The postverbal cases of causal/reason *mat¹* appear with unergative verbs, which in Chinese languages have optional dummy objects (see Cheng and Sybesma (1998)). In the case of *laugh*

Acknowledgement: I would like to thank audiences in the 38th Jahrestagung der Deutschen Gesellschaft für Sprachwissenschaft, the 20th International Conference on Yue Dialects, and Beijing Institute of Technology for comments on preliminary ideas related to this paper. I thank also Wei-tien Dylan Tsai, and Norbert Corver for discussing various aspects concerning this paper with me.

https://doi.org/10.1515/9783110675160-008

(3) a. lei⁵ haam³ *mat¹* aa³? (Cantonese)
   2SG cry what SFP
   b. nǐ kū *shénme*? (Mandarin)
   2SG cry what
   'Why are you crying?'

(4) a. Akiu¹ *dim²* ho²ji³ heoi³ toi⁴bak¹ aa³? (Cantonese)
   Akiu how can go Taipei SFP
   b. Akīu *zěnme* kěyǐ qù táiběi? (Mandarin)
   Akiu how can go Taipei
   'How come Akiu could go to Taipei?'

In addition, both Cantonese and Mandarin can use a sentence-initial *wh*-phrase for questions similar to causal/reason questions. In Cantonese, *mat¹* 'what' is used while in Mandarin, *zěnme* 'how' is used, as we see in (5a,b).

(5) a. *mat¹/*dim²* lei⁵ hai²dou⁶ haam³ ge²? (Cantonese)
   what/how 2SG PROG cry SFP
   Roughly: 'Why are you crying?'
   b. *zěnme/*shénme* nǐ zài kū? (Mandarin)
   how/what 2SG PROG cry?
   Roughly: 'Why are you crying?'

In this paper, we focus on the sentence-initial *mat¹* 'what' in Cantonese, in comparison with other ways of expressing causal/reason questions in Cantonese and Mandarin. I address the question of whether the sentence-initial *zěnme* as in (5b) is similar to the sentence-initial *mat¹* in section 5.

Cross-linguistically, it is not uncommon to find examples where the counterparts of *what* is used to express something similar to what we see in sentence-initial *mat¹* in Cantonese (in particular sentences such as (5a)), as we can see from the examples in German and Dutch in (6).

(6) a. Was lachst du (denn)?! (German)
   what laugh you PRF
   'Why are you laughing?' (you should not laugh!)
   NOT: 'What are you laughing at?'

---

and *cry*, it is sometimes possible to also interpret the questions as 'What are you laughing at/crying about?' See also Cheng and Sybesma (2015).

b. Wat lach je nou? (Dutch)
   what laugh you PRT
   'Why are you laughing?
   NOT: 'What are you laughing at?'

Aside from causal/reason questions, the counterparts of *what* in Dutch and German can also be used in non-questions, in particular, exclamatives (7).

(7) a. Was (der) Otto seine Frau liebt!
       what the Otto his wife loves
       'How Otto loves his wife!' (German; D'Avis (2000): (2a))
   b. Wat heeft hij gewerkt!
       what has he worked
       'Boy, has he worked!' (Dutch; Bennis (1998): (2a))

In the following sections, I first examine the properties of Cantonese sentence-initial *mat*¹ 'what'. I argue that the sentence-initial *mat*¹ differs from both canonical *dim²gaai²* 'why' questions (section 2.1) and the postverbal causal *mat*¹ sentences (section 2.2). I show that *mat*¹-initial sentences are more aligned with exclamatives (section 3.2) than rhetorical questions (section 3.1). In section 4, I discuss further Dutch and German *what*-exclamatives and their similarities with *mat*¹-initial sentences. I argue that *mat*¹-initial sentences in Cantonese can be interpreted as both individual-level exclamatives and event-level exclamatives (based on Nouwen and Chernilovskaya (2015), see also section 3.2). In the concluding section 5, the question of whether sentence-initial *zěnme* 'how' in Mandarin is similar to sentence-initial *mat*¹ is addressed.

2 Properties of sentence-initial *mat*¹

In order to understand sentence-initial *mat*¹, I first consider the distribution of sentence-initial *mat*¹, in comparison with canonical questions with *dim²gaai²* 'why'. In section 2.2, I show that *mat*¹-initial sentences differ from postverbal causal *mat*¹-questions. Section 2.3 reviews the co-occurrence restrictions between sentence-initial *mat*¹ and sentence-final particles.

2.1 Comparison with canonical *dim²gaai²* questions

Before we make a comparison between canonical *dim²gaai²* questions and *mat¹*-initial questions, we need to first clarify the morphology of the counterpart of *what* in Cantonese. As shown in (8), a typical argumental *what*-questions in Cantonese can use either *mat¹* or *mat¹(ye⁵)*, literally 'what thing'.

(8) keoi⁵   maai⁵-zo²   *mat¹(ye⁵)*   aa³?
     3SG   buy-PFV   what   SFP
     'What did he buy?'

However, when sentence-initial *mat¹* is used, *ye⁵* cannot be used:

(9) *mat¹(*ye⁵)*   lei⁵   hai²dou⁶   haam³   ge²?
     what   2SG   PROG   cry   SFP
     'Why are you crying?'

Consider now canonical *dim²gaai²* 'why' questions. Both the postverbal and the sentence-initial *mat¹* differ from the canonical *dim²gaai²* 'why'. First, as (10a) shows, *dim²gaai²* 'why' in an embedded (non-interrogative) clause takes matrix scope (i.e., "long" construal). This is what we expect from *wh*-elements in Chinese languages: *wh*-phrases stay in-situ in narrow syntax, but they can undergo covert movement to take (matrix) scope. When *dim²gaai²* is merged in the matrix, as in (10b), there is no long construal. That is, it cannot be interpreted as construing with the embedded predicate.

(10) a. lei⁵   ji⁵wai⁴   keoi⁵   *dim²gaai²*   wui⁵   lei⁴?   (Long construal)
         2SG   think   3SG   Why   will   come
         'What is the reason x that you think that s/he will come for x?'
     b. lei⁵   *dim²gaai²*   ji⁵wai⁴   keoi⁵   wui⁵   lei⁴   (Short construal)
         2SG   why   think   3SG   will   come
         'What is the reason for your thinking that s/he will come?'
         NOT: 'what is the reason x that you think that s/he will come for x?'

That is, the matrix *dim²gaai²* 'why' in (10b) cannot have moved from the embedded clause. This is not surprising, as Chinese languages typically do not have *wh*-movement (Huang (1982)). Thus, *dim²gaai²* 'why' in Cantonese differs from English 'why', which needs to appear in the matrix to express both short and long construal as in (11) (with both (11a) and (11b) readings).

(11) Why do you think that he is coming?
    a. What is the reason x that you think he is   (Long construal)
       coming for x?
    b. What is the reason that you think that he   (Short construal)
       is coming?

Consider now questions with non-argumental *mat¹* 'what'. Neither the postverbal *mat¹* (12a) nor the sentence-initial *mat¹* (12b) can appear in an embedded (non-interrogative) clause.

(12) a. *lei⁵ ji⁵wai⁴ keoi⁵ haam³ mat¹(ye⁵) aa³?
       2SG think 3SG cry   what   SFP
    b. *lei⁵ ji⁵wai⁴ mat¹ keoi⁵ haam³ ge²?
       2SG think what 3SG cry   SFP
    Intended: 'What is the reason x that you think that s/he is crying for x?'

In other words, non-argumental *mat¹* 'what' do not form long construals. Furthermore, the non-argumental *mat¹* 'what' must appear either postverbally (3a) or sentence-initially (5a). It differs from the canonical *dim²gaai²* 'why' in that it cannot appear after the subject (cf. (1a) repeated in (13b)).

(13) a. *lei⁵ mat¹ hai²dou⁶ haam³ ge²?
       2SG what PROG   cry   SFP
    Intended: 'Why/how come you are crying?'
    b. keoi⁵ dim²gaai² mou⁵ lei⁴?
       3SG   why   not.have come
    'Why didn't s/he come?'

We have seen in (12b) that sentence-initial *mat¹* cannot appear in a non-interrogative embedded clause (to take matrix scope). It should be noted that sentence-initial *mat¹* also cannot appear in an embedded question (taking embedded scope) (14b). This contrasts with *dim²gaai²*, which can be in an embedded question (as in (14a)). It should be noted that non-argument, postverbal *what*-as-*why* in Mandarin (i.e., the *whining-what*) also cannot appear in embedded sentences (see Tsai (this volume)).[5]

---

[5] Note that as Tsai (this volume) points out, if *shénme* 'what' is not the *whining what*, it can appear in embedded questions. This is however not a possibility for sentence-initial *mat¹* in Cantonese, as there is no other interpretation possible of sentence-initial *mat¹* in Cantonese. As shown in (3a), typical argumental *mat¹* appears postverbally, just like typical objects; and like typical

(14) a. ngo⁶ seong² ji¹dou³ *dim²gaai²* lei⁵ mou⁵ heoi³
       1SG want know why 2SG not.have go
       'I wonder why you didn't go.'
   b. *ngo⁵ seong² ji¹dou³ *mat¹* lei⁵ mou⁵ heoi³ (ge²)
       1SG want know what 2SG not.have go SFP
       Intended: 'I wonder why you didn't go.'

Tang (2008) points out that *mat¹* differs from *dim²gaai²* in that the former cannot be in a sluice (compare (15a) and (15b)). This is not surprising, as *mat¹* cannot head an embedded question anyway (as seen in (14b)).

(15) a. keoi⁵ waa⁶ keoi⁵ heoi³ guo³ dan⁶hai⁶ mou⁵ waa⁶ *dim²gaai²*
       3SG say 3SG go EXP but not say why
       'He said that he has been, but he didn't say why.'
   b. *keoi⁵ waa⁶ keoi⁵ heoi³ guo³ dan⁶hai⁶ mou⁵ waa⁶ *mat¹*
       3SG say 3SG go EXP But not say what
       Intended: 'S/he said that s/he has been, but s/he didn't say why.'

We will see in section 3 that *mat¹*-initial questions are also interpreted differently from canonical *dim²gaai²* questions.

2.2 Comparison with postverbal causal *mat¹*-questions

We again start with the form of postverbal causal *mat¹*. We have seen in (8) that when *mat¹* is used as an argument, it can use the form *mat¹(ye⁵)*. This contrasts with sentence-initial *mat¹*, which cannot have *ye⁵* (9). Postverbal causal *mat¹* aligns more with argumental *mat¹*, in that *ye⁵* can be used, as shown in (16).⁶

(16) a. lei⁵ haam³ *mat¹(ye⁵)* aa³?
       2SG cry what SFP
       'Why are you crying?'
   b. lei⁵ hai²dou⁶ fan³ *mat¹(ye⁵)* aa³?
       2SG PROG sleep what SFP
       'Why are you sleeping?

---

in-situ languages, typical argumental *mat¹* can appear in embedded sentences (regardless of whether the embedded clause is a question or not).
6 The colloquial way of pronouncing *mat¹(ye⁵)* is *me¹(ye⁵)*.

The questions in (16a,b) are similar to the Dutch and German examples in (6) in that they also convey a meaning of "you shouldn't have". See Tsai's (this volume) discussion of the Mandarin counterpart, which he calls *whining what*. That is, (16a,b) are not genuine questions of asking for the cause or reason of your crying/sleeping. Instead, it conveys some sort of dissatisfaction of your crying or sleeping. Since Dutch and German place their counterpart of *what* in sentence-initial position (since Dutch and German have *wh*-fronting), one might consider the Cantonese mat^1-initial as a fronted version of the postverbal causal mat^1.

Aside from the fact that *wh*-elements normally do not undergo fronting in Cantonese (or in other Chinese languages), and that the sentence-initial form is restricted to mat^1 only, there are a number of other reasons why it is unlikely that mat^1-initial sentences are derived from postverbal causal mat^1 sentences.

First, the postverbal mat^1 typically appear with unergative verbs such as $haam^3$ 'cry' and fan^3 'sleep' (see footnote 4). In cases where it appears with verbs with an object (including a dummy object), the object is usually bare (without a demonstrative or classifier) (contrast (16b) with (17b,c)),[7] and mat^1 appears right before the bare noun:

(17) a. lei^5 sik^6 $mat^1(ye^5)$ min^6 aa^3?
    you eat what noodle SFP
    'Why are you eating noodles?'/ 'Why are you sitting there eating (noodles)?
b. lei^5 hai^2dou^6 fan^3 $mat^1(ye^5)$ $gaau^3$ aa^3?
    you PROG sleep what sleep SFP
    'Why are you sleeping?'
c. *lei^5 sik^6 (mat^1) li^1-wun^2 (mat^1) min^6 gaa^3?
    you eat what this-CL what noodle SFP
    Intended: 'Why are you eating this bowl of noodle?'

Sentential-initial mat^1 doesn't have restrictions of this sort. It can appear with any verb and any object:

(18) a. mat^1 lei^5 sik^6 (li^1-wun^2) min^6 gaa^3?
    what you eat this-CL noodle SFP
    'Why are you eating (this bowl of) noodle?'
    ('Why are you eating (this bowl of) noodle (at all)?')

---

[7] The lexical item for 'sleep' is fan^3-$gaau^3$, with $gaau^3$ as a dummy object. See Cheng and Sybesma (1998).

b. *mat¹* lei⁵ hai²dou⁶ fan³-gaau³ gaa³?
   what you PROG sleep-sleep SFP
   'Why are you sleeping?'/ 'How come you are sleeping?'

The contrast in interpretation between (17a) and (18a) is clear. Even though both can be interpreted as the addressee should not be eating, (18a) (with or without the demonstrative and classifier) can be interpreted as the addressee should not be eating noodles at all (but rather some other more eatable things).

Sentences in (17) and (18) also illustrate another crucial difference between the two types of *mat¹* sentences. Sentence-initial *mat¹* sentences have restrictions concerning the type of sentence-final particles. In (18a,b), it is not possible to use *aa³*, in contrast with postverbal causal *mat¹* in (17a,b) (see the discussion about the co-occurrence with sentence-final particles in the next section). Furthermore, even though both might have the interpretation that the sentence expresses some kind of dissatisfaction (and therefore the reading that the addresses should not be doing something (as in (17) and (18)), sentence-initial *mat¹* definitely has other interpretations, as we see in (19).

(19) *mat¹* keoi⁵ gam³ gou¹ gaa³
    what he so tall SFP
    'How come he is so tall?'

The sentence in (19) cannot be interpreted as 'he should not be so tall', but rather that his height is above the speaker's expectation. We come back to the interpretation of *mat¹*-initial sentences in section 3.

Lastly, it should be noted that though postverbal *mat¹* cannot appear in a clause with negation (see also the Mandarin counterpart in Tsai (this volume)), sentence-initial *mat¹* can appear with negation, as we see in the contrast between (20a) and (20b).

(20) a. *keoi⁵ m⁴ hai²dou⁶ fan³ *mat¹ye⁵* aa³?
      3SG NEG PROG sleep what SFP
      Intended: 'Why aren't you sleeping?'
    b. *mat¹* keoi⁵ m⁴ hai²dou⁶ fan³ ge²?
      what 3SG NEG PROG sleep SFP
      'How come s/he is not sleeping?'

2.3 Sentence-initial *mat¹* and sentence-final particles

Both Tang (2008) and Lam (2014) discuss the issue of *mat¹* co-occurring with sentence-final particles. Tang (2008) states that the sentence-initial *mat¹* tends to appear with the sentence final particle *ge²*, as in (21).[8]

(21) mat¹   lei⁵   mou⁵   heoi³   *(ge²)?
     what   you   not.have   go   SFP
     'Why didn't you go?/ 'How come you didn't go?'

Further, he shows that certain sentences with the sentence-final particle *ge²* alone can still obtain the same meaning without the presence of *mat¹*, as in (22a,b).

(22) a. lei⁵   mou⁵   heoi³   ge²?
        you   not.have   go   SFP
        'Why didn't you go?/ 'How come you didn't go?'
     b. lei⁵   gam³   hoi¹sam¹   ge²?
        you   so   happy   SFP
        'Why are you so happy?/ 'How come you are so happy?'

This leads Tang (2008) to argue that *mat¹* is not an interrogative element. He argues that it forms a discontinuous construction with sentence-final particles to reinforce the interrogative mood of the sentence. Tang also argues that the co-occurrence of *mat¹* with other sentence-final particles are restricted (see footnote 9).

Lam (2014) examines a long list of sentence-final particles based on Leung (2005), considering all the ones that can appear with sentence-initial *mat¹* and those that cannot. She concludes that *mat¹* not only occurs with sentence-final particles that indicate questions (such as *ge²*, *me¹*, *aa⁴*), but also those that are not interrogative (such as *gaa³*, *wo⁴*). (23) is an example from Lam (2014) showing the co-occurrence with *mat¹* and *gaa³*.[9]

---

8 The sentence-final particle *ge²* indicates assertion with reservation, uncertainty, and surprise (see Sybesma and Li (2007) among others).

9 *Gaa³* is a relevance marker (see Sybesma and Li 2007 among others). Tang (2008) claims that *gaa³* can only occur with *mat¹* if a scalar adverb such as *gam³* 'such' or *gam²* 'such a manner' is present. But the examples in (19) and (23b) show that this is not correct. One may consider that there is a degree expression *gik⁶* in (23b), but this can be replaced by a non-degree expression such as *gong²-lei⁴-gong²-heoi³* 'talking back and forth' without changing the essential interpretation of the sentence.

(23) a. Context: Terrance keeps explaining why Mary does not eat any kind of meat because she is a vegetarian. Nonetheless, John still cannot understand why Mary does not eat beef.
b. (*mat^1*) gong^2 gik^6 keoi^5 dou^1 m^4 ming^4 gaa^3?!
what say peak he still not understand SFP
'Why did he still not understand?'

Lam (2014) provides a long list of particles that are not compatible with *mat^1*. She concludes that these particles violate the requirement of using *mat^1*, namely that the prior expectation of the speaker must be *contrary* to the literal proposition. That is, according to Lam (2014), for a sentence-final particle to co-occur with *mat^1*, it has to indicate speaker bias.

In sum, we have seen in this section that *mat^1*-initial sentences differ from canonical *dim^{2}gaai^2* 'why' questions, and postverbal causal *mat^1* questions in the morphological make-up of the *wh*-element *mat^1* 'what', in distribution as well as in interpretation. In the next section, we explore the interpretation of *mat^1*-initial sentences.

3 The interpretation of *mat^1*-initial sentences

Despite of the fact that we group the sentence-initial *mat^1*-questions with postverbal *mat^1*-sentence as causal/reason questions, they are not interpreted the same way as causal/reason *why* questions. Importantly, *mat^1*-initial sentences not only do not need to be answered, they are also used in a different context. They do not share the same denotation as *why*-questions (which would amount to a set of true propositions/answers). Consider again the sentence in (21) (repeated here as (24a)). First, the sentence can only be uttered if the fact that the hearer didn't go is against the expectation of the speaker. This is similar to the Dutch non-*wh*-exclamative in (24b).

(24) a. mat^1 lei^5 mou^5 heoi^3 *(ge^2)?
what you not.have go SFP
'Why didn't you go?'/ 'How come you didn't go?'
b. dat je daar niet was!
that you there NEG was
'You weren't there!'

Compare these with the canonical *dim^{2}gaai^2* 'why' question in (25). This can be a neutral question, i.e., the speaker has no expectation of the hearer's going.

(25) dim²gaai² lei⁵ mou⁵ heoi³ (ge²)?
    why   you not.have go SFP
    'Why did you not go?'

In this section, we consider two other types of sentences which use *wh*-phrases, but are not interpreted as (real) questions: rhetorical questions and *wh*-exclamatives, in order to understand further the nature and the interpretation of *mat¹*-initial sentences.

3.1 Comparing with rhetorical questions

We first consider rhetorical questions, since these are also questions that do not require an answer (though answers are possible). As the debate concerning the interpretation and illocutionary force of rhetorical questions is not yet settled (see e.g., Han (2002) and Caponigro and Sprouse (2007)), we first consider here the distinction between *why* and *how come* in English. As is known from previous literature, aside from syntactic differences (see Zwicky and Zwicky (1971) and Collins (1991)), these two types of questions differ also as to whether they can be used rhetorically. (26a-c) show that *how come*-questions do not have inversion, have no long-construal and cannot license NPIs:

(26) a. How come John is leaving?
     b. How come you think that Peter is laughing?
     c. *How come John ever said anything?

Moreover, as Fitzpatrick (2005) and Conroy (2006) show, *how come*-questions cannot be used rhetorically. (27a,b) illustrate a question-answer pair. The *why*-question in (27b) has a rhetorical reading, which is negatively biased (i.e., the speaker assumes that a negative answer is correct). It can thus serve as a response to the question in (27a), 'Did John leave?', as it essentially states that John would not leave, and it also goes with the answer particle *no*. This is not the case in (27b); the response with a *how come*-question is not felicitous.

(27) a. Q: Did John leave?
        A: No. Why would John leave?
     b. Q: Did John leave?
        A: #No. How come John would leave?

Fitzpatrick (2005) and Conroy (2006) argue that *how come* selects a factive clause; thus, in (28a), it is a fact that John left early, and in (28b), it is a fact that the addressee thinks that John is late.

(28) a. How come John left early?
b. How come you think that John is late?

This can then explain why the response with the *how come*-questions in (27b) is infelicitous: with the *how come*-question, 'John would leave' is a fact. It is thus infelicitous with the negative answer particle *no*. In other words, *how come*-questions are not negatively biased and they do not have a rhetorical reading.

Let us now turn to Cantonese dim^2gaai^2 and mat^1. As (29a,b) show, dim^2gaai^2 'why' questions, just like *why*-questions in English, can be negatively biased. In other words, dim^2gaai^2 'why'-questions can be rhetorical questions. In contrast, given the same context, mat^1-questions are infelicitous, as shown in (30a,b).

(29) a. Q: keoi⁵ zau²-zo² mei⁶ aa³?
3SG leave-PFV not.yet SFP
'Has s/he left yet?'
b. A: mei⁶-aa³! keoi⁵ dim²gaai² wui⁵ zau²-zo² aa³?
not.yet-SFP 3SG why will leave-PFV SFP
'Not yet! Why would s/he leave?'

(30) a. Q: keoi⁵ zau²-zo² mei⁶ aa³?
3SG leave-PFV not.yet SFP
'Has s/he left yet?'
b. A: # mei⁶-aa³! mat¹ keoi⁵ zau²-zo² ge²?
not.yet-SFP what 3SG leave-PFV SFP

The response in (30b) yields an infelicitous response; the mat^1 sentence indicates that he has left, which is contradictory to the response mei^6-aa^3 'not yet'. Thus, mat^1-initial sentences are on a par with *how come*-questions in that they are not negatively biased and cannot have rhetorical interpretation. Tang (2008) also shows that mat^1-initial sentences take a realis, factive proposition. In other words, sentence-initial mat^1-sentences are similar to English *how come*-questions in that the *wh*-phrase selects a factive clause. This leads us to exclamatives, which are considered to carry a presupposition of factivity.

3.2 Comparing with exclamatives

Aside from rhetorical questions, there is another type of sentences which uses *wh*-expressions and their denotation is not comparable to a question, namely exclamatives, as in (31).

(31) a. What a nice guy he is!
    b. How very tall she is!   (Zanuttini and Portner (2003):(4))

In fact, *why* in English can also be used in exclamations, as in (32), though they are not considered to be part of the *wh*-exclamatives.

(32) a. Why, that's absurd!
    b. Why, it's easy – a child could do it!

Sung (2015) shows that in Budai Rukai, a Formosan language, the counterpart of *why* can be used in exclamatives, as in (33).[10]

(33) a. a-ni   ka-lragi   kai   kaswi-su!
       do.why-3 STAT.NFIN-long this pants-2SG.GEN
       'How long are your pants!'
       (Lit: 'How come your pants are (so) long!')   (Sung (2015): (16b))
    b. a-ni   ka-thariri   turamuru kai Salrabu!
       do.why-3 STAT.NFIN-good very   this Salarabu
       'How nice (handsome) Salrabu is!   (Sung (2015): (18b))

There has been a large amount of work concerning the syntax and semantics of exclamatives. To evaluate whether or not *mat*[1]-initial questions are on a par with exclamatives, we start our discussion with Zanuttini and Portner (2003). They consider factivity, scalar implicature and surprise as the core ingredients of an exclamative. Consider the English exclamative sentences in (34).

(34) a. How tall she is!
    b. What a lot of books John bought!
    c. How fast John drives!

---

10 (33a) also has a question reading: 'Why are your pants (so) long?'

As Zanuttini and Portner (2003) show, exclamatives carry a presupposition of factivity. For (34b), for instance, it presupposes that John bought a lot of books. In addition, there is a contextually given scale, and the exclamative indicates an extreme degree. For (34a), there is a contextually given scale of tallness and the exclamative indicates that her tallness is at the extreme end of the scale. Lastly, they suggest that there is an operation of widening connected to high degree, leading to surprise. The widening operation widens the domain of quantification for the *wh*-operator.

Zanuttini and Portner (2003) have devised tests on the basis of these properties. For instance, in the case of factivity, the test is whether or not exclamatives can be embedded under factive verbs. Nonetheless, as d'Avis (2016) shows, exclamatives in various languages, e.g., German, may not concur with all the tests. He concludes that the recurring aspect of analyses of exclamatives is: " . . . that a certain state of affairs is considered unusual/not normal by the speaker." (D'Avis (2016): 172) (see also Rett (2011)).

This concurs with what Chernilovskaya and Nouwen (2012) (C&N) and Nouwen and Chernilovskaya (2015) (N&C) argue concerning exclamatives. They state that the better characterisation of exclamatives is noteworthiness evaluation. They argue that there are in fact two types of exclamatives. Aside from the traditional type of exclamatives (as we see from the English examples above), which expresses noteworthiness of a referent of a *wh*-word (e.g., tallness, amount of books), there is another type of exclamatives, which expresses noteworthiness of the proposition referenced in the exclamative. This is illustrated by the contrast exhibited in the Dutch exclamatives in (35) (from N&C):

(35) a. Wat een man ik net op straat tegenkwam!
       what a   man I   just on street encountered
     b. Wie ik net op straat tegenkwam!
        who I just on street encountered

N&C show that for (35a) to be felicitous, the man being encountered has to have some gradable property to a remarkably high degree (e.g., tallness). So this is an example of the typical type of exclamatives, where the noteworthiness concerns a referent of the *wh*-word, in this case, 'man'. They suggest that since (35a) concerns an individual property, it is an *i*(ndividual)-level exclamative. In contrast, this is not the case for (35b). They argue that there is no particular gradable property in (35b), but the noteworthiness here concerns the proposition that the speaker encountered a certain person (for example, because the person is expected to be away on holiday). (35b), thus, is not an *i*-level exclamative; rather, it has to do with the event, and thus an *e*(vent)-level exclamative. It should be noted that there is no particular gradable property in (35b) (associated with either an individual or the proposition).[11]

Badan and Cheng (2015) examine exclamatives in Mandarin and argue that there is no *wh*-exclamative in Mandarin. That is, *wh*-phrases are not used for exclamatives. Furthermore, they show that surprise is not a necessary ingredient of exclamatives. (36a,b) show that the counterparts of *wh*-exclamatives in Mandarin have no *wh*-element.

(36) a. tā   zhème   gào   a!
          3SG   this.ME   tall   SFP
          'How tall s/he is!
      b. nǐ   de   wǎncān   duōme   hǎo   a!
          you   DE   dinner   much.ME   good   SFP
          'How delicious your dinner is!'

If having a set of alternatives is a crucial ingredient of exclamatives, it cannot come from a *wh*-operator in Mandarin. Instead, Badan and Cheng (2015) argue that Mandarin exclamatives have scalar focus, which derives a set of alternatives. In particular, the degree adverbs *zhème* 'this much', *nàme* 'that much', and *duōme* '(so) much' function as scalar (focus) operators. Aside from factivity and a set of alternatives, Badan and Cheng (2015) argue that a crucial ingredient of exclamatives is ego-evidentiality, namely a subjectivity/speaker-oriented property. They suggest that this property is spelled out as a low pitch sentence-final particle *a* in Mandarin.

Turning back again to *mat*^{1}-initial sentences, the question that arises is whether they can be considered to be on a par with exclamatives. We have already seen that *mat*^{1} selects for a factive complement. In (37a,b) and (38a,b), we see that *mat*^{1}-initial sentences can contain degree-related expressions such as *gam*^{2} 'such' or *gam*^{3} 'so', the former appearing with verbal predicates while the latter with non-verbal predicates (adjectival and nominal). Furthermore, these sentences all express a bit of surprise or in Chernilovskaya and Nouwen's term, noteworthiness.

(37) a. (*mat*^{1})   lei^5 gam^2 heoi^3 ge^2?
          what   you   such.way   go   SFP
          'Why/how come you went in such a way?'

---

[11] They also indicate that in the case of Dutch *e*-level exclamatives, the verb has to be final (while *i*-level cases can be either verb-second or verb-final).

b. (*mat¹*) lei⁵ gam³ hoi¹sam¹ ge²?
what you so happy SFP
'Why/how come you are so happy?'

(38) a. (*mat¹*) keoi⁵ gam³ gou¹ ge²/gaa³?!
what 3SG so tall SFP/SFP
'Why is s/he so tall?!/ How tall s/he is!'
b. (*mat¹*) keoi⁵ gam³ do¹ syu¹ ge²/gaa³?!
what 3SG so many book SFP/SFP
'What a lot of books s/he has!'

These examples point to similarities with *wh*-exclamatives that we have seen above: the proposition under *mat¹* is a realis, factive proposition (see (30b)); they can have a scale, and there appears to be an extension of the scale since what is expressed is that the degree is higher than expected ((37) and (38)). In other words, on the basis of these examples, we can hypothesize that *mat¹*-initial sentences are in fact exclamatives.

The question that arises is whether *mat¹*-initial sentences in Cantonese are true exclamatives, as degree adverbs are optional in these *mat¹*-sentences. Furthermore, Chinese languages do not have typical *wh*-exclamatives. If these *mat¹*-sentences in Cantonese are indeed exclamatives, is *mat¹* still a *wh*-element? And is there a corresponding ego-evidentiality marker in Cantonese? In the next section, we explore answers to these questions.

4 Understanding *mat¹*-initial sentences

4.1 WHAT-exclamatives

To understand the role of the sentence-initial *mat¹* 'what', let us first consider the counterpart of *what* cross-linguistically. In particular, it is well-known that *what* can be used in various types of sentences, and not necessarily typical *wh*-interrogatives. A good example is German, as illustrated in (39a-c) (from D'Avis (2000) (1a, 2a, 3a)).

(39) a. Was schlägst du schon wieder den Hund?
what beat you PRT again the Dog
'Why are you beating the dog again?'

b. Was (der) Otto seine Frau liebt?
   what the Otto his wife loves
   'How Otto loves his wife!'
c. Was hat Otto gesagt, wen er liebt?
   what has Otto said whom he loves
   'Whom did Otto say that he loves?'

D'Avis (2000) calls the *wh*-element *was* in (39a) a causal *was*, the one in (39b) an exclamative *was* and the one in (39c) a scope-marking *was*. He argues that these are examples of *was* as an expletive.[12] I identify this "expletive" use of *what* henceforth as WHAT. Here, we first concentrate on WHAT in exclamatives. The *was*-causal questions will not be discussed here. I would just like to mention that these causal-questions are similar to the postverbal *mat¹*-questions in Cantonese (e.g., (3a)); the positional difference between Dutch/German causal questions with WHAT and Cantonese postverbal causal *mat¹*-questions (i.e., sentence-initial vs. postverbal) is the result of the known difference between these two types of languages: the presence of *wh*-movement in Dutch/German and the lack of it in Cantonese.

Consider the Dutch data in (40). First, we see in (40a) that the *wh*-phrase *wat een auto's* 'what cars' can be moved as a whole to the left periphery;[13] (40b) shows that the *wh*-phrase can be split up so that only *what* appears in the left periphery, illustrating the so-called 'split exclamatives'.

(40) a. Wat een auto's heeft Jan gekocht!
       what a cars has Jan bought
       'What cars John has bought!'
     b. Wat heft Jan een auto's gekocht
       what has Jan a cars bought
       'What cars John has bought!'   (Corver (1990): 97, (1a,b))

It should be noted that typical *wh*-questions do not allow splits except in the case of *wat ... voor* 'what kind of' questions; compare (41a) with (41b). *Was* 'what' in Dutch differs from other *wh*-elements in its ability to appear in split-exclamatives. As we see in (41b) and (42), this is not possible for *hoe* 'how'.

---

12 D'Avis (2000) suggests that there is a *wh*-chain formation only in the case of scope marking sentences. The causal question reading and the exclamative reading with *was* only arises when the sentences are used as such.
13 See Bennis et al. (1998) for the presence of the indefinite article *een* in exclamatives.

(41) a. Wat_i heeft hij [t_i voor een mooi boeken] gekocht?
what has he for a beautiful books bought
'What kind of beautiful books did he buy?' (Bennis (1998): [9b])
b. *Hoe is hij stom?
how is he foolish
Intended: 'How foolish is he?' (Bennis (1998): [16b])

(42) a. Hoe bijzonder is het dat hij komt!
how special is it that he comes
b. *Hoe is het bijzonder dat hij komt!
how is it special that he comes (Bennis (1998): [18a,b])

It should also be noted that *wat*-split exclamatives differ from regular *wh*-exclamatives in a number of ways. Corver (1990) discusses two differences between typical *wh*-exclamatives and split-exclamatives: (i) split-exclamatives allow an embedded word order (43) (from Rijpma and Schuringa (1978)), while *wh*-exclamatives do not; and (ii) *wat*-split exclamatives can avoid PP-islands (44b).

(43) Wat je toch 'n last hebt met die peuters!
what you yet a trouble have with those nippers
'One has so much trouble with those nippers.'

(44) a. *[Wat een herten]_i heeft de jager [op t_i] geschoten!
what a deers has the hunter at shot
b. Wat heeft deze jager [op [... een herten]] geschoten!
what has this hunter at a deers shot
c. *Wat heeft deze jager [op [... voor een herten]] geschoten!
what has this hunter at for a deers shot
Intended: 'What kind of deers did the hunter shoot at?'

The sentence in (44a) shows that extracting a whole *wh*-phrase out of a PP yields an ungrammatical sentence (hence "PP"-island), while having only *wat* 'what' in the left periphery does not (44b). This can also be compared with the *wat* ... *voor*-question in (44c), which also obeys PP-island condition. What these sentences suggest is that *wat* 'what' may not be "split" from a *wh*-constituent by movement. Corver (1990) suggests that *wat* 'what' in the case of "split-exclamatives" is an exclamative morpheme based-generated in SpecCP. This morpheme then binds one or more phrases in its c-command domain to exclaim a certain property. In other words, the so-called "split"-exclamatives are in fact WHAT-exclamatives, with an expletive like *what* in the left-periphery.

This analysis is supported by the fact that such WHAT-exclamatives do not necessarily have a non-split version, even when there is a scalar adjective in the sentences, as shown in (45).

(45) a. Wat springt zij ver!
     what jumps she far
     'Boy, she jumps far!'
   b. *Wat ver springt zij!
      what far jumps she

In addition, aside from *wh*-exclamatives, it is possible to have *wh*-less exclamatives in Dutch, as in (46a,b). In these sentences, there is no *wh*-element in the left-periphery. Instead, *me toch* 'me yet' is obligatory.[14] As we see in (47), it is also possible to add a sentence-initial *wat* 'what' in the *me toch*-exclamatives. This is also the case in (46a,b).

(46) a. Jan heeft me toch een vrouwen ontmoet in zijn leven!
     John has me yet a women met in his life
     'John has met so many women during his life!'
   b. Hij heeft me toch een hoop kinderen! Dat wil je niet weten!
      he has me yet a lot children that want you NEG know.INF
      'You're not going to believe this, but Boy, does he have a lot of children!'
                                                    (adapted from Martens (2016))

(47) Wat heeft hij me toch een lekkere vlaai gebakken!
     what have.3SG 3SG.M me yet a tasteful flan PTCP.bake
     'What a nice flan he baked!'

The above data further support the analysis of WHAT-exclamatives. The question arises in connection to Cantonese is whether *mat*[1] in Cantonese is similar to *wat* in Dutch WHAT-exclamatives? To answer this question, we need to first turn to WHAT in the scope-marking cases (i.e., the partial *wh*-movement cases).

---

14 Martens (2016) suggests that the role that *me toch* plays is to spell out ego-evidentiality (see e.g., Badan and Cheng 2015).

4.2 WHAT in scope-marking sentences

As we have seen in (39c), in German partial *wh*-movement, the scope is marked with *was* 'what' (while the "real" *wh*-phrase remains in an embedded CP). (48a,b) illustrate the full and partial variants respectively.

(48) a. Mit   wem   glaubt Hans dass Jakob jetzet spricht?
         with   whom   think   Hans that Jakob now   talking
         'With whom does Hans think that Jakob is now talking?'
     b. *Was*   glaubt Hans   mit   wem   Jakob jetzt spricht?
         WHAT   think   Hans   with   whom   Jakob now   talking
         'With whom does Hans think that Jakob is now talking?'

Herburger (1994) argues that partial *wh*-movement questions are interpreted differently from their full-movement counterparts (see also Reis (2000)). In particular, the partial ones are interpreted *de re*, while the full movement yields either *de re* or *de dicto* readings. Consider the question formed with partial *wh*-movement in (49a) and its full movement counterpart in (49b).

(49) a. *Was*   glaubt   der   Georg   wen   die   Rosa   geküßt   hat?
         WHAT   believes DET   Georg   who   DET   Rosa   kissed   has
     b. Wen   glaubt   der   Georg   daß   die   Rosa   geküßt   hat?
         who   believes DET   Georg   that DET   Rosa   kissed   has
         'Who does Georg believe that Rosa has kissed?'   (Herburger (1994): (1a,b))

In (49a), the proposition "Rosa kissed someone" must be interpreted as being part of the speaker's beliefs, rather than part of Georg's belief-state. That is, that Rosa kissed someone cannot just be part of Georg's belief-state. Thus, according to Herburger (1994), (49a) can be paraphrased as "Rosa kissed somebody, who does Georg think it was?". In contrast, though (49b) can also have to the same reading as (49a), it also has a *de dicto* reading. In other words, it is possible to interpret the proposition "Rosa kissed someone" in (49b) as simply a figment of Georg's imagination. Based on this interpretational difference (as well as a number of differences mentioned in the literature), Herburger supports a differential treatment of partial *wh*-movement from full *wh*-movement. In particular, she follows the Indirect Dependency approach (see Dayal (1994, 1996)), and argues that *was* 'what' in (49a) does not form a direct chain with the *wh*-phrase in the embedded clause. Instead, it is linked to the whole embedded question (the CP).

Abstracting away from Herberger's syntactic analysis of the scope-marking sentences, her explanation for why the scope marking sentence in (49a) only has a *de re* reading is as follows (see also Dayal (2000)): *was*, being a *wh*-element is treated as a quantifier (i.e., a *wh*- quantifier). The embedded CP serves as the restriction of the *wh*-quantifier. Quantifier restrictions do not contribute to the assertion part of the sentence, but rather to the presupposition. In other words, in (49a), the proposition "Rosa kissed someone" is the restriction of *was*, and therefore the presupposition.

Dayal (2000) proposes that languages can differ as to how the indirect dependency is realized syntactically. In particular, she suggests that in one variant, the structure involves typical subordination of the embedded CP, as in (50). Crucially, the restrictor of the *wh* (∃)-quantifier is phonologically null, but coindexed with the embedded CP2.

(50)

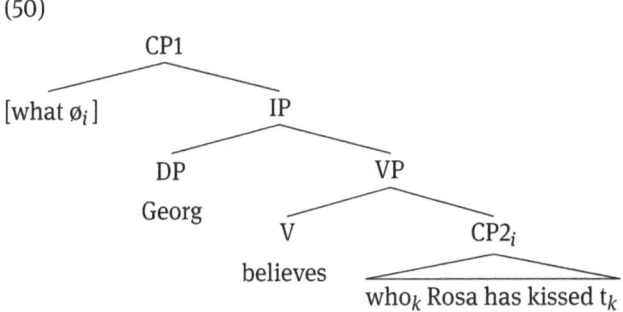

This structure is compatible with Herburger's explanation of the *de re* reading, i.e., that the embedded clause serves as the restriction and thus the presupposition of the whole sentence.

4.3 Relating WHAT-exclamatives and *mat¹*

In the last two sections (sections 4.1 and 4.2), we have seen the workings of the so called "expletive *what*", indicated here as WHAT. We have seen that WHAT can be base-generated in the left-periphery to head an exclamative sentence, and it can also be used to mark the scope of a *wh*-phrase. Let us now turn to *mat¹*-initial sentences in Cantonese. We have already mentioned that the lack of *wh*-movement makes it quite unlikely that *mat¹*-initial sentences in Cantonese are derived from postverbal causal *mat¹*-questions, let alone the fact that there are other differences between the two types of sentences as discussed in section 2.2. In other words, *mat¹* is most likely positioned sentence-initially not because of movement; instead, it is base-generated there. Taking into consideration the similarities between *mat¹*-initial sentences and exclamatives discussed in section 3.2, as well as a base-generated *mat¹* at the left periphery, *mat¹*-initial sentences resemble WHAT-exclamatives in Dutch. In this section, I explore this further.

The potential hurdle to analyse sentence-initial *mat¹*-sentences as exclamatives is the fact that the degree elements are optional. That is, even though there are sentences such as the ones in (37) and (38), where degree-related expressions such as *gam²* 'such' or *gam³* 'so' are present, there are also cases where these expressions are absent, as in (18b), repeated here as (51).

(51) *mat¹   lei⁵   hai²dou⁶   fan-³gaau³   gaa³?*
       what   you   PROG   sleep-sleep   SFP
       'Why are you sleeping?'/ 'How come you are sleeping?'

The question then is whether this type of sentences can also be considered to be exclamatives. We have seen in section 3.2 that according to C&N and N&C, there are two types of exclamatives, and one of which has an e-level noteworthiness, and it also does not have clear-cut scalar expression. Consider now the interpretation of *mat¹*-initial sentences in (52).

(52) a. *mat¹   ngo⁵   gam³   so⁴   gaa³!*
         what   I   so   foolish SFP
         'What am I foolish!'
     b. *mat¹   lei⁵   gam¹jat⁶   jiu³   faan¹hok⁶   aa³?!*
         what   you   today   need   go.to.school SFP
         'How come you have to go to school today?!'   (from Lam (2014): [11])

The sentence in (52a) has the interpretation that my foolishness is at a remarkably high degree (thus *i*-level), while (52b) is exclaiming the noteworthy fact that you have to go to school even today. Lam (2014) offers the following context for (52b): 'Today is a public holiday, so Tom's mother expects that Tom does not need to go to school. Nonetheless, Tom still needs to go to school.' Lam states that '*mat¹* must combine with a proposition with a sentence-final particle that reveals a speaker's former expectation which is contradictory from the [current] proposition.' (Lam 2014, p. 56).

If *mat¹*-initial sentences can be interpreted as indicated above, i.e., it can either express noteworthiness of a particular element or noteworthiness of an event. In other words, *mat¹*-initial sentences in Cantonese in fact instantiate both types of exclamatives argued for by C&N and N&C. The initial hurdle that we encountered when treating *mat¹*-initial sentences as exclamatives has just disappeared.

The next issue we need to address is the role of *mat¹*. Is it similar to WHAT in Dutch and German? Consider the Dutch exclamatives in (53) ((45a) repeated here as (53a); (53b)= N&C:[58]).

(53) a. Wat   springt zij   ver!
        What   jumps   she   far
        'Boy, she jumps far!'
     b. Wat   hij   toen   weer   trok!
        what   he   then   again   picked

As mentioned above, C&N and N&C propose that in the case of *i*-level exclamatives, the noteworthiness is linked to the referent of the *wh*-word, while the noteworthiness is linked to the proposition referenced in *e*-level exclamatives. In the case of (53a), *ver* 'far' can be the referent of *wat* 'what', and that is why the noteworthiness is linked to the distance of jumping. In the case of (53b), *wat* is not linked to a particular referent; rather, it is the whole proposition (i.e., that he then again picked). In N&C, the scenario where (53b) is used concerns the card-trick test. In particular, (53b) can be used when someone picked again and again the same cards out of the playing cards. Importantly, it is not the cards themselves that are remarkable. It is the fact that the person manages to pick the same cards every time. In other words, (53b) is an example of *e*-level exclamative. Bennis (1998) notes that *dat* 'that'-exclamatives in Dutch only has the interpretation where what is exclaimed is the proposition. In other words, *dat* 'that'-exclamatives are *e*-level exclamatives as well, as in (54).

(54) Dat   hij   die   boeken   kan   lezen!
     that he   those   books   can   Read
     'Wow, he can read those books!'   (Bennis (1998): [28])

Bennis considers (54) to be an embedded exclamative, treating *dat* 'that' as a complementizer. Both (53b) and (54) thus have a base-generated element in the left-periphery: *wat* 'what' in (53b) and *dat* 'that' in (54). They both yield *e*-level exclamatives. That is, if the base-generated elements take the proposition below them as the proposition to exclaim, then in both cases we get *e*-level exclamatives. (55) is the Cantonese counterpart of (54).

(55) mat^1 $keoi^5$ sik^1 tai^2 go^2-di^1 syu^1 ge^2/gaa^3
     what   he   know   read   that-CL   book   SFP/SFP
     'Wow, he can read those books!'

The context for a felicitous (55) is that the speaker does not expect that he can read those books. In other words, this has the violation of expectation reading or noteworthiness reading, i.e., exclamative reading.

Mat¹ is thus similar to *wat/dat* in Dutch and *was* in German in heading an exclamative. Furthermore, as we have seen in (52), *mat¹* can yield both *i*-level and *e*-level exclamatives, just like its Dutch counterparts. In the case of an *e*-level exclamative, it takes its complement as the referent to make an exclamative sentence. In the case of an *i*-level exclamative, also similar to its Dutch counterparts, it takes an individual property as a referent.

Recall that what follows *mat¹*or *wat* is factive. The factive presupposition may have the same source as the *de re* interpretation in scope-marking sentences with *was* in German, as discussed in section 4.2. As *mat¹* or WHAT is a quantification element, the proposition following it serves as its restriction, leading to the factive presupposition.

Assuming that sentence-final particles in Cantonese indicate that the IP has moved to the left (see Hsieh and Sybesma (2011) and Sybesma and Li (2007)), *mat¹* is higher in the left-periphery than typical sentence-final particles. (56) and (57) are simplified representations of the sentences in (52). In these representations, the IP has moved to the left of the sentence-final particle in C⁰. *Mat¹* takes either the predicate *gam³ so⁴* 'so foolish', or the whole IP *lei⁵ gam¹jat⁶ jiu³ faan¹hok⁶* 'you need to go to school today' as the restriction (and makes these the presupposition).

(56)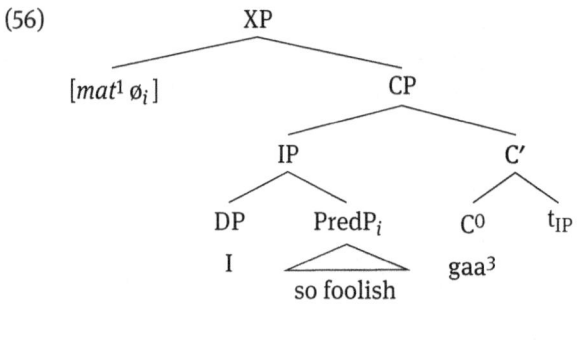

(57)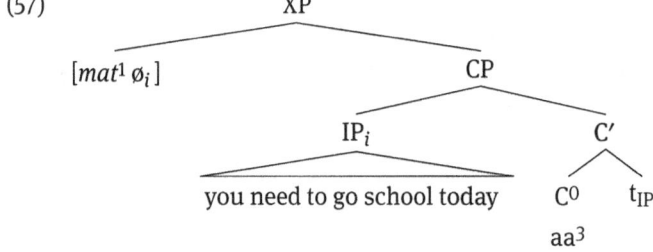

We hypothesise here that *mat¹* may also contribute ego-evidentiality, as *mat¹*-initial sentences have to do with speaker's counter-expectation.[15] In other words, *mat¹*-initial sentences are comparable to exclamatives in Mandarin.

Conclusion

If the direction explored above is correct, *mat¹*-initial sentences are not causal questions; instead they instantiate two types of exclamatives. *Mat¹* appears to be the only *wh*-element which can be used in exclamatives in Cantonese. Considering the fact that in Dutch and German, there is an expletive WHAT that can be used in the left-periphery for exclamatives and scope marking, we can also treat *mat¹* in Cantonese as an expletive WHAT. In other words, *mat¹* is not a typical *wh*-phrase, but rather a *wh*-expletive, on a par with WHAT in Dutch and German. Therefore, Cantonese does not really have true *wh*-exclamatives.

In section 1, we have encountered an example from Mandarin with an initial *wh*-phrase, which looks at first sight quite similar to *mat¹*-initial sentences. The only difference seems to be that instead of using the counterpart of *what*, Mandarin uses the counterpart of *how*. (5b) is repeated here as (58).

(58) zěnme/*shénme nǐ   zài   kū?   (Mandarin)
     how/what   you   PROG cry
     'Why are you crying?'

Tsai (2008) argues that *zěnme* 'how' in Mandarin can be interpreted as 'why' if it precedes a modal (59a) (see also Cheng (2019)). Since *wèishénme* 'why' in Mandarin can be merged in exactly the same position as *zěnme* 'how' (see (2)), we may suggest that *zěnme* 'how' is just a variant of *wèishénme* 'why' in Mandarin. In other words, *zěnme* 'how' differs from *mat¹* in Cantonese, as the latter cannot appear right below the subject (see (13a)).

(59) a. tā   zěnme huì   qù Leiden?
        he   how   will go Leiden
        'How come he will go to Leiden?'

---

[15] It should be noted that the anti-expectation is not necessarily negative. In (55) for instance, the speaker can be pleasantly surprised that he can read those books.

  b. zěnme tā huì qù Leiden?
    how   he   will   go   Leiden
    'How come he will go to Leiden?'

Nonetheless, it is not the case that *zěnme* 'how' can always appear sentence-initially, as we see in (60).

(60) a. tā zěnme kěnéng qù-le Měiguó?
    he   how   possible   go-PFV   U.S.
    'How is it possible that he went to the States?'
  b. *zěnme tā kěnéng qù-le Měiguó?
    how   he   possible   go-PFV   U.S.

The sentences in (61a,b) suggest that *zěnme* 'how' can be used on a par with sentence-initial *mat*[1]; Compare (61b) with (55). Both (61a) and (61b) express noteworthiness, with the former indicating an *i*-level noteworthiness while the latter *e*-level.

(61) a. zěnme tā zhème piào-liàng!
    how   3SG   this.ME   pretty
    'How pretty s/he is!'
  b. zěnme tā kàn-de-dǒng nà-xiē shū?!
    how   he   read-DE-understand   that-CL   book
    'How come he understands those books?'

If this is correct, it means that Mandarin uses *zěnme* as a realization of WHAT (instead of the counterpart of *what*, in contrast with Cantonese, Dutch and German). It should be noted that not all languages use the counterpart of *what* as WHAT in scope-marking constructions. Slavic languages, for instance, use the counterpart of *how* in scope-marking sentences; for example, Russian (62) (Stepanov (2000)).

(62)   Kak vy dumaete, kogo ljubit Ivan?
    how you think   whom loves John
    'Who do you think John loves?'   (Russian, Stepanov (2000): [2a])

If (61a,b) in Mandarin are indeed WHAT-exclamatives, Mandarin is an example of using the counterpart of *how* instead of *what* to mark WHAT-exclamatives, in contrast with Cantonese. The infelicitous (60b) can be due to a clash between the requirement of factivity under exclamative WHAT and the modal expressing possibility. This is of course a tentative conclusion, as more research is needed to determine whether (61a,b) are indeed exclamatives.

References

Badan, Linda & Lisa Lai-Shen Cheng. 2015. Exclamatives in Mandarin Chinese. *Journal of East Asian Linguistics* 24. 383–413.
Bennis, Hans. 1998. Exclamatives! *Linguistics in the Netherlands* 15. 27–40.
Bennis, Hans, Norbert Corver, and Marcel Den Dikken. 1998. Predication in nominal phrases. *Journal of Comparative Germanic Linguistics* 1. 85–117.
Caponigro, Ivano, and Jon Sprouse. 2007. Rhetorical questions as questions. In E. Puig-Waldmüller (ed.) *Proceedings of Sinn und Bedeutung 11*, 121–133. Barcelona: Universitat Popmeu Fabra.
Cheng, Lisa Lai-Shen. 2019. On the interaction between modals and aspects. *English Linguistics* 35. 241–260.
Cheng, Lisa Lai-Shen & Rint Sybesma. 1998. On dummy objects and the transitivity of *run*. *Linguistics in the Netherlands* 81–93.
Cheng, Lisa Lai-Shen & Rint Sybesma. 2015. Transitive psych-predicates. In Audrey Li, Andrew Simpson & Wei tien Dylan Tsai (eds.), *Chinese syntax in a cross-linguistic perspective*, 207–228. Oxford, UK: Oxford University Press.
Chernilovskaya, Anna & Rick Nouwen. 2012. On wh-exclamatives and noteworthiness. In Maria Aloni, Vadim Kimmelman, Floris Roelofsen, Galit W. Sassoon, Katrin Schulz, and Matthijs Westera (eds.), *Logic, language and meaning*, 271–280. Berlin, Heidelberg: Springer Berlin Heidelberg.
Collins, Chris. 1991. Why and how come. In Lisa Lai-Shen Cheng & Hamida Demirdache (eds.), *More papers on wh-movement, MIT Working Papers in Linguistics* 15, 31–45. MITWPL.
Conroy, Anastasia. 2006. The semantics of *how come*: a look at how factivity does it all. In Nina Kazanina, Utako Minai, Philip J. Monahan & Heather L. Taylor (eds.), *University of Maryland working papers in Linguistics* 14, 1–24. UMWPiL.
Corver, Norbert. 1990. *The syntax of left branch extractions*. Katholieke Universiteit Brabant dissertation.
d'Avis, Franz. 2016. Different Languages – Different sentence types? On exclamative Sentences: Different Languages – Different Sentence Types? *Language and Linguistics Compass* 10. 159–175.
D'Avis, Franz-Josef. 2000. On the wh-expletive was in German. In Uli Lutz, Geroen Müller, and Arnim von Stechow (eds.), *Wh-scope marking*, 131–155. John Benjamins Publishing Company.
Dayal, Veneeta. 1994. Scope marking as indirect wh-dependency. *Natural Language Semantics* 2. 137–170.
Dayal, Veneeta. 1996. *Locality in WH quantification*. Dordrecht: Kluwer.
Dayal, Veneeta. 2000. Cross-linguistic variation in indirect dependency. In Uli Lutz, Geroen Müller & Arnim von Stechow (eds.), *Wh-scope marking*, 157–194. John Benjamins.
Fitzpatrick, Justin. 2005. The whys and how comes of presupposition and NPI licensing in questions. In John Alderete, Chung-hye Han & Alexei Kochetov (eds.), *Proceedings of the 24th West Coast Conference on Formal Linguistics*, 183–145. Cascadilla Press.

Han, Chung-hye. 2002. Interpreting interrogatives as rhetorical questions. *Lingua* 112. 201–229.
Herburger, Elena. 1994. A semantic difference between full and partial wh-movement in German. Paper presented at the Linguistic Society of America meeting, January 1994.
Hsieh, Feng-fan & Rint Sybesma. 2011. On the linearization of Chinese sentece-final particles: Max spell out and why CP moves. *Korea Journal of Chinese Language and Literature* 1. 53–90.
Huang, C.T. James. 1982. *Logical relations in Chinese and the theory of grammar*. MIT dissertation.
Ko, Heejeong. 2005. Syntax of Why-in-situ: Merge into [SPEC,CP] in the overt syntax. *Natural Language & Linguistic Theory* 23. 867–916.
Lam, Margaret Nga Yee. 2014. *Scalar mat-construction in Cantonese*. Chinese University of Hong Kong BA Thesis.
Leung, Zhongsen. 2005. *A study of the utterance particles in Cantonese as spoken in Hong Kong*. City University of Hong Kong.
Martens, Gouming. 2016. *Dutch particle exclamatives*. Leiden University MA thesis.
Nouwen, Rick & Anna Chernilovskaya. 2015. Two types of wh-exclamatives. *Linguistic Variation* 15. 201–224.
Reis, Marga. 2000. On the Parenthetical Features of German. *Was... W*-Constructions and how to account for them. In Uli Lutz, Geroen Müller & Arnim von Stechow (eds.), *Wh-scope marking*, 359–407. Amsterdam: John Benjamins Publishing Company.
Rett, Jessica. 2011. Exclamatives, degrees and speech acts. *Linguistics and Philosophy* 34. 411–442.
Rijpma, E & F.G. Schuringa. 1978. *Nederlandse spraakkunst*. Wolters-Noordhoff, 23rd edition edition.
Stepanov, Arthur. 2000. WH-scope marking in Slavic. *Studia Linguistica* 54. 1–40.
Sung, Li-May. 2015. Why exclamatives in Budai Rukai. In Elizabeth Zeitoun, Stacy F. Teng & Joy J. Wu (eds.), *New advances in Formosan Linguistics, AsiaPacific Linguistics* 17, 291–312. Asia-Pacific Linguistics.
Sybesma, Rint & Boya Li. 2007. The dissection and structural mapping of Cantonese sentence final particles. *Lingua* 117. 1739–1783.
Tang, Sze-Wing. 2008. Why *mat* in cantonese? *Zhongguo Yuwen Yanjiu* 1. 9–19.
Tsai, Wei-Tien Dylan. This volume. On applicative *Why*-questions in Chinese. In Gabriela Soare (ed.), *Why is Why Unique? Its Syntactic and Semantic Properties*, Berlin: De Gruyter Mouton.
Tsai, Wei-Tien Dylan. 2008. Left periphery and how-why alternations. *Journal of East Asian Linguistics* 17. 83.
Zanuttini, Raffaella & Paul Portner. 2003. Exclamative clauses: At the syntax-semantics interface. *Language* 79. 39–81.
Zwicky, Arnold M. & Ann D. Zwicky. 1971. How come and what for. In Dale E. Elliott, Michael L. Geis, Alexander Grosu, Barry Nobel, Ann D. Zwicky & Arnold M. Zwicky (eds.), *Working papers in Linguistics* 8, 173–185. Ohio State University.

Part 4: **Some syntactic aspects of *how come***

Yoshio Endo
How come questions and diary English

1 Introduction

In this paper, I will discuss the nature of a null subject in English in the framework of the cartography of syntactic structures (Cinque 1999, Rizzi 1997, among others) with special attention to diary English. I will first discuss some properties of a null subject in diary English like those illustrated in (1) below, where ec stands for empty category. I will next turn to the fact that *how come* questions can exhibit subject drop in diary-style English. The real examples are shown in (2), which were pointed out to me by Andrew Radford (personal communication).[1] I will finally discuss some implications of our approach by looking at a null subject in *wanna* contraction sentences and *that*-trace effect.

(1) a. *ec spent the day at work.*
       (Truman's Diary, 1947, 1 Jan.)
    b. *ec have done 110 pages.*
       (Diary of Virginia Woolf, p. 33; 1.11.)

(2) a. *How come ec can't use iPhoto anymore?*
       (discussions.apple.com)
    b. *How come ec am listening to a part of the book?*
       (goodreads.com)

2 Some properties of diary English

Haegeman (1990) notes various properties of diary English, including the use of a null subject as illustrated in (3) below:

---

[1] After I wrote up an earlier version of this manuscript, Radford (2018) appeared, which makes a detailed discussion of *how come* questions, including my analysis of *how come* questions developed in this paper. Some of the example sentences appearing in the present paper are also discussed in Radford (2018).

https://doi.org/10.1515/9783110675160-009

(3) *A very sensible day yesterday. ec Saw no one. ec Took the bus to Southwark Bridge. ec Walked along Thames Street.*
(Virginia Woolf, Diary, vol.5, 1936–41: 203–4)

There are some important properties of a null subject in diary English. First, the use of a null subject in diary English is not compatible with a root *wh*-question, as we see in (4) below:

(4) **When will <ec> be able to meet him?*
(Haegeman 1990: 163–4)

Second, the subject drop in diary English is not attested in the embedded clause, as illustrated in (5):

(5) *Dreamt that *(I) picked up a New Yorker.*
(Sylvia Plath, *New Yorker* 1982: 304)

Third, the subject drop in diary English is common with a first person pronoun, as shown in Table 1 from Nanyan (2013:100) based on Truman's diary but can also be observed with a third person as in (6a) and the expletive *it* as in (6b):

	Total	Null
1st person SG.	168	108
1st person PL.	39	19
Lexical DP *and* 1st person SG.	6	0
2rd person	2	0
3rd person SG. Lexical DP	65	
3rd person SG. Pronouns	66	8
Expletive	12	5
3rd person PL. lexical DP	25	
3rd person PL. pronouns	17	0
Total	**400**	**135**

http://www.t.rumanlibrary.org/diary/transcript.htm.

Figure 1: Category of person and number of overt and null subjects in root clauses.

(6) a. *ec* studies under [David] Daiches.
(Sylvia Plath, *New Yorker* 1956, 126)
b. *ec* rained in the night, wind, rain and hail.
(Elizabeth Smart, *On the side of the Angels*, 19/01/1945: 27)

Fourth, the subject drop in diary English is different from the subject drop in conversational style. For instance, the subject drop in conversational style is not seen when the subject is followed by an auxiliary verb such as *am*, *have*, etc., as shown in (7), while the subject drop in diary English is possible in such an environment as shown in (8):

(7) a. **ec am thinking of leaving tomorrow.*
b. **ec have been to Turkey.*
c. **ec will rain tomorrow.*

(8) a. *ec am told the men caught another snake this morning – definitely a grass snake this time.*
(Orwell diary 1937, August 11)
b. *ec have done 110 pages.*
(Diary of Virginia Woolf, p. 33; 1.11.)
c. *ec has thrown her wedding ring into the cauldron too.*
(Diary of Virginia Woolf, V: p. 6, 10 January 1936)

Fifth, the subject drop in English is different from the subject drop in Romance languages like Italian where a rich verbal inflectional ending licenses the subject drop. Thus, the subject drop is possible in the embedded clause in Italian as seen in (9):

(9) I   ragazzi   cantano   [quando   ec lavorano].
    the   boys   sing.3PL   when   work.3PL
    'The boys sing while they are working.'
    (Italian)

Finally, the subject drop is also different from the subject drop in Japanese or Portuguese where a discourse familiar pronominal subject may freely drop even in the embedded clause, as illustrated in (10):[2]

---

[2] See Endo (2007) for the nature of subject position in Japanese.

(10) *John-wa* [*zibun-ga/ec sippaisita*]-*to* *omotta*.
John-TOP self-NOM/ec made.mistakes-that thought
'John thought that he made a mistake.'

(Japanese)

3 Phase and cartography of syntactic structures

Haegeman (2017) proposes to derive the various properties noted above in the framework of the cartography of syntactic structures. Before we see Haegeman's specific analysis, let me first introduce some basic background of the cartography of syntactic structures that are relevant to our discussion to follow. Based on the idea that the CP zone is characterized by scope/discourse properties (cf. Chomsky 2001), Rizzi (1997, 2001, 2004) claims that there are various functional heads in the CP zone for topic, focus, and so forth, as shown in (11), and that scope/discourse interpretations are determined by a family of principles, the Criteria, which require a scope- or discourse-related element to enter into a spec-head or head-head agreement relation with respect to features of the relevant class: e.g. Top, Foc, Mod, Subj and so forth for topic, focus, modifier, subject, respectively.

(11)   Force Top* Int Top* Focus Mod* Top* Fin Subj IP

(Rizzi 2004)

With this background in mind, Haegeman proposes to derive the properties of the subject drop in diary English by using Chomsky's (2001) phase theory, according to which the complement of the phase heads C and *v* is sent to PF and LF by the operation Spell-Out. Based on Rizzi's (1997) idea that Force head is occupied by the complementizer *that*, Haegeman derives the properties of null subject in diary English. For instance, in the following sentence in (12a), the complementizer *that* in the embedded clause is spelled out while that in the matrix clause is not. This is because the phase head Force in the embedded clause is necessarily sent to the PF to be spelled out as *that* when the complement of the phase head *v*P in the matrix clause is sent to PF, as shown in (12b). Because the phase head in the matrix clause is not found in the complement domain of the phase head Force in the matrix clause, the Force head is not spelled out as *that* in the matrix clause, as shown in (12c).

(12) a. *(*That)* Bill thinks (that) Mary is sick.

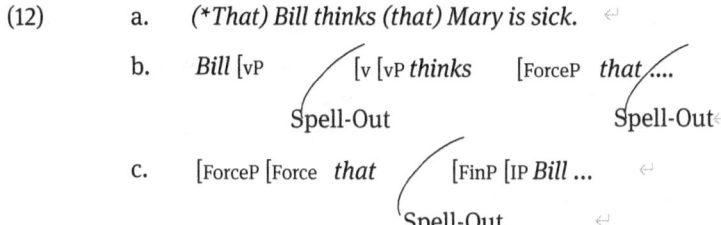

Figure 2: The domain where the complementizer *that* is spelled out in the matrix clause and the embedded clause.

Based on this idea, Haegeman proposes that the derivation in diary English terminates below the CP zone, where the phase head is assumed to be the functional head Subject found immediately above IP, not Force. When the derivation reaches SubjectP (SubjP, hereafter), the complement of SubjP is sent to PF and thus an overt subject like a first person pronoun *I* has no chance to be spelled out because it is not found in the complement of SubjP but the specifier of SubjP, as shown below:

(13) [subjP *I* [subj ⟶ [IP t_i woke to get a letter in the mail]]].
              Spell-out

Figure 3: Derivation related to Spell-Out of SubjP.

With this mechanism, neither the subject, nor an element above the subject like the fronted *wh*-element *when* in (4) may appear in diary English because it is beyond the spell-out domain. Furthermore, because auxiliary verbs like *am* and *have* are found in the IP zone below SubjP, they may appear in diary English as in (8).

4 *How come* questions vs. *why* questions

In this section, we will see some facts which are difficult to explain using Haegeman's observation mentioned in the previous section – namely the fact that *how come* questions can exhibit subject drop in diary-style English.[3] As we saw

---

[3] Andrew Radford (personal communication) points out other problems of phase-theoretic approach to null subject. Consider the sentence *Fancy a drink?* If the sentence is truncated at SubjP, neither LF, nor PF will see the interrogative yes-no question operator above SubjP which (at LF) is crucial to typing the question as a yes-no question, and (at PF) is crucial to assigning the sentence the rising intonation characteristic of a question. It is surely more plausible to say that the whole

above, a fronted wh-element like *when* may not appear in diary English. However, Andrew Radford (personal communication) tells me that, following a query from Liliane Haegeman about whether *how come* allows subject drop, he googled numerous subjectless *how come* questions including those in (14):

(14) a. *How come can't use iPhoto anymore?*
(discussions.apple.com)
b. *How come am listening to a part of the book?*
(goodreads.com)
c. *How come haven't got recon yet?*
(halowaypoint.com)
d. *How come wasn't stopped on the outward journey?*
(whatdotheyknow.com)

Six English teachers I consulted at my university confirmed that such sentences are fine in diary-style written English (though not in spoken English). Andrew Radford also observes that the subject drop is not allowed in *why* questions as shown below:

(15) a. **Why can't ec use iPhoto anymore?*
b. **Why am ec listening to a part of the book?*
c. **Why haven't ec got recon yet?*
d. **Why wasn't ec stopped on the outward journey?*

The null subject sentences in *how come* questions in (14) seem difficult to deal with in the phase theory introduced in the previous section because *how come* is found in a position higher than a subject position and thus *how come* is expected not to be spelled out along with a subject noun phrase. To overcome this problem, I suggest that there is another mode to license a null subject in diary English, which derives the asymmetry between *why* questions and *how come* questions in diary English. Before going directly into this task, let us examine the previous studies of *how come* questions that are relevant to our discussion to follow.

Zwicky and Zwicky (1971) note that *how come* may only be construed with the matrix clause, as in (16). Here *how come* may be associated with the matrix predicate *say*, but not with the embedded predicate *is mad*.

Force structure is visible at LF, but that at PF the highest peripheral projections (from ForceP down to and including SubjP) are given a silent spellout, as a result of some kind of PF economy process. (Whether giving a chunk of peripheral structure a silent spellout involves not sending the relevant material to the PF component at all, or sending it but assigning it a silent spellout is another matter.) See Radford (2018) for discussion of other problems of phase-theoretic approach to null subjects.

(16) *How come you say that John is mad?*
(ok matrix, *embedded)
(Zwicky and Zwicky 1971: 928)

Collins (1991) claims that *how come* is base generated in the C head of the matrix clause, and thus cannot originate in the embedded clause and undergo long-distance movement into the matrix clause, because head movement is generally clause-bound.

Shlonsky and Soare (2011) point out a potential problem with Collins' analysis by observing that *how come* patterns with a phrasal element like *why*, not with a head element like *if* and *whether*, in that it does not allow Sluicing in sentences like the following:

(17) *They thought John left early, but they didn't tell me why/how come/*whether/*if* φ.
(Shlonsky & Soare 2011: 665, ex. 41)

On the basis of this observation in (17), Shlonsky and Soare suggest that *how come* is base generated in a specifier position, not a head position. To be more specific, they adopt Rizzi's (2001) idea that Italian *come mai* 'how come' is base generated in Spec, Int in the CP system we saw in (11), and they also base generate *how come* in Spec, Int, as shown in (18). I will adopt this idea in my analysis of *how come* questions – as shown below.

(18) Force Top* Int (=*how come*) Top* FocP Mod* Top* Fin IP

The question that I would like to ask here is where the complementizer *that* is found in the CP zone. The traditional answer in the framework of the cartography of syntactic structures is found in Rizzi (1997), where it is assumed that the complementizer *that* occupies the head position of ForceP. Here, a problem arises when we look at the observation noticed by Zwicky and Zwicky (1971) that *how come* may be followed by the complementizer *that* as in (19) for many speakers. (See Endo (2018) for inter-speaker variations of the distribution of *how come* and the complementizer *that*).[4]

(19) *How come that she has read the book?*
(Zwicky and Zwicky 1971: 928)

---

4 See Endo (2015) for other properties of *how come* questions.

As we see in (11), ForceP is found in a position higher than IntP, and (if *that* is a Force head) we wrongly expect the complementizer *that* not to follow *how come*, which is found in Spec, Int. This problem can be avoided by a recent view of the complementizer *that*. More recently, Rizzi (2014a) explores the possibility that the complementizer *that* may also be found in the head position of FinP. To be more precise, Rizzi discusses the *that*-trace effect and (following Culicover (1993)) notes that it is alleviated by the presence of an intervening adverbial element, as in the sentence below:[5]

(20)   *This is the man who I think that, next year, ___ will sell his house*

Rizzi attributes this alleviation effect to the fact that recursion of Fin is possible in the presence of an adverbial element (=Mod), as represented in (20') below.[6] Here, we find two Fins, one is higher than the modifier *next year* and the other is lower than the modifier. The lower Fin is nominal Fin[+N] and the higher one is a non-nominal Fin[that] that hosts the complementizer *that*. Here, the lower Fin[+N] can serve the function of satisfying the requirement of a criterial feature on the SUBJ head or what Chomsky calls EPP which requires it to be c-commanded and immediately preceded by a nominal constituent.

(20')   [$_{FINP}$ [$_{FIN[that]}$ that] [$_{MODP}$ [$_{MOD}$ next year] [$_{FINP}$ [$_{FIN[+N]}$ φ] [$_{DP}$ [$_{D\text{-}SUBJ}$ ∅]...who...]]]]

In the absence of an intervening element, Fin recursion is impossible, because it results in an illicit double Fin configuration...*Fin-Fin, which violates the following constraint posited by Rizzi (2014a):

(21)   A head cannot select a categorially non-distinct head.

That is, simple recursion of Fin creates the illicit representation 'Fin-Fin' because the higher Fin selects a categorially non-distinct Fin head in violation of (21). Thus, an intervening element is required between two Fins. To summarize, Rizzi's Fin recursion system has the properties in (22):

---

5 It is interesting to note that some speakers do not find *that*-trace sentences entirely bad, especially with a contracted auxiliary cliticised to the complementiser, as shown below:

(i)   ?? Who do you think that is going to win?
(ii)   (?) Who d'you think that's gonna win?

I am grateful to Andrew Radford (personal communication) for the judgments in (i, ii).
6 See Endo and Haegeman (2019) for the properties of Mod.

(22) a. In the presence of an intervening adverbial element, Fin recursion creates a split Fin structure (=Fin[that] and Fin[+N]);
 b. Fin[that] may host the complementizer *that*;
 c. Fin[+N] does not host the complementizer *that*, but instead licenses the subject position.

With these ideas in mind, recall the statement by Zwicky and Zwicky (1971) that *how come* may be followed by the complementizer *that* for many speakers. However, the informal questionnaire survey I conducted with Andrew Radford shows that many English speakers do not accept *how come* immediately followed by *that*.[7] Following the suggestion by Andrew Radford (personal communication), I suggest that for minority speakers who accept *how come* immediately followed by *that*, Fin[+N] may be spelled out as the complementizer *that*. Speakers who can spell out Fin[+N] as *that* also allow *that*-trace violations, because Fin[+N] (which can be spelled out as *that* by a minority of speakers) licenses subject extraction. In fact, Andrew Radford (personal communication) reports that he allows *that*-trace violations, as in *Who do you think that is most likely to win the race?* And he also allows *how come* to be immediately followed by the complementizer *that*. To summarize so far, I suggested that the complementizer *that* may appear not only in ForceP but also FinP in *how come* questions.

Let us next examine the subject drop in *how come* questions, – namely the fact that they can exhibit subject drop in diary-style English in (14). How can the approach to *how come* questions outlined here deal with these cases? I continue to assume that *how come* directly selects Fin[+N], which in turn licenses the subject head D_{Subj}, as represented below. Thus, a null subject in diary style may be licensed by an immediately adjacent nominal Fin head.

(23) [$_{INTP}$ *how come* [$_{INT}$ ∅] [$_{FINP}$ [$_{FIN[+N]}$ φ] [$_{DP}$ [$_{D\text{-}SUBJ}$ ∅]. . .]]]

Recall that Fin[that], as opposed to Fin[+N], hosts the complementizer *that*. This predicts that we will not find null subjects with *how come that*. This is because *how come* directly selects Fin [+N] that does not spell out the complementizer *that*. It is Fin[+N] that licenses null subjects in diary style English. This prediction is borne out by the observation that all the informants who I consulted said that sentences like (24) below are ungrammatical, where *how come that* is followed

---

7 See Endo (2018) and Radford (2018) for the informal survey.

by a null subject, in sharp contrast with (25) where *how come* questions lack the complementizer *that* and are grammatical in diary English:

(24) a. *How come that ec can't use iPhoto anymore?*
 b. *How come that ec am listening to a part of the book?*
 c. *How come that ec haven't got recon yet?*
 d. *How come that ec wasn't stopped on the outward journey?*

(25) a. How come ec can't use iPhoto anymore?
 b. How come ec am listening to a part of the book?
 c. How come ec haven't got recon yet?
 d. How come ec wasn't stopped on the outward journey?

Why is different from *how come* in several respects. For one thing, *how come* questions generally do not show subject-auxiliary inversion. Following Rizzi and Shlonsky (2007), I assume that an inverted auxiliary verb moves into a non-nominal Fin which is verbal in nature, i.e. Fin[+V], not Fin[+N]. Andrew Radford (personal communication) notes that if we replace *how come* in (25) we saw above by *why*, ungrammaticality arises as in (26) below, where *why* is followed by an inverted auxiliary verb found in the head of Fin[+that]. He also suggests that the ungrammaticality follows if a null subject can only be licensed by an immediately adjacent Fin[+N], not Fin[that].[8]

(26) a. *Why can't <ec> use iPhoto anymore?*
 b. *Why am <ec> listening to a part of the book?*
 c. *Why haven't <ec> got recon yet?*
 d. *Why wasn't <ec> stopped on the outward journey?*

As he notes, the real problem is why only a nominal Fin (not Fin-*that* or a verbal Fin) can license subject drop: he conjectures that the answer may lie in a nominal Fin[+N] carrying agreement properties that can license (and be valued by) a null subject in spec, DP-$_{SUBJ}$. However, more research is needed in this area.

Incidentally, *why* is also different from other wh-expressions like *how*. For instance, Shlonsky and Soare (2011) notes the following asymmetry between *why* and *how* with respect to their base-generated positions and negative islands:

---

8 Andrew Radford reports that he managed to google only one example of *how come that am . . .*, but notes that it contained errors suggesting it was produced by a non-native speaker.

(27) a. *Why didn't Geraldine fix her bike?*
b. **How didn't Geraldine fix her bike?*
(Shlonsky and Soare 2011: 656)

This asymmetry between *why* and *how* stems from the fact that *why* is base-generated in the CP zone without crossing negative islands while *how* is displaced from a position lower than negation (Neg) to cross negative islands. To be more precise, Rizzi (2001, 2004) proposes that *why* is base generated in Spec, Int in a position higher than Neg, and thus does not cross negative islands. Andrew Radford (personal communication) points out (27b) is acceptable for him in the following kind of context in (28a). This is a kind of rhetorical negative question, found in a discourse like (28b). Note that the exclamation mark after the question mark marks this as a rhetorical question. There is something different about rhetorical negative questions – for example, they do not license polarity items like (partitive) *any*, as in (29). In addition, they have a different intonation from operator questions, and are written with *?!* after them rather than just *?* (See Endo (forthcoming) for rhetorical questions in English, German and Japanese.)

(28) a. *He tried every conceivable way to fix his bike – indeed how DIDN'T he try to fix it?*
(= Is there any possible way he could have used but didn't in order to fix the bike?')
b. A: *What does Chomsky know about syntax?*
B: *What DOESN'T Chomsky know about syntax?!*

(29) *Boy, didn't we have some/*any great times together?!*

In our framework of the cartography of syntactic structures, the fact in (28a) can be captured as follows. Rizzi (2001) subsumes negative islands under relativized minimality (RM), where in the configuration. . .X. . .Z. . .Y. . ., movement of Y to X is blocked by Z in cases where X and Z belong to the same feature class.[9] In (27b), *how* and negative islands belong to the same quantification class and thus movement of *how* over negative islands is blocked by RM. Rizzi (2001) claims that when X carries an extra discourse-related feature, movement from Y to X

---

9 Rizzi (2001) proposes four feature classes: (i) quantificational, (ii) modifier, (iii) argumental, (iv) topic, where the quantificational class includes not only quantifiers but also *wh*-elements like *how* and negative elements.

over Z is not blocked by RM by Y belonging to a feature class distinct from the quantificational class, as illustrated by a sentence such as *how didn't he want to eat the dish; with a fork or with Chinese sticks?* (Starke 2001: 93). In the same way, we can consider the element *how* in (28a) to carry an extra feature to escape negative islands. What is the extra feature here? Based on the fact that this type of non-standard questions are suffixed by the exclamation mark *!*, I suggest that the *wh*-element *how* in this use targets the functional head Exclamation[10] in the CP zone by carrying the extra feature related to exclamation, as opposed to a standard wh-question element like *how* in (27b), which targets the functional head Focus in the CP zone.[11] More research is required to identify the exact nature of this extra feature seen in non-standard questions, including the question of what type of feature class the exclamation-related *wh*-elements in question belong to.

5 *Wanna* contraction

In this section, I will discuss some implications of the idea that Fin[+N] may license the subject position by looking at *wanna* contraction, where the word sequence *want to* may be pronounced *wanna* as in (30a) below, but the form is ungrammatical in (30b). The traditional analysis of *wanna* contraction is seen in Lakoff (1970), who attributes a distinction like (30) to the different properties of empty constituents, that is, PRO in (30a) and the variable t_i in (30b) created by a wh-element. Variables, not PRO, block *wanna* contraction.

(30) a. [Who$_i$ do [you want [PRO to meet who$_i$]]] ? →
 Who do you wanna meet?
 b. [Who$_i$ do [you want [t$_i$ to meet the president]]]? →
 *Who do you wanna meet the president?
 (Getz 2018: 119)

Although the ungrammaticality of the *wanna* contraction in (30b) is detected by many speakers, my survey shows that some speakers accept the *wanna* contrac-

---

10 Rizzi (2014b) posits a criterial head for exclamation, where the exact position of the functional head in the CP zone is not clarified.
11 In the system of Rizzi's RM, we need to assume that wh-elements of non-standard questions and standard questions belongs to different feature classes. More research is required on this point. See also Rizi (1990) for RM.

tion in (30b). It is interesting to notice that those speakers who accept *wanna* contraction such as (30b) also accept the *that*-trace sentence that we saw in (20) even in the absence of an intervening adjunct. For instance, Andrew Radford (personal communication) reported to me that he accepts *that*-trace sentences like (31) in very rapid colloquial English, and also accept *wanna* contraction sentence in (30b) as well.

(31) *This is the man who I think that ___ will sell his house.*

How can we capture the correlation of the absence of *that*-trace effect and their acceptance of *wanna* contraction in (30b) by minority speakers? I suggest that the same mechanism that licenses the subject position in *that*-trace sentence in (20) above might be operative in minority speakers' judgement of *wanna* contraction sentences. That is, those minority speakers who allow for *that*-trace sentences in the absence of an intervening adjunct may utilize Fin[+N] even in the absence of an intervening adjunct, which is only available for majority speakers in the presence of an intervening adjunct, as shown below:

(32) . . .[FINP [FIN[+N] φ] [DP [D-SUBJ ∅]. . .who. . .]]]]

Because those minority speakers may license the subject position freely by utilizing Fin[+N], the subject position that follows the verb *want* can be licensed by Fin[+N] without the wh-subject moving in Spec, SubjP. That is, it is not necessary for a wh-subject element base-generated within vP to move into the subject position to satisfy the Subject Criterion, where a *wh*-element may move directly into the CP zone without passing through the subject position, as shown in (33). Here, *want* and *to* are not intermediated by a variable and thus may undergo *wanna* contraction.[12]

(33) . . .want. . .[FINP [FIN[+N] φ] [DP [D-SUBJ ∅] [TP [T to] . . . [vP who. . .]]]]]]

---

[12] Marcel den Dikken (personal communication) pointed out to me that the absence of *that*-trace effect in (31) might be related to the absence of *that*-trace effect in German and Italian. In fact, some of the minority speakers who allow for *that*-trace sentences in the absence of an intervening adjunct and *wanna* contraction in (30b) are quite familiar with German and/or Italian. Thus, it seems that the English grammar by minority speakers have undergone transformation due to immediate or mediated contact with other languages. This is in line with Lightfoot's (2018) idea that syntactic changes of I-language are linked to language acquisition, which are externally driven (E-language).

As a reviewer correctly points out, our approach wrongly predicts that this type of minority speakers would accept a sentence like *John wanna Mary to go*, where Fin[+N] satisfies the subject criterion and thus the referential element *Mary* stays in vP without moving into Spec, SubjP to intervene between *want* and *to*. How would this case be dealt with by our approach? Although I have no clear answer to this important question, my conjecture is as follows: Rizzi (2014b) notes that the subject criterion is endowed with special discourse properties (quasi-topicality, and the like) (Chomsky 2002), and external systems require events to be expressed in subject-predicate format (Rothstein 1983). Thus, some kind of predication is involved in subject criterion, where the subject serves as the starting point of the event description. For instance, in a sentence like *a truck has bumped into a bus in Rome*, a truck serves as the starting point of the car-crash event. With this property of the subject criterion in mind, I suggest that when satisfying the subject criterion, if there are two options, a referential expression and Fin[+N], the minority speakers in question would prefer a referential expression to Fin[+N] because a referential element seems to be more felicitous to serve as a starting point of event description than a non-referential element like Fin[+N]. As a result, a referential expression like *Mary* always intervenes between *want* and *to* by moving into Spec, SubjP from vP. At this point, one may naturally wonder whether the same story holds for the absence of *that*-trace effect in (31) for the minority speakers, where the wh-element *who* does not move into Spec, SubjP. The answer seems to be in the affirmative for the following reason: When satisfying the subject criterion in (31), the minority speakers in question seem to have two options equally, a quantificational wh-element and Fin[+N], because neither qualifies as a referential element. In this sense, both a wh-element and Fin[+N] would be equally suitable for satisfying the subject criterion. Thus, when Fin[+N] meets the subject criterion, a wh-element need not go into Spec, SubjP and may go directly into the CP zone without incurring *that*-trace effect.[13] More research is required in this area.

In the field of language acquisition, Crain & Thornton (1998) claim that the constraint against a variable in *wanna* contraction is also observed in child English, i.e. children do not allow for *wanna* contraction in the sentence in (30b). However, Getz (2019) conducts an experiment on *wanna* contraction with children from 3;09 to 7;03 by carefully controlling various factors revolving

---

13 Needless to say, when Fin[+N] does not satisfy the subject criterion, a *wh*-element moves into Spec, SubjP to give riser to *that*-trace effect. In this respect, Fin[+N] can satisfy the subject criterion as much as *wh*-elements.

around *wanna* contraction sentences that are dismissed in Crain & Thornton, showing that many children use *wanna* contraction sentences like (30b).[14] To be more precise, children use *wanna* contraction sentences like (30b) nearly half the time (47%)—far more than adults (2%).[15] At this point, it is not clear to me whether children and some adult speakers who allow for *wanna* contraction in sentence like (30b) use the same mechanism. More research is required in this area.

6 Summary

To summarize, I have discussed the nature of a null subject in the framework of the cartography of syntactic structures by looking at *how come* questions in diary English. We have seen that *how come* questions can exhibit subject drop in diary-style English. After examining a phase-theoretic approach to the null subject, I have examined an alternative approach to license a null subject by Fin[+N]. An implication of our Fin-based approach has also been discussed by looking at *wanna* contraction, where it is suggested that some minority speakers might use Fin[+N] to license the subject position.[16]

---

[14] I am grateful to David Lightfoot for drawing my attention to Getz (2019).

[15] Our idea that both a wh-element and Fin[+N] would be equally suitable for satisfying the subject criterion fits into Getz's observation that children produce *wanna* contraction and non-*wanna* contraction utterances for a sentence like (30b) in equal proportions.

[16] Part of this paper was presented at Societas Linguistica Europea (SLE) held at University of Zurich in August, 2017 and the third International Workshop of Syntactic Cartography, held at Beijing Language and Culture University in October, 2017. I would like to thank Adriana Belletti, Guglielmo Cinque, Marcel den Dikken, David Lightfoot, Rachael Nye, Ur Shlonsky and Luigi Rizzi for numerous helpful suggestions relating to the form and contents of the paper. Special thanks go to Andrew Radford for fruitful and invaluable comments, tireless discussions and stylistic suggestions on the topic in the present paper. I am also grateful to Timothy Williams for proofreading an earlier version of this paper. This work is supported by Grant-in-Aid for Research (C: 16K02639) and (A: 19H00532).

Appendix

In the main text, we have seen some syntactic properties of *how come* questions with special attention to the null subject. There are some interesting semantic properties of *how come* questions as well. To see my point, consider the following sentence noted by Tsai (2008):

(1) *How come the sky is blue?*

(Tsai 2008: 89)

Attributing the observation to Andrew Simpson (personal communication), Tsai (2008: 89) mentions the expressive meaning of *how come* questions and *why*: *why* involves no special expectation about whether or not some state of affairs should hold, whereas *how come* expresses surprise that a particular state of affairs should hold, as in (1). However, Andrew Radford (personal communication) notes that it is not the case that *how come* always expresses surprise that a particular state of affairs should hold. For instance, there is no surprise in what B says in (2), just curiosity and *how come* sounds less invasive than *why* in this context.

(2) A: *I've gotta go to the doctor this afternoon.*
    B: *How come?*
    A: *Oh, the cut on my finger has got infected.*

Where does this difference come from? To answer this question, it would be helpful to consider the following sentences from Schultz (2015):[17]

(3) a. L: *How come you never send me flowers?*
       S: *Because I don't like you.*
    b. L: *Doo-site   watasi-ni   itido.mo   hana-o*
          how.come   me-to   never   flower-ACC
          okutte   kurenai   no?
          send   benefit   Q
       S: *Kimi-ga   kirai   dakara*[18]
          you-NOM   dislike   because

(Schultz 2015: 24–25)

---

[17] I am grateful to Sony Creative Products for allowing me to use the comic pictures of *Peanuts*.
[18] Here, the direct object *watasi* 'me' is suffixed by the nominative Case particle *ga*. This is because stative predicates in Japanese requires the nominative Case particle *ga* for the direct object.

How come questions and diary English — 265

Figure 4: Conversation in which *how come* is used in a standard question.
©Sony Creative Products

(4) a. S: *How come you never bring me milkshake?*
L: *When he is through, you can lick the straw.*
b. S: *Doosite   boku-ni   milkshake-o*
       how.come   me-to   milkshake-Acc
       mottekitekure   nai   no   sa.
       bring.benefit   NEG   FIN   SFP

(Schultz 2015:124–125)

In (3), Lucy uses a *how come* question to Linus and receives a response with the sentence prefixed by *because*. Here, the corresponding Japanese *how come* question sounds like a standard question suffixed by *no* sentence final particle (SFP), where a mild curiosity by Lucy is felt. In contrast, in (4), although Linus uses a *how come* question to Lucy, he does not receive a response prefixed by *because*, but only a comment from her. The corresponding Japanese *how come* question sounds like a non-standard question or a rhetorical question with strong irritation felt by the speaker, where the sentence is suffixed by the SFP *sa*. Note that Linus's face and gesture show his strong emotion in (4), more than Lucy's face in (3). Based on the fact that the difference between the expressive meaning of curiosity and surprise in *how come* questions is marked by the SFP *sa* in Japanese, I suggest that the two meanings of *how come* questions in English arise through activating or non-activating covert functional head occupied by the SFP *sa* in Japanese: where the functional head occupied by the SFP *sa* in Japanese is responsible for the expressive meaning of surprise. When this functional head is activated in English, the expressive meaning of surprise appears; when this func-

266 — Yoshio Endo

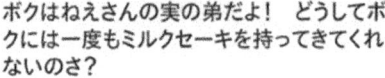

Figure 5: Conversation in which *how come* is used in a non-standard question.
©Sony Creative Products

tional head is not activated in English, *how come* questions express a mild curiosity. What is the SFP *sa*, then? The SFP *sa* is used to report the speaker's familiarity with the proposition, implying that the sentence suffixed by this SFP should be taken as a matter of course. According to Uyeno (1971), the meaning of the particle *sa* is contrasted with the meaning of the particles *yoo* 'appear,' *rasii* 'seem,' and *soo* 'hear,' which are used when the speaker's judgment is made based on appearance. The SFP *sa*, in contrast, is used when the speaker's judgment is made based on his own supposition or inner feeling. Because the speaker's judgment is already made in uttering the SFP *sa*, the speaker's supposition is taken to be discourse-familiar, and thus, we cannot start a discourse with a sentence with the SFP *sa*, as illustrated by the following contrast. (See also Hasunuma (2015) on this point.)

(5) a. *Kore nani?* / *??Kore nani sa?*
    this what   this what SFP
    'What is this?'
 b. **Doo suru sa?*
    how do SFP
    'How are you going to do?'

Based on this fact, I suggest that the SFP *sa* is related to old information or discourse-familiarity. Based on work by Fitzpatric (2005), Radford (2018) emphasizes that *how come* questions are factive in nature and proposes that the complementizer *that* following *how come* in English is FactP. Although more study is required, I suggest that the SFP *sa* might be an overt realization of Radford's FactP.[19] See Endo (forthcoming) for a discussion of expressive meanings seen in non-standard questions revolving around *how come*.

References

Chomsky, Noam. 2001. Derivation by phase. In Michael Kenstowicz (ed.), *Ken Hale: A life in language*, 1–52. Cambridge, MA: MIT Press.
Chomsky, Noam. 2002. *On nature and language*. Cambridge, Cambridge University Press. DOI: https://doiorg/10.1177/003368820303400108.
Cinque, Guglielmo. 1999. Adverbs and *functional heads: A cross-linguistic perspective*. Oxford & New York: Oxford University Press.
Collins, Chris. 1991. Why and how come. *MIT Working Papers in Linguistics* 15. 31–45.
Crain, Stephan & Rosalind Thornton. 1998. Investigations in Universal Grammar: A guide to experiments on the acquisition of syntax and semantics. Cambridge, MA: The MIT Press. DOI: https://doi.org/10.1917/S0022226701238651.
Culicover, Peter W. 1993. Evidence against ECP accounts of the that-t effect. *Linguistic Inquiry* 24. 557–561.
Endo, Yoshio. 2007. *Locality and information structure*. Amsterdam & Philadelphia: John Benjamins. DOI: https://doi.org/10.1075/la.116.
Endo, Yoshio. 2015. Two ReasonPs. In Ur Shlonsky (ed.), *Beyond functional sequence*, 220–231. New York: Oxford University Press. DOI: https://doi.org/10.1093/acprof: oso/9780190210588.003.0012.

---

[19] An important point to notice is the fact that *how come* questions are almost always translated into Japanese sentences suffixed by the element *no*. Makihara (1995) observes that the element *no* always appears in asking for reasons in Japanese when there is a wide difference felt between the speaker's supposition and the real situation that (s)he faces. Thus, the element *no* appears in a sentence like *Kimiha doosite sonna abunai tokoro-ni itta **no***? 'why did you go to such a dangerous place?' in Japanese because there is a wide difference felt between the speaker's supposition that the addressee would not go to a dangerous place and the real situation that the addressee went to a dangerous place. In contrast, in a sentence like *Anata-wa doosite wagasha-o siboosimasitaka*? 'Why did you apply for our position?' the element **no** does not appear, especially in a job interview. (In fact, when we use the element *no* in such a situation, the sentence sounds odd, in *anata-wa doosite wagasya-o siboosimasita **no** desuka*? (This sentence sounds as if the interviewer is implicitly saying that (s)he cannot come up with any reasonable answer to the question.) This is because there is no wide difference felt between the speaker's supposition that the addressee is interested in the position and the real circumstance that the addressee is applying for the position in a typical job interview situation.

Endo, Yoshio. 2018. Variation in wh-expressions asking for a reason, *Linguistic Variation*. [Special Issues on complementizers: Lexical vs. functional variation] 18(2). 299–314. DOI: https://doi.org/10.1075/lv.00024.end.

Endo, Yoshio. 2020. Information structure, null Case particle and sentence final discourse Particle. In Pierre-Yves Modicom & Olivier Duplatre (eds.), *Information structural perspectives on discourse particles,* 223–250. Amsterdam & Philadelphia: John Benjamins. DOI: https://doi.org/10.1075/slcs.213.09end.

Endo, Yoshio. Forthcoming. Non-standard questions in English, German and Japanese. To appear in *Linguistic Vanguard* [Special issue on non-canonical Questions from a comparative perspective].

Endo, Yoshio & Lilian Haegeman, 2019. Adverbial clauses and adverbial concord. Glossa 4(1). 48. 1–32. [Special issues on the internal and external syntax of adverbial clauses: Theoretical implications and consequences]. DOI: http://doi.org/10.5334/gigl.589.

Fitzpatrick, Justin. 2005. The whys and how comes of presupposition and NPI licensing in questions. *Proceedings of the 24th West Coast Conference on Formal Linguistics*, 138–145. Somerville, MA: Cascadilla Press.

Getz, Heidi R. 2019. Acquiring *wanna*: Beyond Universal Grammar, *Language Acquisition*, 26:2. 119–143. DOI: https://doi.org/10.1080/10489223.2018.1470242.

Haegeman, Liliane. 1990. Understood subjects in English diaries: On the relevance of theoretical syntax for the study of register variation. *Multilingua* 9. 157–199.

Haegeman, Liliane. 2017. *Unspeakable Sentences*: Subject Omission in Written Registers: A Cartographic Analysis. Linguistic Variation, 17(2). 229–250. DOI. https://doi.org/10.1075/lv00001.mas.

Hasunuma, Akiko. 2015. Syuuzyosi sa no honsituteki kinoo [Main functions of the sentence final particle sa]. *Nihongo nihonbungaku* 25. 1–27.

Lakoff, George. 1970. Global rules. *Language* 46(3). 627–639. DOI: https://doi.org/10.2307/412310.

Lightfoot, David. 2018. Nothing in syntax makes sense except in the light of change. In Angel J. Gallego & Roger Martin (eds.), *Language, syntax, and the natural sciences,* 224–240. Cambridge: Cambridge University Press. DOI: https://doi.org/10/1017/97812316591529.013.

Makihara, Isao. 1995. Gimonhyoogen niokeru *no* no itisokumen [An aspect of *no* in interrogative sentences]. *Nihongo to Nihonbungaku* 21. 22–30.

Nanyan, Varduhi. 2013. *Subject omission in English diaries*. Doctoral dissertation, Ghent University. https://lib.ugent.be/fulltxt/RUG01/002/060/282/RUG01-002060282_2013_0001_AC.pdf

Radford, Andrew. 2018. *Colloquial English*. Cambridge: Cambridge University Press. DOI: https://doi.org/ 10.1917/9781108552202.

Rizzi, Luigi. 1990. *Relativized minimality*. Cambridge, MA: MIT Press.

Rizzi, Luigi. 1997. The fine structure of the left periphery. In Liliane Haegeman *Elements of grammar: Handbook of generative syntax,* 281–337. Kluwer, Dordrecht. DOI: https://doi.org/10.1007/978-94-011-5420-8_7.

Rizzi, Luigi. 2001. On the Position "Int(errogative)" in the Left Periphery of the Clause. In Guglielmo Cinque and Giampaolo Salvi (eds.), *Current studies in Italian syntax: Essays offered to Lorenzo Renzi,* 267–296. Amsterdam: Elsevier.

Rizzi, Luigi. 2004. Locality and left periphery. In Adriana Belletti (ed.) *Structures and beyond,* 104–131. New York: Oxford University Press.

Rizzi, Luigi. 2014a. Some consequences of Criterial Freezing: Asymmetries, anti-adjacency and extraction from cleft sentences. In Peter Svenonius (ed.), *Functional structure from top to toe*, 19–54. New York: Oxford University Press.
Rizzi, Luigi. 2014b. The cartography of syntactic structures: Locality and freezing effects on movement. In Anna Cardinaletti, Guglielmo Cinque & Yoshio Endo (eds.), *On peripheries: Exploring clause initial and clause final positions*, 29–60. Tokyo: Hituzi Syobo Publishing.
Rizzi, Luigi. & Ur Shlonsky. 2007. Strategies of subject extraction. In Hans-Martin Gartner & Uli Sauerland (eds.), *Interfaces + recursion = language? Chomsky's minimalism and the view from syntax-semantics*, 115–160. Berlin: Mouton de Gruyter.
Rothstein, Susan. 1983. The syntactic forms of predication. Cambridge, MA: MIT dissertation.
Shlonsky, Ur & Gabriela Soare. 2011. Where's 'why'? *Linguistic Inquiry* 42(4). 651–669. DOI: https://doi.org/10.1162/LING_a_00064.
Schultz, Charles. 2015. *Snoopy comic selection 1970's*. [E-book version of Kobo], translated by Shuntaro Tanigawa. Tokyo: Kadokawa.
Starke, Michael (2001) *Move dissolves into Merge: A theory of locality*. Genève: Université de Genève dissertation.
Tsai, Wei-Tien Dylan. 2008. Left periphery and *how-why* alternations. *Journal of East Asian Linguistics* 17(2). 83–115. DOI: DOI: https://doi.org/10.1007/s10831-008-902-0.
Uyeno, Tazuko. 1971. A study of Japanese modality: A performance analysis of sentence particles. Ann Arbor: University of Michigan dissertation.
Zwicky, Arnold M. & Ann D. Zwicky. 1971. How come and what for. In Dale E. Elliott, Michael L. Geis, Alexander Grosu, Barry Nobel, Ann D. Zwicky & Arnold M. Zwicky (eds.), *Working Papers in Linguistics* 8, 173–185. Ohio State University.

Part 5: **A special class of *why* rhetorical questions: Semantics and pragmatics**

Lavi Wolf and Edit Doron
Why rhetorical questions?

1 Introduction

The present work offers a window to understanding the nature of Rhetorical Questions (henceforth RQs) via the analysis of a particular type of RQ, the so-called *Doubly Marked Interrogative*, henceforth DMI. Rhetorical questions (RQ) are not easy to characterize. On the one hand, they have an assertion-like conversational force, as manifested by e.g. their falling intonation (unlike the rising intonation of Ordinary Questions (OQ)) and by their tendency not to require an answer:

(1) a. I know that John is at home. (After all,) Where else can he be? (RQ, no answer required, falling intonation ↓)
 b. I see that John is not at home. (So,) Where else can he be? (OQ, an answer required, rising intonation ↑)

On the other hand, they do retain standard properties of questions, e.g. the syntactic form and the *option* for an answer, unlike standard assertions:

(2) a. SPEAKER: You should stop saying that Luca didn't like the party last night. After all, who was the only one still dancing at 3am?
 ADDRESSEE: Luca. (RQ, answer optional)
 b. SPEAKER: You should stop saying that Luca didn't like the party last night. After all, Luca was the only one still dancing at 3am!
 ADDRESSEE: #Luca. (assertion, answer infelicitous)
(Caponigro & Sprouse 2007)

DMIs may help shed light on several properties of RQs (as well as other nonstandard questions), since they have properties which set them apart from simple RQs, while at the same time retaining all the classical RQ properties. First introduced in Khalaily and Doron (2015) in a descriptive paper reporting examples in Palestinian Arabic (PA), colloquial Modern Hebrew (MH) and other Semitic languages (various dialects of Arabic and Aramaic), we further the discussion on DMIs to show that they involve several non-standard uses of ques-

---

Acknowledgment: This paper is dedicated to Edit Doron, who was always an inspiration, a true mentor, a wonderful colleague to work with and an amazing person to spend time with.

https://doi.org/10.1515/9783110675160-010

tions, combined in a manner which helps draw insights on all RQs, e.g. the distinction between *obvious* and *challenging* RQ types and on the rarely discussed *metalinguistic* aspect of some constituent questions, targeting a previously performed speech act.

The paper is structured are as follows: section 2 introduces the DMI use and structure. Section 3 discusses the unique DMI speech-act properties which are divided into a metalinguistic effect (subsection 3.1), and a rhetorical effect (subsection 3.2) which is further divided into *obvious* (subsection 3.2.1) and *challenging* (subsection 3.2.2) RQ types. Section 4 combines all the DMI properties and provides an account of the DMI combined effect, and section 5 concludes the paper.

2 DMI – use and structure

The following is a basic example of a DMI, much in use in colloquial MH:

(3) lama mi ata
    why who (are) you

This utterance, ostensibly inquiring about the identity of the addressee, is conversationally used as a rejection move. For example, when one conversation participant utters an imperative to another conversation participant, an utterance of of (3) has the effect of rejecting this imperative:

(4) A: Clean the room!
    B: lama mi ata?
       why who (are) you
       'Who are you (to tell me what to do)'

In the above examples, as in all DMI examples, the structure consists of a *wh*-phrase, typically *why*, which embeds a second question Q, where Q can be either a constituent question or a polar question:

(5) [why Q]

The *why*-phrase together with Q forms an amalgamated question. This question, which constitutes the DMI, though introduced by two *wh*-phrases, forms a single interrogative clause which importantly has a continuous falling intonation.[1] This is very different from the intonation contour of a corresponding sequence of two separate interrogative clauses in the following manner:

(6) lama mi ata ↓
    why who (are) you
    'Who are you (to tell me what to do)'

(7) lama?↑ mi ata?↑
    why who (are) you
    'Why? Who are you?'

As will be shown below, the difference between DMIs and a series of two consecutive but separate questions goes deeper than prosodic structure. Another observation we wish to make is that the DMI construction is not a species of multiple non-separate questions as the following:

(8) Who arrived when?

There are several reasons for that. First – *why* does not occur in MH multiple questions (similarly to English). Compare the following two examples:

(9) a. *lama higiaʕ matai?
       why arrived when
       '*Why did when arrive?'
    b. *mi higiaʕ lama?
       who arrived why
       '*Who arrived why?'

(10) a. mi higiaʕ matai?
        who arrived when
        'Who arrived when?'
     b. mi higiaʕ eich?
        who arrived how
        'Who arrived how?'

---

[1] This type of intonation is the hallmark of rhetorical questions (inter alia Sadock 1971; 1974; Han 2002; Progovac 1993).

Second, even if it were possible to have *why* multiple questions, MH does not allow sentence-initial stacked wh-phrases, which is what a DMI requires:

(11) a. *mi matai higiaʕ?
       who when arrived
    b. mi higiaʕ matai?
       who arrived when

Third, phonologically multiple questions consist of the same rising intonational contour that occurs in OQ, while DMIs have a continuous falling intonation.

The DMI construction is highly productive, with many attested examples. The following are taken from Khalaily & Doron (2015). The first, in PA (Palestinian Arabic), is an instance of a mother's reaction to one of her children complaining:

(12) **le:š šu:** sa:yer ʕal-e:k?
     why what is.happening on-you
     'What is happening to you? (And why complain?)'

The DMI in the above example serves to convey to the complaining child that they should not complain because nothing of significance, that merits complaining, has happened to them.

The next example in MH, is from the writer Sayed Kashua's weekly column in the Israeli Haaretz daily newspaper:

(13) **lama matay** hu yadaʕ le-henot me-ha-haclaha ze
     why when he knew to-enjoy fFrom-the-success this.one
     'When did this one know how to enjoy success? (And why expect he would this time?)' (*Haaretz* 5.9.2014)

Kashua is a bilingual speaker of PA and MH. In this example he is reporting the (fictional) words of his mother, a speaker of PA, to his father. The DMI serves to convey to Kashua's father that a presupposition inherent in a previous speech act, namely that Kashua would enjoy his success on the occasion at hand, should be rejected because Kashua never knew how to enjoy success.

The next example, also in Khalaily & Doron (2015), concerns a classroom scenario in which two schoolchildren are having an SMS dialogue. The first asks 'So where are you?', the other responds 'In class'. The first asks 'You are corresponding on the phone while in class?!', with a shocked emoji. To which the other responds with the following DMI:

(14)   **lama ʕeyfo** ʕat?
        why   where   you.FSG
        'Where are you?' (and why assume that your location is more appropriate for phone corresponding than mine?)

As discussed in Khalaily and Doron (2015), the DMI in this example serves to convey to the first that a presupposition inherent in her previous message, namely that she is entitled to express a negative judgment toward the second, should be rejected because she herself is doing exact the same thing he does.

To summarize the DMI properties:

(15)   a. DMIs consist of a *why*-question which embeds an *additional* question Q: [Why Q].
        b. The DMI is a single intonational phrase.
        c. The DMI is not a multiple question.
        d. The DMI is marked by the falling intonation characteristic of rhetorical questions.
        e. Pragmatically, the DMI serves to reject a previous speech-act.

The last property, the conversational end result of the DMI, is discussed at length in the following sections.

3 DMI – speech act properties

DMIs have a common conversational use of rejecting a previous Speech Act (henceforth SA). In this section we discuss the mechanism by which this is done. In order to reject a previous SA, an utterance first needs to refer to this SA. This is the *metalinguistic effect* of DMIs, to be discussed ahead. The *rejection effect*, which is achieved by a combination of pragmatic and semantic factors, is discussed in subsections 3.2. and 4.

3.1 Metalinguistic effect

Metalinguistic operators are ones that do not apply to propositional contents but rather to any facet of the utterance, such as the particular choice of linguistic expressions, their particular sequential order, their implicatures, presuppositions, etc. (cf. Horn 1989). The following is an example of *metalinguistic negation*:

(16) I didn't **read the paper and get up**, I got up and read the paper!

(17) A: Are you happy?
B: I'm not **happy**, I'm **ecstatic**!

(18) A: Max bought two cars.
B: Max didn't buy **two** cars, he bought **seven** cars!

(19) A: John managed to solve the problem.
B: John didn't **manage** to solve the problem – it was quite easy for him to solve!

Another metalinguistic operator[2] is the *metalinguistic comparative* (Rosta & McCawley 2000):

(20) This cat is more stupid than malicious

Since both properties are not on the same scale, the above cannot mean:

(21) This cat's stupidity exceeds its malice

Thus, the intended meaning is metalinguistic, i.e. *stupid* is a more apt description than *malicious*.

Similarly, *metalinguistic questions* are questions which do not apply to propositional contents but rather to any other aspect of the utterance. In this case, these questions refer to the whole SA rather than its content (cf. Ginzburg 2009 for a discussion of metalinguistic questions). The next examples show how metalinguistic questions can be distinguished from ordinary non-metalinguistic questions:

(22) A: John brought something to work today.
B: *What* (did John bring/ did you say)?[3]

(23) A: John came to work today.
B: *What* (#did John come to work/ did you say)?

---

[2] See Horn (1989) for a discussion of several other metalinguistic operators.
[3] Note that there is a clear difference in intonation between ordinary and metalinguistic questions, not further discussed in this paper.

(24) A: John stayed at home today.
B: *Why* (did John stay at home/ did you say it)?

(25) A: John stayed at home today.
B: I know, he is sick. *Why* (#did John stay at home/ did you say it)?

When questions are replied to with questions, the metalinguistic effect becomes even more prominent:

(26) A: Is John in the office?
B: Why (#is John in the office/ did you ask)?

(27) A: Did John bring something to work today?
B: What (#did John bring. . ./ did you ask)?

This effect arises because the questions uttered by B cannot target a propositional content of the previous SA, because unlike assertion, a question's content is not a proposition.

Metalinguistic questions are constrained in various ways. For example, it seems that polar questions cannot be used metalinguistically, at least not simple polar questions.[4] This is because a metalinguistic use of a polar question would be the query whether the first speaker uttered the previous speech act or not:

(28) A: John stayed at home today.

(29) B: Yeah/Indeed/Really? (= did John stay at home/ #did you say that John stayed at home)

Moreover, it seems most constituent questions, with the exception of *why*, and *what* are not suitable as metalinguistic ones:

(30) A: Is John in the office?
B1: Why (did you ask)?
B2: What (did you ask)?

---

4 While metalinguistic polar questions are not felicitous by themselves, they can be performed in combination with non-standard effects, e.g. incredulity:

A: John is so fat.
B: Really (= did you really just say that)?? He is standing right here!

B3: When (#did you ask)?
B4: Where (#did you ask)?
B5: Who (#is asking)?
B6: How (#did you ask)?

We propose that the embedding question in DMIs has a metalinguistic component as it targets the previous speech act. And, unsurprisingly, *why* and *what* are the only constituent questions that serve as embedding DMI questions. While we only deal with *why* DMIs in this paper, the question of the relation between *why* and *what* DMIs is quite intriguing and holds potential for further investigation into the DMI construction as well as metalinguistic questions and their relation with RQs. Coincidentally, Wei-Tien Dylan Tsai and Lisa-Lai Cheng's contributions to this volume analyze questions which on the one hand are *what*-based but on the other hand manifest *why* properties in Mandarin, Cantonese and Taiwanese, (Tsai, this volume; Cheng, this volume), adding to the interest in pursuing this direction further. This direction, especially one which explores the syntactic aspect involving the position of *why* (see also Shlonsky and Soare 2011; Soare 2009) will undoubtedly shed more light on the roles of *why* and *what* in general, and on DMIs in particular.

We represent metalinguistic *why* in the following manner, adopting Karttunen's (1977) traditional question semantics for concreteness:

(31) Standard *why*:
[[Why S]] =
$\lambda p. \exists x[p= x \text{ is reason/justification for } [[S]]] \& p(w_0)$

(32) Metalinguistic *why*:
$SA_A S$ describes a previous speech act SA performed by addressee *A uttering S*
[[Why $SA_A S$]] =
$\lambda p. \exists x[p= x \text{ is reason/justification for } [[SA_A S]]] \& p(w_0)$

In prose, metalinguistic *why* is very similar to ordinary *why* in its denotation, the only difference being that metalinguistic *why*'s denotation is that there is an *x*, which is an answer resolving the *why* question, which constitutes the reason or justification for performing the previous speech-act *S* by the previous conversation participant, while ordinary *why*'s denotation is that there is an *x*, which is an answer resolving the *why* question, which constitutes the reason or justification for *S*.

After having discussed the metalinguistic aspect of the DMI embedding question, we now turn to discuss the rhetorical aspect of the DMI embedded question.

It is important to state again at this point, that the DMI construction itself as a whole is a Rhetorical Question. The following subsection continues our decomposition of the DMI into an embedding metalinguistic question and an embedded RQ, and the subsequent section will show how these two parts combine to create a conventional device with a metalinguistic rejecting RQ effect.

3.2 Rhetorical effect

3.2.1 Obvious RQ

RQs differ from Ordinary Questions (OQs) in various features. Two prominent ones are that:
A. RQ do not require an answer from the addressee.
B. RQ convey a strong bias the speaker has toward a certain answer, typically (but not always) a negative bias.

The second feature has been heavily investigated in the literature. So much so that many have claimed that RQ are not questions at all but rather negative *assertions* (inter alia Han 2002; Progovac 1993; Sadock 1971; Sadock 1974).

Many have traced the source of this negative bias to the relation between RQ and *Strong Negative Polarity Items* (SNPIs) (inter alia Krifka 1995; van Rooij 2003; Guerzoni 2004) e.g. *give a damn, lift a finger*. Indeed, questions containing SNPIs give rise to a rhetorical effect involving a strong negative bias, resembling a negative assertion:

(33) a. Did John help Sue? (= yes / no)

(34) b. Did John lift a finger to help Sue? (= no)

(35) a. Who has shown affection to John? (= the identity of the individual who has shown affection to John)

(36) b. Who gives a damn about John? (= no individual)

These accounts, however, miss certain components of RQ, as discussed in Caponigro & Sprouse (2007). The first of which is that while RQs do not require an answer, they do *allow* answers to be supplies, unlike assertions, as seen in (2), repeated here:

(37) a. SPEAKER: You should stop saying that Luca didn't like the party last night. After all, who was the only one that was still dancing at 3am?
ADDRESSEE: Luca. (RQ, answer optional)
b. SPEAKER: You should stop saying that Luca didn't like the party last night. After all, Luca was the only one that was still dancing at 3am!
ADDRESSEE: #Luca. (assertion, answer infelicitous)

Secondly, it is possible to have a RQ with no SNPIs or any negative bias:

(38) SPEAKER: Of course you should trust Mina. Think about it – was she or wasn't she there for you when you needed her?

(39) ADDRESSEE: She was.
(Caponigro and Sprouse 2007)

Caponigro & Sprouse's conclusion is that RQs are semantically of the same type as OQ. The rhetorical effect is derived pragmatically, via the mutual context, the *Common Ground* (Stalnaker 1978). The Common Ground (CG) is a set of propositions that conversational participants agree upon, i.e. believed by all. Caponigro & Sprouse propose the following condition for a question to be rhetorical:

(40) Q is a RQ iff $[|Q|]^w \in CG_{S\text{-}A}$

In prose, a question Q is a Rhetorical Question RQ iff the denotation of Q in a world w is part of the Common Ground CG, which is mutual to both the speaker s and addressee a. Importantly, Caponigro & Sprouse's denotation of a question, following (Groenendijk & Stokhof 1990), is its true complete answer in a world. This means that any rhetorical question has a true complete answer i.e. a proposition, which is a member of the set of propositions that compose the Common Ground (CG).

One problem of this account is *informativity*. In order for a conversational effect to be informative, items that are added to the CG are required to not exist there beforehand. This constraint, intuitively, prevents redundancy, and is an important principle of rational communication. Stalnaker (1978) lists it as one of the three main principles underlying proper linguistic usage:

(41) A proposition asserted is always true in some but not all of the possible worlds in the context set.

Since the context set is the set of worlds created by intersecting all the propositions in the CG, if a proposition is true in all of the possible worlds in the context set, it is already known to all conversation participants, hence not informative. The same principle is at play in questions, as a question whose answer is already known is clearly infelicitous:

(42) A: Jane is in the office
B: #Where is Jane?

The only way for B's question to be felicitous in the case above would be if B forgot that this information has already been provided. But this, of course, means that the proposition which serves as the answer is no longer part of the CG.

It does not make any conversational sense to ask a question whose answer is already known to all conversation participants just as it does not make conversational sense to utter an assertion whose content is already agreed upon by all conversation participants. It seems, then, that Caponigro & Sprouse's definition of RQs fails *informativity*.

Another more serious problem for Caponigro & Sprouse relates to (40) in its entire, i.e. that the answer to the RQ is a member of CG, importantly the *mutual* set of speaker and addressee's beliefs. While the examples in Caponigro & Sprouse's paper adhere to this condition, some RQs , as the following, do not refer to such mutual beliefs but rather convey a bias of just *one* conversation participant:

(43) Context: Sue is fixing the car and Joe watches. Both Sue and Joe share the belief that Sue knows how to fix the car, but both do not share the belief that Joe knows how to fix the car as well.

Joe: Let me help you fix the car.
Sue: What the hell do you know about fixing cars?!

Note that there is no need for an SNPI to convey Sue's bias in this RQ and that the RQ is completely felicitous in this context. This would be puzzling if indeed the answer to the RQ is a member of the CG, because that would require the CG to contain the proposition that Joe does not know anything about fixing cars. While this proposition might be true *for Sue,* it is clearly not true in the given context as far as Joe is concerned.

To conclude this section, we find Caponigro & Sprouse's account to be very much on the right track and adopt the view that most RQs are semantically of the same type as OQs. However, not all RQs are derived pragmatically. We propose a distinction between two types of RQs, one of which has an *obvious* answer and is derived in the same manner proposed in Caponigro & Sprouse and discussed here. The other type, a *challenging* RQ, is discussed in the next section.

3.2.2 Challenging RQ

We propose a second type of RQs, termed *challenging* following Krifka (1995), termed so because in these RQs, speech act performers are (or present themselves as being) very certain that there can be no positive answer (or no answer at all) and thus pose a challenge to the addressee to supply even one congruent answer, as in the following:

(44) Who (the hell) likes John?!

Semantically, the above question is represented in the same manner as ordinary constituent questions:

(45) [[Who likes John]] = $\lambda p.\ \exists x[p=$ x is a person that likes John & $p(w_0)]$

The semantics dictates that a congruent answer to this question would be any answer that supplies a name of person who likes John, i.e. it would be enough that there exists one such person. An incongruent answer, therefore, in which the addressee does not know even one such person or stronger yet that the addressee does know that there is no such person, is therefore much less likely than a congruent one. We will return to this element shortly.

The second element that differentiates challenging RQ from ordinary ones lies in the information structure, specifically a certain kind of stress – *emphatic* – which marks a speaker's bias. Note the difference between (44) and the following, with the same question:

(46) Context: John is a candidate for a part in a play. A committee that reviews all candidates, votes on each one separately. The following is a call for a vote regarding John:

Sue: OK, so with a raise of hands – who likes John?

The above example does not indicate a speaker bias. There is also an apparent difference in intonation, marked in (44) as an exclamation mark following the question mark, which does not manifest in 44. In order to see how this difference in intonation indicates a speaker bias, we turn to similar cases involving *emphatic stress* in assertions, discussed in Krifka (1995). One such case is the following:

(47) John would distrust ALBERT SCHWEITZER!

The effect of this type of stress, marked in all-caps, is that Albert Schweitzer is *the least likely* person to be distrusted. Krifka (1995) proposes the following *emphatic principle* (simplified) for this type of stress, applied to assertions:

(48) Emphatic Assertion(p): for all p' A(p) :p<$_c$p'
    A(p) = alternative set to *p*

In prose, the emphatic effect is to mark a proposition *p* and contrast it with a set of alternative propositions *p'*, indicating that *p* is less likely than any p'. In (44), this effect leads to the speaker's intended *biased* meaning that out of all possible and relevant individuals Albert Schweitzer is the least likely person to be distrusted. The speaker's conveyed bias, therefore, is that if John would distrust even Albert Schweitzer, the least likely of all (relevant alternative) individuals, he would distrust anyone.

We propose that the same effect underlies challenging RQs, like (44). But since we deal with questions rather than assertions, we first need to spell out what constitutes an alternative set to a question. The answer lies in the manner by which questions are represented.

We argue that emphaticness is actually not applied to the question itself but rather to another speech act, an imperative. Following Sauerland & Yatsushiro (2014), the question SA is decomposed into an imperative, i.e. an order or request presented to the addressee, to make the answer to the question known conversationally and added to the CG. This process is represented as follows:

(49) IMP *addressee* DO [CG [Q]]

    IMP = imperative
    DO = imperative force[5]
    CG = common ground
    Q = question denotation[6]

Applying this account to (44) above, repeated here, would yield:

(50) Who (the hell) likes John?!
    IMP *addressee* DO [CG [λp. ∃x[p= x is a person that likes John & p(w$_0$)]]]

---

[5] For further details, see Sauerland & Yatsushiro (2014). For the current paper's purposes, the imperative force is the conversational effect the imperative has on the context, however achieved.
[6] As discussed above, we assume that the denotation of a question is its full answer.

In prose, a speaker who performs the above challenging RQ, tasks the addressee with the imperative to make the answer to the question 'who likes John' a member of the CG.

Applying an emphatic stress to the imperative results in a bias that the likelihood of fulfilling the imperative goal i.e. making the answer known, is very low. We propose the following expansion of emphatic assertion to speech acts in general:

(51) Emphatic Speech-Act(SAC):
for all SAC' ∈ A(SAC) :SAC$<_c$ SAC'

SAC = Speech Act Content
A(SAC) = alternative set to SAC

By virtue of stressing a question emphatically, the speaker is conveying their bias that the act they request the addressee to perform is not really achievable.

4 The DMI effect

The DMI effect is brought upon by the interplay between the metalinguistic embedding RQ and the embedded RQ, which can be either challenging or obvious, which yields a challenging RQ DMI in the manner discussed shortly.

Recall the DMI structure:

(52) [why Q]

Decomposing this structure into the elements discussed in the previous sections yields the following:

(53) [why^{metalinguistic} Q$^{obvious/challenging\ RQ}$]

Further decomposed into:

(54) [IMP *addressee* DO [CG [why^{metalinguistic}]] IMP *addressee* DO
[CG [Q$^{obvious/challenging\ RQ}$]]]

We assume a standard pragmatic rhetorical relation which holds between the embedding and the embedded question, adhering to the *cooperative principle* (Grice 1975).

The meaning of DMIs is created by conventionally joining two questions together, not giving the addressee any time to answer the first before proceeding with the second. In such a case, by virtue of combining both questions into the same unit, the answer to the second question must be *relevant* to the answer to the first question. And since the embedding question is always metalinguistic and the embedded question can be either an obvious RQ or a challenging one, this leaves us with two combination options. We will address each option by formally explaining two examples which were presented above.

The first, addressing example (14), the pupils texting in class, is repeated here:

(55) A: You are texting while in class?!
 B: lama eifo at?
 Why where (are) you
 'And where are you texting from?'

[IMP *addressee* DO [CG [why^{metalinguistic}]] IMP *addressee* DO [CG [Q^{obvious}]]]

[IMP *addressee* DO [CG [λp. ∃x[p= x is a justification for SA_AS] & $p(w_0)$]]

IMP *addressee* DO [CG [λp. ∃x[p= addressee is located at x] & $p(w_0)$]]]

In prose, the embedded RQ is of an *obvious* type here. The DMI performer tasks the addressee with providing a justification for her previous SA by virtue of the *why* question, and then without any pause tasks the addressee with providing the location of her whereabouts. Since the embedded question is an obvious RQ, the answer, is which supplied pragmatically, is that the addressee is (nowhere other than) in a classroom as well.

The DMI effect is derived by a combination of both parts of the DMI in accordance with the maxim of *relevance*. The (mutually known) fact that the addressee is in class is relevant to inquiring about the justification for performing the previous SA i.e. the shocked "You are texting while in class?!", because given that the addressee is in class, it is not justified in any way to be shocked.

As for the classical DMI example repeated here:

(56) A: Clean the room!
 B: lama mi ata?
 why who (are) you
 'Who are you (to tell me what to do)'

[IMP *addressee* DO [CG [why^{metalinguistic}]]   IMP *addressee* DO [CG [Q^{challenging}]]]

[IMP *addressee* DO [CG [λp. ∃x[p= x is a justification for SA$_A$S] & p(w$_0$)]]

IMP *addressee* DO [CG [λp. ∃x[p= the addressee is x] & p(w$_0$)]]]

In prose, the embedded RQ is of a *challenging* type here. The DMI performer tasks the addressee with providing a justification for her previous SA by virtue of the *why* question, and then without any pause tasks the addressee with providing their identity. Since the embedded question is a challenging RQ, the speaker's bias is that it is very unlikely that the addressee can provide an answer. In this case, the unlikelihood to provide an answer is due to a felicity condition according to which the only individuals for whom it is felicitous to order the DMI performer to clean the room are ones of authority over the DMI performer, and since the addressee is not a member of this set, they are essentially a 'nobody' – a person of no importance. The imperative tasking the addressee to felicitously say who they are, thus, is a challenge to provide an 'authority' name, and since the embedded question is pragmatically related to the embedding question, i.e. tasking the addressee to supply a justification for the previous SA which is the order "clean your room!", if it is unlikely for the addressee to supply an 'authority' name, it is as unlikely for the addressee to be justified in uttering an authority-dependent imperative.

5 Conclusion

This paper discusses and analyses the DMI, a construction which is unique in form and function, in Palestinian Arabic (PA), colloquial Modern Hebrew (MH) and other Semitic languages. The DMI construction has both a rhetorical effect and a metalinguistic one. It is composed of two consecutive questions when the first one is metalinguistic i.e. it addresses a previous speech act, and the other rhetorical i.e. it challenges and effectively rejects the speech act which had been addressed.

The analysis in this paper, which provides insights into the realm of metalinguistic and rhetorical questions with their various types, shows how the relation between the two questions that compose the DMI gives rise to a challenging effect which rejects a previously performed speech act.

References

Caponigro, Ivano & Jon Sprouse. 2007. Rhetorical questions as questions. *Proceedings of Sinn und Bedeutung, vol.* 11, 121–133.
Cheng, Lisa L-S. This volume. *What-as-Why* Sentences in Cantonese. In Gabriela Soare (ed.), *Why is 'Why' Unique? Its Syntactic and Semantic Properties*, Berlin: De Gruyter Mouton.
Ginzburg, Jonathan. 2012. *Meaning for Conversation*. Oxford: Oxford University Press.
Grice, Herbert Paul. 1975. Logic and conversation. In Cole, P. & Morgan, J.L. (eds.), *Syntax and Semantics, volume 3: Speech acts*, 225–242. New York: Seminar Press.
Groenendijk, Jeroen & Martin Stokhof. 1990. Partitioning Logical Space. 02(August).
Guerzoni, Elena. 2004. Even-NPIs in YES/NO Questions. *Natural Language Semantics* 12(4). 319–343.
Han, Chung Hye. 2002. Interpreting interrogatives as rhetorical questions. *Lingua*, vol. 112, 201–229.
Horn, Laurence. 1989. *A natural history of negation*. Chicago: University of Chicago Press.
Karttunen, Lauri. 1977. Syntax and semantics of questions. *Linguistics and Philosophy* 1. 3–44.
Khalaily, Samir & Edit Doron. 2015. Colloquial Modern Hebrew Doubly-marked Interrogatives and Contact with Arabic and Neo-Aramaic Dialects. *Journal of Jewish Languages*. Brill 3(1–2). 116–131.
Krifka, Manfred. 1995. The semantics and pragmatics of polarity items. *Linguistic analysis* 25(3–4). 209–257.
Progovac, Ljiljana. 1993. Negative polarity: Entailment and binding. *Linguistics and Philosophy* 16(2). 149–180.
Rosta, Andrew & James D. McCawley. 2000. The Syntactic Phenomena of English. *Language* 79 (3). 614–625.
Sadock, Jerrold. 1971. Queclaratives. *Seventh Regional Meeting of the Chicago Linguistic Society, vol. 7*, 223–232.
Sadock, Jerrold. 1974. *Toward a linguistic theory of speech acts. Language*. Vol. 52. New York: Academic Press.
Sauerland, Uli & Kazuko Yatsushiro. 2014. *Remind-me presuppositions and Speech-Act Decomposition: Japanese kke and German wieder*. Berlin, ZAS: Ms.
Shlonsky, Ur & Gabriela Soare. 2011. Where's 'Why'? Linguistic Inquiry 42(4). 651–669.
Soare, Gabriela. 2009. The Syntax-Information Structure Interface: A view from Romanian. Université de Genève dissertation.
Stalnaker, Robert. 1978. Assertion. In Peter Cole (ed.), *Syntax and Semantics, volume 9: Pragmatics*. 315–322. New York: Academic Press.
Tsai, Wei-Tien Dylan. This volume. On Applicative Why-Questions in Chinese. In Gabriela Soare (ed.), *Why is 'Why' Unique? Its Syntactic and Semantic Properties*, Berlin: De Gruyter Mouton.
van Rooij, Robert. 2003. Negative polarity items in questions: Strength as relevance. *Journal of Semantics* 20(3). 239–273.

Part 6: ***Why*** **and the syntax-prosody interface**

Giuliano Bocci, Silvio Cruschina and Luigi Rizzi
On some special properties of *why* in syntax and prosody

1 Introduction

Syntactic research over the last twenty years has uncovered numerous peculiarities in the syntactic behaviour of *why*, in comparison with other wh-elements (see Soare (this volume); cf. also the discussion in Stepanov & Tsai 2008). An important difference, for instance, concerns word order. In some languages requiring subject inversion in wh-interrogatives, *why* is exceptional in that it allows the non-inverted order wh–subject–inflected verb (Rizzi 1997, 2001a). This can be illustrated by the contrast between the Italian equivalents of *what* and *how* on the one hand (1a,b), and *why* on the other (1c):

(1) a. *Che cosa Gianni dice a Piero
 What Gianni says to Piero
 b. *Come Gianni contatterà Piero
 How Gianni contact.FUT.3SG Piero
 c. Perché Gianni contatterà Piero
 Why Gianni contact.FUT.3SG Piero
 'Why will Gianni contact Piero?'

To account for this syntactic asymmetry Rizzi (2001a) proposed that, while other wh-elements are extracted from the IP, *perché* (*why*) is externally merged in the left periphery. More precisely, *why* is first merged in the Spec of Int(errogative), a dedicated left-peripheral position also hosting *se* (if), the marker of embedded yes/no questions.[1] Whereas other wh-elements target the lower Foc(us) position, which in turn attracts the inflected verb endowed with +Q, Int° is inherently

---

[1] See Shlonsky and Soare (2011) for a revised version of this analysis, according to which *why* is externally merged in the left periphery, but in a lower dedicated functional layer. In this analysis, *why* reaches its final position in Spec of Int via movement. Crucially, this approach maintains that *why* is not extracted from the IP since it is first merged in the left periphery.

Acknowledgements: We would like to thank Valentina Bianchi and the audience of SLE 2017 for their constructive comments and suggestions, as well as the editor of this volume, Gabriela Soare, for her assistance and guidance through the publication process.

endowed with +Q, hence it does not trigger movement of a verbal element to the left periphery. This captures the absence of obligatory inversion with *why*.

The main aim of this paper is to show that, in Italian, *why*-questions are different from other wh-questions not only syntactically, but also prosodically. We argue that the same formal apparatus explaining the special syntactic behaviour of *why* can be used to also capture the prosodic peculiarities of *why* with respect to prominence distribution. In particular, we will discuss two phenomena: (i) subject inversion, and (ii) the assignment of main prominence, i.e. sentential stress and the nuclear pitch accent (henceforth, NPA). Our argument for the special status of *why* will be supported by experimental findings related to both phenomena. For subject inversion in *why*-questions, we will rely on the studies by Bocci & Pozzan (2014) and Bianchi, Bocci & Cruschina (2017), where the position of the subject in *why*-questions is tested also against information-structure conditions. As for prominence distribution in wh-questions, our starting point will be the experimental findings discussed in Bocci, Bianchi & Cruschina (2021) on wh-questions introduced by bare wh-elements other than *why*. We will then present the results of our own experiment specifically aimed at testing prominence distribution in *why*-questions as opposed to other types of wh-questions.

Prosodically, *why*-questions are different from questions with other wh-elements. Bocci, Bianchi & Cruschina (2021) show that in wh-questions, with wh-elements other than *why*, the NPA is always assigned, in Italian, to the lexical verb and never to the wh-element itself (see also Marotta 2001). This somehow unexpected property is taken to be a reflex of the derivational history of the wh-element, in that in Italian the main prominence (i.e. the NPA and sentential stress) tracks the intermediate positions of the wh-element, which moves stepwise from a vP internal position to the vP edge, and then to the CP system. The *wh*-phrase is endowed with a [wh, focus] feature bundle, which the wh-phrase shares with every phase head that intervenes along its movement path. Prominence assignment to the verb is then a "memory" of this transition event, couched in formal featural terms.

A different pattern emerges with *why*: in direct interrogative sentences introduced by *why*, the main prominence typically falls on *why* itself, and not on the verb, as in the pattern observed with other wh-elements. We take this prosodic asymmetry to be directly linked to the different syntactic derivation of *why*, which, unlike other wh-elements, does not undergo cyclic movement from a clause internal position, but is externally merged in a left-peripheral dedicated position.[2]

---

[2] In this paper, we will not discuss cases in which *why* is construed long distance with an embedded clause, an interpretation that is possible, for instance, in the following example, which can be interpreted as a question about the reason of the firing:
(i) Why did you say he was fired?

2 The syntax of Italian wh-questions

Before turning to *why*-questions, let us first consider the general syntactic behaviour of wh-questions. In Italian direct wh-questions with bare wh-elements other than *why*, neither subjects nor other constituents can intervene between the wh-phrase and the inflected verb – the subject, for instance, must occur postverbally (Calabrese 1982, Rizzi 1996, 2001a), as shown in (2):[3]

(2) a. Che cosa (*Gianni) ha fatto Gianni?
       what   Gianni   has done Gianni
    b. Dove   (*Gianni) ha dormito (Gianni)?
       where   Gianni   has slept   Gianni
    c. Come   (*Gianni) ha dormito (Gianni)
       how   Gianni   has slept   Gianni

Unlike English, in Italian the subject does not necessarily undergo inversion: it can be dislocated to the left or simply omitted. In line with the previous literature, however, we use the term subject inversion to refer to this syntactic restriction.[4]

A second syntactic property discussed in Rizzi (1997, 2001a) is that fronted foci are incompatible with a wh-phrase within the left periphery of the clause, irrespective of the linear order, as shown in (3). See the experimental evidence presented in Bocci, Rizzi, and Saito (2018). More generally, we can say that wh-phrases are incompatible with any narrow focus, insofar as this restriction also operates when the focus is *in situ*, as in the example in (4) (from Bocci 2013:19), at least in genuine direct wh-questions with an interrogative interpretation.

Cases like this inevitably involve movement. Since why in (i) moves through the CP phase of the embedded clause and the vP phase of the matrix clause, our analysis – to be presented in Section 6 – predicts that the prosodic system of Italian should keep trace of these intermediate steps in the derivation. We leave the discussion of these cases for future work.

3 On the distribution of the subject in indirect questions, see Bocci & Pozzan (2014) and Bocci & Cruschina (2018).

4 Some apparent exceptions are discussed in Cardinaletti (2007) where it is shown that specific types of adverbs, can indeed intervene between the wh-phrase and the verb. For simplicity, here we describe subject inversion in its traditional terms as an adjacency requirement and refer to her work for the relevant exceptions. Note also that in Italian, unlike Germanic languages, subjects cannot occur between the auxiliary and the verb in analytic forms (see, e.g., Rizzi 1996).

(3) a. *A chi   QUESTO hanno   detto?
       to whom   this   have.3PL Said
    c. *QUESTO   a chi   hanno   detto?
       why   to whom have.3PL Said

(4) *Quando   hanno   consegnato IL LIBRO a   Leo?
    to whom have.3PL given   the book   to Leo

Why-questions behave differently in this respect: they admit the non-inverted order wh–subject–inflected verb, that is, they allow either a preverbal (5a) or a postverbal subject (5b). The two positions for the subject are not in free variation, but are sensitive to information structure conditions, much as in declarative sentences (cf. § 3 below). *Why*-questions show a second relevant difference with respect to other wh-questions: they are compatible with a narrow focus, as shown in (6) (see Rizzi 1997, 2001a):

(5) a. Perché Stefano balla?
       why   Stefano dances
    b. Perché balla   Stefano?
       why   dances   Stefano
       'Why is Stefano dancing?'

(6) Perché QUESTO avremmo   dovuto   dirgli?
    why   this   have.COND.1PL must.PP say.INF=him.DAT
    'Why should we have said *this* to him?'

From a syntactic viewpoint, Rizzi's (2001a) analysis of *perché* in Italian *why*-questions is able to capture both exceptional behaviours in a straightforward way. Contrary to other wh-operators, *perché* 'why' does not move from a position within the IP, but it is externally merged in a dedicated position in the left periphery, namely, the Spec of Int(errogative)P, above the landing site of the other bare wh-operators, that is, Spec/Foc:[5]

(7) FORCE (TOP*) INT (TOP*) FOC (TOP*) FIN IP

---

[5] Along the same lines, but with a slightly different implementation of this idea, Shlonsky & Soare (2011) assume that *why* moves locally to Spec/Int from another left-periphery position. In embedded indirect yes-no questions, Int° hosts the interrogative complementizer corresponding to English *if* (see Rizzi 2001a).

This positional difference, immediately supported by the ordering in (6), is also instrumental in capturing the observed difference with respect to inversion. Foc, attracting other wh-elements, is not inherently endowed with a +Q feature. Therefore, it must acquire such a feature through head movement of the inflected verb (assumed in the system of Rizzi 1996, 1997, 2001a to be a potential carrier of +Q), whence the obligatory inversion. On the contrary, Int is a position specialized for questions, hence it is inherently endowed with +Q. Therefore it does not trigger head movement of the inflected verb. Along these lines, the special position of *why* explains its compatibility with a preverbal subject (no inversion required), and its compatibility with a lower narrow focus (because the lower Foc head remains available to trigger focus movement or to license a focus *in situ*).

The derivation of a *why*-question (8) as opposed with a wh-question introduced by *dove* 'where' (9) is illustrated in (10) and (11), respectively:

(8) Perché Gianni è partito?
    why Gianni is left
    'Why did Gianni leave?'

(9) Dov' è andato Gianni?
    where is gone Gianni
    'Where did Gianni go?'

(10) [$_{FP}$ Force [$_{IntP}$ *perché*$_Q$ [Int$_Q$ [$_{FocP}$ [$_{IP}$ Gianni è partito]]]]]?

(11) [$_{FP}$ Force [$_{IntP}$ Int [$_{FocP}$ *dove*$_Q$ [$_{I°}$è]$_Q$ [$_{IP}$ pro <è> andato Gianni <dove>]]]]?

On the basis of Rizzi's analysis, we can thus expect two types of subject inversion in Italian wh-questions: (i) in *why*-questions, where subject inversion is not enforced by a syntactic constraint, we expect the possibility of the regular kind of subject inversion sensitive to information structure which is also found in Italian declaratives; as will be shown below (cf. § 3), in this type of wh-questions the position of the subject depends on the information structure of the sentence, so that inversion is associated with a focal status of the subject, as is generally the case for the so called 'free' subject inversion in Italian (see Belletti 2004); (ii) with the other bare wh-operators, subject inversion is triggered by a specific syntactic requirement of the construction, and information structure plays no role.

In the following section we present the result of the syntactic experiment described and discussed in Bianchi, Bocci & Cruschina (2017) and that was specifically designed to test this distinction.

3 Subject inversion in *why*-questions

In order to investigate the focal nature of postverbal subjects in *why*-questions, Bianchi, Bocci & Cruschina (2017) carried out a web-based two-alternative forced choice experiment with 64 native speakers of Italian. The experimental material consisted of 72 written fictional scenes introduced by a brief description and the task was to choose the sentence that sounded more natural in the provided context between two alternatives that only differed with respect to the position of the subject: preverbal *vs* postverbal. Three conditions were tested: (i) *why*-questions in neutral contexts (12), (ii) *why*-questions in contexts that favoured a focus interpretation of the subject (13) and (iii), as a control condition, wh-questions introduced by other bare wh-adjuncts – *dove* 'where' and *come* 'how' – presented in a neutral context (14), where the context was in fact the same as in the first condition with *why*-questions:

(12) <u>Neutral context</u> (broad focus):

[*A causa di un problema tecnico hanno dovuto spostare la prova generale e le aule per le prove individuali sono state riassegnate, per cui Giulia chiede al direttore*: 'Because of a technical problem the dress rehearsal was postponed and the rooms for the individual rehearsals have been reallocated, so Giulia asks the director:']

    a. Perché Stefano balla?
        why Stefano dances
    b. Perché balla Stefano?
        why dances Stefano
        'Why is Stefano dancing?'

(13) <u>Contexts favouring subject focalization</u> (narrow focus):

[*Giulia non sa che hanno cambiato il primo ballerino per il pas à deux e chiede stupita*: 'Giulia doesn't know that the lead dancer for the pas à deux has been replaced and, surprised, asks:']

    a. Perché Stefano balla?
        why Stefano dances
    b. Perché balla Stefano?
        why dances Stefano
        'Why is *Stefano* dancing?'

(14) Neutral context (broad focus):

[*A causa di un problema tecnico hanno dovuto spostare la prova generale e le aule per le prove individuali sono state riassegnate, per cui Giulia chiede al direttore*: 'Because of a technical problem the dress rehearsal was postponed and the rooms for the individual rehearsals have been reallocated, so Giulia asks the director:']

    a. Dove Stefano balla?
        where Stefano dances
    b. Dove balla Stefano?
        where dances Stefano
        'Where is Stefano dancing?'

The results of this experiment are illustrated in Figure 1. As expected, postverbal subjects were almost always preferred in the control condition with *dove* 'where' and *come* 'how'. This suggests that subject inversion is obligatory in this condition, which was tested in neutral contexts. We can thus conclude that subject inversion in this condition is due to structural requirements and has nothing to do with information structure (see also Bianchi, Bocci & Cruschina 2018 and Leonetti 2018).

    Let us now turn to *why*-questions. In neutral contexts, that is, in the very same context as the control condition, we only observe a preference rate of 37% for subject inversion: preverbal subjects are indeed preferred in 63% of the cases. However, when the context is set so as to induce narrow focus on the subject, postverbal subjects are preferred in 66% of the cases, suggesting that the distribution of the subject in *why*-questions is indeed sensitive to information structure. Following Belletti (2004), we believe that the inverted focal subject (cf. e.g. in (13b)) targets a dedicated focus project in the periphery of the vP.

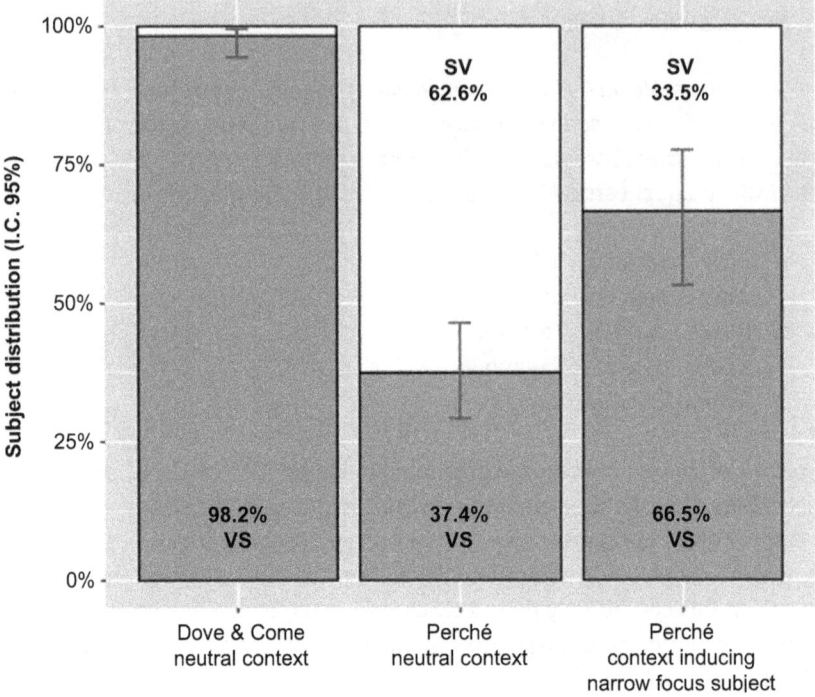

Figure 1: Preference for postverbal subjects (VS) over preverbal subjects (SV) across conditions (Bianchi, Bocci & Cruschina 2017).

Summing up, Bianchi, Bocci & Cruschina's (2017) experimental findings confirm that subject inversion is not obligatory in *why*-questions, as opposed to other types of wh-questions introduced by a bare wh-element. In addition, they show that, even if not mandatory, subject inversion is still possible in *why*-questions and that in that case, the position of the subject is to be related to its focal status. Let us now move to the prosodic properties of wh-questions.

4 Prosodic properties of wh-questions in Italian

To understand the special properties of *why*-questions at the prosodic level, we have to start from the general prosodic behaviour of wh-questions. In Italian, main prominence is by default assigned *rightmost* (Nespor & Vogel 1986, Avesani 1990). This can be observed in neutral, broad focus, declarative sentences, where the rightmost constituent bears main phrasal stress and the nuclear pitch accent (NPA). In direct wh-questions, however, the NPA distribution exhibits a deviant pattern. In the presence of bare wh-elements, the NPA neither falls on the rightmost constituent, in contrast to the default pattern observed in declaratives, nor does it associate with the wh-element, as we may expect if the wh-element qualifies as focal. In bare wh-questions, the NPA is systematically assigned to a lexical verb. This is true of bare wh-questions with short distance wh-movement where the wh-element is an argument of the matrix verb (15a), which bears the NPA. In cases of long distance wh-movement where the wh-word is extracted from an embedded clause (15b), the embedded verb bears the NPA (see Calabrese 1982, Ladd 1996, Marotta 2001, 2002, Bocci, Bianchi & Cruschina 2021).

(15) a. *Short-distance movement*
Chi **pen**sa che ti dovrei presentare al
who thinks that you.DAT should.1SG introduce to-the
direttore?
directot
'Who thinks that I should introduce you to the director?'
b. *Long-distance movement*
Chi pensi che dovrei presen**ta**re al direttore?
who think.2SG that should.1SG introduce to-the director
'Who do you think that I should introduce to the director?'

Bocci, Bianchi & Cruschina (2021) propose to link the NPA-assignment in Italian wh-questions to the successive cyclic nature of wh-movement. Wh-movement must pass through the edge of every *v*P and CP phase between the base-generation position and the final landing site in the left periphery of the sentence. In direct wh-questions, moreover, an interrogative wh-phrase bears a [wh/focal] feature, which can be viewed as a feature bundle. When the wh-phrase passes through the edge of a phase (v° or C°), it shares the [wh/focal] feature with the relevant phase head.[6] As for the principles of the syntax-prosody interface that determine the mapping between syntactic and prosodic structure, Bocci, Bianchi & Crus-

---

6 This mirrors at the prosodic level what is expressed morpho(phono)logically in "wh-agreement" constructions in languages like Chamorro (Chung 1998) and Welsh (Willis 2000). More specifically, the NPA is assigned to the phase head (most typically, the lexical verb) adjacent to the intermediate position at the edge of vP through which the wh-phrase moves. Note also that, for Bocci, Bianchi & Cruschina (2021), the precise agreement process is immaterial for the purposes of their analysis, that is, they do not commit themselves as to whether the whole feature bundle acts as a probe, or rather whether the [focus] feature is transmitted by the wh-phrase to the phase head via dynamic agreement in the sense of Rizzi (1996).

china (2021) assume that the following rules are at the basis of the algorithm responsible for the NPA assignment:

(16) i. The NPA must be assigned to an element that is phonologically overt (and non-clitic; see Calabrese 1982, Nespor & Vogel 1986). Thus, among the *wh*-copies in a *wh*-movement chain, only the highest copy is eligible for NPA assignment, the lower ones being subject to phonological deletion.
   ii. When the syntactic structure contains one or more occurrences of the [focus] feature, the NPA must be assigned to a syntactic element that is marked with this feature (irrespective of whether the feature is interpretable or not on that element).
   iii. The NPA is assigned to the rightmost element that satisfies (i) and (ii). If the sentence does not contain any occurrence of the [focus] feature, the NPA is assigned to the rightmost element by default (see Katz & Selkirk 2011).

In other words, at the syntax-prosody interface, the NPA is assigned to the rightmost element in the sentence that is endowed with the [wh/focal] feature and that is not phonologically null.

A question featuring short-distance movement such as (15a) is thus analysed as illustrated in (17). The wh-phrase starts off from within the vP of the matrix clause and only shares its [wh/focal] feature with the phase heads in the matrix clause. Crucially, the v^0 and C^0 heads of the embedded clause do not bear the [focus] feature, and hence they do not qualify for NPA assignment. Since traces are phonologically deleted, according to principle (16i) they are not possible targets for NPA assignment. As a consequence, the rightmost phonologically-realized element that is specified for the [wh/focal] feature is the matrix lexical verb *pensa* 'thinks', as indicated by the arrow ((17) is reproduced from Bocci, Bianchi & Cruschina 2021: (28), without adapting the structure to the more cartographic representation adopted in the current paper; the same considerations hold for (18)):

(17)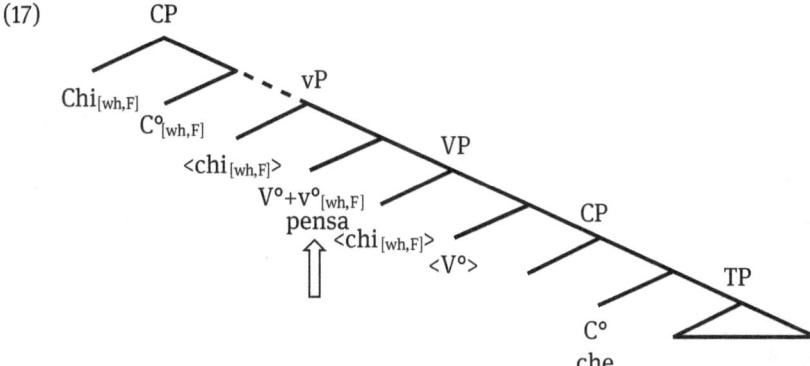

By contrast, in the case of long-distance movement like (15b), the wh-element is cyclically extracted from the vP of the embedded clause and, on its way to the CP of the matrix clause, it shares its [wh, focal] feature bundle with the head of each higher phase, as illustrated in (18):

(18)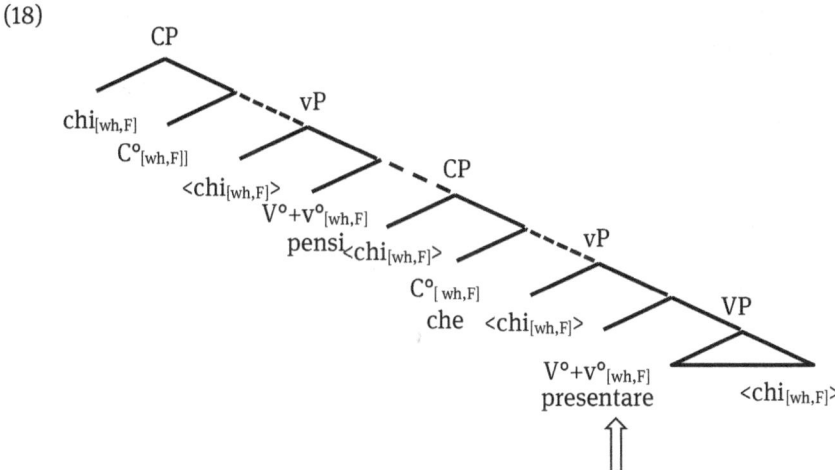

The rightmost phonologically realized position that is specified for the [focus] feature is the v^0 in the embedded clause. This head incorporates the matrix lexical verb, so the NPA is associated with the infinitive *presentare* 'introduce' which counts as the rightmost element endowed with the [wh/focal] feature and is not phonologically null.

This analysis predicts that when no wh-movement takes place, the [wh/focal] feature is not shared within the clause and there is thus only one element that is visible to the phonological component, that is, the interrogative wh-phrase itself, which bears a [wh/focal] feature. In this case, only principle (16ii) becomes relevant and the NPA must be assigned to a syntactic element that is marked with this feature.[7] This prediction is indeed borne out by *why*-questions.

We saw that in bare wh-questions, the NPA is systematically assigned to the lexical verb, either to the matrix verb with short-distance movement or to the embedded verb in the cases of long-distance movement.[8] Crucially, Marotta (2001) reports that direct questions with *perché* 'why' do no obey this generalization that holds for other bare wh-elements: in Italian *why*-questions the NPA does not associate with the lexical verb, but rather with *perché*. At first sight, one might conjecture that this asymmetry between *perché*, on the one hand, and the other wh-elements, on the other, may result from the phonological weight that characterizes *perché*: being disyllabic and phonological heavy, it is able to bear main prominence, while phonological lighter elements fail to do so. However, as originally discussed by Marotta (2001) Italian has other disyllabic wh-elements (like *quando* 'when', *dove* 'where', *come* 'how', *cosa* 'what') and they, unlike *perché*, pattern with monosyllabic, light elements like *chi* 'who' and *che* 'what'.

Pushing forward this line of reasoning, Bocci (2013: § 6.7) advances another argument to reject the hypothesis that phonological weight may account for the peculiar patterns observed in bare-wh questions with *why* and the other wh-elements. He proposes the generalization that in aggressively non-D-linked wh-questions, the NPA cannot naturally associate with the wh-element, but rather targets the lexical verb, as in case of bare wh-questions, whereas in D-linked wh-questions, the wh-phrase tends to attract main prominence, as in *why*-questions. For aggressively non-D-linked wh-questions and D-linked questions it is possible to construct near minimal pairs in which the wh-element features are equivalent in terms of phonological weight, that is, with respect to the numbers of syllables and presence of lexical stress. If different classes of wh-questions, but with similar phonological weight show opposed prosodic patterns, prominence distribution cannot be merely accounted for in terms of phonological weight.

In this paper, we propose that the same algorithm responsible for the assignment of the NPA in other wh-questions operate in the case of *why*-questions, but in the lack of wh-movement from the IP, a different outcome is expected. As shown in the next section, the results of our prosodic experiment confirm this expectation and the opposition between *why*-questions and other wh-questions.

---

[7] We return to the application of the algorithm for the NPA assignment in *why*-questions in Section 6.

[8] See Bocci, Bianchi & Cruschina (2021) for a discussion of some degree of optionality, whereby in some instances of long-distance movement, the NPA may fall on the verb of the matrix clause.

5 NPA distribution in *why*-questions: The prosodic experiment

To explore the prosodic properties of Italian *why*-questions, we carried out a production experiment in which we tested 8 native speakers of (Tuscan) Italian (two men and eight women from the area around Siena). The experiment consisted in a reading task.

We tested a single independent factor, 'wh-type' with three levels: (i) *why*-questions, (ii) D-linked wh-questions, and (iii) aggressively non D-linked wh-questions. A set of the experimental target sentences exemplifying the three conditions is given in (19).

(19) a. Perché hai lavato il divano? (*why*-question)
       why have.2sg washed the couch
       'Why did you wash the couch?'
   b. Chi di voi ha lavato il divano? (*D-linked wh-question*)
       who of you have.3SG washed the couch
       'Who of you washed the couch?'
   c. Chi diavolo ha lavato il divano? (*aggressively non*
       who devil has washed the Couch   *D-linked wh-question*)
       'Who the hell washed the couch?'

The D-linked wh-question and the aggressively non D-linked wh-question in each item formed a near-minimal pair, with an analogous number of syllables. *Diavolo* 'devil' and *cavolo* 'cabbage' are swear words in Italian and clearly feature lexical stress. In terms of phonological weight, *chi diavolo* and *chi cavolo* are somehow equivalent to wh-phrases of the type *chi di loro* 'who of you'. We created 5 items consisting of triplets analogous to (19) and we obtained 15 experimental stimuli.

The target sentences were inserted at the end of short fictional dialogues between two interlocutors. In order to minimize the impact of the linguistic context, for each item we used the same dialogue to introduce the target sentences. The dialogues were meant to introduce a 'neutral' wh-question. In order to use the same dialogues for different types of wh-questions and to preserve the coherence of the discourse, we used personal pronouns in the D-linked condition. This guaranteed the appropriateness of the discoursed-linked interpretation even if the previous dialogues did not mention a direct antecedent.

The factor 'wh-type' was manipulated within participant and within item. In order to prevent possible carry-over effects, we arranged the stimuli in 3 blocks so that within each block, each item was presented only once, under a single experimental condition. The 15 experimental stimuli were interspersed with 15 filler trials with an analogous dialogical structure. The order of the trials was pseudorandomized. Participants were asked to read aloud the dialogues, taking the role of both characters alternately. The sequence of the 30 trials were presented three times in order to collect three repetitions of each stimulus. No feedback was provided to the participants. If they reported that they felt unsatisfied with their production and wanted to repeat the production, we allowed them to read the sentence again. In these cases, we rejected the first production and we kept the new one. The recording took place individually in a quiet room in Siena (Italy).[9] The experiment lasted between 45 and 60 minutes.

We collected and analysed a total of 352 target sentences (8 speakers * 5 items * 3 conditions * 2/3 repetitions).[10] The sentences were segmented into phonemes and intonationally transcribed with a ToBi-like transcription system, within the theoretical framework of the Autosegmental-Metrical Theory of Intonation (Beckman & Pierrehumbert 1986, Ladd 1996). The phonetic analyses were carried out using Praat (Boersma & Weenink 2018) and the annotations were extracted via scripts.

The perceptual analysis of the sentences revealed that the target questions were all realized within a single intonational phrase. Moreover, the metrical head of the intonational phrase, i.e. the element endowed with main sentential stress, was also assigned the Nuclear Pitch Accent (NPA), i.e. the most prominent pitch accent in the prosodic constituent. Following Gili Fivela et al. (2015: 156), we labelled as NPA the rightmost pitch accent after which the pitch contour is completely compressed and no subsequent fully-fledged pitch is observable.[11] In what follows we will mainly discuss distribution of the NPA, but since its location coincides with that of main phrase stress, the same considerations hold true for the latter notion.

The results of this experiment concerning the distribution of the NPA in the three types of wh-questions are reported in Figure 2.1. As we can see, in all conditions, the NPA is never assigned to the rightmost constituent of the clause, that is, to the prominence default position in broad focus declaratives. In *why*-questions

---

[9] To record the materials, we used a head-mounted microphone (Shure Beta 53) and a solid state recorder (Zoom H-4) set a t 48KHz and 16 bits. The recordings were subsequently resampled to 16KHz.
[10] We had to discard 8 sentences from the collected corpus because they featured clear segmental disfluencies.
[11] In our data, no compressed PAs were identified in the post-nuclear region. As a consequence, the NPA in our data corresponds also to the rightmost PA before the right-boundary (and the possible edge tones) of the prosodic constituent.

with *perché*, the NPA is virtually always assigned to the wh-element. In case of D-linked questions, we observe a partially similar pattern: the NPA is assigned to the wh-element in 85% of cases, while in the rest of the cases the NPA has been transcribed on the lexical verb (12.8%) or not identified (2.4%). In contrast with the two previous conditions, aggressively non-D-linked wh-elements behave like regular bare wh-questions: the NPA is virtually never assigned to the wh-element (2.6%), even though the wh-phrase is phonologically heavy; it is instead assigned to the lexical verb in the overwhelming majority of cases (94.83%).

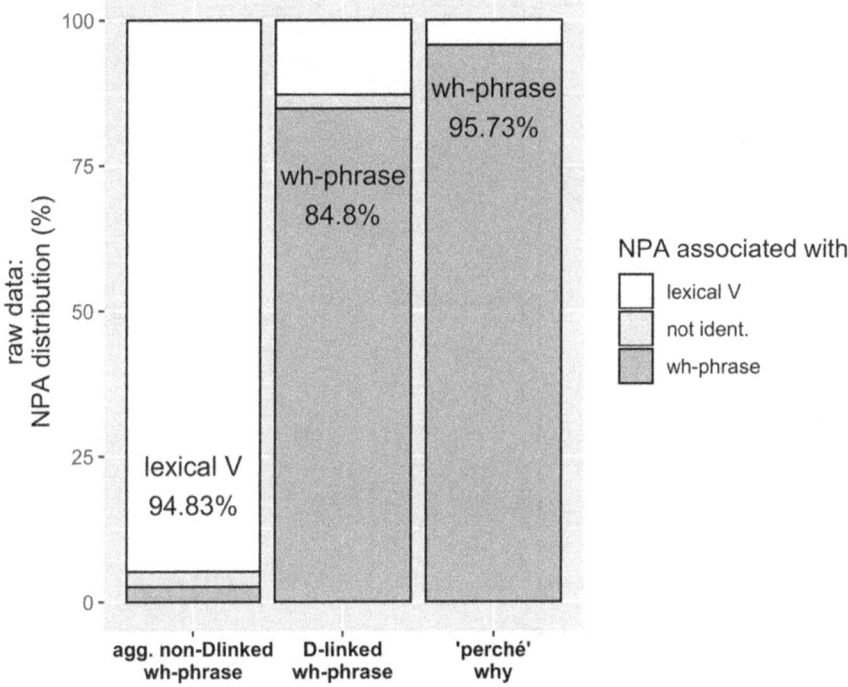

Figure 2.1: NPA distribution (%) in direct wh-questions: aggressively non D-linked, Dlinked, and *perché*-questions.

To statistically test the NPA distribution across conditions, we excluded from the analysis the 6 sentences in which the NPA was not clearly identified. In this way, we could reduce the association site of the NPA to a binary variable: the NPA associated either with the wh-element or with the lexical verb. We built a multi-level mixed effects regression with the log odds of NPA on the wh-element as the dependent variable. We specified as independent factor the type of wh-questions, with a dummy coding, with aggressively non D-linked question as a reference category. The error structure included by-participant and by-item intercepts. The statistical test revealed that the NPA is significantly more likely to associate with the wh-element in D-linked questions (Est. 7.51, Std. Error 1.06, z value 7.07, p <.001) and in *perché*-questions (Est. 8.96, Std. Error 1.20, z value 7.48, p <.001), rather than in aggressively non-D-linked questions. The coefficients extracted from the model are plotted in Figure 2.2 (along with the calculated confidence interval at 95%).[12]

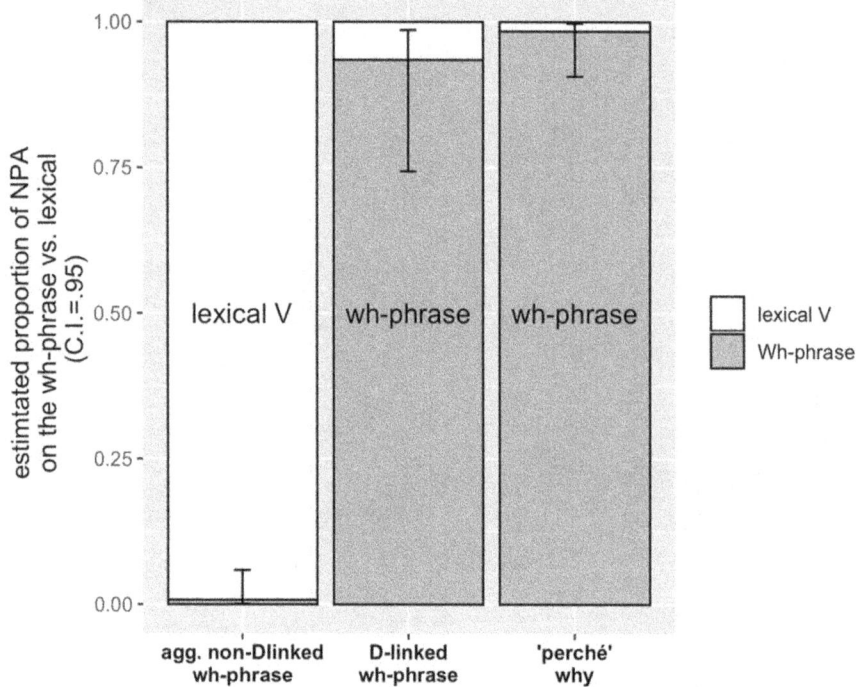

Figure 2.2: Estimated distribution of the NPA in direct wh-questions: aggressively non D-linked, D-linked, and *perché*-questions.

---

12 In Tuscan Italian, the presence of a high boundary tone in wh-questions is reported to be optional (Marotta 2001, Bocci, Bianchi & Cruschina 2021). Our data confirm this observation: overall, a final rise L-H% is observed in 50% of the data. In order to ascertain that the presence of the final rise is not related to the placement of the NPA, we built a multi-level mixed effects regression with the NPA placement as a dependent variable and two independent factors: wh-type and presence of the final rise. The test showed that the type of wh-question is a significant predictor of NPA placement, while the presence of L-H% does not affect NPA distribution (z value < 1). The interaction between final rise and wh-type also appeared to be non-significant.

Let us now consider some examples of pitch contours. As shown in Figure 3, in a *why*-question such as that in (19a), *perché* bears the NPA, the rightmost fully fledged pitch accent in this case (in this case, the only PA present in the sentence). More specifically, we observe that a H* pitch accent is aligned with word-final stressed syllable of *perché*. No other pitch accent occurs in the rest of the clause. The only pitch movement we observe corresponds to the question final rise (resulting from the sequence of the phrase accent L- and the boundary tone H%) that culminates in the last (unstressed) syllable of the sentence-final word (i.e. *divano*).

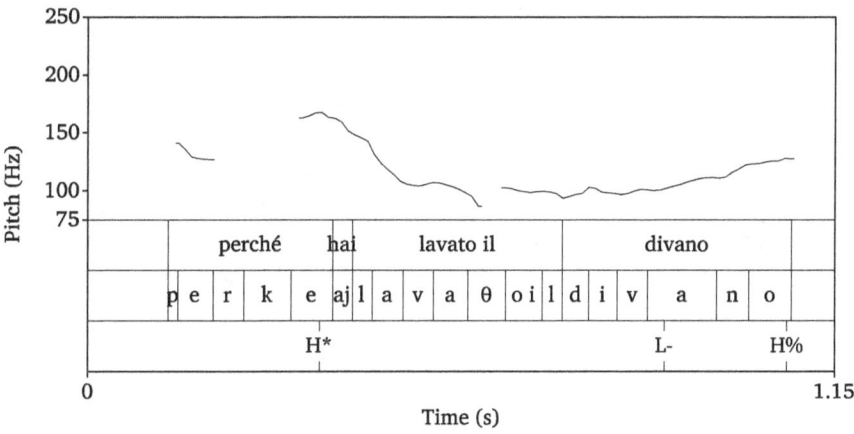

Figure 3: Pitch contour of an utterance produced after the *why*-question in (19a).

In the case of D-linked wh-phrases like (19b), the NPA is more likely to align with the wh-element. This is shown in Figure 4 , where H*, the only PA present in the sentence, is assigned to the complex wh-phrase *chi di voi* 'who of you'. After the NPA H* realized on *voi*, no other pitch accent occurs before final rise L-H%.

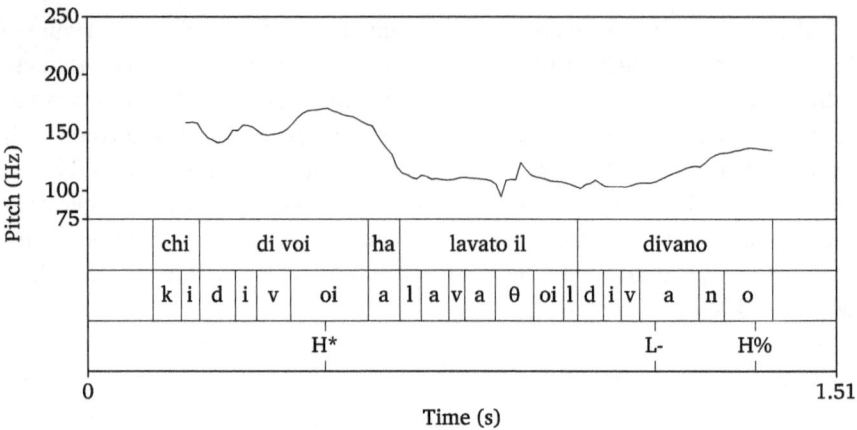

Figure 4: Pitch contour of an utterance produced after the D-linked wh-question (19b).

Finally, the pitch contour of an utterance produced after (19c) (see Figure 5) shows that in aggressively non-D-linked wh-questions behave like wh-questions introduced by bare wh-phrases, in that the NPA systematically falls on to the lexical verb: observe a NPA of the type H* associated with *lavato* 'washed'.

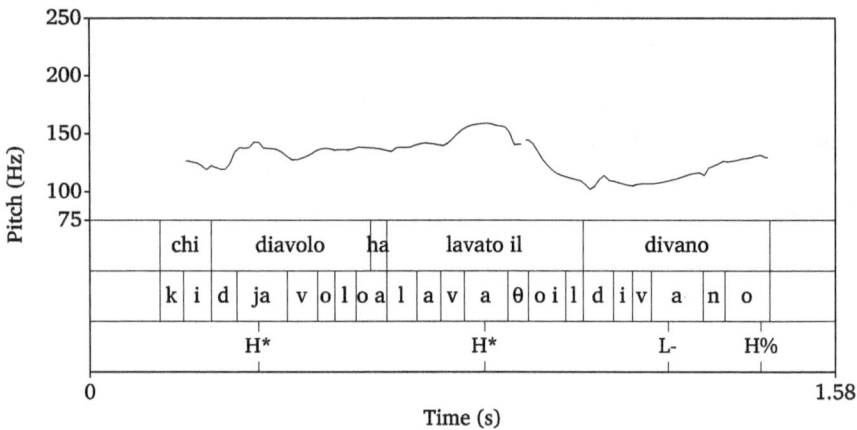

Figure 5: Pitch contour of an utterance produced after the aggressively non-D-linked wh-question (16c).

In this paper we will not directly address and compare the prosodic behaviour of D-linked and aggressively non-D-linked wh-phrases, simply using them as terms of comparison with *why*-questions, our main focus here.[13] The results of our prosodic experiment suggest that in direct *why*-questions, *why* is typically associates with the NPA, much as D-linked wh-phrases,[14] and in contrast with aggressively non-D-linked wh-phrases. The sharp contrast between *why* and (phonologically complex) aggressively non-D-linked wh-phrases argues against an analysis of the property of *why* in terms of phonological weight, and calls for a syntactic explanation.

The explanation we offer to account for the NPA distribution in *why*-questions relies on a combination of the syntactic analysis by Rizzi (2001a) with the interface account by Bocci, Bianchi & Cruschina (2021): unlike other wh-elements, *perché* 'why' does not undergo movement from a clause internal position and is externally merged in the left periphery (cf. § 2). In *why*-questions, thus, the phase head little *v* is not crossed over by *perché* and the lexical verb in little v° then fails to attract NPA.

6 The special prosodic behaviour of *why*

In Section 4, we saw that in wh-questions with bare wh-elements other than *why*, the NPA is always assigned to the lexical verb and never to the wh-element itself. *Why*-questions, on the contrary, exhibit a different pattern: as shown in Section 5, the NPA predominantly falls on *why* itself. The special behaviour of *why*-questions can be taken to be the consequence of their different syntactic derivation. In other wh-questions the assignment of the NPA to the lexical verb is a reflex of the successive cyclic movement of the bare wh-element, which tracks the intermediate positions. Since the syntactic derivation of *why* is different from that of the other wh-elements, in that it does not undergo cyclic movement from a clause inter-

---

[13] A possible interpretation of the exceptional behaviour of D-linked wh-phrases that could be explored in future work is the following: when they pass through the edge of the vP phrase they do not share the focal feature with the phase head (cf. § 4). A further aspect that we leave to future work is that the similarity between D-linked wh-questions and *why*-questions goes beyond the prosodic level and the assignment of the NPA: at the syntactic level, both D-linked wh-questions and why-questions do not strictly require subject inversion (see Rizzi 2001b).

[14] It is important to restrict this generalization to the context we tested, that is, to neutral contexts. Even if we did not include it as a further condition in our experiment, we expect that in *perché*-questions the NPA can associate with another constituent of the sentence for independent focalization purposes, provided the relevant contexts (cf. the syntactic experiment in § 3).

nal position but is directly merged in the left periphery, the asymmetry between *why*-questions and other wh-questions is expected. We argue, however, that the algorithm responsible for the NPA assignment is the same for all wh-questions, including *why*-questions. The difference lies in the application conditions of the principles regulating the same algorithm. Let us consider again these principles, repeated here below as (16'):

(16') i. The NPA must be assigned to an element that is phonologically overt (and non-clitic). Thus, among the *wh*-copies in a *wh*-movement chain, only the highest copy is eligible for NPA assignment, the lower ones being subject to phonological deletion.
ii. When the syntactic structure contains one or more occurrences of the [focus] feature, the NPA must be assigned to a syntactic element that is marked with this feature (irrespective of whether the feature is interpretable or not on that element).
iii. The NPA is assigned to the rightmost element that satisfies (i) and (ii). If the sentence does not contain any occurrence of the [focus] feature, the NPA is assigned to the rightmost element by default.

Condition (16i) is not relevant in the case of *why*-questions. *Why* is externally merged in the left periphery; since no wh-movement occurs, no wh-copies and chains are involved in the derivation of *why*-questions. For the same reasons, no feature sharing between *perché* and phrase heads can take place. The question to be addressed now is whether *why*-questions involve at least one occurrence of the focus feature, presumably born by *why* itself. This constitutes a precondition for the application of (16ii) and for preventing (16iii).

A positive answer to this question comes from a comparison with yes/no questions. In Italian neutral yes/no questions, when no narrow focus occurs, the NPA is assigned to the rightmost constituent of the sentence, namely, to the default prominence position of Italian (Gili Fivela et al. 2015). Since the derivation of yes/no questions does not crucially involve a focus feature (Bianchi & Cruschina 2016), it is expected that prominence distribution in these structures patterns with what we observe in broad focus declaratives. Suppose now that no focus feature is present in *why*-questions: we would then expect the default prominence placement similar to that found in neutral yes/no questions and declarative clauses. As a matter of fact, however, our experimental findings and those reported in Marotta (2001) clearly show that neutral *why*-questions are characterized by a marked prosodic pattern in which the NPA is systematically assigned to *perché* 'why', while the rest of the clause is prosodically subordinate to it. This marked prosodic pattern strongly suggests that a focus feature is assigned to *perché*, much as it is assigned to all other wh-elements.[15] Algorithm (16) will thus assign NPA to *perché* itself, the rightmost overt element carrying [focus].

Exceptions to this general pattern of NPA assignment in *why*-questions are possible if an independent [focus] feature is present on another element of the syntactic structure. Recall that in Italian *why*-questions are compatible with a narrow focus, as shown in (20) (which repeats example (6) above):

(20) Perché QUESTO avremmo dovuto dirgli?
 why this have.COND.1PL must.PP say.INF=him.DAT
 'Why should we have said *this* to him?'

This configuration is syntactically possible because *perché* and the fronted narrow focus do not compete for the same position, as would be the case with other wh-questions (Rizzi 1996, 1997). Prosodically, it is the narrow focus that associates with the NPA because it qualifies as the rightmost element that satisfies the interface principles in (16). In conclusion, *why* is the carrier of the [focus] feature and, as such, in neutral *why*-questions it acquires main prominence. But, if why cooccurs with another element bearing the [focus] feature, as in (20), the NPA is 'shifted' to that element, which is typically to its right (on the ban of the order Focus–Why, see Rizzi 2001a).[16]

---

15 Alternatively, one could speculate that the marked prosodic distribution observed in neutral *why*-questions is not linked to the presence of focus, but rather to the fact that what follows *perché* is given/presupposed information and that as such must get destressed and deaccented. As a result, the NPA would surface on *perché* simply by virtue of the fact that *perché* would be the only element that is not given. There are two main arguments to reject this alternative hypothesis. First given information in Italian fails to be destressed prosodically (Bocci 2013 and references cited therein). Second, according to our intuitions, *perché* consistently associates with the NPA even when the proposition p is clearly non-presuppositional, as in negative why-questions like (i):

(i) Perché non chiedi un congedo?
 'Why don't you ask for a leave?'

16 This analysis raises the issue of how the [focus] feature on *why* satisfies the Focus Criterion if the focal head remains in a lower position. One possibility is that the Foc head may move to Int, and create the Spec-head configuration required for the satisfaction of the Focus criterion (in the case of (20) this would happen after the Foc head has satisfied the Focus Criterion for QUESTO). Alternatively, given the close association of Q and Foc in the wh-system, one could consider the possibility that the satisfaction of the Q Criterion by *why* in Spec-Int suffices to also satisfy the criterial requirements of its [focus] feature. We intend to explore these options in future work.

7 Conclusions

The experimental studies reviewed in this paper clearly show that Italian *why*-questions behave differently from other types of wh-questions. At the syntactic level, *why*-questions do not require subject inversion and are compatible with a narrow focus, while at the level of the prosody, *why* typically associates with the NPA.

In our analysis, both properties can be accounted for if we assume that, unlike other wh-operators, *why* does not involve wh-movement from IP and is directly merged within the left periphery. This syntactic difference is also at the basis of our account of the special prosodic behaviour of *why*-questions. In other wh-questions, the NPA associates with the lexical verb, a reflex of the syntactic derivation of the wh-element through the vP periphery before reaching its final landing site: the phase head v° is the rightmost element carrying the [focus] feature, hence the lexical verb (ultimately associated with v° via head movement) is assigned the NPA under (16). By contrast, the derivation of *why* involves no movement, so that the association of the NPA with a verbal element is correctly predicted not to hold. We have suggested that the assignment of the NPA to *why* itself also is the outcome of the syntax-prosody algorithm that assigns the NPA to the rightmost element in the structure that carries a [focus] feature. On the one hand, *why* stands out in that it is the only bare wh-element that is externally merged in the left periphery. On the other hand, like other wh-elements, and in opposition with the yes/no operator, *why* too is inherently assigned the [focus] feature. This determines the consequence that *why* carries the NPA in *why* questions like (19), under algorithm (16). As the results of our prosodic experiment show in section 5, this prediction is correct. On the whole, the empirical findings discussed in this paper support the view that the syntactic structure guides computational processes at the interfaces with meaning and sound, as in much cartographic work (Cinque & Rizzi 2010, Rizzi & Bocci 2017). In particular, some aspects of the syntactic structures directly condition phonological operations such as the assignment of the NPA.

References

Avesani, Cinzia. 1990. A contribution to the synthesis of Italian intonation. *Proceedings of the 1st International Conference on Spoken Language Processing*, vol. I. 833–836.

Beckman, Mary E. & Janet B. Pierrehumbert. 1986. Intonational structure in Japanese and English. *Phonology Yearbook* 3. 255–309.

Belletti, Adriana. 2004. Aspects of the low IP area. In Luigi Rizzi (ed.), *The Structure of IP and CP. The Cartography of Syntactic Structures, Vol. 2*, 16–51. New York: Oxford University Press.

Bianchi, Valentina & Silvio Cruschina. 2016. The derivation and interpretation of polar questions with a fronted focus. *Lingua* 170. 47–68.

Bianchi, Valentina, Giuliano Bocci & Silvio Cruschina. 2017. Two types of subject inversion in Italian wh-questions. *Revue roumaine de linguistique* 62 (3). 233–252.

Bianchi, Valentina, Giuliano Bocci & Silvio Cruschina. 2018. The syntactic and prosodic effects of long-distance *wh*-movement in Italian. In Delia Bentley & Silvio Cruschina (eds), *Non-Canonical Postverbal Subjects*, Special issue of *Italian Journal of Linguistics* 30(2). 59–78.

Bocci, Giuliano. 2013. *The Syntax–Prosody Interface: A cartographic perspective with evidence from Italian*. John Benjamins.

Bocci, Giuliano & Lucia Pozzan. 2014. Questions (and experimental answers) about Italian subjects. Subject positions in main and indirect question in L1 and attrition. In Carla Contemori & Lena Dal Pozzo (eds), *Inquiries into Linguistic Theory and Language Acquisition. Papers offered to Adriana Belletti*, 28–44. Siena: CISCL Press.

Bocci, Giuliano & Silvio Cruschina. 2018. Postverbal subjects and nuclear pitch accent in Italian wh-questions. In Rorberto Petrosino, Pietro Cerrone & Harry van der Hulst (eds.), *From Sounds to Structures. Beyond the Veil of Maya*, 467–494. Berlin: De Gruyter.

Bocci, Giuliano, Valentina Bianchi & Silvio Cruschina. 2021. Focus in wh-questions: Evidence from Italian. *Natural Language & Linguistic Theory* 39. 405–455. DOI: https://doi.org/10.1007/s11049-020-09483-x

Boersma, Paul & David Weenink. 2018. Praat: doing phonetics by computer [Computer program]. http://www.praat.org

Calabrese, Andrea. 1982. Alcune ipotesi sulla struttura informazionale della frase in Italiano e sul suo rapporto con la struttura fonologica. *Rivista di Grammatica Generativa* 13. 489–526.

Cardinaletti, Anna. 2007. Subjects and wh-questions. Some new generalizations. In Jose Camacho, Nydia Flores-Ferrán, Liliana Sánchez, Viviane Déprez & María José Cabrera (eds.), *Romance linguistics 2006: Selected papers from the 36th Linguistic Symposium on Romance Languages (LSRL)*, 57–79. Amsterdam/Philadelphia: John Benjamins.

Chung, Sandra. 1998. *The Design of Agreement: Evidence from Chamorro*. Chicago: University of Chicago Press.

Cinque, Guglielmo & Luigi Rizzi. 2010. The cartography of syntactic structures. In Heine Bernd & Narrog Heiko (eds.), *The Oxford Handbook of Linguistic Analysis*, 65–78 Oxford: Oxford University Press.

Gili Fivela, Barbara, Cinzia Avesani, Marco Barone, Giuliano Bocci, Claudia Crocco, Mariapaola D'Imperio, Rosa Giordano, Giovanna Marotta, Michelina Savino & Patrizia Sorianello. 2015. Intonational phonology of the regional varieties of Italian. In Sonia Frota & Pilar Prieto (eds.), *Intonation in Romance*, 140–197. Oxford: Oxford University Press.

Ladd, D. Robert. 1996. *Intonational phonology*. Cambridge University Press.

Laka, Itziar. 1990. *Negation in Syntax: On the Nature of Functional Categories and Projections*. Cambridge, MA: MIT dissertation.

Leonetti, Manuel. 2018. *Two types of postverbal subject*. In Delia Bentley & Silvio Cruschina (eds.), *Non-Canonical Postverbal Subjects*, Special issue of *Italian Journal of Linguistics* 30(2). 11–36.

Marotta, Giovanna. 2001. I toni accentuali nelle interrogative aperte (wh-) dell'italiano di Lucca. In Camilla Bettoni, Antonio Zampolli & Daniela Zorzi (eds.), *Atti del II congresso di studi dell'Associazione Italiana di Linguistica Applicata*, 175–194. Perugia: Guerra Edizioni.

Marotta, Giovanna. 2002. L'Intonation des énoncés interrogatifs ouverts dans l'italien toscan. In *Speech Prosody 2002, International Conference*.

Nespor, Marina & Irene Vogel. 1986. *Prosodic Phonology*. Berlin: Mouton de Gruyter.

Poletto, Cecilia & Raffaella Zanuttini. 2013. Emphasis as reduplication: Evidence from *sì che/no che* sentences. *Lingua* 128. 124–141.

Rizzi, Luigi & Giuliano Bocci. 2017. The left periphery of the clause: primarily illustrated for Italian. In Martin Everaert & Henk C. van Riemsdijk (eds.), *The Wiley Blackwell Companion to Syntax, Second Edition*, Oxford: Blackwell.

Rizzi, Luigi. 1996. Residual Verb-second and the Wh-criterion. In Adriana Belletti and Luigi Rizzi (eds.), *Parameters and Functional Heads. Essays in Comparative Syntax*. 63–90. Oxford/New York: Oxford University Press.

Rizzi, Luigi. 1997. The fine structure of the left periphery. In Liliane Haegeman (ed.), *Elements of Grammar*, 281–337. Dordrecht: Kluwer.

Rizzi, Luigi. 2001a. On the position 'Int(errogative)' in the left periphery of the clause. In Guglielmo Cinque & Giampaolo Salvi (eds), *Current studies in Italian syntax. Essays offered to Lorenzo Renzi*, 287–296. Amsterdam: Elsevier.

Rizzi, Luigi. 2001b. Reconstruction, weak island sensitivity, and agreement. In Carlo Cecchetto, Gennaro Chierchia & Maria Teresa Guasti (eds.), *Semantic Interfaces*, 145–76. Stanford, CA: CSLI.

Shlonsky, Ur & Gabriela Soare. 2011. Where's 'why'?. *Linguistic Inquiry* 42(4). 651–669.

Stepanov, Arthur & Wei-Tien Dylan Tsai. 2008. Cartography and licensing of wh-adjuncts: a cross-linguistic perspective. *Natural Language & Linguistic Theory* 26(3). 589–638.

Willis, David. 2000. On the distribution of resumptive pronouns and wh-trace in Welsh. *Journal of Linguistics* 36. 531–573.

Index of subjects

applicative construction 14, 206
applicative *shenme* 211, 210

Basque 1, 2, 5, 11, 12, 63, 64, 65, 67, 73, 75, 84, 85, 88, 89, 90, 91, 92, 93, 94, 95, 96, 98
bipartite nature 23, 36
bipartite nature of *núkàtà...qó* 23, 36

Cantonese 7, 9, 13, 14, 15, 198, 219, 220, 221, 222, 225, 230, 234, 235, 237, 239, 240, 241
Chinese 1, 2, 7, 51, 197, 198, 201, 202, 206, 207, 213, 214

diary English 15, 249, 250, 251, 252, 253, 254, 258
Doubly Marked Interrogative 273
Dutch 5, 11, 12, 15, 27, 115, 119, 129, 132, 134, 135, 136, 137, 138, 139, 141, 142, 144, 145, 151, 152, 153, 154, 157, 160, 163, 167, 170, 174, 179, 181, 185, 191, 220, 221, 225, 228, 232, 235, 237

exclamatives 14, 221, 229, 230, 231, 232, 233, 234, 235, 236, 237, 239, 240, 241, 242, 243
experimental study 17, 202
expletive *what* 239

German 8, 13, 15, 115, 118, 119, 122, 123, 124, 127, 129, 130, 132, 134, 135, 136, 138, 139, 140, 141, 142, 143, 144, 145, 220, 221, 225, 232, 234, 235, 238, 241

Hebrew 16, 17
high reason adverbials 152, 175, 176, 179
high *zergatik* 98, 99, 101, 102, 103, 104, 105, 106, 107, 109
how come questions in diary English 254

inner light verb construals 199, 202
Italian 1, 2, 4, 6, 10, 11, 17, 18, 23, 34, 35, 36, 41, 42, 43, 47, 51, 58, 59, 78, 90, 115, 116, 117, 119, 126, 128, 293, 294, 295, 296, 297, 298, 300, 301, 304, 305, 312, 313

Kwa languages
– Ewe 9, 203

low reason adverbials 12, 175

Mandarin 7, 9, 13, 14, 15, 197, 198, 199, 201, 203, 206, 207, 212, 214, 215, 219, 220, 221, 223, 225, 226, 233
metalinguistic effect 274, 277, 279
modal particles 120, 121, 122, 123, 13, 130, 143
morphological alternation 24, 28

NPA 17, 294, 300, 301, 302, 303, 304, 305, 306, 307, 308, 309, 310, 311, 312, 313

postverbal *mat*[1] 198, 223, 225, 226, 228, 235
prominence distribution 294, 304, 312
prosodic asymmetry 2, 294
prosodic pattern 18, 202, 312

rhetorical effect 274, 281, 282, 288
rhetorical questions 16, 17, 99, 108, 221, 229, 230, 231, 259

sentence final particle (SFP) 265
sentence-initial *mat*[1] 198, 220, 221, 222, 223, 224, 226, 227, 228, 230, 234, 240, 244
sentence-initial *zenme* 198
silent applicative head 198, 199
speech act 209, 210, 274, 276, 277, 279, 280, 284, 285, 17, 288
subject drop 7, 15, 249, 250, 251, 252, 253, 254, 257
syntax-prosody algorithm 314

Taiwan Southern Min 198, 211
the maxim of *relevance* 287

V2 effects 84, 94, 104, 109
van daar 189, 190, 191
van waar 189, 190
verb copying 201, 202, 204, 205, 208, 214, 215

waar XP 165
waarom 12, 132, 133, 134, 135, 138, 142, 144, 145, 151, 153, 154, 155, 156, 157, 158, 159, 160, 161, 163, 164, 165, 166, 172, 173, 175, 176, 185, 187
Waarom XP 151, 152, 153, 154, 155, 156, 157, 159, 161, 162, 164, 165, 174, 175, 179, 191

wanna contraction 16, 249, 260, 261
Wanneer XP 152, 181
what-exclamatives 221
whining force 14, 208, 209
whining *what* 197, 198, 200, 202, 203, 204, 208, 210, 212, 214, 225
why-questions with V2 63
Why-Stripping 12
wieso 139, 140, 141, 143, 144, 145

zenme 7, 8

www.ingramcontent.com/pod-product-compliance
Lightning Source LLC
Chambersburg PA
CBHW031421150426
43191CB00006B/345